THE EMERGENTLY ILL CHILD

Dilemmas in Assessment and Management

Edited by

Roger M. Barkin, MD, MPH, FAAP, FACEP
Director, Pediatric Emergency Services
Rose Medical Center
Denver, Colorado

Associate Attending Physician
Department of Emergency Medicine
Denver General Hospital

Associate Professor of Pediatrics and Surgery
University of Colorado Health Sciences Center
Denver, Colorado

AN ASPEN PUBLICATION
Aspen Publishers, Inc.
1987
Rockville, Maryland
Royal Tunbridge Wells

Library of Congress Cataloging-in-Publication Data

The Emergently ill child.

"An Aspen publication."
Includes bibliographies and index.
1. Pediatric emergencies. I. Title. I. Barkin,
Roger M. [DNLM: 1. Emergencies—in infancy & childhood.
2. Emergency Medicine—in infancy & childhood.
WS 200 E535]
RJ370.E45   1987   618.92 '0025   87-14391
ISBN: 0-87189-862-4

Diagnostic and therapeutic approaches to specific clinical conditions may change because of alterations in our understanding of the pathophysiology of a clinical process or indications and dosages of medications. Every effort has been made to ensure the accuracy of the information herein; however it remains the responsibility of the practitioner to evaluate the appropriateness of a particular opinion in the context of actual clinical situations and with due considerations to new and evolving developments and data. Authors, editors, and the publisher cannot be held responsible for any typographical or other errors found in this book.

Editorial Services: Marsha Davies

Library of Congress Catalog Card Number: 87-14391
ISBN: 0-87189-862-4

Printed in the United States of America

1   2   3   4   5

To Suzanne, who has maintained her equanimity throughout this effort;

To Adam and Michael, for their patience and willingness to let me sit at the computer;

To clinicians at the cutting edge, for whom we hope this book will provide new perspectives; and

To children, who will, we hope, be served by this book.

Table of Contents

Contributors

Jean T. Abbott, MD
Attending Physician
Emergency Department
Assistant Professor of Surgery
Department of Surgery, Section of
   Trauma and Emergency Medicine
University of Colorado Health Sciences
   Center
Denver, Colorado

Steven H. Abman, MD
Assistant Professor
Department of Pediatrics
University of Colorado Health Sciences
   Center
Denver, Colorado

Elizabeth M. Allen, MD
Division of Pediatric Pharmacology and
   Critical Care
Case Western Reserve University School
   of Medicine
Dayton, Ohio
Rainbow Babies and Childrens Hospital
Cleveland, Ohio

M. Douglas Baker, MD
Attending Physician
Emergency Department
Assistant Professor of Pediatrics
University of Pennsylvania School of
   Medicine
Children's Hospital of Philadelphia
Philadelphia, Pennsylvania

Roger M. Barkin, MD, MPH
Director, Pediatric Emergency Services
Rose Medical Center
Associate Attending Physician
Department of Emergency Medicine
Denver General Hospital
Associate Professor of Pediatrics and
   Surgery
University of Colorado Health Sciences
   Center
Denver, Colorado

Suzanne Z. Barkin, MD
Chief Resident
Department of Radiology
University of Colorado Health Sciences
   Center
Denver, Colorado

Louis M. Bell, MD
Attending Physician, Emergency
   Department and Division of Infectious
   Diseases
Children's Hospital of Philadelphia
Assistant Professor of Pediatrics
University of Pennsylvania School of
   Medicine
Philadelphia, Pennsylvania

Carol D. Berkowitz, MD
Director, Pediatric Clinic and Group
    Practice
Harbor/UCLA Medical Center
Adjunct Associate Professor of Pediatrics
UCLA School of Medicine
Torrance, California

James B. Besunder, DO
Division of Pediatric Pharmacology and
    Critical Care
Case Western Reserve University School
    of Medicine
Dayton, Ohio
Rainbow Babies and Childrens Hospital
Cleveland, Ohio

Jeffrey L. Blumer, PhD, MD
Associate Professor of Pediatrics
Assistant Professor of Pharmacology
Case Western Reserve University
Dayton, Ohio
Chief, Division of Pediatric Pharmacology
    and Critical Care
Rainbow Babies and Childrens Hospital
Cleveland, Ohio

Joel D. Blumhagen, MD
Associate Professor of Radiology
Department of Radiology
Children's Hospital and Medical Center
Seattle, Washington

Dianna M. Burns, MD
Attending Physician
East San Antonio Pediatric Association
East San Antonio Medical Center
San Antonio, Texas

Patrick L. Carolan, MD
Attending Physician
Department of Emergency Services
Minneapolis Children's Medical Center
Clinical Instructor of Pediatrics
University of Minnesota Affiliated
    Hospitals
Minneapolis, Minnesota

Henry E. Cooper, Jr., MD
Director, Adolescent Clinic
Associate Professor
Department of Pediatrics
University of Colorado Health Sciences
    Center
Denver, Colorado

Diana J. Becker Cutts, MD
Attending Physician
Department of Emergency Services
Minneapolis Children's Medical Center
Clinical Instructor of Pediatrics
University of Minnesota Affiliated
    Hospitals
Minneapolis, Minnesota

James A. Dernocoeur
Paramedic
Prehospital Quality Assurance Consultant
Fitch and Associates, Inc.
Kansas City, Missouri

**Ronald A. Dieckmann, MD,
    MPH**
Attending Physician
Emergency Department
San Francisco General Hospital
Director of Pediatric Emergency Medicine
University of California, San Francisco

**Pamela M. Downey, MD, BSc
    Med**
Senior Resident
Emergency Medical Services
Denver General Hospital
Denver, Colorado

David Elkayam, MD
Fellow in Allergy and Clinical Immunology
National Jewish Center for Immunology
    and Respiratory Medicine
University of Colorado Health Sciences
    Center
Denver, Colorado

Jeffrey L. Goldhagen, MD, MPH
Associate Director, Medical Education
Minneapolis Children's Medical Center
Minneapolis, Minnesota

LeRoy M. Graham, MD
Fellow, Pediatric Pulmonary Medicine
Department of Pediatrics
University of Colorado Health Sciences
  Center
Denver, Colorado

Steven K. Greenholz, MD
Clinical Research Fellow
Instructor in Surgery
Pediatric Surgery Section
University of Colorado Health Sciences
  Center
Denver, Colorado

Esequiel C. Guevara, MD
Associate Director
Emergency Department
Brackenridge Hospital
Austin, Texas

Anthony J. Haftel, MD
Chief, Division of Emergency Medicine
Children's Hospital of Los Angeles
Associate Professor of Pediatrics
University of Southern California School
  of Medicine
Los Angeles, California

Glenn C. Hamilton, MD
Chair and Program Director
Department of Emergency Medicine
Professor of Emergency Medicine
Associate Professor of Internal Medicine
Wright State University School of
  Medicine
Dayton, Ohio

Stephen Heinz, MD
Attending Physician
Emergency Medical Services

Rose Medical Center
Denver, Colorado

Jeffrey H. Hill, MD, PhD
Attending Physician, Division of Pediatric
  Pharmacology and Critical Care
Rainbow Babies and Childrens Hospital
Cleveland, Ohio
Assistant Professor of Pediatrics
Case Western Reserve University
  School of Medicine
Dayton, Ohio

Dee Hodge III, MD
Associate Director, Division of Emergency
  Medicine
Children's Hospital of Los Angeles
Clinical Assistant Professor of Pediatrics
University of Southern California School
  of Medicine
Los Angeles, California

**J. Gerard Horgan, MB, MRCP,
FRCR**
Assistant Professor
Department of Radiology
University of Colorado Health Sciences
  Center
Denver, Colorado

Martin D. Klatzko, MD
Attending Physician
Department of Emergency Services
Minneapolis Children's Medical Center
Clinical Instructor of Pediatrics
University of Minnesota Affiliated
  Hospitals
Minneapolis, Minnesota

Kenneth W. Kulig, MD
Medical Director
Rocky Mountain Poison and Drug Center
Denver General Hospital
Director, Clinical Toxicology Fellowship
  Program
University of Colorado School of Medicine
Denver, Colorado

Donald J. Lefkowits, MD
Attending Physician
Emergency Medical Services
Rose Medical Center
Denver, Colorado

John R. Lilly, MD
Chief, Pediatric Surgery Section
Professor of Surgery
University of Colorado Health Sciences
    Center
Denver, Colorado

Deborah M. Lince, MD
Attending Physician
Department of Radiology
The Mason Clinic
Seattle, Washington

Richard G. Lucht, MD
Senior Resident and Clinical Instructor
Wright State University School of
    Medicine
Dayton, Ohio

Robert C. Luten, MD
Director, Pediatric Emergency Services
University Hospital of Jacksonville
Assistant Professor of Surgery and
    Pediatrics
University of Florida
Jacksonville, Florida

Dawn L. Martin, MD
Attending Physician, Children's Clinic
Minneapolis Children's Medical Center
Minneapolis, Minnesota

Frank J. Martorano, MD
Director, Pediatric Services
Porter Memorial Hospital
Denver, Colorado

John A. Marx, MD
Research Coordinator
Department of Emergency Medicine
Assistant Professor of Surgery
University of Colorado Health Sciences
    Center
Denver, Colorado

Ann R. McGravey, MD
Assistant in Medicine
Boston Children's Hospital
Instructor in Pediatrics
Harvard Medical School
Boston, Massachusetts

Janet E. McNally, RN, MS
Nursing Unit Administrator
Pediatric Ambulatory Care Center
University of Colorado Health Sciences
    Center
Denver, Colorado

John D.G. Neufeld, MD
Senior Resident
Emergency Medical Services
Denver General Hospital
Denver, Colorado

Kim A. Ogle, MD
Associate Director, Pediatric Emergency
    Services
University Hospital of Jacksonville
Jacksonville, Florida

N.E. Peterson, MD
Associate Director, Surgery
Division Chief, Urology
Denver General Hospital
Associate Professor of Surgery
University of Colorado Health Sciences
    Center
Denver, Colorado

Ronald R. Pfister, MD
Director of Pediatric Urology
Professor of Surgery
University of Colorado Health Sciences
    Center
Denver, Colorado

Michael E. Pichichero, MD
Elmwood Pediatric Group
Rochester, New York
Clinical Associate Professor of Pediatrics
University of Rochester Medical Center

Peter T. Pons, MD
Director of Paramedic Division
Department of Emergency Medicine
Denver General Hospital
Assistant Professor of Surgery
University of Colorado Health Sciences
 Center
Denver, Colorado

Michael Radetsky, MD, CM
Director, Pediatric Critical Care Services
Tucson Medical Center
Associate, Pediatric Infectious Disease
Associate Professor of Pediatrics
University of Arizona School of Medicine
Tucson, Arizona

Peter Rosen, MD
Acting Deputy Manager, Medical Affairs
Director, Emergency Medical Services
Denver General Hospital
Professor of Surgery
University of Colorado Health Sciences
 Center
Denver, Colorado

Ronald P. Ruffing, MD
Senior Resident
Emergency Medical Services
Denver General Hospital
Denver, Colorado

Carol M. Rumack, MD
Associate Professor
Department of Radiology
University of Colorado Health Sciences
 Center
Denver, Colorado

Jeffrey S. Schiff, MD
Acting Director, Emergency Department
Minneapolis Children's Medical Center
Minneapolis, Minnesota

Nancy A. Schonfeld, MD
Attending Physician
Division of Emergency Medicine
Children's Hospital of Los Angeles
Los Angeles, California

Steven M. Selbst, MD
Associate Director
Emergency Department
The Children's Hospital of Philadelphia
Assistant Professor of Pediatrics
University of Pennsylvania School of
 Medicine
Philadelphia, Pennsylvania

Jonathan I. Singer, MD
Associate Professor
Departments of Emergency Medicine and
 Pediatrics
Wright State University School of
 Medicine
Dayton, Ohio

Martin J. Smilkstein, MD
Attending Physician
Emergency Medical Services
New York University Medical Center
Bellevue Hospital
New York City Poison Center
Clinical Toxicology Fellow
Rocky Mountain Poison and Drug Center
Denver, Colorado

Gary R. Strange, MD
Acting Director
Emergency Medicine Residency Program
University of Illinois
Chicago, Illinois

Richard W. Talley, MD
American Heart Association National
 Faculty for Advanced Life Support
Attending Physician
Emergency Medical Services
Rose Medical Center
Denver, Colorado

Andrew M. Wiesenthal, MD
Chief of Pediatrics
Arapahoe Medical Offices
Colorado Permanente Medical Group
Littleton, Colorado
Clinical Assistant Professor of Pediatrics
University of Colorado Health Sciences
 Center
Denver, Colorado

Madolin K. Witte, MD
Attending Physician, Division of Pediatric
  Pharmacology and Critical Care
Rainbow Babies and Childrens Hospital
Cleveland, Ohio

Donald Demetrios Zukin, MD
Attending Physician
Children's Hospital of Oakland
Oakland, California

Foreword

Pediatricians are responsible for promoting health, preventing disease, and treating illnesses among the infants, children, and adolescents for whom they provide medical care. These are broad and heavy responsibilities that require extensive knowledge and skill to discharge properly. The treatment of acute, life-threatening illnesses is a particularly heavy burden for pediatricians and other physicians and allied professionals who deal with them. Anticipating such illnesses generates continuous stress and the need to know how best to treat them. These illnesses constitute the major *raison d'etre* of pediatric practice—the carrots chased and sought in almost every encounter with young patients who are acutely ill or seemingly so. Not only is it necessary to make the correct diagnosis and to institute the proper treatment, but one must be sure to do no harm. One needs to know what to do, when to do it, and why it should be done, for under these circumstances the potential for significant morbidity and mortality is very high.

The subjects covered in *The Emergently Ill Child* constitute the major reasons for acute illness visits by infants, children, and adolescents. There are others, of course, including anaphylactic shock, diabetic ketoacidosis, appendicitis, testicular torsion, and various neonatal emergencies, but no one book, save the major pediatric texts, can address all critical conditions. Barkin and his colleagues have focused on diseases and situations for which there has been some controversy in terms of management, controversy that has, for the most part, been resolved through new knowledge generated by recent studies. Where controversy still exists, two or even three opinions are presented in separate chapters to provide the reader with different perspectives on the same subject, much as one might gain through consultations in practice. This method serves to stimulate thinking, to challenge shibboleths, and to change behavior appropriately.

Although algorithms are presented for managing some of the critical conditions discussed, this book is not a cookbook to be referred to under emergent circumstances. Rather, it should be read at one's leisure when there is time to reflect on what is presented (1) in order to understand the rationale for the recommendations made by the authors and, in some instances, (2) to decide which of the various management courses to take. In so doing, the likelihood of acutely ill patients benefiting from the reader's treatment will be enhanced.

Robert A. Hoekelman, M.D.
Professor and Chairman
Department of Pediatrics
University of Rochester School of Medicine and Dentistry

Foreword

Over time, many attitudes toward the care of the critically ill child have developed. The perception that only a pediatrician can care for a sick child grew as pediatrics evolved into an autonomous specialty. With the evolution of emergency medicine came the attitude that only the emergency physician knows how to approach the critically ill patient, adult, or child.

As I have watched the care rendered to children by pediatricians and emergency physicians, I have realized that both groups show an enormous amount of anxiety about the care of the critically ill child, the appropriateness of that care, and the likelihood of facing the tragedy of a child's untimely death.

There is a genuine desire within both fields to define more accurately the parameters of diagnosis and care. While there is always some interspecialty competition and friction in communication, there has been less between emergency medicine and pediatrics than between emergency medicine and many other specialties. Interaction is essential to the effective practice of medicine. We must, therefore, continue our efforts to define initial response to pediatric emergencies within the context of the patient's total care.

The critical problem is to achieve effective education as approaches to care are defined. Even if it were possible or desirable to train all emergency physicians and pediatricians both in emergency medicine and pediatrics, the problems of how to stay current and how to avoid confusion based on daily experience would remain. In addition, technical tasks are more difficult to perform on small children. While no book can do more than address the facts of "how to do it," a book can teach "when to do it" and present an organized approach that will permit greater confidence. The principal limitation to the performance of a technical task is rarely motor inability, but rather lack of self confidence that the procedure is needed.

The literature is a difficult source of knowledge. Even if we have the self discipline to go to the library and seek out material about which we feel inadequate, it is still almost impossible to judge whether we are reading accurate research. We have grown accustomed to demanding a triply blinded, prospective, controlled series of at least 1,500 patients in order to believe any new clinical truths. However, most clinical doctrines of diagnosis and therapy have not been subjected to this kind of research, probably will not be, and even ethically cannot be.

How do we integrate astute observations based on experience without being accused of being anecdotal? While virtually all physicians learn more from a real patient for whom they have had direct responsibility than from large clinical trials, they also learn well from case conferences concerning morbidity and mortality (the M and M conference). Perhaps this is because it is always painful to have to present the patient at such a conference; we may learn best from pain.

Unless we use the observations of practicing physicians, we never will be able to change but will be permanently imprisoned in the current "standard of care." We need not look back very far in the practice of medicine to find therapies that today appear to be quackery. For instance, looking back a hundred or more years, it is hard to accept that any intelligent physician could have believed in the widely practiced purgative and bleeding therapies of the Benjamin Rush school of thought.

The studied observations of some very experienced physicians are expressed in this book. The fact that these experts disagree reflects the reality that there is no single truth in clinical medicine. There is room for much thought after studying these observations and different points of view. For the experienced reader, the result may be a modification of both ends of the spectrum.

I certainly did not agree with everything I read in this book, but it did make me think. And the challenge to accepted truths keeps one from believing in purgatives and leeches.

The approach to fever is one example. I personally cannot understand the need to argue about fever in the child under two months of age. The incidence is low, and in the time spent deciding what to do, a complete septic workup could be performed. Moreover, it is so difficult to define normal values in this age group that there cannot be a parameter that will effectively guide judgment. In an older child the limits of the septic workup become much harder to define, and the increased incidence of febrile cases necessitates an organized approach.

There are other areas of controversy where some data is available, but we still base treatment on what has worked well for others and ourselves. For example, the esophageal foreign body is a problem in which arguing from the last memorable case is unwise. Here the expertise of consultants from other specialties directly affects patient management. I have been fortunate to be able to work both with highly competent radiologists and otolarlyngologists. Therefore my approach is usually based on who is available.

Asthma is so common that we take it for granted. There is an endless variety of ways to treat asthma, yet each year we experience deaths in very young asthmatics. The articles in this book should be mandatory reading for anyone who encounters this condition.

My favorite chapters are the ones on cardiac arrest. Nowhere in medicine has such a rigid cult appeared with such a paucity of data. The difference between adult and pediatric arrests must be stressed, but common to both is a lack of knowledge about what can be accomplished and which drugs are effective or dangerous. The current controversy over calcium administration is an example. The answer is probably so complex in its origin that at present it is outside the realm of possible experimentation. I have seen both calcium infusion and calcium channel blockers "work." I have seen both recommended with the same degree of enthusiasm. Perhaps both sides are right and it is the calcium ratio across the cell membrane that needs to be altered rather than any absolute quantity of calcium ions. The arguments presented in this book about the appropriate amount of bicarbonate to use are long overdue. I believe that within a decade, the past twenty years' use of bicarbonate will be considered the modern equivalent of purgatives.

I recommend this book not only for residents in training for whom it is absolutely mandatory, but also for practicing emergency physicians, pediatricians, and family practitioners. It would be also of interest to any surgeon who has responsibility for acute pediatric emergencies. Finally, while this book will cause some discomfort to medical students who need absolutes and who do not possess the experience to sort out truths, it will introduce the concept of a multipotential practice. It will also familiarize students with the reality that there is no single set of facts that can be acquired to ensure a permanently sound practice. All practice must evolve, and what better way than through the controversy of observations based on thoughtful experience.

This is not a hard book to read because it will remind the clinician of his or her own painfully encountered cases. It is not an easy book to read because it mandates thought, possible change in what was taken for granted, and the realization that sick children are always going to induce anxiety unless we are willing to modify and improve our practice. If read more than once—with care, with thought, and perhaps with some irritation at having to question what was expected as golden and unchanging—then this book will provide pleasure, analgesia, and self confidence that will enable triumph rather than tragedy in the care of the critically ill child.

Peter Rosen, MD

Preface

Those who care for emergently ill children have developed approaches to management that are unique to children, often extrapolated from clinical experience in adults. The increasing recognition of the unique diagnostic and management issues in pediatric patients has led to a rapid expansion of clinical experience and pathophysiologic understanding in approaching potentially life-threatening or worrisome situations.

Children are a special challenge; their illness may progress rapidly, but they are generally treatable with timely and appropriate care. Effective management leaves the child with a full life ahead and no sequelae.

The Emergently Ill Child: Dilemmas in Assessment and Management has been exciting to edit. The focus is on areas that are controversial, problematic, or require the re-evaluation of traditional approaches. It reflects the expansion of knowledge and the dilemmas that have evolved in our care of ill children. It very specifically covers areas that have changed markedly in recent years and for which changes in clinical approaches are significant.

The proper assessment and management of ill children are evolving rapidly and reflect new knowledge, new technology, and the evolution of a new body of clinical experience. Because of the rapidity of this data explosion, many issues in clinical practice have become controversial as a result of new information superimposed upon years of clinical experience. New pharmacologic agents and altered uses and routes for existing drugs have expanded our alternatives.

The contributions are a compilation of the views of experts with different training and specialties, from different institutions. Editorial perspectives are also included. Obviously, by allowing individual clinicians the opportunity to present their own views, approaches are presented that are not uniformly accepted by all physicians. In this way, however, the reader is provided with a remarkably balanced presentation that allows individual and collective re-evaluation of clinical problems.

This approach is meant to stimulate thought, discussion, and further exploration of key issues. It is not a primary text; other sources of useful and current information are available. This book is designed to provide in-depth, timely coverage of topics that are changing rapidly and for which new knowledge may affect management.

We hope you will find the material informative, interesting, and useful in your practice. Only through maintaining an awareness and true understanding of new trends and directions can we remain at the cutting edge in providing our patients with optimal care.

Roger M. Barkin, MD, MPH, FAAP, FACEP

Acknowledgments

This book is largely a reflection of the many discussions over the last few years between pediatricians, emergency physicians, family practitioners, and intensivists about how to treat specific problems. These have been heated and exciting. It is our hope that we have captured in these pages the dilemmas that exist and the evolving data base that should assist us in caring for children.

The contributors and their respective staffs have been gracious in sharing perspectives and insights about dilemmas that confront us daily. Their dedication to the care of children has made this book possible and we are appreciative.

I am grateful to the Department of Emergency Medical Services at Rose Medical Center for supporting this effort, and the Departments of Pediatrics and Surgery at the University of Colorado Health Sciences Center and the Department of Emergency Medical Services of the Denver Department of Health and Hospitals for providing environments that allow open discussion and questioning of old approaches and evolving new practices.

R.M.B.

Part I

Infections in Children

Section 1

The Febrile Child

Fever is the most common cause of children being seen in an ambulatory setting. The febrile child under 2 months of age presents unique problems because of the subtlety of systemic infection and the nonspecific nature of signs and symptoms. The absence of uniformity in managing these children underlines the difficulties of making judgment decisions. An aggressive workup is required, commonly necessitating hospitalization and broad-based antibiotic treatment pending the results of cultures.

The older child under 2 years of age is more easily examined, but may have associated occult bacteremia; specific clinical and laboratory tests may be useful.

Paramount to managing the febrile child is the recognition that the elevated temperature reflects an underlying infection. Controversy exists regarding what constitutes an elevated temperature, what is the optimal site for measurement, and how aggressive antipyretic therapy should be. The significance of an elevation must partially reflect the child's age, toxicity, and clinical condition; differential considerations; and site and technique of measurement.

On the basis of recent data, although axillary temperatures are useful in thermostable environments, problems are inherent in the less constant setting of the office, clinic, or emergency department. If differentiating a low grade fever from a normal temperature is essential to clinical practice, as it is in the infant, rectal temperatures are the "gold standard."

Control of the fever may combine antipyretics and sponging.

1. Assessment and Management of the Febrile Infant under 2 Months of Age

Carol D. Berkowitz, MD

A number of controversies surround the appropriate assessment and management of the febrile infant under 2 months of age. These issues include the degree of temperature elevation that constitutes a fever; the role of clinical judgment in the assessment of young, febrile infants; the spectrum of illnesses manifested by these infants; predictors of serious bacterial disease; the extent of the laboratory evaluation; and appropriate management strategies.

FEVER

We[1] conducted a survey of pediatric training programs in the United States. There was little agreement on what constitutes a fever in this age group. Of 154 respondents, 20% felt that a temperature greater than 38 °C was sufficiently elevated to warrant a diagnostic investigation. Forty percent set the temperature between 38.1 °C and 38.4 °C. However, three respondents (1.5%) felt the temperature should be at least 39.1 °C before a "rule out sepsis" workup is initiated.

Is there a rational way to determine what constitutes a significant temperature elevation in this age group? Infants under 6 months old normally maintain a higher body temperature.[2] Pantell et al[3] retrospectively reviewed records from 1,341 visits of infants under 6 months of age to a family medicine clinic. There were both well and sick infants, and mild temperature elevations between 37.8 °C and 38.2 °C were common. Temperatures greater than 38.3 °C were distinctly unusual in infants under 3 months of age (about 1%) and were associated with 21.5 times the risk of serious underlying infection. No infant in this series had a temperature greater than 40 °C. In another retrospective review, McCarthy and Dolan,[4] specifically looking at hyperpyrexia (temperature greater than 40 °C) in infants under 3 months old, found

3

only 22 cases of 150,000 emergency department visits. However, about one third of these infants had life-threatening infections, including bacterial meningitis, sepsis, gastroenteritis with severe dehydration, and pneumonia. Of 147 infants with temperatures between 37.8 °C and 39.9 °C, 9.5% had serious illnesses, and none had meningitis.

It is not surprising that high temperatures are unusual in this age group. Elevation of body temperature results from behavioral actions (eg, putting on warm clothes), peripheral vasoconstriction, central pooling, and shivering. Shivering, however, is not noted for several months after birth, although other sources of heat generation (eg, brown fat) may contribute to the young infant's ability to generate a febrile response. It is important to appreciate, however, that high temperatures are uncommon in this age group, and that a *young infant may have a serious life-threatening infection with only a low-grade fever.*

CLINICAL JUDGMENT

The extent of the appropriate workup is also an area of disagreement. Approximately 10% of training programs we[1] surveyed were willing to leave the extent of the laboratory assessment to the clinical judgment of the physician. Most of us would agree that physician judgment can vary widely, depending on the experience of the individual physician. But can even the most experienced physician clinically assess young infants? It is important for the practitioner to recall that the child's social skills, such as a smile, may not appear until the infant is 6 to 8 weeks old.

Roberts and Borzy[5] prospectively studied the ability of clinical judgment to differentiate between ill and well infants. Evaluating physicians were asked to assign febrile infants under 8 weeks of age to one of three groups: group I, ill; group II, uncertain; and group III, well. The incidence of bacteremia was the same in the ill and the uncertain groups, and was 18.5%. One infant was felt to be clinically well but had group B streptococcal bacteremia. The authors concluded that *clinical judgment is not useful in the assessment of the young febrile infant.*

SPECTRUM OF DISEASE

In the studies of McCarthy and Dolan[4] and Roberts and Borzy,[5] the incidence of bacteremia and other serious infections in children under 2 months of age ranged from 10% to 33%. Pantell et al[3] also noted an increased risk of serious infections in this age group. The relatively high incidence suggested the need for extensive diagnostic workup and universal hospitalization.

However, subsequent studies involving larger numbers of infants revealed a lower incidence. In a retrospective study[6] involving 434 infants under 2 months old evaluated in five emergency departments in Southern California, documentable bacterial infection was found in 3.5%. Of significance, infection with *Hemophilus influenzae* type B accounted for about one half of the cases of meningitis and about one third of the cases of bacteremia. This finding suggests that treatment with ampicillin and gentamicin sulfate (as was done with the majority of infants in the study) is inappropriate. Other recent studies[7-9] of outpatient neonates revealed a similar incidence of documentable bacterial infection.

Of importance, however, is the fact that although only 3% to 4% of the infants had culture-proven bacterial infections, approximately 30% had some other serious illness (eg, pneumonia, gastroenteritis with dehydration, or aseptic meningitis).

Krober et al[10] in a prospective study at Tripler Army Medical Center of febrile infants under 2 months old reported a number of interesting findings: bacterial pathogens were isolated from 15% of the infants, but no infant had bacteremia, and only one had meningitis. Forty-one percent of the infants had documentable viral infections. Aseptic meningitis was the single most frequently made diagnosis; however, eight infants had positive viral cerebrospinal fluid (CSF) cultures in the absence of CSF pleocytosis. In addition, pyuria was absent in three fourths of infants with positive urine cultures, and one third of infants with salmonellosis did not have diarrhea. Clinical signs of pneumonia (rales, rhonchi, tachypnea) were absent in all infants with abnormal chest film findings. The investigators were unable to delineate any factor that distinguished ill from well febrile young infants, but clearly these children experienced the entire range of viral and bacterial disease.

PREDICTORS OF SERIOUS DISEASE

Although most infants may appear appropriately ill, infants with serious occult infection may appear remarkably well. This is obviously problematic and has led to studies attempting to define predictive variables. Six variables seemed to be associated with bacterial disease in one study[6]: (1) age under 1 month, (2) history of lethargy, (3) no contact with an ill person, (4) breast-feeding, (5) polymorphonuclear white count $\geq 10,000/mm^3$, and (6) band count $\geq 500/mm^3$. Other investigators[7,11] also noted that the incidence of serious infection is twice as high in infants under 1 month of age as compared with infants between 1 and 2 months old.

Crain and Shelov[7] reported somewhat different findings. They prospectively studied 175 febrile infants under 8 weeks of age. Culture-positive bacterial infections occurred in 6.3%, and bacteremia was detected in 3.4%. Individual variables of white blood cell (WBC) count $\geq$ 15,000/mm³, band count $\geq$ 500/mm³, temperature, irritability, tone, cry, and activity level did not correlate with bacteremia. An erythrocyte sedimentation rate (ESR) $\geq$ 30 mm/hr was found in 4 of 5 infants with bacteremia compared with 6 of 94 nonbacteremic infants. The combination of clinical impression of sepsis, WBC count $\geq$ 15,000/mm³, and ESR $\geq$ 30 mm/hr identified all bacteremic infants and excluded 82% of nonbacteremic infants.

Dagan et al[12] in a prospective study of 233 young infants identified four factors, the *absence* of which was predictive of no serious bacterial infection in 99.3%. These factors were (1) no soft tissue infection, (2) WBC count between 5,000/mm³ and 15,000/mm³, (3) band count < 1,500/mm³, and (4) no pyuria (< 10 WBC per high-power field) on urinalysis. Anbar et al,[13] however, reported in a subsequent study that these variables were predictive in only 95.7% of the cases; therefore, 4.3% of infants with serious bacterial infections were not identified. This represented three infants with bacteremia, including one with group B streptococcus, and two with *Salmonella typhimurium*. These two organisms were reported by others to cause fever without other clinical symptoms. In spite of suggestive data, *there are no clear factors that are sensitive and specific to be relied upon in decision making.*

LABORATORY ASSESSMENT

Although there is no agreement about the significance of specific laboratory findings, it would nevertheless seem appropriate to assess the febrile young infant with a comprehensive laboratory assessment.

What should this assessment include, and how should this evaluation be influenced by the physical findings? For instance, if the patient has respiratory symptoms, should the evaluation be limited to a chest x-ray film, a complete blood count (CBC), and a blood culture; or is there a need to perform a "rule out sepsis" workup, including a lumbar puncture?

We surveyed 93 physicians (house staff, clinical, and full-time faculty) at Harbor/UCLA Medical Center. Ninety-six percent said they routinely perform a lumbar puncture on infants under 1 month of age with fever without an identified source; one physician said his decision to perform a lumbar puncture would depend on the appearance of the infant. The figure dropped to 58% if either otitis media or pneumonia was present. Greene et al[8] noted that two thirds of chief residents, but only 16% of practitioners, included the lumbar puncture as a routine part of the workup of the febrile infant under 2 months old, and that the febrile infant was 4 times as likely to receive a lumbar puncture in a university setting.

Although there is no consensus on the appropriate laboratory evaluation, common sense dictates that the assessment be guided by the clinical findings and a knowledge of the potential systemic spread of certain diseases. Conversely, the presence of certain physical findings might suggest the need for studies not routinely included in a "rule out sepsis" evaluation. For instance, young infants with otitis media should be examined with tympanocentesis.

Should one be selective in culture material? The data of Kröber et al[10] show that both bacterial and viral infections can exist even in the absence of inflammatory response. It would therefore seem appropriate to submit cultures (eg, of urine and CSF) even if no WBCs are present. Additionally, stool cultures in the absence of diarrhea, and chest x-ray studies in the absence of respiratory symptoms may be warranted. Although the laboratory evaluation may justifiably be individualized, it should be comprehensive.

MANAGEMENT

Most physicians would agree that young febrile infants are at risk for an assortment of serious illnesses, and clinical judgment and laboratory tests are poor at identifying the infant with occult infection. What then is a rational approach to the management of the febrile infant under 2 months of age? One approach would be universal hospitalization of all such infants. This approach would assure that all infants are appropriately treated so long as the correct antibiotics are used. However, only 62% of the infants we[1,6] studied were admitted, and only 69% of the training programs we surveyed routinely admitted febrile infants under 2 months old.

Are there drawbacks to universal hospitalization? Many infants experience a prolonged hospital stay because of contaminated cultures, infiltrated intravenous solutions, and nosocomial infections.[11,14] The psychologic issues of mother-infant separation and its effect on bonding and the fostering of the vulnerable infant syndrome have also been raised.[6] Last, there is the tremendous cost of hospitalization: A three-day hospital stay at our institution in 1987 cost approximately $2,700, and a five-day stay cost $4,500.

What does one do after admission? Should all admitted infants be managed expectantly with antibiotics pending culture outcome? What antibiotics should be used and for how long should they be administered? The incidence of *H influenzae* as a pathogen in this age group suggests that ampicillin and gentamicin sulfate may not provide adequate antimicrobial treatment. Concern about potential toxicity precludes the use of chloramphenicol in this age group. Cefotaxime sodium and other third generation cephalosporins have been recommended in lieu of gentamicin because of their broad spectrum against most bacterial causes of meningitis (excluding *Listeria*, which necessitates the addition of ampicillin to all therapeutic regimens). Caution should be exercised so that these drugs are not overused. It would be inappropriate to administer cefotaxime to every "rule out sepsis" admission. It also now appears that waiting 3 days to be certain cultures are negative is unnecessary. Recent studies[15] showed that waiting 48 hours is sufficient.

CONCLUSION

It is obvious that all *ill-appearing* infants should be hospitalized. Is there another approach for the *well-appearing,* young febrile infant? An alternative management strategy would include a comprehensive history and physical examination with a full laboratory workup including CBC and differential cell and platelet counts, ESR, urinalysis, urine culture, lumbar puncture, and analysis including bacterial and viral cultures, stool culture, and chest x-ray study. If any result suggests a site of bacterial or serious viral (ie, aseptic meningitis) infection, the infant should be admitted and begun on parenteral antibiotics. If the evaluation is normal, the infant may be sent home, but only if appropriate monitoring and follow-up in 8 to 12 hours on an ambulatory basis can be assured. The child should be observed for clinical resolution and continuing negative laboratory assessment with specific instructions regarding the signs and symptoms that require earlier re-evaluation.

REFERENCES

1. Berkowitz CD, Orr DP, Uchiyama N, et al: Variability in the management of the febrile infant under 2 months of age. *J Emerg Med* 1985;3:345–351.

2. Gundy JH: *Assessment of the Child in Primary Health Care.* New York, McGraw-Hill Book Co, 1981, pp 35–36.

3. Pantell RH, Naber M, Lamar R, et al: Fever in the first six months of life: Risks of underlying serious infection. *Clin Pediatr* 1980;19:77–82.

4. McCarthy PL, Dolan TF: The serious implications of high fever in infants during their first three months. *Clin Pediatr* 1976;15:794–796.

5. Roberts KB, Borzy MS: Fever in the first eight weeks of life. *Johns Hopkins Med J* 1977;141:9–13.

6. Berkowitz CD, Uchiyama N, Tully SB, et al: Fever in infants less than two months of age: Spectrum of disease and predictors of outcome. *Pediatr Emerg Care* 1985;1:128–135.

7. Crain EF, Shelov SP: Febrile infants: Predictors of bacteremia. *J Pediatr* 1982;101:686–689.

8. Greene JW, Hara C, O'Connor S, et al: Management of febrile outpatient neonates. *Clin Pediatr* 1981;20:375–380.

9. Caspe WB, Chamudes O, Louie B: The evaluation and treatment of the febrile infant. *Pediatr Infect Dis* 1983;2:131–135.

10. Krober MS, Bass JW, Powell JM, et al: Bacterial and viral pathogens causing fever in infants less than 3 months old. *Am J Dis Child* 1985;139:889–892.

11. DeAngelis C, Joffe A, Willis E, et al: Hospitalization *v* outpatient treatment of young, febrile infants. *Am J Dis Child* 1983;137:1150–1152.

12. Dagan R, Powell KR, Hall CB, et al: Identification of infants unlikely to have serious bacterial infection although hospitalized for sepsis. *J Pediatr* 1985;107:855–860.

13. Anbar RD, Richardson-de Corral V, O'Malley PJ: Difficulties in universal application of criteria identifying infants at low risk for serious bacterial infection. *J Pediatr* 1986;109:483–485.

14. DeAngelis C, Joffe A, Wilson M, et al: Iatrogenic risks and financial costs of hospitalizing febrile infants. *Am J Dis Child* 1983;137:1146–1149.

15. Rowley AH, Wald ER: Incubation period necessary to detect bacteremia in neonates. *Pediatr Infect Dis* 1986;5:590–591.

2. Fever in the First 8 Weeks of Life

Dianna M. Burns, MD

Fever in the first 2 months of life is a perplexing problem for the clinician. The infant under 3 months of age has 21 times the risk of serious infection when compared with the older child.[1] Distinguishing between the infected infant requiring immediate hospitalization and the infant who can be managed as an outpatient is a challenge to even the most experienced physician. The difficulty of diagnosing potentially life-threatening infections in febrile infants under 2 months of age based on clinical and laboratory criteria available at the initial encounter dictates variable policies regarding the extent of evaluation and the necessity for admission.

The reported percentage of serious infection in this age group varies. Some studies[2,3] found bacteremia to be as high as 12% to 14% in febrile infants under 6 weeks of age. There seems to be a decrease in the percentage of occult infection and an increase in the reliability of the clinical evaluation after 30 days of life.[2,4]

Although acquired at the time of delivery, often in association with prolonged rupture of membranes, group B streptococcus and *Listeria monocytogenes* can cause late onset of sepsis and meningitis. Gram-negative bacteria are important pathogens, as is *Staphylococcus aureus* associated with infection acquired in the nursery. Congenital toxoplasmosis may appear after birth with fever, poor feeding, rales, and even seizures.

Metabolic and anatomic defects may predispose the infant to increased risk. Galactosemic infants are at risk of gram-negative sepsis, whereas children with ectodermal dysplasia cannot maintain heat normally in a warm environment. Furthermore, neonates are relatively immunocompromised because of immature cellular function.

CLINICAL EXAMINATION

Any examination of the febrile neonate must start with a history of the pregnancy, delivery, and postnatal experience. Exposures to infection in either the nursery or the home must be sought. General habits and behavior should be reviewed and deviations defined.

The physical examination should assess the general state of the infant, often facilitated by early antipyretic therapy. The alert, active febrile infant is less likely to be harboring a serious occult infection.

Signs suggestive of focal infection must be sought. Ten percent of infants under 3 months of age experience an episode of otitis media.[5] Although examination of the middle ear is difficult, the tympanic membrane of the febrile neonate must be visualized and tested for mobility. Unlike in the older child, gram-negative organisms including *Escherichia coli*, *Klebsiella pneumoniae*, and *Pseudomonas aeruginosa* are important pathogens in the neonate. These organisms, along with group B streptococcus and *S aureus*, account for one third of the cases of otitis media in the first few weeks of life; *Streptococcus pneumoniae* and *Hemophilus influenzae* account for another third. No organism is found in the remainder. Conjunctivitis may be suggestive of *Chlamydia*, *S. aureus*, or *Neisseria gonorrhoeae* infections.

The degree of temperature should be noted. Mild elevations are common. Fifty percent of infants with temperatures greater than 37.8 °C but less than 38.3 °C had no serious illness in one study.[1] Some of the elevations could be related to logistical problems such as the infant being overdressed or in a hot room. However, 1% to 2% of these infants have a bacterial infection, particularly given the relative rarity of temperatures greater than 38.3 °C. McCarthy and Dolan[4,6] found that 8 of 22 (36%) infants under 3 months of age with temperatures greater than 40 °C had either bacterial meningitis, sepsis, pneumonia, or gastroenteritis with dehydration.

LABORATORY EVALUATION

Laboratory findings are poor predictors. The white blood cell (WBC) count is too variable. Infants with uncomplicated neonatal courses have an initial leukocytosis that usually resolves within the first 4 days of life. The absolute neutrophil count is normally between 1,350 and 8,840/mm^3; counts outside this range are associated with serious bacterial infection. However, 1% of normal newborns have neutrophil counts greater than 9,000/mm^3, particularly when the neonate was stressed after surgery or transfusions.[7] More alarming perhaps is the infant with a neutrophil count less than 1,350/mm³; severe neutropenia is often associated with sepsis.

In the older child, a left shift in the WBC count is indicative of a bacterial infection; this shift is not consistent in the neonate.[8] The ratio of immature cells to total neutrophil count is a more useful measurement in the neonate. Noninfected infants have a ratio of 0.339 to 0.476; ratios exceeding 0.800 are very worrisome.[9] Vacuolization and toxic granulations of the neutrophils are frequently found in infants with culture-proven bacterial sepsis. In fact, persistence of these changes correlates with inadequate antibiotic therapy or a resistant focus of infection.[10]

Since systemic infection is always a concern, a blood culture(s) should be taken in the febrile child under 2 months of age. Lumbar puncture should be considered because of the nonspecific signs of meningitis. However, if the child is bright, alert, and active with unremarkable laboratory findings after optimizing the reliability of the examination with control of fever and allowing the infant to be comfortable, the lumbar puncture may on occasion be delayed. Urinalysis and culturing should always be done. If sepsis is suspected, the ideal specimen is obtained by suprapubic aspiration or in-and-out catheterization. A chest x-ray film is usually appropriate because of the unreliability of clinical examination.

The erythrocyte sedimentation rate (ESR) is a nonspecific test for tissue damage. Normal newborns without sepsis or hemolytic disease during the first week of life have ESRs below 5 mm/hr, and below 10 mm/hr in the second week of life.[11] It is elevated in the infected infant.[6]

MANAGEMENT

Crain and Shelov[8] evaluated febrile infants under 8 weeks of age at an urban emergency department and determined that a combination of WBC ≥15,000/mm³, ESR ≥30 mm/hr, and clinical impression identified all infants with sepsis and excluded 82% of infants without bacteremia.

Many advocate admission for all febrile infants under 2 months of age; in practice one third of such infants are not admitted. This group is primarily infants with temperatures less than 38.3 °C (rectally). The private practitioner seems to be less likely to admit the febrile neonate than is the university-based physician.[12] Boys under 30 days of age and those with temperatures greater than 38.5 °C are more likely to be admitted for inpatient management.[2] Outpatient management is possible only if on initial examination the infant appears well, the physical examination is normal (except for possibly a mild upper respiratory tract infection or minimal gastrointestinal findings unassociated with tachypnea, dehydration, or vital sign abnormalities), and the laboratory findings are normal, including cerebrospinal fluid (CSF) and urine cultures, chest x-ray film, and laboratory screening. Good follow-up must be assured with re-examination scheduled within 12 to 24 hours or sooner if the condition worsens. Such observation without immediate treatment does not seem to endanger infants.[13]

However, it must be emphasized that the vast majority of febrile infants under 2 months of age are admitted. If admission is warranted, antibiotic therapy is initiated for at least 2 days until cultures are negative. In the infant who clinically looks well, and the need for admission is determined solely because of age or lack of good follow-up, withholding antibiotic therapy should be considered after appropriate cultures are obtained. This may decrease the hospital stay, decrease the chances of iatrogenic complications, and lessen the financial burden.[5,13] This patient must be monitored closely and constantly re-examined; any change in condition should lead to the initiation of antibiotic therapy.

Antibiotic therapy must cover group B streptococcus, *E coli*, and *L monocytogenes*. Ampicillin and an aminoglycoside are used extensively. Term infants without urinary tract infections rarely have gram-negative baccillus sepsis after 4 weeks of age, whereas the problem of *H influenzae* commences at this time. Chloramphenicol should probably replace the aminoglycoside in the term infant at 4 weeks of age. In contrast, pre-term infants with perinatal complications should be covered with ampicillin and an aminoglycoside until 2 months of age.[5] The third generation cephalosporins offer alternative drug coverage while providing good penetration into the CSF. Cefotaxime or other cephalosporins are used extensively with excellent success and should be combined with ampicillin in children under 2 months of age.[14]

CONCLUSION

Infants *under 1 month* of age require special consideration; the incidence of occult infection is greater, the clinical assessment is less reliable, and the host reserves are more easily depleted. Perhaps inpatient management of all infants under 1 month of age with parenteral antibiotics is indicated.

After 1 month of age, the clinical assessment along with laboratory screening lends some support to the acceptability of outpatient management of some of these patients, provided the physical and laboratory examinations are unremarkable and follow-up is assured.

There is no clear-cut approach or diagnostic scheme permitting the security of 100% sensitivity. Each child must be assessed individually, and the risks, benefits, and clinician's level of comfort based on clinical judgment and experience must be weighed.

REFERENCES

1. Pantell RH, Naber M, Lamar R, et al: Fever in the first six months of life. *Clin Pediatr* 1980;19:77.

2. Radetsky M: The clinical evaluation of the febrile infant. *Prim Care* 1984;11:395.

3. Amio J, Alpent G, Reisner SH: Fever in the first month of life in Israel. *J Med Sci* 1984; 5:447.

4. McCarthy PL, Dolan TF: The serious implications of high fever in infants during their first three months: Six years experience at Yale-New Haven Hospital emergency room. *Clin Pediatr* 1976;15:794–798.

5. Klein JO, Schlesinger PC, Karasio RB: Management of the febrile infant three months of age or younger. *Pediatr Infect Dis* 1984;3:75.

6. McCarthy PL: Controversies in pediatrics: What tests are indicated for the child under two with fever. *Pediatr Rev* 1979;1:51.

7. Gregory J, Hey E: Blood neutrophil response to bacterial infection in the first month of life. *Arch Dis Child* 1972;47:747.

8. Crain EF, Shelov SP: Febrile infants: Predictors of bacteremia. *J Pediatr* 1982; 101:686.

9. Christensen RD, Bradley PP, Rothstein G: The leukocyte left shift in clinical and experimental neonatal sepsis. *J Pediatr* 191;98:101.

10. Liw CH, Lehan C, Speer ME, et al: Degenerative changes in neutrophils: Indicator of bacterial infection. *Pediatr Rev* 1979;1:51.

11. Adler SM, Denton RL: The erythrocyte sedimentation rate in the newborn period. *J Pediatr* 1975;86:942.

12. DeAngelis C, Jolfe A, Willis E: Hospitalization versus outpatient treatment of young febrile infants. *Am J Dis Child* 1983;137:1150.

13. Greene JW, O'Connor S, Altemeier WA: Management of febrile outpatient neonates. *Clin Pediatr* 1981;20:375.

14. Kaplan, Sheldon: Current management of common bacteria meningitides. *Pediatr Rev* 1985;7:77.

3. The Febrile Child under 2 Years of Age: Assessment and Management

Pamela M. Downey, MD, BSc Med

Assessment of the febrile child aged 2 months to 2 years is a common pediatric problem accounting for one fourth to one third of pediatric patient visits in pediatric ambulatory clinics.[1,2] Fever may be a symptom that heralds a trivial illness or the harbinger of serious disease. Indeed, the child with a potentially life-threatening illness may be obscured by the large number of children with fever and self-limited disease. This is further complicated by the difficulty in assessing the signs, symptoms, and physical condition of children under 2 years of age. Data are obtained from the parent, the child is often frightened, and the examination may be difficult and time consuming. What guidelines exist to assist in this evaluation?

DEFINITION OF FEVER

Most clinicians define fever as a temperature greater than 37.8 °C orally or 38.3 °C rectally without prior antipyretic therapy.[1] Mothers who state that their child has a "subjective" fever are correct 52.3% of the time when they use palpation. When they feel their child is not febrile, they are correct 93.9% of the time.[3]

Axillary temperatures are insensitive and inaccurate in assessing a fever; one third of fevers are not detected by an axillary temperature.[4] The skin temperature is influenced by ambient temperature. Skin vasoconstriction accompanies fevers as part of the mechanism through which fever is mounted. Hence, while the core temperature is rising, the skin temperature is falling.

CATEGORIES OF FEBRILE CHILDREN

Children with fever can be grouped into five categories based on the duration of fever and underlying host characteristics.[2] The *first* category is children with a fever of less than 2 weeks duration and no localizing signs. It is this category around which most of the controversy exists and this will be the main focus of a later discussion. The *second* group is children with fever and a localized infection. These two groups account for the vast majority of children with fever.

The *third* category is children with underlying conditions such as heart disease, malignancy, postsplenectomy, sickle cell disease, and other immuno-compromised states. These children all require aggressive evaluation and management. They usually require hospitalization and presumptive antibiotic therapy. Group *four* includes children with fever and nonspecific signs such as weight loss, lymphadenopathy, organomegaly, etc. These children require investigation for an underlying malignancy, connective tissue disease, or chronic infection. The *fifth* category is children with fever of unknown origin (FUO) for more than 2 weeks.[2]

ETIOLOGY

The vast majority of febrile illnesses in children are respiratory, although a host of conditions can cause fevers. In one series[5] of children under 24 months of age who had an acute onset of temperatures of 40 °C or above, the diagnostic categories and their relative incidence are presented in Table 3-1.

Table 3-1 Diagnostic Categories and Their Frequencies in the Febrile Child

Category of Illness		Percent of Total
Otitis media		36.9%
Nonspecific illness		25.5%
Pneumonia		15.5%
Recognizable viral illness		12.7%
Exanthem/enanthem	5.8%	
Meningitis/encephalitis	3.6%	
Gastroenteritis	1.8%	
Croup	1.5%	
Recognizable bacterial illness		9.4%
Bacteremia	6.1%	
Cellulitis	0.9%	
Meningitis	1.2%	
Urinary tract infection	0.6%	
Other	0.6%	

Source: Reprinted with permission from *Pediatrics in Review* (1979;1:51), Copyright © 1979, American Academy of Pediatrics.

Viral infections account for the majority of illness in children. The most common bacterial pathogens include *Streptococcus pneumoniae* and *Hemophilus influenzae*, the latter accounting for the majority of invasive disease in children under 9 years of age. Group A streptococcus, *Neisseria meningitidis*, *Staphylococcus aureus*, and *Salmonella* species are also frequent pathogens.

ASSESSMENT OF THE FEBRILE CHILD

History

The history may delineate specific useful symptoms such as ear tugging, diarrhea, vomiting, respiratory problems, urinary symptoms, rash, or significant household or day-care exposures. Substantial current medical problems need to be elucidated, but usually the symptoms are nonspecific with children having fever, poor appetite, irritability, or lethargy.

The past medical history is also important, focusing on underlying problems, previous heart or lung disease, sickle cell disease, or any immunocompromised state.

Clinical Judgment

Observation of the child is invaluable in making an assessment. Antipyretic therapy with acetaminophen (10 to 15 mg/kg) every 4 to 6 hours should be started *early* to facilitate the examination. Many children appear lethargic and irritable when their temperatures are elevated; rapid improvement in responsiveness is noted with defervescence. The child should interact with its environment, looking at the examiner and around the room, smiling, and interacting.[6] Another valuable observation includes the amount of motor activity the child exhibits.

Physical Examination

The physical examination should determine how sick the child is and if there is evidence of dehydration. Foci of infection may become evident, and associated infections such as meningitis must be excluded.

A careful history and physical examination identify approximately 70% of serious illnesses in the child under 2 years old.[5]

Laboratory Assessment

Identifying the child who requires extensive laboratory evaluation is the subject of lively debate. The clinical assessment, based on history and physical examination and observation, is central to deciding to pursue laboratory evaluation. If the child has focal symptoms or signs, the evaluation should focus on that entity as well as excluding concurrent infection. Children commonly have an easily defined infection such as otitis media, but may also have accompanying meningitis or pneumonia.

The presence of otitis media, an upper respiratory tract infection (URI) or fever without a source in a child with a high fever should not be a diagnostic endpoint. The incidence of occult bacteremia in the febrile child between 3 and 24 months of age is between 3% and 10%.[1,7–10] The risk of bacteremia parallels the increase in fever; using 38.9 °C as a temperature cutoff, it is approximately 6%. Clinical evaluation in children under 2 years of age can identify only about two thirds of a group at high risk for bacteremia; therefore, children in this age group who have a temperature greater than 38.9 °C should be further assessed with a white blood cell (WBC) count. If the WBC count is more than 15,000/mm³, a blood culture is normally obtained because this elevation is associated with an increased risk of bacteremia (Table 3-2 and Figure 3-1).[5,8] Usually the blood culture is obtained while the WBC count is drawn, and the culture is later discarded if the cell count is not elevated.

These laboratory tests may be postponed if close follow-up is available, the parents are reliable observers, and the child looks well. The child can then be reassessed by history and physical examination in 8 to 12 hours, and a laboratory evaluation performed if the child is still febrile or looks ill. Children with a temperature less than 38.9 °C who look well, have a WBC count between 5,000 and 15,000/mm³, and interact with their environment have a greater than 96% chance of having a sterile culture.[2]

The risk of developing meningitis in a child under 2 years old is estimated at 0.1%. Bacteremia as a risk factor increases the probability of subsequent meningitis by 40 times.[2] Children with a temperature greater than 41.1 °C have a 10% incidence of meningitis.

Lumbar puncture is essential to making the diagnosis of meningitis. Several studies[11,12] have suggested that the risk of subsequent meningitis is increased in children who receive a lumbar puncture at their initial evaluation. Subsequent reports[12] retrospectively looked at 1,483 bacteremic children and revealed that the development of meningitis correlated best with the bacterial species involved. The risk of meningitis was highest with meningococcemia, followed by *H influenzae* bacteremia and *S pneumoniae*. Lumbar puncture at the first visit was not strongly associated with an increased risk of meningitis. A lumbar puncture should be performed if a diagnosis of meningitis is consid-

Table 3-2 Occult Bacteremia: Major Pathogens and Risk Factors

Author	Major Pathogens (% of Total Pathogens)	Significant Associations
Waskerwitz and Berkelhamer[9]	S pneumoniae 3% H influenzae 1.7% Group B streptococcus 0.3% Salmonella sp 0.3% N meningitidis 0.3%	Physician's assessment
Teele et al[10]	S pneumoniae 2.5% H influenzae 0.33% K pneumoniae 0.16% C perfringens 0.16%	Age 7–18 mo WBC >15,000/mm³ Temp >38.9 °C Pneumonia, URI, FUO
McGowan et al[1]	S pneumoniae 2.68% H influenzae 0.85% S aureus 0.28% S pyogenes 0.14% S micros 0.14% N meningitidis 0.14% Salmonella sp 0.14%	Age 7–12 mo Temp > 38.9 °C WBC > 20,000/mm³ Pulmonary infiltrate
McCarthy et al[5]	S pneumoniae 2% H influenzae 2.3% Salmonella sp 0.6% N meningitidis 0.5% Other 0.95%	Age 3–18 mo Age 36–46 mo Temp > 40 °C WBC > 15,000/mm³ URI, FUO, otitis media

ered.[1] A repeat lumbar puncture should be considered if the bacteremic child appears ill at follow-up (Section 5).

Urinary tract infections in children under 2 years old may be subtle. Children may have only fever, lethargy, or vomiting and diarrhea as presenting symptoms. Pyuria is not a reliable indicator of the presence or absence of infection. Approximately one third of urine samples from young children with less than 10 WBC per high-power field will grow a significant pathogen.[13] Children whose fever does not have an obvious source should have their urine cultured (Section 4).

Follow-Up

Studies of the outcome of children with unsuspected bacteremia have shed some light on the significance of this illness, although the natural history needs to be more clearly defined. A retrospective study[14] of children with pneumococcal bacteremia revealed that meningitis developed in three, whereas two

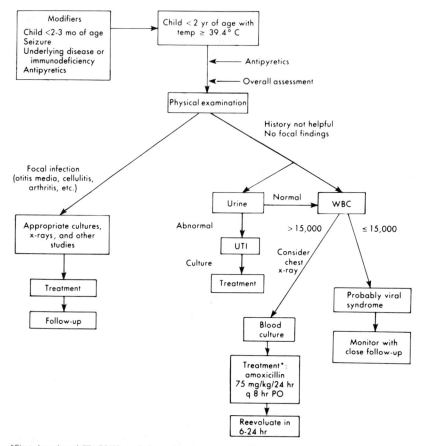

*First dose (ampicillin 50-75 mg/kg) may be given parenterally.

Figure 3-1 Evaluation of febrile child under 2 years of age. *Source:* Reprinted from *Emergency Pediatrics*, ed 2 (p 180), by RM Barkin and P Rosen with permission of CV Mosby Company, © 1986.

developed an identifiable respiratory focus. In a prospective study[15] of children well enough to go home at the initial visit and subsequently found to have pneumococcal bacteremia at follow-up, 12.5% had persistent bacteremia, 2.5% pneumonia, and 2.5% meningitis. Thus, pneumococcal bacteremia is not an entirely benign disease. Follow-up of 94 episodes of *H influenzae* bacteremia showed that in one third, severe focal infections developed.[16]

Prophylactic antibiotic administration has been suggested as a means of reducing these complications. The answer to this question is at present unresolved. Teele et al[10] showed that children sent home on oral antibiotic therapy improved more often than those who did not receive antibiotics. Meningitis developed with equal frequency in both groups. A prospective study[17] comparing penicillin therapy (Bicillin C-R 50,000 units benzathine/kg followed by oral penicillin, 100 mg/kg/d) with no antibiotics in children with fever greater than 40 °C and no identifiable focus of infection concluded that antibiotic therapy is appropriate in children at risk of occult bacteremia without a focus. Ten of 96 patients were bacteremic. Four of the 5 treated patients were improved at the follow-up visit, whereas the 5 untreated bacteremic patients were unimproved in the untreated group, two developed otitis media, and two developed meningitis. Although the numbers are small, the authors conclude that antibiotic therapy is warranted for children who have no focus of infection and are at risk for occult bacteremia. A third study by Jaffee[12] (discussed by McLellan) compared the outcomes of 475 children from 3 to 36 months of age with a temperature greater than 39 °C, one half of whom were treated with amoxicillin and the remainder with placebo. Nineteen were bacteremic, and in the treated group, 9 of 13 patients were improved at follow-up, but three patients had persistent bacteremia and one child developed periorbital cellulitis. In the untreated group, 3 of 6 were better.

Oral antibiotics may retard the development of less serious disease but do not seem to prevent the development of subsequent meningitis.[2]

MANAGEMENT CONSIDERATIONS

A systematic approach is mandatory, requiring an understanding of the clinical data summarized above and clinical judgment (Figure 3-1).

Several conclusions are worthy of emphasis:

- Children with underlying disease (asplenia, malignancy, etc) who have a fever and no focus of infection should have a complete blood count (CBC), blood culture, and lumbar puncture before being hospitalized for presumptive antibiotic therapy.
- In the previously well child between 2 months and 2 years old with a temperature greater than 38.9 °C, no focus of infection (including otitis media or URI), and who *looks well* by clinical assessment, a CBC should be obtained. If the WBC count is between 5,000 and 15,000/mm^3, the child probably has a viral illness and may be monitored with close follow-up.[18] If the WBC count is more than 15,000/mm^3, a blood culture should be obtained. As meningeal signs are unreliable in children under 12 to 18 months of age, a lumbar puncture should be considered.

- Previously well children who are febrile, who have no focus of infection, and *appear ill* should have a CBC, blood culture, lumbar puncture, and be hospitalized for observation. Antibiotic coverage for *S pneumoniae, H influenzae*, and *N meningitidis* should be provided. Immunocompromised children require broader coverage.

- Do not rely on urinalysis to rule out urinary tract infection (UTI) in young children. Culture the urine in those for whom the diagnosis of UTI is a consideration.

- The question of prophylactic antibiotics is difficult because of the lack of consistent data. Prophylactic antibiotic administration may reduce morbidity in these children, but does not seem to prevent serious illness. It is important that the use of prophylactic antibiotics not provide a false sense of security to the clinician. Remember that as many as one significantly febrile infant in ten is bacteremic, and the risk of meningitis in bacteremic children is increased 40 times.

- Reliable follow-up and close monitoring of children who appear well on initial examination are essential, with reassessment in 6 to 12 hours. If their condition changes earlier, more prompt evaluation is necessary.

REFERENCES

1. McGowan Jr, Bratton L, Klein JO, et al: Bacteremia in febrile children seen in a 'walk-in' pediatric clinic. *N Engl J Med* 1973;25:1309.

2. Radetsky M: The clinical evaluation of the febrile infant. *Prim Care* 1984;11:395.

3. Banco L, Veltri D: Ability of mothers to subjectively assess the presence of fever in their children. *Am J Dis Child* 1984;138:976.

4. Kresch MJ: Axillary temperature as a screening test for fever in children. *J Pediatr* 1984; 104:596.

5. McCarthy P, Jekel JF, Dolan TF: Temperature greater than or equal to 40 °C in children less than 24 months of age: A prospective study. *Pediatrics* 1977;59:663.

6. McCarthy P, et al: Further definition of history and observation variables in assessing febrile children. *Pediatrics* 1981;67:687.

7. Crain EF, Shelov SP: Febrile infants: Predictors of bacteremia. *J Pediatr* 1982;101:686.

8. Teele D, et al: Bacteremia in febrile children less than two years of age: Results of cultures of 600 consecutive febrile children seen in a walk-in clinic. *J Pediatr* 1975;87:227.

9. Waskerwitz S, Berkelhamer JE: Outpatient bacteremia: Clinical findings in children under two years with initial temperatures of 39.5 °C or higher. *J Pediatr* 1981;99:231–233.

10. Teele DW, Marshall R, Klein JO: Unsuspected bacteremia in young children. *Pediatr Clin North Am* 1979;26:773.

11. Teele DW, Dashefsky B, Rakusan T, et al: Meningitis after lumbar puncture in children with bacteremia. *N Engl J Med* 1981;305:1079.

12. McLellan D, Giebink GS: Perspectives on occult bacteremia in children. *J Pediatr* 1986; 109:1.

13. Ginsburg CM, McCracken GH: Urinary tract infections in young infants. *Pediatrics* 1982; 69:409.

14. Myers MG, et al: Complications of occult pneumococcal bacteremia in children. *J Pediatr* 1974;84:656.

15. McCarthy P, et al: Bacteremia in children: An outpatient clinical review. *Pediatrics* 1976; 57:861.

16. Marshall R, Teele DW, Klein JO: Unsuspected bacteremia due to *Hemophilus influenzae*: Outcome in children not initially admitted to hospital. *J Pediatr* 1979;95:690.

17. Carroll WL, et al: Treatment of occult bacteremia: A prospective randomized clinical trial. *Pediatrics* 1983;72:608.

18. Barkin RM, Rosen P: *Emergency Pediatrics*, ed 2. CV Mosby Co, 1986, pp 178–183.

4. Management of the Febrile Child under 2 Years of Age

Louis M. Bell, MD

The identification of serious infection is the primary concern when examining the young febrile child between the ages of 3 and 24 months. Infections with *Streptococcus pneumoniae* and *Hemophilus influenzae* type B (including meningitis) have a peak incidence in this age group. Because of the potentially devastating sequelae of these infections and the often subtle nature of the presentation, it is essential that the physician understand the risk factors for serious infection, the laboratory tests needed in the evaluation, and the indications for treatment.

EVALUATION AND RISK FACTORS FOR SERIOUS INFECTION

The initial examination of the febrile child should include consideration of five factors: (1) age, (2) degree of the temperature, (3) severity of illness, (4) immunocompetence, and (5) the presence or absence of a focus of infection. Consideration of these factors will make identifying the child at risk for bacteremia or sepsis easier and will direct management and treatment.

Age

Febrile children under 24 months of age are at greater risk for serious bacterial infections, particularly with encapsulated bacteria. It is the encapsulated structure of these bacteria (*S pneumoniae, H influenzae* type B, *Neisseria meningitidis*, and *Salmonella* sp) and the poor antibody responses to the antigenically distinct polysaccharide capsules that are the likely explanations for the virulence of these organisms in this age group. Maturation of the antibody response occurs over the first 2 years of life and reaches adult levels by 18 to 24 months. In one study[1] of pneumococcal infections in children, 88% of meningitis, 70% of bacteremia, and 85% of otitis media occurred before the age of 2 years. Recently, in surveillance of *H influenzae* disease, approximately 88% of meningitis and 82% of other invasive types occurred in children younger than 24 months of age.[2]

Fever

The degree of elevation of the temperature is also important in assessing risk. Although a temperature less than 38.9 °C reassures the physician that bacteremia is not present (a negative predictive value of 99%), as the temperature climbs above 39 °C, the child's risk for sepsis, bacteremia, or meningitis increases.[3] Three to five percent of children aged 3 to 24 months with temperatures greater than 39 °C to 40 °C will be bacteremic with either *S pneumoniae* (50% to 60%), *H influenzae* (20% to 30%), or other organisms (10% to 20%) including *N meningitidis* and *Salmonella* sp.[3] In addition, McCarthy and Dolan[4] found that as temperatures rise even higher ($\geq$ 41.1 °C), the number of patients with meningitis significantly increases as compared with a group of patients with temperatures of 40.5 °C to 41.0 °C. The physician cannot use a decrease in temperature after antipyretic therapy as a reassuring indication that bacteremia or sepsis is less likely. Torrey et al[5] studied children 3 to 24 months of age with temperatures greater than 38.9 °C, and compared one group with bacteremia with a group without bacteremia. There was no difference in response to antipyretic therapy between the two groups.

Severity of Illness

Assessing the severity of illness or toxic condition of the febrile child is a clinical skill that comes with experience and is subjective and difficult to teach to medical students and house staff. Clearly the younger the child the harder it may be to judge the severity of illness. McCarthy and co-workers[6] attempted to translate the physician's subjective observations into a "severity of illness scoring system." With this system, clinicians generate a score based on quality of cry, reaction to parent stimulation, state of variation (ie, wakefulness), color, hydration, and response to social overtures. Ninety-two percent of children with a high score (ie, they appeared severely ill) were found to have serious illness including meningitis, pneumonia, cellulitis, septic arthritis, and infections of the urinary tract.[6] Regardless of the physician's method, an impression of severity of illness in the febrile child is vital for proper management.

The Immunocompromised Child

Obviously, an important part of the initial examination of the febrile child is a careful history of any condition that might affect immune function. In the 3- to 24-month-old child, a congenital immunodeficiency, although rare, should be considered in the child with recurrent serious bacterial infections or failure to thrive. Children undergoing cancer chemotherapy or with other chronic diseases such as nephrosis have increased risk of infection. A history of any illness or trauma that results in the removal of the spleen (idiopathic thrombocytopenia purpura, Hodgkin's disease, trauma) or a decrease in splenic function (sickle cell anemia) increases the risk of overwhelming infection, particularly with encapsulated organisms. Septicemia in these children may have a rapid onset and progression. The febrile child with sickle cell anemia has a 400 fold increased risk of pneumococcal septicemia if under 5 years old and a 4 fold risk of *H influenzae* septicemia if under 9 years of age.[7] Any febrile child with a sudden onset of fever and a history suggesting immunocompromise should be admitted to the hospital and placed on antibiotic therapy after appropriate bacterial cultures are done.

MANAGEMENT AND TREATMENT OF THE FEBRILE CHILD

Based on examination findings as outlined above, the febrile child 3 to 24 months of age can be placed into one of four categories:

1. well-appearing with a focus of infection
2. ill-appearing with a focus of infection
3. ill-appearing without a focus of infection
4. well-appearing without a focus of infection.

The Febrile Child with a Focus of Infection

Management of the well-appearing child with an identifiable focus of infection is directed by the history, site of infection, and the risks of subsequent spread to other vital organs. For example, outpatient management with oral antibiotics for the febrile child with an extremity cellulitis that developed after mild trauma is appropriate. However, a well-appearing child with fever and periorbital cellulitis requires hospitalization and intravenous antibiotic therapy. The diagnosis of otitis media has special implications and is reviewed later.

Conversely, the child who appears severely ill with a focus of infection should be hospitalized. Laboratory studies (complete blood count [CBC], differential cell and platelet counts, erythrocyte sedimentation rate [ESR], and cultures) aimed at defining the bacterial cause and extent of the infection should be obtained. Once again, the appropriate tests and cultures are governed by the site of infection.

The Febrile Child without a Focus of Infection

The child who appears severely ill without a focus of infection should have a complete series of tests to rule out sepsis and meningitis. A "sepsis workup" includes a CBC with differential cell and platelet counts. Evidence of leukocytosis or leukopenia ($< 5,000/mm^3$) increases the chances of sepsis or bacteremia. Additional tests include bacterial cultures of the blood, urine, and cerebrospinal fluid (CSF), urinalysis, and chest roentgenogram. There has been controversy recently about the risks of causing meningitis when a lumbar puncture is performed during an episode of bacteremia. However, in reviewing the data, Shapiro et al[8] controlled for the confounding effects of other clinical variables and found that the development of bacterial meningitis in children with occult bacteremia is dependent only on the bacterial species causing the infection. Therefore, the physician should perform a lumbar puncture at the slightest suspicion of meningitis without fear of inducing or increasing the risk of subsequent meningitis.

Once the sepsis workup is completed, broad-spectrum antibiotics should be administered pending the results of the laboratory tests. In the ill patient without an apparent focus of infection who is not immunocompromised, ampicillin and chloramphenicol, given intravenously, are still used in our hospital. However, in comparative trials, the newer third generation cephalosporins were shown to be as effective in providing broad-spectrum coverage and may be an appropriate alternative.

OCCULT BACTEREMIA

Management of the febrile but well-appearing child without a focus of infection presents a challenge to the physician. The management and treatment of these patients remain controversial, but a plan of action can be formulated based on available clinical information. The issue of occult bacteremia is the basis for the controversy. As we stated earlier, 3% to 5% of children between the ages of 3 and 24 months with a temperature greater than 39.4 °C who look clinically well are bacteremic.

Complications of occult bacteremia include such serious infections as meningitis, cellulitis, and epiglottitis. Blood culture tests remain the only reliable method of diagnosing occult bacteremia. The risk factors discussed earlier, although helpful, fail to identify patients with bacteremia. At most, two thirds of cases are correctly predicted by experienced clinicians, and then only at the expense of misdiagnosis in others with viral infections.

Laboratory Tests

Unfortunately, no laboratory test result can reliably predict bacteremia on the initial evaluation. Based on clinical studies, however, we know that the 3- to 24-month-old child with a temperature greater than 39.4 °C and white blood cell count (WBC) of more than 15,000/mm³ has a 10% chance of bacteremia. These children are 5 times more likely to have bacteremia, and 2 times more likely to have pneumonia, than children with lower counts.[9] The diagnosis of otitis media in these circumstances (ie, 3 to 24 months, $\geq$ 40 °C, > 15,000/mm³) *increases* the likelihood of bacteremia or pneumonia to 8 times that of similar children with WBC counts less than 15,000. Although the WBC count is somewhat helpful, we should remember that although 60% of bacteremic patients have WBC counts greater than 15,000/mm³, so do 30% of those with negative blood cultures. Children with *H influenzae* or *N meningitidis* occult bacteremia, which have the highest complication rates, stand an even chance of having a WBC count less than 15,000/mm³. Additional tests such as ESR, latex agglutination, and differential counts have not increased the identification of these children to a great degree.

Presumptive Treatment of Occult Bacteremia

The relatively high incidence of bacteremia among young febrile children, combined with the inability to diagnose bacteremia clinically at the time of the visit and the risk of serious focal complications, led several investigators to study presumptive antibiotic therapy in susceptible populations. Although early retrospective investigations[10,11] of bacteremia suggested a beneficial effect from antibiotics, these data *were* retrospective, the patients were not randomized and differed clinically, and the type and route of antibiotic administration varied, the incidence of meningitis was not influenced. Jaffee et al[12] in a randomized, double-blind study of oral amoxicillin for presumed bacteremia in 1,500 febrile children found no difference in incidence of major sequelae between the groups. However, expectant antibiotic therapy did reduce fever and improved the clinical appearance of bacteremic children.

The only other prospective trial[13] was a nonblind study with a combination of penicillin G benzathine and penicillin G procaine suspension given intramuscularly, which found a significant reduction of complications in the treated group. This study was flawed, however, because it was nonblind and included otitis media (a minor complication) in the list of major complications such as meningitis.

Recommendations for Treatment of Occult Bacteremia

Although there are many different reasonable approaches to management and treatment of the febrile child at risk for occult bacteremia, the following conservative approach is recommended: Any child 3 to 24 months of age with a temperature greater than 39.4 °C, no focus of infection (or otitis media), and who appears clinically well should have a CBC done and blood taken for culture. If the WBC count is greater than 15,000/mm³, the blood culture should be sent for processing. If the temperature is less than 39.4 °C and the WBC count is in the normal range, the child will be at low risk for bacteremia, and a viral syndrome is likely.

Because pneumonia is common and often difficult to diagnose in this age group, we recommend that if the WBC count is elevated (greater than 15,000/mm³) in the child with a high fever, a chest film should be strongly considered if the respiratory rate is greater than 40 breaths per minute, even in the absence of localizing chest finding on physical examination.

If the chest x-ray film shows no abnormalities, a urinalysis and urine culture should be done if the child is a girl.[14] If at any time during the evaluation a focus is found (ie, pneumonia, urinary tract infection), it should be treated appropriately.

The management of the child at risk for bacteremia with otitis media may be amended somewhat. Since the decision to treat this focal infection is already made, a CBC is not so important. However, a blood culture should be sent because these patients are still at risk for bacteremia and pneumonia. The decision to send the child for a chest x-ray film can be based on the WBC count and the presence or absence of tachypnea.

Based on the prospective study by Jaffee et al,[12] I believe presumptive treatment is warranted for children at risk for occult bacteremia. Although the study showed that treatment had no effect on major sequelae, the patients had a reduction in fever and clinical symptoms. Treatment using oral amoxicillin is based on patient weight (125 mg three times daily for children ≤ 10 kg, and 250 mg three times daily for children > 10 kg). Parenteral antibiotics (ampicillin sodium 50–75 mg/kg or ceftriaxone 50 mg/kg) may be an alternative. Follow-up in 24 to 48 hours is necessary.

MANAGEMENT OF THE CHILD WITH A POSITIVE BLOOD CULTURE

If the child is bacteremic, treatment depends on the clinical symptoms and the bacteria isolated. If *S pneumoniae* is isolated, and the child is *febrile* with no focal infection or otitis media, a complete septic workup and admission for IV antibiotic therapy is necessary. Children who are *afebrile* should have a repeat blood culture taken and can be discharged to home on oral penicillin V potassium for 10 days if they are well appearing. Daily follow-up is essential. Any other pathogen isolated from the blood (ie, *H influenzae*, *N meningitidis*, or *Salmonella* sp) necessitates admission, a complete septic workup, and appropriate IV antibiotic therapy.

REFERENCES

1. Gray BM, Converse GM III, Dillon HC Jr: Serotypes of *Streptococcus pneumoniae* causing disease. *J Infect Dis* 1979;140:979–983.

2. Murphy TV, Osterholm MT, Pierson LM, et al: Prospective surveillance of *Haemophilus influenzae* type B disease in Dallas County, Texas and in Minnesota. *Pediatrics* 1987;79:173–180.

3. McLellan D, Grebink GS: Perspectives on occult bacteremia in children. *J Pediatr* 1986;109:1–8.

4. McCarthy PL, Dolan TF: Hyperpyrexia in children. *Am J Dis Child* 1976;130:849–851.

5. Torrey SB, Henretig F, Fleisher G, et al: Temperature response to antipyretic therapy in children. *Am J Emerg Med* 1985;3:190–192.

6. McCarthy PL, Sharpe MR, Spresel SZ: Observation scales to identify serious illness in febrile children. *Pediatrics* 1982;70:802–809.

7. Powars D, Overturf G, Turner E: Is there an increased risk of *H influenzae* septicemia in children with sickle cell anemia? *Pediatrics* 1983;71:927–931.

8. Shapiro ED, Aaron NH, Wald ER, et al: Risk factors for development of bacterial meningitis among children with occult bacteremia. *J Pediatr* 1986;109:15–19.

9. McCarthy PL: Controversies in pediatrics: What tests are indicated for the child under 2 with fever. *Pediatr Rev* 1979;1:51–56.

10. Bratton L, Teele DW, Klein JO: Outcome of unsuspected pneumococcemia in children not initially admitted to the hospital. *J Pediatr* 1977;90:703–706.

11. Marshall R, Teele DW, Klein JO: Unsuspected bacteremia due to *Haemophilus influenzae*: Outcome in children not initially admitted to hospital. *J Pediatr* 1979;95:690–695.

12. Jaffee DM, Fleisher GR, Henretig F: A preliminary report of a randomized trial: The effect of early oral antibiotic therapy on febrile children with bacteremia. Abstracts of the 23rd Annual Meeting of the Ambulatory Pediatric Association, Washington, DC, 1983.

13. Carroll WL, Farrell MK, Singer JI, et al: Treatment of occult bacteremia: A prospective randomized clinical trial. *Pediatrics* 1983;72:608–612.

14. Roberts KB, Charney E, Sweren RJ, et al: Urinary tract infection in infants with unexplained fever: A collaborative study. *J Pediatr* 1983;103:864–867.

5. Fever: Management and Measurement

Janet E. McNally, RN, MS

It is estimated that one fourth of all encounters in private offices and clinics are prompted by febrile illnesses. Many parents believe that fever in and of itself can be harmful and cause life-threatening injury to their children. Focusing on fever is not limited to parents alone. Health care providers may contribute to misconceptions; fever is an important diagnostic criterion.

The measurement of temperature varies from practitioner to practitioner and from setting to setting. It is understandable that parents become concerned about their child's fever when their care provider obtains a temperature with each visit, and may even remeasure it with a different instrument to check the initial accuracy. The ideal site and instrument for temperature measurement and the management strategies for fever remain controversial.

THE SITE

The criteria for choosing a site for temperature measurement include proximity to major arteries, insulation from external influences (eating, drinking, etc), absence of inflammation, degree of precision required, overall status of the patient, the patient's age, and safety of the technique.[1] In the case of rectal temperatures, the care provider must also consider the impact of the procedure on the child with respect to the nature of invasiveness and discomfort.

Rectal temperatures have been considered the most accurate determination of core temperature. Studies done over the past 20 years have challenged this perception. Rectal perforation and trauma to the fragile rectal mucosa are real threats to the young infant or struggling toddler. Buntain et al[2] reported nine instances of rectal perforation by thermometers. The emotional impact on the young child must be considered when data support the accuracy of axillary and oral routes for temperature measurement in specific circumstances. In children too young to master oral temperature taking (generally under the age of 4 years), the rectal route has traditionally been used. Nurses, other health care providers, and parents involved in temperature taking have noted that children in this age group find the procedure uncomfortable and, for the most part, show behaviors that indicate discomfort such as crying, fussing, and struggling.

The *oral or sublingual* site is close to the branches of the lingual artery and a branch of the external carotid artery. However, the temperature can be affected by food and fluids as well as muscular activity. These factors may be controlled. Most children 4 years of age and older can learn to cooperate with this method; otherwise, an accurate reading cannot be obtained, and if a glass thermometer is used, it may break.

Axillary temperatures remain controversial from the perspective of accuracy. In children under 4 years old, the oral temperature is not practical, and in many settings, the axillary temperature is preferred to the rectal route because of the ease and lack of invasiveness. Trauma and discomfort are thereby minimized, and the technique is easily taught. Furthermore, the large deposits of brown fat found in the axilla render this site an accurate indicator of deep body temperature.

Buntain et al[2] studied the differences between rectal and axillary temperatures using both glass, mercury thermometers and electronic thermometers. Neonates were studied in the controlled environment of the nursery. Temperatures at 3, 5, and 10 minutes using the two techniques correlated well. The authors recommended the axillary site over the rectal site in the nursery setting, and again stressed safety, hygiene, and diminished vagal stimulation as advantages of the axillary route when environmental factors can be controlled. The oral route was still considered optimal in children old enough to cooperate, as well as in adults.[1]

Haddock et al[3] studied 31 neonates and found that for 52% of the infants, axillary and rectal temperatures were the same; none differed by more than 0.8 °F. Eoff et al[4,5] found a similar correlation.

Perhaps the study most relevant to the acutely ill child seen in the office or emergency department was the study by Kresch[6] of 109 children ranging from 10 days to 6 years of age. The environment was less controlled than in the nursery, and room temperature varied by as much as 10 °F. The sensitivity of axillary temperatures in detecting fevers was 33%; 37.3 °C was defined as a febrile axillary value.

The *tympanic membrane* was recently explored as an additional site using newly developed technology. The proximity to the internal carotid artery, the location within the cranium, relative freedom from moisture, and ease make this a technique for further exploration.

The duration of time required for accurate measurement of temperature remains controversial. Haddock et al[3] in a nursery setting found that the maximum axillary temperature was reached between 3 and 12 minutes, with 94% reached within 10 minutes. Maximum rectal temperatures were reached between 1 and 6 minutes, with 87% reached at 3 minutes.[3,5]

THE INSTRUMENTS

The glass, mercury thermometer has for many years been the only instrument used as a standard in measuring temperature. It has unquestioned reliability, although standardization of the routinely used thermometer is inconsistent, with tremendous variability noted.[7] Breakage of the instrument poses a potential danger.

During the last decade, electronic instruments were introduced and widely accepted. Their reliability, time saving features, and safety are outstanding, and their price has dropped significantly, making them widely available to both care providers and parents.

MANAGEMENT OF FEVER

Several factors must be considered in determining appropriate management of the febrile child. First, guidelines must be established regarding what is abnormal; second, the pathophysiology and cause of the fever must be determined; and finally, the overall condition of the child and the importance of the relative accuracy of the measurement must be assessed. The literature supports various temperature levels as indicators of serious illness in infants. These factors, when considered together, form the basis for a rational and appropriate approach to management.

Fever is a physiologic response, and is a symptom, not a primary disease entity. Fever must be viewed with this perspective, and the focus must be on evaluating and diagnosing the underlying process causing the fever rather than reducing it empirically without evaluation. Often, the major value of early antipyretic therapy is to facilitate assessment.

Body Temperature

Body temperature actually varies throughout the day and from person to person. Oral temperatures greater than 37.6 °C obtained with the patient at rest are considered elevated. Diurnal variation may account for as much as 1° of elevation late in the day. Rectal temperatures are usually 0.5 °C to 1.0 °C higher than oral or axillary temperatures.

Kresch[6] defined fevers as temperatures greater than 37.6 °C orally and 38.1 °C rectally. In contrast, Younger and Brown[8] used the levels of 36.1 °C orally and 37.2 °C rectally.

Pathophysiology

The hypothalamus regulates temperature, establishing a set point based on blood temperatures. The set point may be raised by infection or malignancy, and is lowered by antipyretics. Excessive heat production, such as is noted in hyperthyroidism, may elevate the temperature in the presence of a normal set point. This elevation responds to tepid sponging. A normal set point is also found in heat stroke, in which heat loss mechanisms are defective.

A rational approach to fever therapy should be based on a knowledge of the body's physiologic responses. Bacteria, viruses, and fungi seem to induce fever by activating phagocytes, which release endogenous pyrogens that circulate to the hypothalamus and reset the body temperature to a higher point. Aspirin and acetaminophen act directly on the hypothalamus to counter the effects of endogenous pyrogens. When the mechanism of the fever is identified as the result of infection, the use of aspirin or acetaminophen is the appropriate approach to reduce the fever.

Intervention

Aspirin reduces fever effectively and has the advantage of diminishing pain, swelling, and inflammation. The therapeutic dosage for infants is 10 to 15 mg/kg every 4 to 6 hours for a total dosage of 60 to 80 mg/kg/24 hr. Aspirin was reported to increase the risk in specific patients of Reye's syndrome and should not be prescribed for children with varicella (chicken pox) or influenza.

In a comparison study, Lovejoy[9] showed that aspirin and acetaminophen reduce fever equally well. The recommended dosage of acetaminophen is 10 to 15 mg/kg every 4 to 6 hours. When aspirin and acetaminophen were combined using the therapeutic dose of each drug, the combination extended the antipyretic effect to 6 hours, and no toxicity was noted. In instances in which aspirin is not contraindicated, this combination may be advantageous.[9]

In conditions in which the body temperature is elevated and the set point is normal, sponging with tepid water may be useful. However, Hunter[10] found that tepid sponging was less effective than antipyretic drug therapy, and that the combination of sponging and drug therapy produced no additional effect.

This is indeed controversial. Donahue[11] recommended selective use of tepid sponging, particularly if the physiologic mechanisms causing the fever were identified, and found that tepid sponging was most beneficial if the set point had been lowered.

CONCLUSIONS

1. Glass and electronic thermometers are accurate; the latter has the advantages of speed and safety.
2. Axillary temperatures can be an appropriate site for measurement when the environment is thermostatically controlled. In less thermostable environments, axillary temperatures may be used to determine markedly elevated temperatures but is less reliable with low-grade elevations in environments that are not thermostable. When determining instances where the degree of fever is crucial, the axillary site is questionable.
3. Although there are variations between instruments and sites, the paramount issue concerning the febrile child is the importance of observing behavior, focusing particularly on feeding, activity, spontaneous motions, visual contact, and comfort. Antipyretic therapy may help in the early assessment of the child and is essential to appropriate assessment and disposition.

REFERENCES

1. Blainey CG: Site selection in taking body temperature. *Am J Nurs* 1974;74:1859–1861.
2. Buntain WL, Pregler M, O'Brien, et al: Axillary versus rectal temperature: A comparative study. *J Louisiana State Med Soc* 1977;129:5–8.
3. Haddock B, Vincent P, Merrow D: Axillary and rectal temperatures of full term neonates: Are they different? *Neonatal Network* 1986;5:36–40.
4. Eoff MJF, Meier RS, Miller C: Temperature measurement in infants. *Nurs Res* 1974;23:457–460.
5. Eoff MJF, Joyce B: Temperature measurements in children. *Am J Nurs* 1981; 81:1010–1011.
6. Kresch MJ: Axillary temperature as a screening test for fever in children. *J Pediatr* 1984;104:596–599.
7. Knapp HA: Accuracy of glass clinical thermometers. *Am J Surg* 1966;112:139.
8. Younger JB, Brown BS: Fever management: Rational or ritual. *Pediatr Nurs* 1985;11:26–29
9. Lovejoy FH Jr: Aspirin and acetaminophen: A comparative view of their antipyretic and analgesic activity. *Pediatrics* 1978;62:904–909.
10. Hunter J: Study of antipyretic therapy in current use. *Arch Dis Child* 1973;48:313–315.
11. Donahue AM: Tepid sponging. *J Emerg Nurs* 1983;9:78–82.

Section 2

Pharyngitis

Exciting developments have occurred in evaluating and treating the child with group A beta-hemolytic streptococcus. Rapid streptococcal antigen assays facilitate confirmation when positive, but require culture follow-up when negative. The efficacy of early treatment remains somewhat controversial, but recent data confirm the clinical impression that the symptoms are foreshortened with early antibiotic therapy; this treatment, however, may increase the frequency of reinfection.

The choice of antibiotics is broad, reflecting allergies, sensitivity, concomitant infections, and previous experience. Parenteral antibiotics may improve compliance but do not normally speed recovery.

6. Group A Beta-Hemolytic Streptococcal Pharyngitis: Immediate Treatment with Penicillin, Rapid Diagnosis, and Antibiotic Selection

Michael E. Pichichero, MD

Group A beta-hemolytic streptococcus (GABHS) is a common pathogen in children causing morbidity in terms of illness and lost days of day care, school, and work.

BENEFICIAL AND ADVERSE EFFECTS OF IMMEDIATE TREATMENT

The question of the effect of antibiotic therapy on the clinical course of GABHS pharyngitis has resurfaced as a controversial issue. Recent reports challenge the widely held view that penicillin produces minimal improvement, at best, in reducing the clinical symptoms of acute pharyngitis caused by GABHS. Still, some physicians remain unconvinced, arguing that these studies are flawed by the absence of a placebo control group and clinician "blindness," sample size, and the absence of a control group on a more realistic alternative therapy, such as aspirin or acetaminophen. More important, the potential adverse effect of early antibiotic treatment of GABHS pharyngitis by predisposing the patient to more frequent reinfection was not considered.

Early treatment of scarlet fever with penicillin may substantially suppress streptococcal antibody production. Type-specific streptococcal antibody responses are diminished by early penicillin treatment. The risk of a second attack of streptococcal scarlet fever is 2 to 9 fold higher (depending on the child's age) in children who have been treated early in their clinical course with penicillin. The risk of recurrence is related to diminished streptococcal immunity in the treated children, which could be modified by postponing penicillin treatment.[1]

Note: This work was supported by the Elmwood Pediatric Research Fund.

The availability of a "rapid strep test," whereby GABHS pharyngitis can be diagnosed in 15 to 20 minutes, increases the pressure to treat the patient immediately to facilitate a rapid return to day care, school, or work. The desire to make the patient feel better faster also prompts the initiation of antibiotic therapy for patients clinically determined to be infected. Is this the best course of action? In light of the frequency with which this diagnosis is considered, questions of treatment affecting both symptomatic response and recurrent infection deserve further study.

Despite earlier studies showing that penicillin produced marked improvement in symptoms, Peter and Smith[2] concluded in 1977 that penicillin treatment had little effect on the clinical course of this disease. The controversy surfaced again with Nelson's[3] 1984 publication of data collected in 1958–59 showing greater clinical improvement in children receiving penicillin compared with those receiving placebo. Unfortunately, the sample size was small, observers of clinical responses were not "blinded" as to treatment group, the placebo was not identical in physical appearance with penicillin, and GABHS carriers were not excluded.

Recognizing the need for a double-blind evaluation of clinical response to treatment, Krober et al[4] reported their experience with children at two army medical centers. This study occasioned considerable commentary because of its very small number of patients (26 with positive cultures). Randolph et al[5] undertook a double-blind, placebo-controlled evaluation of antibiotic effect on the acute clinical course of GABHS pharyngitis in 194 culture-positive cases. Regrettably, the placebo employed (grape syrup) did not physically resemble the antibiotics used (penicillin and cefadroxil monohydrate). Patients or parents with prior experience with antibiotic suspensions would easily have discerned the group to which the child has been "randomly" assigned. Furthermore, patients in the penicillin and placebo groups were instructed to avoid aspirin and acetaminophen (28% did not comply). Therefore, the study did not answer the more clinically practical question of whether penicillin relieves symptoms of streptococcal pharyngitis better than ad libitum use of antipyretic/analgesic drugs.

We have recently completed a prospective, randomized, double-blind study involving 142 children with presumed GABHS pharyngitis[6] that addresses many of the shortcomings of these recent studies. The children had predetermined classic clinical symptoms and signs of bona fide GABHS pharyngitis. The groups were comparable in all clinical, epidemiologic, and laboratory parameters; 114 were culture positive and approximately one half received penicillin in the initial 48–56 hours following diagnosis. All children received ad libitum aspirin or acetaminophen, the use of which was carefully monitored. The placebo and penicillin (125–250 mg administered 3 times daily) were identical in physical characteristics, and study nurses dispensed all medication. Symptomatic response to the initial 48 hours of treatment was assessed by the patient or parent using a questionnaire which was validated as reliable. Penicillin produced a reduction of fever (data not shown) and all symptoms of GABHS pharyngitis greater than that achieved with aspirin or acetaminophen alone, thereby answering the more clinically practical question of whether penicillin relieves symptoms of streptococcal pharyngitis better than ad libitum use of antipyretic/analgesic drugs (Figure 6-1). No response to treatment was detected in patients with negative cultures.

Despite the apparent beneficial effect of penicillin in relieving symptoms of acute GABHS pharyngitis, there appeared to be an important concomitant adverse effect not considered in any of the recent reports, which related to the incidence of recurrences of GABHS infection. We examined this issue in the recently completed study.[6]

Following the delay of initiation of antibiotic treatment for 48–56 hours as opposed to immediate initiation of treatment on making the presumptive diagnosis of GABHS pharyngitis, children were monitored for GABHS recurrences. Recurrences were defined chronologically as early (< 30 days after initial diagnosis) or late (> 30 days but < 4 months, in the same streptococcal season). We found that a child receiving immediate treatment with penicillin was up to 8 times more likely to experience a GABHS reinfection within 4 months than was a child for whom penicillin treatment was delayed for 48–56 hours (Table 6-1).

Thus, our findings and those of others document that delay in initiating antibiotic treatment results in persistent acute symptoms. Although the patient suffers somewhat during the delay, postponing treatment may well reduce the frequency of GABHS reinfection.

Is the immediate price worth the long-term concern? Patients are becoming increasingly aware of the availability of the rapid strep test. Physicians previously unwilling to invest the time and effort to take and process office throat cultures now can avail themselves of a rapid diagnostic kit that will allow the patients to receive immediate antibiotic treatment for "laboratory-confirmed" GABHS pharyngitis. These physicians will join the already large group that treats pharyngitis empirically with antibiotics; starts antibiotics presumptively while awaiting results of a throat culture, and receives a report of a negative throat culture, but continues empirically-started antibiotics for a complete therapeutic course, anyway, out of concern for a false-negative culture or because the patient starts feeling better coincident with treatment. The clinician should consider both the beneficial and the adverse consequences of such action.

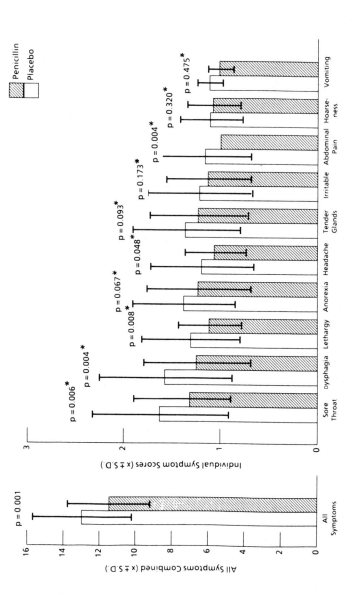

Figure 6-1 Effect of penicillin treatment on clinical symptoms of GABHS pharyngitis, day 3, in 114 patients. Symptom scoring was 1 = absent, 2 = moderate, 3 = severe. Treatment groups were compared by Student's *t* test using a one-tailed probability; an *asterisk* indicates a significant difference (*p* < .05). *Source:* Adapted with permission from "Adverse and Beneficial Effects of Immediate Treatment of Group A Beta Hemolytic Streptococcal Pharyngitis with Penicillin" by ME Pichichero et al, *Journal of Pediatric Infectious Diseases* (1987;6), Copyright © 1987, Williams & Wilkins Company.

Table 6-1 Adverse Effects of Immediate Treatment of GABHS Pharyngitis with Penicillin

	Treatment Group		
Variable	Penicillin (n = 59)	Placebo (n = 55)	P Value[1]
Early recurrence	14 (24%)	8 (15%)	0.115
Late recurrence	8 (14%)	1 (2%)	0.035*
Early and late recurrence	22 (37%)	9 (16%)	0.025*

[1]Treatment groups compared by chi-square or Fisher's exact test as appropriate; one-tailed probability.
*Indicates significant difference ($p < .05$).

Source: Adapted with permission from "Adverse and Beneficial Effects of Immediate Treatment of Group A Beta Hemolytic Streptococcal Pharyngitis with Penicillin" by ME Pichichero et al, *Journal of Pediatric Infectious Diseases* (1987;6), Copyright © 1987, Williams & Wilkins Company.

RAPID DIAGNOSTIC TESTS

The signs and symptoms of GABHS pharyngitis can be difficult to distinguish from those of viral pharyngitis and the sore throat that accompanies mononucleosis syndrome. The Breese[7] scoring system uses a combination of epidemiologic (season of the year and patient age), laboratory (white blood cell count), and acute clinical features (fever, sore throat, abnormal pharynx and cervical glands, and headache) to improve clinical diagnostic acumen.

However, the most accurate and reliable "gold standard" of GABHS diagnosis has, for many years, been the throat culture. Culturing throat swabs on sheep blood agar plates requires some degree of technical expertise and causes a delay of 24 to 48 hours (for incubation) before results are known. A number of commercial antigen detection tests for the rapid identification of GABHS on throat swabs are now available. All depend on extraction of group A carbohydrate from GABHS scraped from the throat during the swabbing process. Coagglutination and latex agglutination assays cause precipitation, whereas the mixture changes color with enzyme immunoassay methods.

Several studies[8–25] compared the accuracy of these rapid strep tests and conventional blood agar culture tests in hospitals or microbiology laboratories. In these settings under study conditions, the rapid tests generally showed a sensitivity of 82% to 95% and a specificity of 84% to 100% (Table 6-2). Under study conditions, in office practice–based studies, results were similar. Yet, caution is to be taken since under field conditions, such as in an actual emergency room setting, rapid strep test performance may plummet. For example, Lieu et al[26] in studying 556 children at Boston Children's Hospital Emergency Department found rapid test sensitivity to be no more than 45%.

The incidence of false-negative rapid strep tests is greatest when the patient has ten or fewer colonies of GABHS isolated by culture. If such cultures for

Table 6-2 Summary of Published Studies Evaluating the Accuracy of Latex Agglutination Testing under Study Conditions in Detecting GABHS Pharyngitis

Study Site/Author	Number of Patients	Sensitivity (%)	Specificity (%)	Overall Accuracy (%)
Hospital-Based				
Slifkin and Gil[8] (1984)	557	95	100	99
Rosenfeld[9] (1984)	171	94	99	98
Fieber et al[10] (1985)	186	95	96	95
Forbes et al[11] (1984)	324	84	99	98
Janda et al[12] (1984)	571	90	99	98
Chang and Mohla[13] (1985)	435	90	99	98
Staneck et al[14] (1984)	200	88	86	86
Miceika et al[15] (1985)	813	92	93	93
Gerber et al[16] (1984)	339	83	99	94
Gerber et al[17] (1984)	263	84	99	94
McCusker et al[18] (1984)	500	91	99	97
Miller et al[19] (1984)	147	91	98	97
Shruptar et al[20] (1986)	200	76	88	75
Shruptar et al[20] (1986)	200	75	91	78
Office Practice-Based				
Forbes et al[21] (1984)	202	85	92	89
Gangemi et al[22] (1985)	309	92	98	97
Staneck et al[23] (1984)	366	87	75	79
Schwartz et al[24] (1985)	425	93	90	92
Weiner et al[25] (1986)	93	73	98	91
Weiner et al[25] (1986)	93	74	89	83

GABHS (1 +) are excluded from the comparisons of culture and rapid tests, then the sensitivity of the rapid detection test significantly improves. These findings have rekindled an old argument about the clinical importance of GABHS (1 +) throat cultures. Patients who are GABHS carriers frequently have low numbers of bacteria isolated on cultures. Such patients are not truly infected, are minimally contagious, and are not at risk for nonsuppurative sequelae. However, this is not true for all patients with positive (1 +) cultures since such patients are sometimes truly infected as confirmed by a bona fide increase in antistreptococcal antibodies.

The blood agar culture method is not perfect. Simultaneously obtained swabs can produce a disparity in culture positivity in as many as 5% to 10% of patients. Such variation is probably related to throat swabbing technique. Culture findings based on duplicate swabs obtained by the same person with one processed in an office-based laboratory and the other in a reference laboratory may vary in GABHS recovery by as much as 15% to 20%. Yet the culture method remains the "gold standard" of GABHS detection.

Thus, in evaluating the potential use of the new rapid strep test kits, the clinician is left to determine an acceptable limit of false-negative results. This is difficult. A false-negative rapid test could result in a patient suffering from a more prolonged illness; a period of greater contagion to others; and the consequences of acute rheumatic fever. Further work is needed.

What about false-positive rapid strep tests? The highest published incidence of false-positives is 43.1%[26]; the lowest 0%.[8] False-positive results cause unnecessary use of antibiotics and perhaps missed school or work. With regard to the former, the adverse consequences of antibiotic use include expense, side effects, and potentially, anaphylaxis.

Some authorities in the GABHS field argue that the incidence of false-positive rapid strep tests is sufficiently low (overall about 5%) and the risks sufficiently rare that this issue can be reasonably ignored. In contrast, whereas the incidence of false-negative tests is also low (overall about 10%), the risk of missing such a case is viewed as too great. Therefore, one suggested means of using the rapid test method is as follows: *Obtain duplicate throat swabs from acutely ill patients. Perform a rapid test. If the test is positive, presume the patient has GABHS infection and discard the duplicate swab. If the test is negative, presume the patient does not have GABHS infection, but send the second swab for confirmatory culturing.*[27]

A final issue to be addressed is practicality. Use of rapid strep test kits in offices or emergency departments requires a quick turn-around time. For the patient to tie up an examining room for 75 minutes while a rapid strep test is performed can be a real problem in some settings. Furthermore, if the physician, physician's assistant, or nurse is to perform the test, it must be easy to master; require minimal preparation time; require minimal technical skill; have clear instructions, illustrations, and endpoints; have positive and negative controls for ease of interpretation; and require not more than a few minutes of hands-on time. A comparison of ten commercially available kits by Radetsky et al[28] led to the conclusion that no test was ideal and further improvements should be sought.

ANTIBIOTIC SELECTION

Numerous studies independently have described bacteriologic or clinical failure rates as high as 20% to 30% in children with GABHS pharyngitis who received oral or parenteral penicillin. These bacteriologic failures might be explained by the presence of beta-lactamase–producing strains of *Staphylococcus aureus, Hemophilus influenzae, Hemophilus parainfluenzae, Branhamella catarrhalis,* or anaerobes, particularly *Bacteroids* sp, which inactivate penicillin at the local site of infection.

Table 6-3 Summary of Previous Studies That Examined the Effectiveness of Penicillin Compared to Cephalosporins in the Treatment of GABHS Pharyngitis

Reference	Number of Patients	10-Day Treatment Regimen 125–250 mg/dose	Bacteriologic Failure Rate (%)
Stillerman[30]	79	Cephaloglycin qid	10
(1970)	36	Penicillin V qid	17
	33	Benzathine penicillin once	9
Stillerman and Isenberg[31]	38	Cephalexin tid	11
(1970)	39	Penicillin V tid	26
Disney et al[32]	89	Cephalexin tid	5
(1971)	76	Penicillin G tid	9
Gau et al[33]	25	Cephalexin tid	4
(1972)	25	Penicillin V qid	8
Stillerman[34]	84	Cephalexin tid	10
(1972)	89	Penicillin V tid	22
Rabinovitch et al[35]	43	Cephalexin qid	0
(1973)	54	Penicillin V or G qid	6
Matsen et al[36]	66	Cephalexin tid	3
(1974)	34	Penicillin tid	3
	38	Benzathine penicillin once	4
Derrick and Dillon[37]	73	Cephalexin tid	4
(1974)	74	Penicillin V tid	8
	74	Benzathine penicillin once	5
Stillerman[38]	49	Cefatrizine tid	10
(1976)	52	Penicillin V tid	19
Disney et al[39]	15	Cefaclor tid	7
(1979)	15	Penicillin tid	7
Ginsburg et al[40]	44	Cefadroxil bid	5
(1980)	52	Penicillin V tid	15
Ginsburg et al[41]	49	Cefadroxil bid	5
(1982)	50	Penicillin V tid	12
	49	Benzathine penicillin once	12
	50	Erythromycin estolate bid	2
Henness[42]	76	Cefadroxil bid	1
(1982)	67	Penicillin V qid	2
Stillerman[43]	51	Cefaclor tid	14
(1986)	53	Penicillin V tid	30
Pichichero et al[44]	60	Cefuroxime bid	15
(1987)	30	Penicillin V tid	12
Pichichero et al[45]	75	Cefadroxil qd	10
(1987)	75	Penicillin V tid	24

Source: Adapted with permission from "A Multicenter, Randomized, Single-Blind Evaluation of Cefuroxime Axetil and Phenoxymethyl Penicillin in the Treatment of Streptococcal Pharyngitis" by ME Pichichero, FA Disney, GH Aronovitz et al, *Clinical Pediatrics,* © JB Lippincott Company (in press).

Patients who are GABHS-infected, penicillin-treatment failures may harbor greater numbers of penicillin-resistant *S aureus* in their throats than those who are penicillin-treatment successes. In a study by Brook[29] of 98 children with GABHS pharyngitis who were treated with penicillin for 10 days, 62 were bacteriologic cures and 35 failures. Among the children who were cured, 26 harbored penicillinase-producing bacteria before treatment; among the children who failed on penicillin treatment, 69 harbored such organisms. The number of penicillinase-producing strains increased as a consequence of penicillin therapy.

Use of cephalosporins as alternative oral agents in the treatment of GABHS pharyngitis dates to 1967. Since that time, at least 16 comparative trials have been performed (Table 6-3). All show cephalosporins to be as effective as or more effective than penicillin.

A number of clinical trials showed superior efficacy of lincomycin hydrochloride monohydrate and clindamycin palmitate hydrochloride (active against *S aureus* and anaerobes) over penicillin in the treatment of GABHS pharyngitis. In four separate studies by three different groups, the bacteriologic failure rate for clindamycin phosphate or lincomycin hydrochloride *v* penicillin was 16% *v* 41%,[46] 0% *v* 12%,[47] 8% *v* 14%,[48] and 7% *v* 21%.[49]

The relative role of penicillinase-producing bacteria in precluding effective treatment of GABHS pharyngitis with penicillin seems worthy of additional research. For now, considerations of cost and the broader antimicrobial activity than is perhaps necessary for GABHS eradication lead to the continued recommendation of penicillin as the treatment of choice. However, when confronted with a patient who is allergic to penicillin and intolerant of erythromycin; whose infecting GABHS strain is resistant to erythromycin or penicillin; or who continues to get reinfected with GABHS after penicillin therapy; treatment with an alternative agent is recommended. Although the 5% to 10% crossreaction rate between penicillins and cephalosporins should be noted, a cephalosporin should be considered.[50]

REFERENCES

1. Strom J: Penicillin treatment and immunity to scarlatina. *Acta Paediatr* 1954; 43:267–279.

2. Peter G, Smith AL: Group A streptococcal infections of the skin and pharynx. *N Engl J Med* 1977;297:365–370.

3. Nelson JD: The effect of penicillin therapy on the symptoms and signs of streptococcal pharyngitis. *Pediatr Infect Dis* 1984;3:10–13.

4. Krober MS, Bass JM, Michels GN: Streptococcal pharyngitis. Placebo-controlled double-blind evaluation of clinical response to penicillin therapy. *JAMA* 1985;253:1271–1274.

5. Randolph MF, Gerber MA, DeMeo KK, Wright L: Effect of antibiotic therapy on the clinical course of streptococcal pharyngitis. *J Pediatr* 1985;106:870–875.

6. Pichichero ME, Disney FA, Talpey WB, Green JL, Francis AB, Roghmann K, Hoekelman RA: The adverse and beneficial effects of immediate treatment of group A beta-hemolytic streptococcal pharyngitis with penicillin. *Pediatr Infect Dis* 1987;6.

7. Breese BB: A simple scorecard for the tentative diagnosis of streptococcal pharyngitis. *Am J Dis Child* 1977;131:514–517.

8. Slifkin M, Gil GM: Evaluation of the culturette brand ten-minute group A strep ID technique. *J Clin Microbiol* 1984;20:12–14.

9. Rosenfeld J: Rapid detection of group A streptococcal antigen from throat swabs. *Intersci Conf Antimicrob Agents Chemoth* 1984;24:629.

10. Fieber L, Stevens G, Drew L, Mintz L: Clinical evaluation of a rapid agglutination test for the detection of group A streptococcus. *Am Soc Microbiol* 1985;85:223.

11. Forbes B, Corwin R, Pettit D, McMillan J, Mollica M, Wiener L: Clinical evaluation of the 10-minute group A ID (MGA) latex agglutination test for the detection of group A streptococcus in throat swabs. *Intersci Conf Antimicrob Agents Chemoth* 1984;24:630.

12. Janda WM, Fritz B, Shrenberber P, Dathe K, Lebeau L: Rapid detection of group A streptococci on throat swab specimens. *Intersci Conf Antimicrob Agents Chemoth* 1984;24:633.

13. Chang MJ, Mohla C: Ten-minute detection of group A streptococci in pediatric throat swabs. *J Clin Microbiol* 1985;21:258–259.

14. Staneck J, Weckbach L, Dine M, Friedberg D: The 10-minute culturette test for group A streptococcus in the hospital and office laboratory. *Intersci Conf Antimicrob Agents Chemoth* 1984;24:14.

15. Miceika BG, Vitous AS, Thompson KD: Detection of group A streptococcal antigen directly from throat swabs with a ten-minute latex agglutination test. *J Clin Microbiol* 1985;21:467–469.

16. Gerber MA, Spadaccini LJ, Wright LL, et al: Latex agglutination tests for the rapid identification of group A streptococci directly from throat swabs. *J Pediatr* 1984;105:702–705.

17. Gerber MA, Randolph MF: Effect of antimicrobial therapy on the clinical course of group A beta-hemolytic streptococcal (GABHS) pharyngitis in children. *Intersci Conf Antimicrob Agents Chemoth* 1984;84:237.

18. McCusker JJ, McCoy EL, Young CL, et al: Comparison of directigen group A strep test with a traditional culture technique for detection of group A beta-hemolytic streptococci. *J Clin Microbiol* 1984;20:824–825.

19. Miller JM, Phillips HL, Graves RK, et al: Evaluation of the directigen group A strep test kit. *J Clin Microbiol* 1984;20:846–848.

20. Shruptar S, Bretl T, Gilchrist M: Comparison of a new latex agglutination (LA) test, INSTA KIT for group A strep ID (IK) (Mead Johnson) and culturette brand 10-minute group A strep ID (CB) (Marion) versus culture (CX) for detection of group A streptococci (GAS) in throat swabs. *Intersci Conf Antimicrob Agents Chemoth* 1986;26:108.

21. Forbes B, Corwin R, Pettit D, et al: Clinical evaluation of the 10-minute group A ID (MGA) latex agglutination test for the detection of group A streptococcus in throat swabs. *Intersci Conf Antimicrob Agents Chemoth* 1984;24:630.

22. Gangemi JD, Gibson J, Krech L, et al: Clinical evaluation of a latex agglutination test for group A streptococcus in throat swab specimens. *Am Soc Microbiol* 1985;85:C-59.

23. Staneck J, Weckbach L, Dine M, Friedberg D: The 10-minute culturette test for group A streptococcus in the hospital and office laboratory. *Intersci Conf Antimicrob Agents Chemoth* 1984;24:14.

24. Schwartz RH, Hayden GF, McCoy P, et al: Rapid diagnosis of streptococcal pharyngitis in two pediatric offices using a latex agglutination kit. *Pediatr Infect Dis* 1985;4:647–650.

25. Weiner LB, McMillan JA, Higgins AP, Keller K: Clinical evaluation of two latex agglutination (LA) tests for identification of group A streptococcus (GAS). *Intersci Conf Antimicrob Agents Chemoth* 1986;26:108.

26. Lieu TA, Fleisher GR, Schwartz JS: Clinical performance and effect on treatment rates of latex agglutination testing for streptococcal pharyngitis in an emergency department. *Pediatr Infect Dis* 1986;5:655–659.

27. Gerber MA: Rapid diagnosis of streptococcal pharyngitis. *Infect Med* 1986;3:75–82.

28. Radetsky M, Wheeler RC, Roe MH, Todd JK: Comparative evaluation of kits for rapid diagnosis of group A streptococcal disease. *Pediatr Infect Dis* 1985;4:274–281.

29. Brook I: Role of beta-lactamase-producing bacteria in the failure of penicillin to eradicate group A streptococci. *Pediatr Infect Dis* 1985;4:491–495.

30. Stillerman M: Comparison of cephaloglycin and penicillin in streptococcal pharyngitis. *Clin Pharmacol Ther* 1970;11:205–213.

31. Stillerman M, Isenberg HD: Streptococcal pharyngitis therapy: Comparison of cyclacillin, cephalexin and potassium penicillin V. *Antimicrob Agents Chemoth* 1970;270–276.

32. Disney FA, Breese BB, Green JL, et al: Cephalexin and penicillin therapy of childhood beta-hemolytic streptococcal infections. *Postgrad Med J* 1971;47(Suppl):47–51.

33. Gau DW, Horn RFH, Solomon RM, et al: Streptococcal tonsillitis in general practice: A comparison of cephalexin and penicillin therapy. *Practitioner* 1972;208:276–281.

34. Stillerman M, Isenberg HD, Moody M: Streptococcal pharyngitis therapy: Comparison of cephalexin, phenoxymethyl penicillin and ampicillin. *Am J Dis Child* 1972;123:4571.

35. Rabinovitch M, MacKenzie R, Brazeau M, Marks MI: Treatment of streptococcal pharyngitis: I. Clinical evaluation. *CMA J* 1973;108:1271–1274.

36. Matsen JM, Torstenson O, Siegel SE, et al: Use of available dosage forms of cephalexin in clinical comparison with phenoxymethyl penicillin and benzathine penicillin in the treatment of streptococcal pharyngitis in children. *Antimicrob Agents Chemoth* 1974;6:501–506.

37. Derrick CW, Dillon HC: Therapy for prevention of acute rheumatic fever. *Circulation* 1974;50:38.

38. Stillerman M: Comparison of cefatrizine and penicillin V potassium in group A streptococcal pharyngitis. Presented at the 16th Interscience Conference on Antimicrobial Agents and Chemotherapy, Chicago, 1978.

39. Disney FA, Breese BB, Francis AB, et al: The use of cefaclor in the treatment of beta-hemolytic streptococcal throat infections in children. *Postgrad Med J* 1979;55(Suppl 4):50–52.

40. Ginsburg CM, McCracken GH Jr, Crow SD, et al: A controlled comparative study of penicillin V and cefadroxil therapy of group A streptococcal tonsillopharyngitis. *J Int Med Res* 1980;8(Suppl 1):82–86.

41. Ginsburg CM, McCracken Jr GH, Steinberg JB, et al: Treatment of group A streptococcal pharyngitis in children: Results of a prospective, randomized study of four antimicrobial agents. *Clin Pediatr* 1982;21:83–88.

42. Henness DM: A clinical experience with cefadroxil in upper respiratory tract infection. *J Antimicrob Chemoth* 1982;10(Suppl B):125–135.

43. Stillerman M: Comparison of oral cephalosporins with penicillin therapy for group A streptococcal pharyngitis. *Pediatr Infect Dis* 1986;5:649–654.

44. Pichichero ME, Disney FA, Aronovitz GH, et al: A multicenter, randomized, single-blind evaluation of cefuroxime axetil and phenoxymethyl penicillin in the treatment of streptococcal pharyngitis. *Clin Pediatr* 1987; in press.

45. Pichichero ME, Disney FA, Aronovitz GH, et al: A randomized, single-blind evaluation of cefadroxil and phenoxymethyl penicillin in the treatment of streptococcal pharyngitis. *Antimicrob Agents Chemoth* 1987;in press.

46. Breese BB, Disney FA, Talpey WB: Beta-hemolytic streptococcal illness: Comparison of lincomycin, ampicillin, and potassium penicillin treatment. *Am J Dis Child* 1966;112:21–27.

47. Breese BB, Disney FA, Talpey WB, Green J: Beta-hemolytic streptococcal infection: Comparison of penicillin and lincomycin in the treatment of recurrent infections or the carrier state. *Am J Dis Child* 1969;117:147–152.

48. Randolph MF, DeHaan RM: A comparison of lincomycin and penicillin in the treatment of group A streptococcal infection. *Del Med J* 1969;41:51–62.

49. Randolph MF, Redys JJ, Hibbard EW: Streptococcal pharyngitis. III Streptococcal recurrence rates following therapy with penicillin or with clindamycin (7-chlorolincomycin). *Del Med J* 1970;42:87.

50. Gerber MA, Markowitz M: Management of streptococcal pharyngitis reconsidered. *Pediatr Infect Dis* 1985;4:518–526.

7. A Clinical Approach to the Diagnosis of Streptococcal Pharyngitis

Michael Radetsky, MD, CM

Acute pharyngitis occurs repeatedly throughout a lifetime. Although many adults stoically tolerate this passing discomfort, children with painful throats, especially if febrile, are routinely brought to clinics or offices for examination. An estimated 11% of all school-age children visit physicians with this complaint annually. In response, physicians obtain a large number of throat cultures for the isolation of group A beta-hemolytic streptococci (GABHS), as many as 30 million annually by some estimates. These numbers reflect the popular fear that a sore throat, in particular a "strep throat," may be the harbinger of more serious disease, and the general assumption that some therapy offered uniquely by physicians might ameliorate the illness or its sequelae. The facts are otherwise.

Of all children who seek medical attention for a sore throat, or who have clinical pharyngitis diagnosed on examination, only 60% have pathogenic organisms isolated on their culture. Influenza virus, respiratory syncytial virus, herpes simplex virus, parainfluenza virus, and adenovirus are the pathogens that, as a group, are most commonly isolated in cultures from patients with acute pharyngitis. GABHS account for the remainder of definable cases. There is no convincing evidence that other serogroups of streptococci, *Mycoplasma pneumoniae*, *Chlamydia trachomatis*, or *Corynebacterium hemolyticum*, are common causes of acute pharyngitis at any age. Thus, in the majority of instances, there is either no identifiable cause of the acute pharyngitis, or the cause identified is an organism for which there is no specific therapy.[1] Symptomatic treatment, with analgesics, salt-water gargling, hard candy, or lollipops, and distraction form the basis of management; and the physician, with assurance, can predict an uneventful recovery.

Nevertheless, the collective memory of widespread severe scarlet fever, acute rheumatic fever, poststreptococcal glomerulonephritis, and postpharyngeal quinsy remains alive. For many parents, the possibility of "strep throat" in their child engenders a sense of dread; for others, it is the perceived cause of the majority of childhood illnesses. Physicians still feel the urgent obligation to ward off acute rheumatic fever and other complications with antimicrobials. Yet the risk of these untoward complications of streptococcal pharyngitis has declined dramatically over the last three decades. With the exception of isolated outbreaks, the yearly incidence of acute rheumatic fever in urban areas is estimated to be less than 1 per 200,000 population aged 5 to 19 years. Up to one third of all cases of acute rheumatic fever are not preceded by symptomatic pharyngitis and, consequently, cannot be prevented with antimicrobials. The risk of acquiring acute rheumatic fever after untreated streptococcal pharyngitis in the 1980s is not known, but is likely to be less than the 0.4% figure of the early 1960s. Similarly, severe scarlet fever and peritonsillar abscess (quinsy) are becoming more infrequent. Finally, poststreptococcal glomerulonephritis cannot be prevented with specific therapy. The reality, then, is that streptococcal pharyngitis, even if left untreated, is an infection with infrequent sequelae.[2]

The detection of streptococcal pharyngitis has its own difficulties. Although a clinical impression of nonstreptococcal pharyngitis is quite accurate (negative predictive value = 97% when prevalence is 15%), even the most experienced clinician can rarely predict the presence of streptococcal pharyngitis more than one third of the time. There are no good data to support the contention that pharyngitis caused by streptococci is inevitably more severe than that caused by other pathogens. On the contrary, during nonepidemic conditions, in which the prevalence of streptococcal isolation from throat cultures is less than 20%, pharyngitis thought severe enough to warrant a throat culture yields streptococci no more than 30% of the time.[3,4] Furthermore, it is well known that the presence of pharyngeal streptococci in cultures, even from the symptomatic patient, is accompanied less than one half the time by an increase in antistreptococcal antibodies, and that at least one of six patients whose throat cultures are negative for group A streptococcus on conventional sheep blood agar plates subsequently shows serological evidence of a streptococcal infection.[5] Even worse, one third of patients admitted with acute rheumatic fever during the epidemic at Fort Warren Air Force Base did not even recall having had symptoms of an antecedent sore throat.

Finally, the conclusion that antimicrobials meaningfully shorten the symptomatic course of streptococcal pharyngitis is exaggerated. Although most studies designed to validate this contention have been flawed, there is now ample support for the revised conclusion that early antimicrobial therapy abbreviates the course of illness in direct proportion to the severity of symptoms. Mild illness gains little from specific therapy; severe symptoms regress 1 to 2 days more rapidly with treatment.[6]

Thus, in 1987, in North America, streptococcal pharyngitis can best be characterized as a restricted subset of a common illness (pharyngitis)—a subset that is usualy self-resolving, infrequently debilitating, and rarely dangerous; that is difficult to diagnose clinically and whose laboratory detection can be misleading; and whose symptoms are inconstantly relieved by the use of antimicrobials.

ANTIGEN DETECTION

The introduction of antigen detection tests for group A streptococcus was hailed as a major advance in laboratory technology. Claims of improved diagnostic accuracy and parent-pleasing diagnostic rapidity held out the promise of an attractive new solution to the manifold difficulties associated with the diagnosis of streptococcal pharyngitis. There are now more than 15 rapid streptococcal detection kits commercially available. Rather than simplifying the approach to clinical pharyngitis, however, this new technology introduces yet another variable into the clinical equation. Even though streptococcal antigen testing has now been available for 3 years, there are still large gaps in our knowledge: how accurate these test kits are when used under office conditions; whether a backup culture on selective media might be advisable; which patients would benefit most; what will be the true effect of such testing on office revenues and work flow. As of this writing, only 14 peer-reviewed studies have been published that compare antigen detection kits with conventional throat cultures. So far, these studies have tested only products that use the latex agglutination technique for antigen detection. The results are variable. In most cases, specificity, and positive and negative predictive values were 90% or greater. However, sensitivities were regularly less than 90%, with false-negative agglutination tests occurring most frequently when the paired throat culture yielded less than ten colonies (1+ growth). Such light growth is unusual in symptomatic streptococcal pharyngitis, occuring less than 10% of the time. Nevertheless, these patients with only a few colonies of streptococcus have a 30% chance of developing antistreptococcal antibodies. It appears that false-negative antigen detection tests may indeed be missing meaningful streptococcal infections. The newer solid-phase enzyme immunoassay technology now beginning to appear on the market may have an enhanced capacity to detect low numbers of streptococci, but no peer-reviewed publications have yet appeared to validate this claim.[7–9]

Rapid streptococcal antigen detection technology has yet to provide relief from the clinical perplexities already enumerated. Instead, these new kits offer a compromise to the practitioner: they provide rapid identification of pharyngeal streptococci, but at the cost of microbiological inaccuracy. Similarly, when throat swabs are processed on demand, the clinical advantages and "peace of mind" provided by early diagnosis are bought at the price of the diversion of personnel from their accustomed duties. Yet there is no denying that the rapid diagnosis of streptococcal pharyngitis does offer benefits: It allows for the prompt use of antimicrobials to ameliorate severe symptoms; infected children are allowed back in school sooner so that their caretaking parents can return to work; and infected individuals can be quickly identified during streptococcal outbreaks or when there is a family or patient history of acute rheumatic fever.

DIAGNOSTIC STRATEGY

Given the benign nature of most streptococcal pharyngitis, but acknowledging the need to provide protection against these uncommon but serious consequences of untreated infection, each physician must construct a reasonable diagnostic strategy that includes the best aspects of clinical examination and laboratory detection. One such strategic plan is presented in Figure 7-1. This strategy is based on certain assumptions:

- The identification of streptococcal pharyngitis is for the purpose of preventing acute rheumatic fever by the use of antimicrobials.
- The risk of acute rheumatic fever after untreated streptococcal pharyngitis is low, but local outbreaks can still occur, and a familial predilection increases this risk.
- Laboratory testing for pharyngeal streptococci should be restricted to those patients in whom either yield of positives or risk of sequelae is high.
- Clinical judgment is more accurate in determining who does not have streptococcal pharyngitis than who does.
- Rapid streptococcal antigen tests are reliable when positive, but untrustworthy when negative.
- A properly performed throat culture on selective sheep blood agar plates remains the gold standard for laboratory detection of streptococci.

The diagnostic sequence is initiated when the patient complains of fever or respiratory symptoms. If a family or patient history of acute rheumatic fever exists, or if epidemic conditions prevail, then a special consideration pertains, and laboratory testing is indicated. If no such consideration exists, then the clinician must decide if the patient *does not* have clinical streptococcal pharyngitis based on the absence of such findings as fever, sore throat, or an inflamed throat. For these patients, symptomatic therapy alone is adequate. However, if

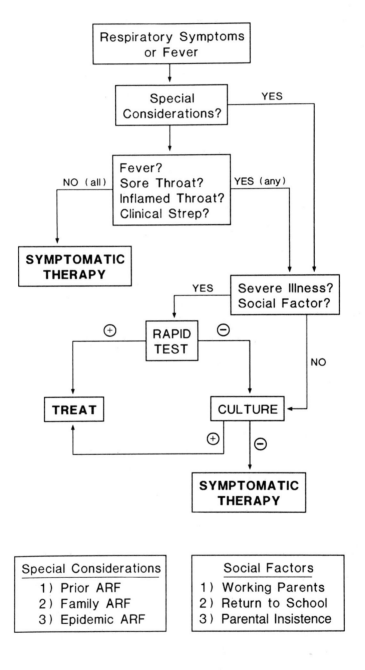

Figure 7–1 Diagnostic strategy for the evaluation of streptococcal pharyngitis.

the clinician *is not* convinced that streptococcal infection is absent, then laboratory testing is necessary. If the illness is severe, or if social factors demand the earliest possible conclusion regarding the presence or absence of streptococci, then a rapid antigen test should be performed, with throat culture backup for all negative tests. On the other hand, if the illness is mild, and social equanimity reigns, then a proper throat culture on selective sheep blood agar is the laboratory test of choice.

This diagnostic scheme, if followed, would avoid any laboratory testing in more than 70% of those children who have fever or respiratory symptoms. It would also detect at least 80% of all cases of pharyngeal streptococci and 88% of those illnesses capable of causing a titer rise in antistreptolysin O antibody. Finally, under endemic conditions, the risk of acute rheumatic fever in a symptomatic patient population evaluated according to this diagnostic strategy would be less than 1 in 1,000.

CONCLUSION

Streptococcal pharyngitis is commonly feared but only occasionally present. Patient protection and appropriate antimicrobial therapy are best guaranteed by a rational diagnostic strategy that combines clinical triage with the rapidity of antigen detection and the proven accuracy of throat culture tests. Such a scheme will provide the best balance between disease prevention and economic prudence.

REFERENCES

1. McMillan JA, Sandstrom C, Weiner LB, et al: Viral and bacterial organisms associated with acute pharyngitis in a school-aged population. *J Pediatr* 1986;109:747–752.

2. Peter G, Smith AL: Group A streptococcal infections of the skin and pharynx. *N Engl J Med* 1977;297:311–317, 365–370.

3. Honikman LH, Massell BF: Guidelines for the selective use of throat cultures in the diagnosis of streptococcal respiratory infection. *Pediatrics* 1971;48:573–582.

4. Todd JK: Throat cultures in the office laboratory. *Pediatr Infect Dis* 1982;1:265–270.

5. Roe MH, Tolliver PR, Lewis PL, et al: Primary plate identification of group A *Streptococcus* on a selective medium. *Am J Dis Child* 1984;138:589–591.

6. Randolph MF, Gerber MA, DeMeo KK, et al: Effect of antibiotic therapy on the clinical course of streptococcal pharyngitis. *J Pediatr* 1985;106:870–875.

7. Radetsky M, Todd JK: Criteria for the evaluation of new diagnostic tests. *Pediatr Infect Dis* 1984;3:461–466.

8. Radetsky M, Wheeler RC, Roe MH, et al: Comparative evaluation of kits for rapid diagnosis of group A streptococcal disease. *Pediatr Infect Dis* 1985;4:274–281.

9. Radetsky M, Solomon JA, Todd JK: Identification of streptococcal pharyngitis in the office laboratory: Reassessment of new technology. *Pediatr Infect Dis* June 1987; (in press).

Section 3

Periorbital Cellulitis

Differentiating periorbital or preseptal cellulitis from other differential considerations is fundamental to the management of periorbital swelling. Worrisome findings indicative of orbital involvement include diplopia, limited eye motion, and proptosis and mandate a rapid ophthalmologic referral and intervention. Therapy must reflect the age of the child, concurrent illness, and predisposing conditions that impair the skin's integrity.

8. Evaluation of Periorbital Swelling

Robert C. Luten, MD

Periorbital swelling is a common problem confronting the physician seeing acutely ill children. When presented with undifferentiated swelling in the periorbital area, the primary responsibility of the physician is to distinguish the serious and potentially life-threatening causes of this finding from those that are less serious. Failure to recognize periorbital cellulitis and deeper orbital involvement and to treat the infection aggressively may lead to devastating complications.[1–8]

MECHANISM OF SWELLING

The anatomy of the orbit and periorbital region explains the nature of the pathologic process. The orbit is a bony cavity surrounded by sinuses. Superiorly, the orbit is bound by the frontal sinus, inferiorly by the maxillary sinus, and medially by the ethmoid and sphenoid sinuses. The sinuses and orbit, besides being contiguous, have a venous drainage system devoid of valves and lymphatic drainage. These veins also receive drainage from the face and have common drainage into the cavernous sinus.[9] This anatomical relationship explains the occurrence of reactive periorbital edema because of pressure on the vessels of the sinuses from sinusitis, causing impeded blood flow in the vessels of the orbit and subsequent edema, without actual infection. Infection may propagate via these valveless veins from the sinuses to the orbital and periorbital area.

The connective tissue in the periorbital area is rather loose. This explains the exaggerated response to infection or inflammation in this region.

The orbital septum is a fascial plane located in the eyelid. It separates the soft tissues of the eyelid anteriorly and the contents of the orbit posteriorly.

Cellulitis of this area is *preseptal* if there is no involvement of the orbit, and *septal* if the orbital structures are involved.

Periorbital cellulitis, the most common infectious presentation, is produced by two distinct mechanisms. Trauma may produce a portal of entry for bacteria, particularly *Staphylococcus aureus* and group A streptococcus. Infection may also spread via the valveless venous system from the paranasal sinuses. This latter route of infection usually has a greater degree of systemic toxicity. *Hemophilus influenzae* and gram-positive organisms have been cultured. Accompanying sinusitis has been documented by radiographs.

DIFFERENTIAL DIAGNOSIS

The causes of periorbital swelling are multiple. Separating those that are acute, or may have serious complications if unrecognized, from those that are less acute, or not serious in nature, is imperative. Those in the latter category, although needing adequate treatment and workup, may be approached in a less aggressive fashion. The most frequent diagnostic problem is distinguishing periorbital swelling because of periorbital or orbital cellulitis from swelling produced by trauma, insect bites, allergic reactions, or reactive edema (Table 8-1 and Figure 9-1).

These entities can be partially distinguished on the basis of history and physical examination (Table 8-2). Two tips that may be helpful are: (1) Swelling and erythema may be demarcated with a pen and observed for a couple of hours in questionable cases. Cellulitis frequently spreads across the lines. Allergic swelling may recede with administration of diphenhydramine or adrenaline. (2) When the diagnosis cannot be made with certainty, but the

---

Table 8-1 Differential Considerations of Periorbital Swelling Based on Acuteness and Severity

	Acute or Serious	*Less Acute or Nonserious*
Most common	Conjunctivitis/ blepharitis	Trauma
		Insect bites
	Periorbital cellulitis	Allergic reaction
	Orbital cellulitis	Contact dermatitis
		Reactive edema
Less common	Lacrimal duct/ gland infection	
	Erysipelas	Tumor
	Osteomyelitis	Renal disease
	Sinusitis with direct extension	

Table 8-2 Periorbital Swelling: Differential Considerations

	Onset	Appearance	Palpation	Fever	Remarks
Periorbital/Orbital Cellulitis	Rapid, less than one day, sometimes hours only	Reddish, may be violaceous	May be tense, painful	Almost always present	Usually unilateral
Trauma	History of trauma, variable onset	Reddish blue	May be tense or soft; usually nontender	Afebrile	Variable
Insect Bite	Variable, hours to days		Nontender, variable tenseness	Afebrile	Bite may be present, usually unilateral
Allergic Reaction	Can be rapid, minutes to hours		Nontender, variable tenseness	Afebrile	Allergen usually not found, often bilateral
Reactive Edema	Usually days, recedes as the day progresses	No color	Soft, nontender	Variable	Evidence of sinusitis, usually unilateral

suspicion of an infectious origin is low, a child may be observed at home for progression.

PERIORBITAL VERSUS ORBITAL CELLULITIS

If an infectious origin is defined, it is critical that the clinician distinguish between periorbital (or preseptal) cellulitis and orbital cellulitis or abscess. The key to making this distinction is examination of the mobility of the globe, its position, and visual acuity. Lack of mobility of the globe as well as a more anterior or proptotic position suggests orbital involvement. Decreased visual acuity, when this can be tested, also strongly suggests orbital rather than periorbital involvement.

An elevated or normal white blood cell count does little to aid the clinician in distinguishing between orbital and periorbital cellulitis. Plain radiographs of the orbit and sinuses, although of value in the recognition of sinusitis, offer very little help.

With the advent of computed tomography (CT), orbital involvement may be detected. Indications for a CT scan of the orbital area include the following:

- Definite orbital involvement on physical examination. This is done to exclude complications or orbital cellulitis including abscess formation and extension.
- Questionable orbital involvement on physical examination. A CT scan should be done to definitively exclude orbital involvement.
- Inability to examine the globe because of periorbital swelling. If the primary clinician or ophthalmologist cannot visualize the globe, it is imperative that examination of the region be done by CT.[10]

CONCLUSION

The consequences of misdiagnosis and subsequent inappropriate management can be devastating. The most serious complications of an infectious process are cavernous sinus thrombosis as well as abscess formation, osteomyelitis, blindness and injury to the eye, as well as meningitis. Appropriate and aggressive management can forestall progression and make these complications exceedingly rare (Figure 8-1).

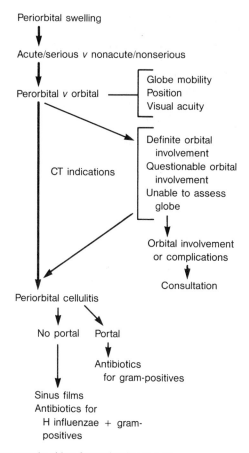

Periorbital swelling

Acute/serious *v* nonacute/nonserious

Perorbital *v* orbital ——— Globe mobility / Position / Visual acuity

CT indications — Definite orbital involvement / Questionable orbital involvement / Unable to assess globe

Orbital involvement or complications

Consultation

Periorbital cellulitis

No portal / Portal

Antibiotics for gram-positives

Sinus films / Antibiotics for H influenzae + gram-positives

Figure 8-1 Management algorithm for periorbital swelling.

REFERENCES

1. Barkin RM: Facial and periorbital cellulitis in children. *J Emerg Med* 1984;1:195–199.

2. Teele DW: Management of the child with a red and swollen eye. *Pediatr Infect Dis* 1983;2:258–262.

3. Middleton D, Ferrante J: Periorbital and facial cellulitis. *Am Fam Physician* 1980;2:98–103.

4. Barkin RM, Todd JK, Amer J: Periorbital cellulitis in children. *Pediatrics* 1978;61:272–277.

5. Gellady AM, Shulman ST, Ayoub EM: Periorbital and orbital cellulitis in children. *Pediatrics* 1978;62:272–277.

6. Jackson K, Baker SR: Clinical implications of orbital cellulitis. *Laryngoscope* 1986; 96:568–574.

7. Weiss A, Friendly D, Eglin K, et al: Bacterial periorbital and orbital cellulitis in childhood. *Ophthalmology* 1983;90:195–203.

8. Rubinstein J, Handler ST: Orbital and periorbital cellulitis in children. *Head Neck Surg* 1982;5:15–21.

9. Chandler J, Langenbrunner DJ, Stevens ER: The pathogenesis of orbital complications in acute sinusitis. *Laryngoscope* 1970;9:1414–1428.

10. Goldberg F, Berne AS, Oski FA: Differentiation of orbital cellulitis from preseptal cellulitis by computed tomography. *Pediatrics* 1978;62:1000–1005.

9. Periorbital Cellulitis

Richard G. Lucht, MD
Glenn C. Hamilton, MD

Periorbital cellulitis is commonly seen during childhood, usually resolving rapidly with appropriate antimicrobial therapy. Prompt recognition and treatment can prevent systemic and ocular complications.

Periorbital cellulitis involving infections of the superficial tissue layers surrounding the eye must be distinguished from the less common, but more severe orbital cellulitis. The critical plane separating periorbital cellulitis from orbital cellulitis is the facial layer termed the orbital septum (Figure 9-1). The preseptal region is bordered anteriorly by the skin, superiorly and inferiorly by vertical fibrous attachments from the skin to the orbital rim, and posteriorly by the tarsus and orbital septum.

PRESENTATION

Infection anterior to the orbital septum is described as preseptal or periorbital cellulitis. Although reported at any age, it most commonly occurs in children under 6 years of age with a mean age of 2.8 years.[1,2] It is characterized by erythema, edema, tenderness, and warmth of the lid often with an associated purplish hue; the eye itself is uninvolved, vision and mobility being normal. The cellulitis is unilateral in more than 94% of patients.[3,4] One fourth of patients have mild conjunctival hyperemia without purulent discharge. Seventy-three percent of children have temperatures greater than 37.8 °C; 48% have temperatures greater than 38.3 °C.[5] Sinusitis with marked nasal drainage, pain, or tenderness over the paranasal sinuses may also occur.[4] Severe infection of the orbit is associated with higher temperatures and a prolonged febrile course.[6]

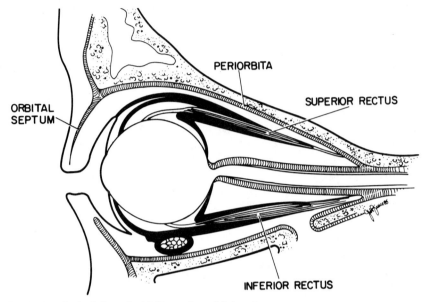

Figure 9-1 Sagittal view of orbit illustrating orbital septum.

PATHOPHYSIOLOGY AND ETIOLOGY

Predisposing conditions are found in 50% to 90% of children with periorbital cellulitis.[1,7] The majority of patients show one of three clinical patterns:

1. A history of trauma, skin infection, or insect bite in close proximity to the eye is present, commonly in children over 3 years of age.[8] *Staphylococcus aureus* and group A beta-hemolytic streptococcus are the most common causes. *Hemophilus influenzae* infection can occur after surgical repair of skin lacerations as well as superficial tissue injury to the eyelid.[2] Anaerobic organisms such as *Bacteroides,* peptostreptococcus, and Veillonella are pathogenic as well.
2. A history of an antecedent upper respiratory tract infection (URI) or an examination revealing coryza, pharyngitis, or otitis media may be noted. Since the conjunctival surface is an extension of the upper respiratory tract via the lacrimal cannaliculi and nasolacrimal ducts, it is understandable that a URI may involve the conjunctiva and periorbital soft tissues. Most of these patients are under 3 years of age and have a preceding mild URI followed by preseptal swelling and fever.[8,9]
3. Paranasal sinusitis may be a third predisposing condition. Some regard it as a complication of the process that initiated the cellulitis, whereas

others imply direct causation.[2,5,8,10] Except for the ethmoid sinuses, there is normally no direct communication between the sinuses and preseptal tissues; however, the bony walls are extremely thin, providing a potential for penetration in cases of severe inflammation.

Periorbital cellulitis associated with sinusitis may be described as an inflammatory process caused by venous obstruction.[9] The course is subacute, often with little fever, tenderness, or induration. The etiologic organisms are those associated with acute sinusitis reflecting normal respiratory pathogens, although anaerobic bacteria may be important with severe or resistant disease.[9]

Other factors predisposing to periorbital cellulitis include leukemia, hordeolum, herpes, epiglottitis, odontogenic abscess, and varicella.[11,12] Infants under 4 months old may have nasolacrimal duct obstruction. Osteomyelitis of the maxilla caused by *S aureus* has progressed to involve the preseptal tissues in an infant under 9 months old.[1,12]

DIAGNOSIS

Cultures

The specific diagnosis depends on the history, clinical examination, and recovery of the causal organism from blood or adjacent skin aspirate. The value of the tissue aspirate Gram's stain and culture are controversial.[2,4,9,13] The low yield of positive cultures among children with periorbital cellulitis and prior URI suggests that skin aspiration is generally not useful. Tissue aspiration culturing is common practice and may be of value in certain settings.[14]

Blood cultures are frequently useful. Forty-two percent of patients with periorbital cellulitis had positive blood cultures for *H influenzae* and, less commonly, *Streptococcus pneumoniae*.[2] Many patients without bacteremia had been pretreated with systemic antibiotics before a culture was obtained, suggesting that the true incidence may be higher.

Nasopharyngeal and conjunctival cultures and the use of Gram's stain are poorly correlated with detection of causative organisms and are therefore not recommended.[5]

Radiologic Studies

Radiologic studies may be helpful to assess both the degree and location of the inflammatory process. Sinus radiographs often show abnormal findings because of the underdevelopment of the sinuses and the concurrent URI, independent of whether true sinusitis exists. Inflammatory edema associated with sinusitis and venous obstruction commonly has ipsilateral ethmoid sinus opacification as well as ipsilateral or bilateral involvement of the maxillary sinuses.

Ultrasonography helps differentiate periorbital cellulitis from more extensive infections. Foreign bodies and abscesses as small as 3 mm may be identified; however, lesions immediately adjacent to the globe are difficult to differentiate.[1] Computed tomography assists in distinguishing periorbital from orbital cellulitis in patients in whom the extent of orbital disease is not clinically definable.[15]

DIFFERENTIAL DIAGNOSIS

The involvement of deeper orbital structures must be clarified. The differential diagnoses include orbital cellulitis, facial cellulitis, blepharitis, or lacrimal gland or sac infection. Allergic reactions and insect bites may produce prominent lid edema. Trauma may appear as periorbital swelling and erythema (Table 9-1).[13]

Ocular vaccinia without skin manifestations may produce marked periorbital erythema and edema. Corneal ulcers, vesicular lesions of the conjunctiva, or preauricular adenopathy may be present. Malignancy such as retinoblastoma or rhabdomyosarcoma may show relatively rapid onset of lid swelling.[11]

Table 9-1 Differentiating Periorbital Cellulitis and Orbital Cellulitis

Condition	Periorbital Cellulitis	Orbital Cellulitis
Lid edema	Present	Severe
Lid erythema	Present	Present
Ophthalmoplegia	Absent	Present
Chemosis	Mild or absent	Present
Proptosis	Mild or absent	Present
Pain with eye movement	Absent	Present
Loss of vision	Normal	Often decreased
Fever	Present	Present
Leukocytosis	Present	Present
Age	Usually < 5 years old	Usually > 5 years old
Additional findings:	Sinusitis	Sinusitis
	Adjacent skin lesions	Subperiosteal or orbital
	Recent mild URI	abscess formation

TREATMENT

Management remains controversial. Therapy must reflect the patient's age, predisposing factors, likely etiologic agents, and the results of cultures of tissue aspirate and blood (Table 9-2). The majority of children with periorbital cellulitis require parenteral antibiotics while being monitored in a hospital setting. Patients remain febrile a mean of 38 hours, with marked resolution of erythema and swelling in 48 hours. A total course of 10 days of antibiotics is required, the hospital stay ranging from 4 to 7 days.[1,5]

Antimicrobial agents must have a broad spectrum, usually combining chloramphenicol and a semisynthetic penicillinase-resistant penicillin such as nafcillin (100 to 200 mg/kg/24 hr q 4 hr IV). Chloramphenicol (100 mg/kg/24 hr q 6 hr IV) is preferred over ampicillin because of the high incidence of beta-lactamase–producing *H influenzae*.[1] Because of the increasing incidence of chloramphenicol-resistant *H influenzae*, combination therapy with both ampicillin and chloramphenicol may be the initial therapy of choice in nontraumatized patients. In children with known penicillin allergy, third generation cephalosporins such as cefotaxime, cefuroxime or ceftriaxone may be effective. Primary monotherapy with a second or third generation cephalosporin may be relatively safe and effective.

In children with a history of eyelid trauma or skin infection, a semisynthetic penicillin or cephalosporin derivative provides effective coverage for *S aureus* and group A streptococcus. If there is a history of human or animal bite, or repair of a skin laceration, antimicrobial coverage should include agents effective against gram-negative and anaerobic organisms.[2]

Table 9-2 Periorbital Cellulitis: Common Causes and Organisms

Trauma
  Group A streptococci
  S aureus
  S pneumoniae
  H influenzae
  Anaerobes

Upper Respiratory Infection
  H influenzae
  S pneumoniae
  Group A streptococci

Sinusitis
  Group A streptococci
  Anaerobes
  H influenzae
  S aureus

Some physicians suggest that mild cases of periorbital cellulitis, with an obvious adjacent skin lesion, may be treated with oral antibiotics such as dicloxacillin (50 mg/kg/24 hr q 6 hr PO). Occasionally, older children may be treated as outpatients with oral therapy initially in situations in which compliance and close follow-up are possible.[5,13]

Prompt incision and drainage is appropriate for initial management of a preseptal abscess.

Decongestants, topical ophthalmic antibiotics, or local therapy are not beneficial in expediting resolution. Warm soaks, nasal decongestants, and acetaminophen or aspirin may provide symptomatic relief. Early ophthalmologic and otolaryngologic consultations may be useful in severe or complex cases.[5]

CONCLUSION

Periorbital cellulitis requires early recognition and aggressive management. Careful evaluation must differentiate periorbital cellulitis from deeper orbital involvement. Antecedent conditions such as trauma, skin infection, URI, or concurrent sinusitis suggest likely causal agents and appropriate antibiotic management.

REFERENCES

1. Spires JR, Smith RJ: Bacterial infections of the orbital and periorbital soft-tissues in children. *Laryngoscope* 1986;96:763–767.

2. Weiss A, Friendly D, Eglin K, et al: Bacterial periorbital and orbital cellulitis in childhood. *Ophthal* 1983;90:195–203.

3. Gellady AM, Shulman ST, Ayoub EM: Periorbital and orbital cellulitis in children. *Pediatrics* 1978;61:272–277.

4. Barkin RM: Facial and periorbital cellulitis in children. *J Emerg Med* 1984;1:195–199.

5. Barkin RM, Todd JR, Amer J: Periorbital cellulitis in children. *Pediatrics* 1978;62:390–392.

6. Robie G, O'Neal R, Kelsey DS: Periorbital cellulitis. *J Pediatr Ophthal* 1977;14:354–363.

7. Rubinstein JBV, Hanoler SD: Orbital and periorbital cellulitis in children. *Head Neck Surg* 1982;5:15–21.

8. Smith TF, O'Day D, Wright PF: Clinical implications of preseptal (periorbital) cellulitis in childhood. *Pediatrics* 1978;62:1006–1009.

9. Shapiro ED, Wald ER, Brozanski BA: Periorbital cellulitis and paranasal sinusitis: A reappraisal. *Pediatr Infect Dis* 1982;1:91–95.

10. Herman J, Katzuni E: Periorbital cellulitis complicating adenovirus infection. *Am J Dis Child* 1986;8:745.

11. Middleton DB, Ferrante JA: Periorbital and facial cellulitis. *Am Fam Phys* 1980;21:98–103.

12. Noel LP, Clarice WN, Peacocke TA: Periorbital and orbital cellulitis in childhood. *Can J Ophthal* 1981;16:178–180.

13. Shackelford PG, Smith M: Preseptal and orbital cellulitis, in Feigin RD, Cherry JD (eds): *Textbook of Pediatric Infectious Disease*. Philadelphia, WB Saunders Co, 1981, pp 663–665.

14. Epperly TD: The value of needle aspiration in the management of cellulitis. *J Fam Prac* 1986;23:337–340.

15. Goldberg F, Berne AS, Oski FA: Differentiation of orbital cellulitis from preseptal cellulitis by computed tomography. *Pediatrics* 1978;62:1000–1005.

Section 4

Urinary Tract Infection

Diagnosing urinary tract infections in children requires reliance on careful examination of a properly collected urine and quantitative culture. Although there has been enthusiasm for shortening the therapeutic course, the evidence does not support this approach in the majority of children.

Radiologic evaluation has evolved rapidly, ultrasonography and voiding cystourethrogram being the least invasive approaches to the initial evaluation. Further experience may increase the utility of other modalities.

10. Urinary Tract Infections: Assessment and Management

Andrew M. Wiesenthal, MD

Urinary tract infections (UTIs) are among the most common childhood illnesses treatable with antimicrobial therapy. The incidence varies with the age and sex of the child and the presence or absence of symptoms. Two to three percent of pre-term newborns, for example, have asymptomatic bacteriuria, whereas only 1% of term newborns do. The incidence in boys in these populations is greater than that in girls. In boys who are school-age or older, the incidence is 0.03% or less, whereas roughly 2% of girls the same age have asymptomatic bacteriuria. The incidence of symptomatic UTI in newborns is 0.14%; girls outside the newborn period have a symptomatic incidence of 2.8%. The comparable figure in boys is 0.7%.[1]

The risk of recurrence of UTI ranges from 30% to 75%, depending on the number of prior infections.[1] The subset of these children with vesicoureteral reflux shown radiographically is at risk for renal scarring and further symptomatic infection. They do not seem to have an increased risk of hypertension or reduced renal function over many years of follow-up, but the children of women with recurrent UTI may be at increased risk of such infections themselves.[2]

ETIOLOGY

Urinary tract infection in newborns is commonly hematogenous, as the causative organisms reflect. They include *Staphylococcus aureus, Staphylococcus epidermidis, Enterobacteriaceae*, and other gram-negative enteric bacteria.

In older infants and children, infection is generally ascending, from the perineum via the urethra to the bladder and subsequently by the ureters, if

71

reflux is present, to the kidneys. Accordingly, the implicated bacteria are *Enterobacteriaceae*, other gram-negative organisms, and *S epidermidis*.[3]

CLINICAL PRESENTATION

Clinicians often make reference to "classic" symptoms and signs of UTI: frequency and dysuria with fever and costovertebral angle tenderness if upper tract disease, or pyelonephritis, is present. There is, unfortunately, no correlation between either of the latter two findings and the presence or absence of upper tract disease and concomitant renal damage. Asymptomatic children may have ongoing renal infection, whereas febrile, systematically ill children may have disease restricted to the bladder. Urinary tract infection needs to be considered in any febrile child, especially girls. In a recent study[4] of infants under 2 years of age with fever and no identifiable focus of infection on physical examination, 7.4% of the girls had UTI, but none of the boys did.

LABORATORY ASSESSMENT

With children showing some or all of the classic symptoms and signs, genital trauma, sexual abuse, sexually transmitted diseases, and bacterial vaginosis should be considered in the differential diagnosis when appropriate.

Examination of the urine remains the cornerstone of laboratory evaluation. *The quality of the specimen submitted is the most important determinant of the quality of any laboratory test result.* Urinalysis and urine cultures are prime examples of this rule. In general, the less invasive the means of specimen collection, the greater the likelihood of contamination and the less interpretable the results. Suprapubic bladder aspiration is a preferred method for obtaining specimens because of the relatively low incidence of contamination. Bladder catheterization is next most acceptable from the standpoint of the laboratory but is still uncomfortable. A clean-catch midstream specimen in continent children is perhaps the most reasonable compromise. Clean-bag specimens, obtained after thorough cleaning of the perineum and the application of an adhesive urine collection bag, are very likely to be contaminated. However, this technique may be the only method acceptable under certain circumstances to the parents of infants and other incontinent children.

Once a specimen is obtained, there are several ways to examine the urine that may be helpful in diagnosis and management. First, a chemical dipstick is generally employed by most laboratories. The leukocyte esterase and nitrite tests are most useful in the diagnosis of UTI.[5] Positivity of the former correlates with the presence of pyuria, which is often, but not always, present with

UTI. If the nitrite test is positive, it implies that bacteria capable of fixing the nitrate normally found in urine have been in contact with the urine in large enough numbers for long enough to do so. This test may therefore not be positive in a child who is voiding frequently and thus not allowing sufficient time for the conversion of nitrate to nitrite by bacteria in the bladder. For this reason, among others, a first-morning void specimen (urine that has been in the bladder for at least several hours) is most likely to be positive.

After the dipstick examination is performed, many laboratories micro-scopically examine the sediment of a centrifuged aliquot of urine. Generally they report on the presence or absence of white blood cells, white and red blood cell casts, and bacteria. None of these findings is particularly sensitive or specific. A Gram's stain of the sediment can be helpful: One or more organisms per high-power microscopic field is a sensitive indicator; if ten or more organisms are present, the finding is quite specific for UTI. In addition, knowing whether the organisms are gram-negative or positive aids in the choice of initial antimicrobial therapy.[6]

Finally, the urine may be cultured quantitatively. The growth of more than 10^5 colonies of a single organism per mm^3 has been the sine qua non of UTI for many years. However, there may be children with clinically important infections whose urine cultures grow fewer than 10^5 colonies per mm^3 (Table 10-1).[7,8]

INITIAL MANAGEMENT

All newborns and very young infants, as well as older children who are especially toxic or dehydrated, should be admitted to the hospital. Appropriate fluid resuscitation should be instituted, and therapy with ampicillin and an aminoglycoside initiated. A more specific antimicrobial agent can be selected, if necessary, once urine culture and susceptibility results become available.

Older, symptomatic but nontoxic children can usually be treated as outpatients. An appropriate initial oral antimicrobial agent might be sulfisoxazole, amoxicillin, trimethoprim-sulfamethoxazole, or nitrofurantoin. The duration of this therapy should be 10 days.[9]

Despite the fact that many adult women can be successfully treated with single-dose antimicrobial therapy, such management has not been nearly so effective in children, either in terms of the initial cure rate or the rate of subsequent relapse or reinfection.[10,11] It may be possible (and practical) to treat adolescent girls with a single dose or short (3-day) course if good follow-up can be assured, but until more encouraging data on the use of such strategies in younger children become available, they should be treated more conservatively.[12]

Table 10-1 Criteria for Diagnosis of UTI

Method of Collection	Colony Count/mL (Pure Culture)	Probability of Infection
Suprapubic aspiration	$\geq 10^3$	Highly likely
	$< 10^3$	Unlikely
Catheterization	$\geq 10^4$	Highly likely
	$10^3 - 10^4$	Probable
	$< 10^3$	Unlikely
Voided		
Male-continent	$\geq 10^4$	Highly likely
	$10^3 - 10^4$	Suspicious
	$< 10^3$	Unlikely
Female-continent	$\geq 10^5$	Likely
	$10^4 - 10^5$	Suspicious
	$10^3 - 10^4$	Indeterminate
	$< 10^3$	Unlikely
Incontinent	$\geq 10^3$	Indeterminate
	$< 10^3$	Unlikely

Source: Reprinted with permission from WA Durbin et al, "Management of Urinary Tract Infections in Infants and Children," *Pediatric Infectious Disease* (1984;3:564–574), Copyright © 1984, Williams & Wilkins Company.

If bacteriuria is detected in asymptomatic children, they should be treated as described above until the urinary tract can be proven to be normal radiographically. Once such information is available, no treatment is necessary for asymptomatic bacteriuria.

ONGOING MANAGEMENT

There is no substitute for good follow-up of UTI in children. All should have a repeat culture to verify cure. All boys should have radiologic studies (renal ultrasound, which has supplanted the intravenous pyelogram,[13] and either a renal scan or a voiding cystourethrogram) 4 to 6 weeks after initial diagnosis. Many authorities feel that the same rule should apply to girls, but others state that such studies can wait until the child has had a second proven infection. Children with radiographic abnormalities should have blood pressure determinations and renal function tests, and, depending on the extent of those abnormalities, may require referral to a urologist. Children with many recurrences of UTI may benefit from suppressive therapy with trimethoprim--

Table 10-2 Management of Schoolgirls with Recurrent Bacteriuria

Radiologic Category	Antibiotic Suppression	Therapy*	Monitor Urine	Repeat Radiologic Studies	Urologic Consultation
Normal or Grade I Reflux	No	Yes	Yes	4-5 Yrs	No
Grades II or III Reflux	Yes	Yes	Yes	2-5 Yrs	?
Grade IV Reflux	Yes	Yes	Yes	Yes	Yes

*Therapy for overt disease.

Source: Reprinted with permission from GA McCracken Jr, "Recurrent Urinary Tract Infections in Children," *Pediatric Infectious Disease* (1984;3:S28–S30), Copyright © 1984, Williams & Wilkins Company.

sulfamethoxazole or nitrofurantoin, the former being preferred. It may be useful for parents of such children to screen first-morning voided specimens regularly at home using a nitrite dipstick test.[14] School-aged girls with recurrent infection require specific evaluation (Table 10-2).

The importance of follow-up must be clearly emphasized to the parents of all children with UTI.

REFERENCES

1. Hellerstein S: Recurrent urinary tract infections in children. *Pediatr Infect Dis* 1982;1:271–281.

2. Gillenwater JY, Harrison RB, Kunin CM: Natural history of bacteriuria in schoolgirls: A long-term case-control study. *N Engl J Med* 1979;301:396–399.

3. Ogra PL, Faden HS: Urinary tract infections in childhood: An update. *J Pediatr* 1985;106:1023–1028.

4. Roberts KB, Charney E, Sneren RJ: Urinary tract infection in infants with unexplained fever: A collaborative study. *J Pediatrics* 1983;103:864–867.

5. Perry JL, Matthews JS, Weesner DE: Evaluation of leukocyte esterase test as a rapid screening technique for bacteriuria. *J Clin Microbiol* 1982;15:852–854.

6. Jenkins RD, Fenn JP, Matsen JM: Review of urine microscopy for bacteriuria. *JAMA* 1986;255:3397–3403.

7. McCracken GH Jr: Recurrent urinary tract infections in children. *Pediatr Infect Dis* 1984;3:S28–S30.

8. Todd JK: Diagnosis of urinary tract infections. *Pediatr Infect Dis* 1982;1:126–131.

9. Durbin WA, Peter G: Management of urinary tract infections in infants and children. *Pediatr Infect Dis* 1984;3:564–574.

10. Avner ED, Ingelfinger JR, Herrin JT, et al: Single-dose amoxicillin therapy of uncomplicated pediatric urinary tract infections. *J Pediatr* 1983;102:623–627.

11. Shapiro ED: Short course antimicrobial treatment of urinary tract infections in children: A critical analysis. *Pediatr Infect Dis* 1982;1:294–297.

12. Fine JS, Jacobson MS: Single-dose conventional therapy of urinary tract infections in female adolescents. *Pediatrics* 1985;75:916–920.

13. Johnson CE, DeBaz BP, Shurin PA: Renal ultrasound evaluation of urinary tract infections in children. *Pediatrics* 1986;78:871–878.

14. Kunin CM, et al: Detection of urinary tract infections in 3- to 5-year-old girls by mothers using a nitrite indicator strip. *Pediatrics* 1976;57:829–835.

11. Urinary Tract Infections: Diagnosis and Management

Donald J. Lefkowits, MD

Urinary tract infections (UTIs) in the pediatric patient present perhaps the clearest example of modern medicine's ultimate dilemma: "to heal but do not harm." The challenge is to diagnose accurately and treat optimally with minimal invasiveness and risk to the patient while providing cost-effective and efficient care.

This bacterial infection involving the urethra and bladder (*lower*) or the ureters and kidney (*upper*) is more common in women than in men (10:1 ratio). However, in children under 1 year of age, boys are infected more commonly (5:1). Between 5% and 10% of all girls will have at least one UTI by 18 years of age.[1]

MAKING THE DIAGNOSIS

Nonspecific signs and symptoms are common in children under 2 years of age. Neonates and infants may have generalized symptoms including irritability, fever or hypothermia, failure to thrive, and lethargy, or gastrointestinal findings such as poor feeding, vomiting, diarrhea, abdominal distension, and jaundice.

Predisposing factors exist:

- reflux
- stasis
- obstruction
- pregnancy
- recent sexual intercourse
- recent instrumentation
- recent treatment with antibiotics.

The most prominent are incompetent valves at the ureterovesicular junction and stasis.[2] Causes of stasis are:

- congenital anomalies of the ureter or urethra (valves, bands, stenosis)
- neurogenic bladder or dysfunctional voiding
- calculi
- external compression of the bladder or ureter.

Older children may have more classic findings of fever, frequency, dysuria, abdominal or flank pain, hematuria, and enuresis. Boy toddlers who must strain to void, or develop a diminished stream or dribbling, should be considered to have an anatomic abnormality.

The initial physical examination may reveal a toxic condition, dehydration, or sepsis, as well as localized findings such as flank or suprapubic tenderness. Hypertension, abdominal masses, spinal deformities, and evidence of neurologic compromise of the lower extremities should be excluded.

In the septic or acutely ill-appearing child, a suprapubic or straight-catheter specimen should be obtained. Bag specimens are inappropriate in such patients who will require empiric, parenteral antibiotics. Midstream clean-catch (MSCC) specimens may be appropriate for the older child who can cooperate with careful collection techniques. Blood cultures and serum chemistry tests to assess acid-base status and renal function may be needed.

For the less ill child, obtaining an MSCC or a double-repeated bag specimen is less invasive and probably adequate for diagnosis. Resulting colony counts should be considered with the overall clinical picture to determine appropriate therapy. Strict adherence to the oft-given standards of growth of more than 10^5 colonies for bag and MSCC specimens, 10^3 for catheter specimens, and 10^1 for suprapubic specimens may result in misdiagnosis.[3]

Ancillary data from the urinalysis can be useful in the differential diagnosis of patients with urinary symptoms. One or more white blood cells per high-power field (HPF) in an unspun urine is supportive for UTI. One or more bacteria per HPF in a carefully collected unspun specimen is highly sensitive and specific for UTI.[4]

Leukocyte esterase activity in an MSCC or catheter specimen correlates highly with the presence of UTI. A recent study by Chernow et al[5] using the leukocyte esterase test strip showed 100% sensitivity and 76% specificity in detecting positive cultures. Dipstick tests for nitrites show a fairly high rate of false-positives and are thus of less value. All these studies are improved by using a first-morning void.

Differentiating upper from lower UTI was attempted using a variety of laboratory tests without uniform success:

- individual ureteral catheterization
- bladder washout
- antibody coating
- urinary lactic dehydrogenase (LDH) tests
- C-reactive protein.

Initial clinical findings combined with close observation of response to therapy is likely to be of greater value to the clinician.

MANAGEMENT

Beginning empiric therapy without awaiting identification of the causative agent is essential in treating UTIs in the newborn and any child appearing ill, septic, or with signs and symptoms suggestive of acute pyelonephritis. Initial therapy includes gentamicin sulfate or other aminoglycosides (5 to 7.5 mg/kg/24 hr q 8 to 12 hr IV) combined with *one* of the following: ampicillin (100 to 200 mg/kg/24 hr q 4 to 6 hr IV), sulfisoxazole (150 mg/kg/24 hr q 6 hr PO), or trimethoprim (TMP) with sulfamethoxazole (SMZ) (8 mg TMP + 40 mg SMZ/kg/24 hr q 12 hr PO). Sulfonamides should be avoided in the newborn. These patients generally require initial hospitalization for hydration and parenteral administration of antibiotics.

Appropriate initial therapy for the less acutely ill child includes amoxicillin (30 to 50 mg/kg/24 hr TID PO), sulfisoxazole (120 to 150 mg/kg/24 hr QID PO), or TMP/SMZ (8 mg TMP + 40 mg SMZ/kg/24 hr BID PO).

Duration of therapy is a current issue of some debate. Although therapy for 10 days has been the "gold standard," recent pediatric literature[6–8] suggests potential advantages of 1- and 3-day therapy regimens. These are associated with lower costs, improved compliance, decreased risk of side effects, and lesser incidence of emergence of resistant strains. These studies suggest the initial cure rates and recurrence rates are roughly equivalent in short-term and long-term therapy groups. However, the results of some studies are not so conclusive, and short-term therapy cannot yet be considered standard. It may be appropriate to consider single or short-term therapy in the older girl with a clear-cut, uncomplicated lower tract UTI who is assured of careful follow-up. Further studies are needed, however, before short-course therapy can be considered in most cases.

All patients require long-term follow-up to monitor for recurrences and impairment of renal function.

Recurrences occur in 10% to 70% of patients, varying with the age at the first infection and presence of underlying anatomic abnormalities.[1–3] Recurrences are most frequent in the first 6 months after infection and are rare after 18 months without previous reinfection. Recurrences may be asymptomatic even when the initial infection was accompanied by symptoms.

Surveillance to identify recurrences requires monthly repeat MSCC cultures for 3 to 6 months, and then cultures every 3 months for an additional year. Reinfection requires prompt therapy, radiologic evaluation if not already performed, and investigation of personal hygiene and sexual activities. Suppressive therapy may be required.

RADIOLOGIC EVALUATION

Studies[1-3] report marked anatomic abnormalities in 15% to 50% of children who develop UTI. This may approach 90% in children under 2 years old.[9] All infants and any boy experiencing a first UTI should be studied. Older girls experiencing one uncomplicated lower UTI may be followed with surveillance cultures and referred only if there is a recurrence.

There is evidence that the once standard intravenous pyelogram may be replaced by ultrasound examination and a voiding cystourethrogram as adequate means of evaluating for anatomic abnormalities.[10,11] Such a combined approach spares the child exposure to intravenous contrast materials as well as decreasing the exposure to ionizing radiation (Chapter 12).

CONCLUSION

Treatment must reflect the age and toxic condition of the child, with therapy indicated for 10 days. Radiologic evaluation should be done for selected patients, and careful follow-up is required for all. A team effort is required to ensure that what may initially be perceived as a benign and short-lived problem remains so.

REFERENCES

1. Cunningham RJ III: Urinary tract infection in infants and children. *Postgrad Med* 1984;75:59–64.

2. Krugman S, et al: *Infectious Diseases of Children*. St. Louis, CV Mosby Co, 1985, pp 421–432.

3. Weir MR, Lampe RM: Urinary tract infections in children. *Am Fam Prac* 1984;29:147–153.

4. Kunin CM: The quantitative significance of bacteria visualized in the unstained urinary sediment. *N Engl J Med* 1961;265:589–590.

5. Chernow B, Zaloga GP, et al: Measurement of urinary leukocyte esterase activity: A screening test for urinary tract infections. *Ann Emerg Med* 1984;13:150–154.

6. Stahl GE, Topf P, et al: Single dose treatment of uncomplicated urinary tract infections in children. *Ann Emerg Med* 1984;13:705–708.

7. Avner ED, Ingelfinger JR, et al: Single dose amoxicillin therapy of uncomplicated pediatric urinary tract infections. *J Pediatr* 1983;102:623–627.

8. Roberto U, D'Eufemia P, et al: Effects of 3- vs 10-day treatment of urinary tract infections. *J Pediatr* 1984;104:483–484.

9. McKerrow W, Davidson-Lamb N, Jones PF: Urinary tract infections in children. *Br Med J* 1984;289:299–303.

10. Kangarloo H, Gold RH, et al: Urinary tract infection in infants and children evaluated by ultrasound. *Radiology* 1985;154:367–373.

11. Leonidas JC, McCauley RGK, et al: Sonography as a substitute for excretory urography in children with urinary tract infections. *AJR* 1985;144:815–819.

12. Radiologic Evaluation after Urinary Tract Infections

Suzanne Z. Barkin, MD
Roger M. Barkin, MD, MPH
J. Gerard Horgan, MB, MRCP, FRCP
Carol M. Rumack, MD

The child seen for evaluation and treatment of signs and symptoms consistent with a urinary tract infection (UTI) requires careful follow-up. One of the most important reasons for this ongoing care is to preclude the existence of anatomical and functional abnormalities that require intervention. This has historically been done using an excretory urogram (IVP) and voiding cystourethrogram (VCUG), but recent advances give alternatives that provide good anatomic definition with reduced risk and exposure of the child to ionizing radiation.

Children with UTI who are generally studied radiologically 4 to 6 weeks after a documented infection include:

- those under 1 year of age
- males, as they have an increased risk of associated anomaly
- those with clinical signs and symptoms and laboratory confirmation of pyelonephritis
- those with clinical evidence of renal disease (ie, high blood pressure, BUN, or creatinine)
- females, after second documented UTI, although many authorities recommend they be studied after the first infection.

RADIOLOGIC TECHNIQUES

Voiding Cystourethrography

The classic VCUG is appropriate for all patients with infections to evaluate vesicoureteral reflux, and bladder and urethral anatomy. Reflux is a dynamic phenomenon, occurring in waves and, in 20% of children, only during urination; the VCUG remains the most sensitive and specific test available.[1]

The VCUG provides anatomic evidence of bladder and urethral anomalies; radionuclide cystography (see below) is excellent in showing reflux and may be useful to follow reflux once the anatomy is defined because of its accuracy and low radiation dose.

Sonography

Real time sonography can identify some anomalies of the upper urinary tract (ie, number, position), particularly if obstruction is present. Other anomalies including duplicity,[2] mild calyceal dilatation, or blunting and mild scarring may be missed. Ultrasonography can also provide accurate measurements of present and serial evaluation of future renal growth; normal growth implies a normal kidney.[3] The sensitivity and specificity reflect the quality of the equipment and personnel.

Hydronephrosis can also be identified. Abnormalities found by sonography in 29 patients correlated 100% with those found on excretory urogram, with the exception of one patient who had focal renal scarring missed on ultrasonography.[4]

Information can also be obtained about the bladder, vesicoureteral junction, and proximal urethra. Ureteropelvic junction obstruction, which is the commonest cause of obstruction,[5] appears as dilatation of the renal pelvis and calyceal structures without identifiable dilatation of the ureter. A study[5] showed that 12 of 13 patients with obstruction of the proximal ureter had congenital stricture at the ureteropelvic junction. Lower urinary tract obstruction commonly caused by posterior urethral valves is associated with a dilated, tortuous ureter. Although severe reflux may be suspected, mild grades may be missed.[6] Hydroureter associated with obstructed or nonobstructed primary megaureter may also be defined. Bladder anomalies such as ureteroceles are noted as cystic structures communicating with the bladder. Posterior urethral valves have an accompanying bladder wall of increased thickness as well as dilatation of the posterior urethra.

Excretory Urography

The IVP is a standard component in the evaluation of renal anatomy and collecting system after UTI. Such imaging is useful in identifying anomalies that predispose the patient to infection, but has limited use in confirming the diagnosis of acute pyelonephritis. Abnormal excretory urograms were found with only 24% to 28% of patients with acute pyelonephritis.[7] Although a relatively safe procedure, the technique does expose children to ionizing radiation, a solute load, and the anaphylactic risk of intravenous administration of contrast material.

To reduce the radiation exposure, many clinicians reduce the number of exposures, taking a scout film before administration of contrast material, a 25-second postinjection film, and 10-minute postinjection film only. This normally provides adequate visualization of renal anatomy.

Radionuclide Scintigraphy

Technetium-99m-DTPA is very sensitive in the functional evaluation of the functioning renal mass, tubular transit time, and glomerular filtration rate. Its high concentration in the urine allows excellent visualization of the pelvicalyceal systems, ureters, and bladder. It is visualized independently of bowel gas and feces. Because of its low resolution, it may not define small cortical lesions. It does not show blunting of the calyces until the pathologic condition is severe.[8] Anomalies are unlikely to be seen unless obstruction is present. It is useful in monitoring pre- and postoperative patients.

Technetium-99m-glucoheptonate identifies renal parenchymal involvement and thereby may differentiate upper from lower tract disease because of its excellent visualization in the renal cortex.[9] Acute pyelonephritis causes focal defects in the parenchyma, which are often not seen on sonography; cystitis does not. These focal defects may be secondary to parenchymal scars; DTPA helps differentiate involvement of the upper from the lower tract.

ASSESSMENT OF THE CHILD

Increasing importance is being placed on the VCUG as the primary screening test in children after UTI. The VCUG reliably indicates reflux and its severity and permits visualization of the urethra with its potentially surgically correctable lesions (Figure 12-1). If the VCUG shows *no abnormalities,* then ultrasonography should be performed, evaluating renal size, evidence of obstruction, and vesicoureteral junction abnormalities. If these examinations show no abnormalities, further studies are not indicated; if any abnormality is detected, an IVP should be done.[10,11]

If the VCUG shows *abnormalities,* an excretory urethrogram should be done to determine the nature and extent of nephropathy.[1,12–14]

Some clinicians use ultrasonography as the primary study after UTI. However, Jequier et al[11] studied 240 patients between 2 days and 15 years of age

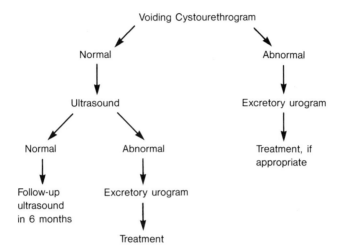

Figure 12-1 Radiologic evaluation of child with a urinary tract infection.

following a UTI. Seventy-one patients had ultrasonograms that showed abnormalities confirmed by radiographic (IVP and VCUG) studies. However, 51 patients had discrepant ultrasonographic and radiographic findings, all of which were because of missed reflux; the authors suggested that the evaluation of UTIs be accompanied by a VCUG.

There is still widespread use of the excretory urogram in the evaluation of children after UTI. The technique has been used for years and is reliable. It optimally defines the extent of renal scarring, which may be vital in making surgical decisions in cases of severe reflux nephropathy and calyceal deformity. However, it is not to be regarded as a simple examination.

Where expertise exists, ultrasonography may be used instead of the excretory urogram except in patients with reflux who are prone to progressive nephropathy.

There is no consensus on the long-term follow-up of patients with recurrent UTI. Radionuclide cystography may be used for follow-up for reflux as well as to complement the first ultrasound examination in girls. Children under 5 years of age should also have follow-up ultrasound examinations to assess renal size.

CONCLUSION

Greater experience with newer imaging techniques provides alternatives to traditional approaches. Obviously, the selection of any study must reflect the information required, the sensitivity and specificity desired, the equipment and expertise available, and individual experience. Ultrasound provides an increasingly useful modality in the evaluation of children following UTIs.

REFERENCES

1. Blickman JG, Taylor GA, Lebowitz RL: Voiding cystourethrography: The initial radiologic study in children with urinary tract infection. *Radiology* 1985;156:659–662.

2. Horgan JG, Rosenfield N, Rosenfield AT: Is renal ultrasound a reliable indicator of a nonobstructed duplication anomaly? *Pediatric Radiology* 1984;14:388–391.

3. Han BK, Babcock DS: Sonographic measurements and appearance of normal kidneys in children. *AJR* 1985;145:611–616.

3. Sty JR, Starshak RJ: Sonography of pediatric urinary tract abnormalities. *Sem Ultrasound* 1981;11:71–87.

4. Kangarloo H, Gold RH, Fine RN, et al: Urinary tract infection in infants and children evaluated by ultrasound. *Radiology* 1985;154:367–373.

5. Chopra A, Teele RL: Hydronephrosis in children: Narrowing the differential diagnosis with ultrasound. *J Clin Ultrasound* 1980;8:473–478.

6. Schneider K, Jablonski C, Wiessner M, et al: Screening for vesicoureteral reflux in children using real-time sonography. *Pediatr Radiol* 1984;14:400–403.

7. Silver TM, Kass EJ, Thornbury JR, et al: The radiological spectrum of acute pyelonephritis in adults and adolescents. *Radiology* 1976;118:65–71.

8. Ash JM, Antico VF, Gilday DL, et al: Special considerations in pediatric use of radionuclides for kidney studies. *Sem Nucl Med* 1982;12:345–369.

9. Handmaker H: Nuclear renal imaging in acute pyelonephritis. *Sem Nucl Med* 1982;12:246–253.

10. Hayden CK, Swischuk LE, Fawcett HD, et al: Urinary tract infections in childhood: A current imaging approach. *RadioGraphics* 1986;6:1023–1038.

11. Jequier S, Forbes PA, Nogrady MB: The value of ultrasonography as a screening procedure in first-documented urinary tract infection in children. *J Ultrasound Med* 1985;4:393–400.

12. Mason WG: Urinary tract infections in children: Renal ultrasound evaluation. *Radiology* 1984;153:109–111.

13. Leonides JC, McCauley RGK, Klauber GC, et al: Sonography as a substitute for excretory urography in children with urinary tract infection. *AJR* 1985;144:815–819.

14. Ben-Ami T: The sonographic evaluation of urinary tract infections in children. *Sem Ultrasound CT, MR* 1984;5:19–34.

Section 5

Meningitis

In the febrile child, meningitis may accompany a seemingly minor infection such as otitis media.

The lumbar puncture is the diagnostic test for meningitis since clinical signs and symptoms may be misleading. On rare occasions, the study may be delayed, but antibiotics should not be withheld. A blood culture obtained before antibiotic therapy often identifies the causative organisms. Interpretation of the cerebrospinal fluid analysis varies with the age of the child; previous antibiotic therapy and blood introduced secondary to an intracranial bleed or traumatic puncture may alter the findings.

Initial antibiotics must be age specific, reflecting changes in bacterial etiologies. Third generation cephalosporins are increasingly becoming the primary antibiotic therapy of choice.

13. Diagnosis and Initial Management of Bacterial Meningitis in Infants and Children

Nancy A. Schonfeld, MD

Bacterial meningitis remains an important cause of death and neurologic sequelae in infants and children. Improvement in the morbidity and mortality is dependent on early diagnosis and aggressive therapy. The signs and symptoms associated with meningitis are, however, often subtle and nonspecific.

Meningitis is often preceded by a respiratory tract infection, leading to bacteremia and subsequent seeding of the meninges. Pyarthrosis, cellulitis, pericarditis, or pneumonia may also lead to bacteremia. Less commonly, direct extension from sinusitis, mastoiditis, otitis media, or head trauma occurs.

BACTERIOLOGY AND CHANGING RESISTANCE PATTERNS

Neonates

Meningitis in the neonate is most often caused by organisms acquired from the mother during birth. Seeding of the meninges occurs after invasion of the blood from a colonized site such as the umbilicus or respiratory tract. Meningitis is usually associated with septicemia in the neonate. Group B streptococcus and *Escherichia coli* account for about 70% of cases of neonatal septicemia and meningitis. Other causes include *Listeria monocytogenes,* other streptococcus, other gram-negative enteric bacilli, and coagulase-negative staphylococcus. The incidence of neonatal infections with *Hemophilus influenzae* and *Streptococcus pneumoniae* acquired via horizontal transmission has been rising. *H influenzae* type B is the leading cause of meningitis in infants between 1 and 2 months of age. However, in this same age group, group B streptococcus is the second most frequent causal agent of meningitis.

Infants and Children

Children up to 2 years of age have the highest incidence of meningitis. In infants and toddlers (2 months to 2 years), the leading causes of meningitis are *H influenzae* type B, *S pneumoniae*, and *Neisseria meningitidis*. Approximately 20% to 25% of isolates of *H influenzae* are beta-lactamase positive and resistant to ampicillin. In addition, reports[1] of relatively penicillin-resistant pneumococcus are increasing. In school-age children and adolescents, the incidence of bacterial meningitis decreases, and there is an increased incidence of meningitis caused by *N meningitidis*.[2,3]

CLINICAL SYMPTOMS AND SIGNS

Neonates and Young Infants

The signs and symptoms of meningitis depend on the duration of the illness and the age of the child. Neonatal infections with group B streptococcus and *L monocytogenes* can be divided into early and late onset forms. The early onset form usually occurs within the first 72 hours of life and is fulminant. The late forms are more insidious in onset and may not present until 2 months of age. In older infants and children, the onset of meningitis usually follows one of two patterns: (1) the illness develops over several days as a nonspecific viral illness or (2) the illness is fulminant with the development of signs and symptoms over a few hours. Increased intracranial pressure secondary to diffuse cerebral edema is not uncommon. This course typifies disease caused by *N meningitidis*, although any organism may be associated with a fulminant course.

The symptoms and signs of meningitis in neonates and infants are often nonspecific: restlessness, irritability, decreased feeding, emesis, diarrhea, lethargy, decreased tone, elevated heart rate, a full fontanelle, respiratory distress, and seizures. In this age group, fever is present in only about 50% of patients with meningitis. The presence of a fever, however, in an infant under 2 months old requires a lumbar puncture to rule out meningitis. In studies with experienced house staff, 10% to 20% of young infants with meningitis were clinically judged not to have meningitis.

Toddlers and Older Children

In children over 18 months old, the signs and symptoms of meningitis may include headache, nausea, vomiting, evidence of increased intracranial pressure, focal neurologic signs, fever, alteration in consciousness, irritability, photophobia, seizures, and a stiff neck with positive Kernig's or Brudzinski's signs. However, it still may be difficult to differentiate early meningitis from a viral syndrome. A stiff neck is a late finding and is not a reliable indicator in children under 18 months of age.[1,2]

THE LUMBAR PUNCTURE

Indications for a Lumbar Puncture

The lumbar puncture is the sine qua non for the diagnosis of meningitis. It should be performed whenever the diagnosis of meningitis is suspected clinically with very few exceptions. Because the early diagnosis of meningitis is crucial, a large number of lumbar punctures are negative. Multiple centers report a ratio of 10:1 of negative versus positive results of lumbar punctures.

Forty percent of newborns and 20% to 30% of children with meningitis experience seizures. These children are usually febrile. Because of the nonspecific and variable clinical manifestations of meningitis, a lumbar puncture is usually indicated in any child under 18 months old with a first febrile seizure. The decision to perform a lumbar puncture in children over 18 months of age may be left to careful clinical judgment. Postictal children are often difficult to assess clinically.

Seizures with fever occur in about 5% of children aged 6 months to 6 years[4] (see Chapter 27). In one series, 20% of children with a first-time febrile seizure who were not clinically suspected of having meningitis did have meningitis.

Reasons for Withholding the Lumbar Puncture

The lumbar puncture is a diagnostic rather than a therapeutic tool in the evaluation of suspected meningitis. There are situations in which delaying the lumbar puncture is necessary for the safety of the child. *Withholding antibiotic therapy is inappropriate.* Often, a blood culture obtained before initiating antibiotics will identify the causative organism. Reasons for withholding the lumbar puncture include hemodynamic instability, evidence of a mass lesion or increased intracranial pressure, thrombocytopenia or significant bleeding disorder, persistent seizure activity, infection in the area over the lumbar region, and, less commonly, inexperienced medical personnel, or equipment (usually involving subsequent transport).

If an infant or child is in shock or experiencing respiratory difficulties, the lumbar puncture should be delayed until resuscitation and stabilization is completed. Placing infants and children in the flexed position for a lumbar puncture may contribute to hypoxia, impaired venous return, and respiratory compromise. Antibiotics should be administered to any ill-appearing or unstable patient suspected of having meningitis if the lumbar puncture is delayed.

Focal neurologic signs such as hemiparesis, facial palsy, or gaze preference, or evidence of increased intracranial pressure such as altered pupillary reactions, decreased heart rate, elevated blood pressure, apnea, and posturing may occur in up to 15% of patients with bacterial meningitis. These patients need to be assessed for the presence of cerebral edema, brain abscess, acute hydrocephalus, subdural empyema, and arterial or venous thrombosis. In addition, infants and children with mass lesions such as brain tumors may have fever and focal neurologic signs, evidence of increased intracranial pressure or seizures. Although herniation from the withdrawal of cerebrospinal fluid (CSF) is rare in children, a CT scan is indicated before lumbar puncture in children suspected of having meningitis if there is evidence of increased intracranial pressure or an intracranial mass. The lumbar puncture and CT scan are diagnostic and not therapeutic modalities and should not delay therapy. Antibiotics should be administered if there is any delay in obtaining and completing the CT scan.

The lumbar puncture should be delayed in patients with thrombocytopenia or bleeding disorders such as hemophilia only until a platelet or factor transfusion can be completed. Abnormal bleeding at the site of the lumbar puncture may cause cord compression. Again, if there is any delay in obtaining platelets for the child suspected of meningitis, antibiotics should be administered. This is especially important in immunocompromised hosts such as patients on chemotherapy.

Infection of the structures overlying the site for the lumbar puncture is an unusual reason for withholding the procedure. Infection could be transmitted to the CSF by the needle.

Children with a clinical diagnosis of meningitis are often transported to a tertiary care facility. Children with clinically suspected or laboratory documented meningitis should never be transported by their parents. Transport by ambulance, helicopter, or plane should always be arranged. The medical team necessary will vary with the child's condition. The referral physician or institution may be unable to perform the lumbar puncture before transfer because of inadequate personnel or equipment. If the child's transport will be prolonged, the referring physician should initiate antibiotic therapy after consultation with physicians at the receiving hospital. Antibiotics should also be administered before transport if a lumbar puncture is performed at the primary hospital and the results are consistent with meningitis. A blood culture should also be obtained.

INTERPRETATION OF CSF TEST RESULTS

All evaluations of CSF should include a Gram's stain, culture and sensitivity, cell count, and protein and glucose determinations. Delay in the examination of the CSF more than 90 minutes may result in lysis of the white blood cells (WBCs). Serum glucose levels should be determined before the lumbar puncture. The stress of the lumbar puncture may transiently elevate serum glucose levels. Approximately 30 minutes is required for equilibration of serum and CSF glucose levels.[5]

Neonates

Interpretation of test results for neonates differs from those for the older infant or child. Although the average WBC count in the CSF during the first 7 days of life is 8 cells/mm^3, as many as 30 cells/mm^3 may be found in the first month of life in uninfected infants. Up to 60% of the cells may be polymorphonuclear leukocytes. Normal cell counts by 1 month of age are the same as for older infants and children. The CSF protein and CSF glucose–to–serum glucose ratios are higher for infants under 1 month of age. The CSF protein ratio ranges from 20 mg% to 170 mg%, with a mean of 90 mg%. The CSF glucose ratio ranges from 44% to over 100% of the serum level with an average of 87%.[6]

The CSF Gram's stain is positive for organisms in 83% of neonates with culture proven group B streptococcal meningitis and in 78% with gram-negative meningitis. The Gram's stain for organisms may be negative for up to 50% of patients with culture-proven *L monocytogenes*. Countercurrent immunoelectrophoresis is available for detection of group B streptococci and K1 strains of *E coli* and *L monocytogenes*. A latex particle agglutination test is also available for group B streptococci. A repeat lumbar puncture 4 to 6 hours after the initial tap may be helpful when the results of the CSF tests are ambiguous. Antibiotic therapy, however, should not be delayed if sepsis and meningitis are suspected clinically.

Infants and Children

Cerebral edema may accompany meningitis. An opening pressure should be measured whenever possible. A pressure greater than 180 to 200 mm H$_2$O is abnormal and may indicate the need for cerebral resuscitation measures.

In infants and children over 1 month of age, more than 6 to 8 WBCs/mm^3 is abnormal. The presence of any polymorphonuclear leukocyte is probably abnormal as 95% of uninfected children have no polymorphonuclear leukocytes in the CSF. The WBC count in the CSF of infants and children with viral meningitis usually ranges from 10 to 1,000 cells/mm^3 with a predominance of lymphocytes. WBC counts up to 2,500 cells/mm^3 are documented with viral meningitis infrequently. The WBC count in the CSF of infants and children with bacterial meningitis is usually in the range of 1,000 to 20,000 cells/mm^3 with a predominance of polymorphonuclear leukocytes.

A normal CSF protein level in infants and children is less than 40 mg%. In viral meningitis, the range is 40 mg% to 100 mg%, while in bacterial meningitis the CSF protein is frequently greater than 100 mg%. The CSF glucose level in infants and children is usually two thirds of the serum level. In viral meningitis, this CSF glucose–to–serum glucose ratio is usually maintained. The ratio is frequently much lower in patients with bacterial meningitis with CSF glucose levels less than 30 mg%. The depressed CSF glucose levels with bacterial meningitis may be caused by increased cerebral glucose use and an altered glucose transport mechanism.[7]

No organisms are detected on Gram's stain of specimens from patients with viral meningitis. Ninety-seven percent of CSF Gram's stains will be positive for organisms if the concentration of bacteria in the fluid is greater than 100,000 colony-forming units per mL. There is a decreasing rate of detection with lower concentrations. In overwhelming infections, organisms may be seen on the Gram's stain of the CSF in the absence of a CSF pleocytosis. The astute physician may identify signs and symptoms of meningitis clinically before there is a detectable inflammatory reaction or positive Gram's stain of the CSF.

A repeat lumbar puncture of an untreated, stable child 4 to 6 hours after the initial tap may help when results are consistent with either a viral or early bacterial meningitis. Other tests such as latex particle agglutination and countercurrent immunoelectrophoresis for *H influenzae, S pneumoniae* and *N meningitidis* are also available for use with blood, CSF, and urine.

Traumatic Lumbar Punctures

Blood present in the CSF may be secondary to an intracranial bleed or traumatic tap. If it is the result of a traumatic tap, the number of red blood cells (RBCs) will decrease as the tubes of CSF are collected. The WBC/RBC ratios in the peripheral blood and CSF have been used to determine if a CSF pleocytosis is present. If the ratios are comparable, it is assumed there is no CSF pleocytosis. If the WBC/RBC ratio is greater for the CSF than for the peripheral blood, it is assumed that a CSF pleocytosis is present. This method suggests that there is a fixed relationship between the number of RBCs and WBCs when blood is present in the CSF. In one series, however, only 20% of the expected number of WBCs was found in the CSF of patients with traumatic taps. These data suggest that a CSF pleocytosis could escape detection by this method.[8] The results of a traumatic tap are ambiguous, and the reliability of any interpretation is limited.

The clinical course of patients with blood-contaminated CSF needs to be followed closely regardless of the cellularity. Often, the ultimate interpretation must rest on the results of bacterial cultures.

The Partially Treated Patient

The interpretation of the CSF test results in a child treated with oral antibiotics before the initial lumbar puncture is a great concern to clinicians. Short-term antibiotic therapy for children with bacterial meningitis does not significantly alter the biochemistry or cytology of the CSF. In a retrospective study[9] of 68 patients with acute bacterial meningitis, the results of the CSF studies obtained at admission and the results of the CSF studies obtained 44 to 68 hours after initiation of appropriate intravenous antibiotics were compared. The CSF WBC counts, the differential, and protein and glucose determinations were not statistically different for all patients with *H influenzae* or *S pneumoniae* meningitis and for 13 of 16 patients with meningococcal meningitis. The CSF studies obtained 44 to 68 hours after initiation of intravenous antibiotics retained their bacterial character and would not have been interpreted as showing aseptic meningitis. However, the culture and Gram's stain of the CSF may be negative, especially when meningococcal or pneumococcal meningitis was pretreated with effective antibiotics. This is less common with meningitis caused by *H influenzae*.

CHOICE OF ANTIBIOTICS

The mortality of bacterial meningitis is less than 5% with early diagnosis and treatment. The initial choice of antibiotics depends on the age of the child and the expected pathogens. Broad-spectrum antibiotics should be continued until the culture and sensitivity results are available.

Neonates under 1 Month Old

The expected pathogens are group B streptococci, *E coli*, and *L monocytogenes*. Conventional therapy is ampicillin and an aminoglycoside, commonly gentamicin sulfate. In the first week of life the dosage for ampicillin is 50 mg/kg every 12 hours, and the dosage for gentamicin sulfate is 2.5 mg/kg every 12 hours. After the first week of life the dosage for ampicillin is 50 mg/kg every 6 hours, and the dosage for gentamicin sulfate is 2.5 mg/kg every 8 hours.[2] Aminoglycoside levels should be monitored, especially in infants with renal compromise or a history of hypotension. An alternative regimen that is equally effective in the treatment of neonatal meningitis is ampicillin and cefotaxime sodium. The dosage for cefotaxime sodium in the first week of life is 50 mg/kg every 12 hours, and after the first week of life is 50 mg/kg every 6 hours.[10,11]

Infants 1 to 3 Months Old

In this age group, the most common cause of meningitis is *H influenzae* type B. However, group B streptococcus, *S pneumoniae, L monocytogenes,* and *N meningitidis* are also potential pathogens. The use of ampicillin and gentamicin in this age group may be inadequate for the treatment of *H influenzae* type B since penicillinase-producing organisms represent 20% to 25% of isolates. Similarly, the use of ampicillin and chloramphenicol sodium succinate would not adequately cover gram-negative enterics. Ampicillin and cefotaxime would provide the broadest coverage in this age group. The dosage for ampicillin and cefotaxime sodium is as above. The dosage for chloramphenicol in infants 1 week to 1 month of age is 25 mg/kg every 12 hours, and for infants and children over 1 month old is 20 to 25 mg/kg every 6 hours. Chloramphenicol levels must be measured.[10,11]

Infants over 3 Months Old and Children

The most important pathogens are *H influenzae* type B, *S pneumoniae,* and *N meningitidis.* Conventional therapy consists of ampicillin and chloramphenicol.[2] Chloramphenicol has substantial side effects, especially on the hematopoietic system. Its metabolism is unpredictable in infants and may be influenced by the presence of hepatic dysfunction and interactions with other drugs such as phenobarbital. Chloramphenicol should probably not be used in children unless chloramphenicol levels can be obtained to guide therapy.

Equally effective regimens for the treatment of bacterial meningitis include ceftriaxone sodium, cefuroxime sodium, or cefotaxime alone. The results of multiple studies[12–14] indicate that these cephalosporins are as effective as ampicillin and chloramphenicol in the treatment of acute bacterial meningitis with no increase in complications, mortality, or long-term sequelae. They are effective against beta-lactamase–positive *H influenzae* as well as the relatively penicillin-resistant pneumococcus. The primary use of the third generation cephalosporins, cefotaxime and ceftriaxone, is gaining more general acceptance as the treatment of choice in bacterial meningitis.[12–14]

CONCLUSION

Bacterial meningitis is a life-threatening infection that requires prompt recognition and diagnostic evaluation. The lumbar puncture remains the diagnostic method of choice, being both highly specific and sensitive. If there are delays in performing the lumbar puncture, antibiotics should be initiated.

Antibiotic therapy should reflect the age of the child and the causative organisms. Therapy must reflect the changing sensitivity patterns of *H influenzae* and *S pneumoniae* as well as the availability of third generation cephalosporins.

REFERENCES

1. Jackson MA, Shelton S, Nelson JD, et al: Relatively penicillin-resistant pneumococcal infections in pediatric patients. *Pediatr Infect Dis* 1984;3:129–132.

2. Klein JO, Feigin RD, McCracken GH: Report of the task force on diagnosis and management of meningitis. *Pediatrics* 1986;78:959–982.

3. Kaplan SL, Feigin RD: Clinical presentations, prognostic factors and diagnosis of bacterial meningitis, in Sande M, Smith AL, Root RK (eds): *Bacterial Meningitis.* New York, Churchill Livingston Inc, 1985, pp 83–84.

4. Rutter N, Smales ORC: Role of routine investigations in children presenting with their first febrile convulsion. *Arch Dis Child* 1977;52:188–191.

5. Donald PR, Malan HC, Van der Walt A: Simultaneous determination of cerebrospinal fluid glucose and blood glucose concentrations in the diagnosis of bacterial meningitis. *J Pediatr* 1983;103:413–415.

6. Weisman LE, Merenstein GD, Steenbarger JR: Effect of lumbar puncture position on the sick neonate. *Am J Dis Child* 1983;137:1077–1079.

7. Portnoy JM, Olson LC: Normal cerebrospinal fluid values in children: Another look. *Pediatrics* 1985;75:484–487.

8. Rubenstein JS, Yogev R: What represents pleocytosis in blood contaminated (traumatic tap) cerebrospinal fluid in children. *J Pediatr* 1985;107:249–251.

9. Blazer S, Berant M, Alon U: Effect of antibiotic treatment on cerebrospinal fluid. *Am J Clin Pathol* 1983;80:386–387.

10. Odio CM, Faingezicht I, Salas JL, et al: Cefotaxime vs conventional therapy for the treatment of bacterial meningitis of infants and children. *Pediatr Infect Dis* 1986;5:402–407.

11. Enzenauer RW, Bass JW: Initial antibiotic treatment of purulent meningitis in infants 1 to 2 months of age. *Am J Dis Child* 1983;137:1055–1056.

12. Steele RW, Bradsher RW: Comparison of ceftriaxone with standard therapy for bacterial meningitis. *Pediatrics* 1983;103:138–141.

13. Schaad UB, Krucko J, Pfenninger J: An extended experience with cefuroxime therapy of childhood bacterial meningitis. *Pediatr Infect Dis* 1984;3:410–416.

14. Jacobs RF, Wells TG, Steele RW, et al: A prospective randomized comparison of cefotaxime vs ampicillin and chloramphenicol for bacterial meningitis in children. *J Pediatr* 1985;107:129–133.

Section 6

Pelvic Inflammatory Disease

The incidence of pelvic inflammatory disease has markedly increased. *Neisseria gonorrhoeae* and *Chlamydia trachomatis* are the important pathogens requiring early and aggressive treatment. Antibiotic selection has evolved to reflect the changing causative agents.

Specific criteria for hospitalization have been suggested to be marked toxicity, poor response, complications, and diagnostic problems. However, many recommend that all adolescents be hospitalized and treated parenterally to maximize subsequent fertility, minimize complications, and provide an intense educational experience to reduce recurrences.

14. Pelvic Inflammatory Disease: Management in the Adolescent

Jean T. Abbott, MD

Pelvic inflammatory disease (PID) is epidemic in sexually active adolescents. The disease is difficult to diagnose, requires a close working relationship between patient and physician for appropriate management, and may be followed by significant morbidity, even after optimal treatment. There are currently little scientific data to help the clinician decide if a patient should be admitted, and what treatment would be optimal. Treatment problems are magnified by the increased impact of sequelae early in reproductive years, and by the special management problems of working with adolescent patients who may be relatively unsophisticated about their bodies and the seriousness of this disease.

EPIDEMIOLOGY

About 1 million cases of PID are diagnosed annually in the United States. Of these, about one third occur in patients under the age of 20. PID is almost always a disease of sexually active women, and more than one half of the patients have never been pregnant. Youth (15 to 19 years old), multiple sexual partners, presence of lower genital tract infection, exposure to a partner with a sexually transmissible disease, history of prior PID, and use of an intrauterine device (IUD) increase the risk of PID. In Sweden (where detailed epidemiologic data are available), sexually active 15-year-olds have an average of four sexual partners per year and an annual risk of contracting PID of 1 in 8; this risk drops to 1 in 40 by age 20 years.[1]

The sexually active adolescent is at increased risk of contracting PID for a number of physiologic and sociologic reasons. Immaturity of the cervical mucus and epithelium is believed to persist for several years after menarche, and provides a less solid barrier to cervical penetration of lower genital tract

99

organisms. Sexual promiscuity is more common in the teenage years, leading to increased risk of exposure to various genital tract pathogens. In addition, birth control methods that might limit the spread of sexually transmitted organisms are less likely to be used by adolescents, and the person is less likely to recognize and seek medical attention for lower genital tract infections or PID.[1] Thus, not only is the disease more likely to occur in this age group, but it is less likely to be recognized and to receive timely treatment.

Complications of PID are considerable. Infertility caused by tubal occlusion occurs in about 17% of patients after a single episode of PID, and increases to 52% of women aged 15 to 24 years after three or more episodes of PID. Pelvic pain from adhesions and scarring in the pelvis is estimated to occur in 18% of women (5% in a control group of women without PID). The risk of ectopic pregnancy increases about 6 times after PID, giving a ratio of ectopic to intrauterine pregnancies of 1 to 24.[2]

DIAGNOSIS

Many studies over the past 20 years have shown the difficulties of diagnosing PID by clinical criteria. The classic clinical picture of pelvic pain, cervical discharge, fever, and pain on cervical and adnexal palpation is neither sensitive nor specific. Laparoscopically confirmed PID is found in only 65% of patients in whom the diagnosis is made on clinical grounds. In a series of more than 800 Swedish patients with a clinical diagnosis of PID, 35% had other findings at laparoscopy: 12% had normal pelvic organs, and the other 23% had pain and symptoms caused by appendicitis, ectopic pregnancy, rupture of an ovarian cyst, torsion of the adnexa, or endometriosis.[1] This rate of clinical inaccuracy has not improved over 20 years of continued laparoscopic correlation, and has been encountered by other investigators.[3]

How, then, should PID be diagnosed clinically? Sexual activity, particularly with multiple partners or with known exposure to sexually transmitted organisms, places the adolescent at high risk for PID. If the patient has truly not had intercourse, is pregnant, or has not undergone a recent procedure penetrating the cervical os (eg, dilation and curettage, IUD insertion, or other procedure that introduces organisms to the upper genital tract), PID is very unlikely. On physical examination, abdominal pain and cervical motion tenderness are the most universal findings. Vaginal discharge is present in 50% to 60% of patients on inspection, with almost all patients having microscopic evidence of an inflammatory vaginal discharge (white blood cells (WBCs) > epithelial cells by wet mount).[4] Fever is present about one half of the time. Unilateral pelvic pain is unusual (10% of patients) and should prompt consideration of ectopic pregnancy, appendicitis, cyst disease, or a urinary origin for symptoms.

Adnexal masses may be present (about 50% of the time), but it is often difficult to differentiate an inflammatory mass from an actual adnexal abscess or mass, either clinically or by ultrasonography.[3]

Selective laboratory tests may be useful in diagnosis. The erythrocyte sedimentation rate (ESR) and WBC count are not as useful as commonly believed. An elevated ESR (> 15 mm/hr) is seen 75% of the time, and WBC counts are elevated in about 60% of patients. A serum pregnancy test may also be useful if complications of pregnancy such as ectopic pregnancy are considered in the patient's differential diagnosis (Chapter 35).

A vaginal wet mount may be very useful; a normal WBC count virtually excludes PID, since a lower genital tract infection almost always accompanies upper tract disease. Gram's stain of a cervical culture (GC) can be useful in identifying gram-negative intracellular diplococci of *Neisseria gonorrhoeae*; the multiple other organisms in the vaginal flora do not correlate with upper tract pathogens or the presence of disease. Gram's stain is positive for gonorrhea if gram-negative diplococci are present in or closely associated with polymorphonuclear leukocytes, and it is equivocal if only extracellular organisms or atypical intracellular gram-negative diplococci are seen. Finding *N gonorrhoeae* identifies a patient at high risk for PID, but correlation with the actual infecting organisms of an upper tract infection is too poor to use this as a basis for treatment.[5] If the Gram's stain is negative for *N gonorrhoeae,* a GC culture should be obtained and clinical PID still must be treated to cover the usual spectrum of pathogens.

Other ancillary studies will rarely make the diagnosis of PID and are useful on a selective basis when the clinician has a specific alternate diagnosis. Culdocentesis may show purulent cul-de-sac fluid in either ruptured appendicitis or in an extensive PID. Unclotted blood would suggest adnexal cyst rupture or an ectopic pregnancy. A clear tap (serous fluid) would be consistent with PID, ruptured ovarian cyst, or other diagnoses that do not involve peritoneal extension, but is most helpful in excluding emergent surgical disease.

Laparoscopy can be very useful in distinguishing PID from other surgical and nonsurgical causes of abdominal pain and is probably underused in the United States for patients with uncertain diagnoses. Ultrasonography can be used to detect and follow masses or abscesses associated with the inflammatory process, or in the rare pregnant patient with PID, but cannot identify patients with simple PID.[6]

ORGANISMS CAUSING PID

PID can be caused by many organisms and is probably polymicrobial in most patients. *N gonorrhoeae* and *Chlamydia trachomatis* are most frequently identified as pathogens. Other aerobic and anaerobic bacteria and *Mycoplasma* species have also been isolated from the fallopian tubes of patients with PID; the relationship between these organisms is widely debated. The correlation between cervical organisms, cul-de-sac isolates, and organisms harvested from the fallopian tubes at laparoscopy is poor. The organisms isolated during the evolution of a case of PID may change as opportunistic colonization by secondary invaders takes place.

The epidemiologic spectrum of PID isolates has varied over years and in different geographic locations, probably reflecting the sexually transmitted organisms most prevalent in a given community.[5] In Sweden, where most of the laparoscopy has been performed to identify pathologic organisms in the fallopian tubes, *Chlamydia*, with or without other organisms, is currently isolated in about 60% of PID patients, and has overtaken *Neisseria* as the most common pathogen in PID.[1] In the United States, where control of gonorrhea has been slower and less successful, gonococcal PID is seen more commonly, and it has been suggested that *Chlamydia* will become a more frequent isolate as (or if) gonorrhea is controlled. Without aggressive use of laparoscopy and with a more heterogeneous population, characterization of PID in the United States has been difficult.

Although the severity of clinical disease may reflect the pathogen, correlation of the clinical picture with the amount of organ damage is poor. Gonococcal PID more often appears with abrupt onset of purulent cervical discharge and moderately severe, acute pain in a patient who appears moderately ill. In contrast, the patient with *Chlamydia* may have minimal signs, may come for treatment after several days of smoldering, low-grade symptoms, and with an equivocal clinical picture. Evaluation of the fallopian tubes by laparoscopy reveals a prompt response to appropriate antibiotics in most patients with gonococcal PID, whereas patients with *Chlamydia* have prolonged infection of the tubes, considerable scarring, and continued evolution of the disease process, even after seemingly good clinical response to therapy.[7,8] Patients with mixed anaerobic infections have the most severe course, both clinically and at laparoscopy, with a high incidence of abscess and inflammatory mass formation, and a prolonged clinical course.

HOW SHOULD THE PATIENT WITH PID BE TREATED?

Since identification of the causative organism or organisms is difficult, antibiotic treatment must be directed against a large number of organisms known to be implicated in patients with PID who have been studied laparoscopically. *N gonorrhoeae* and *Chlamydia* coexist in about 25% of patients,[9] so recognition of one organism still requires treatment of both in any given patient. In the toxic patient or the patient with an IUD, coverage should be directed at anaerobic organisms that may coexist, and this requires parenteral therapy.

The current Centers for Disease Control recommendations for treating PID[10] (Appendix 14-A) are reasonable, but it should be remembered that they are based on scant data and must be modified if more accurate identification of organisms is available by laparoscopy or other means.

SHOULD THE ADOLESCENT WITH PID BE HOSPITALIZED?

Indications for hospitalization of adolescents with PID vary widely. Several obvious indications exist:

- inability to tolerate oral antibiotics
- vomiting or other significant systemic toxicity
- inability to exclude surgical disease, ie, ectopic pregnancy, ovarian torsion, or appendicitis
- complicated PID: abscess, inflammatory mass, or significant peritonitis requiring parenteral antibiotic coverage against potential anaerobic pathogens and close monitoring for possible surgical intervention
- physical signs of peritonitis
- failure to respond to an outpatient regimen.[1,7]

Three social considerations may also mandate admission: (1) inability to follow-up the patient in 2 to 3 days to evaluate the response to therapy, (2) inability of the patient to comply with an outpatient treatment regimen, and (3) any consideration of child abuse. Although these indications are much less universally accepted, they must be recognized if complications are to be prevented, particularly in the young patient.

In uncomplicated PID, pressure for the clinician to treat the patient *out* of the hospital comes from several directions. First, there is no clear evidence that parenteral antibiotics alter the natural history or limit the sequelae of uncomplicated PID. Second, a large number of patients want outpatient treatment; they have limited systemic toxicity, poor understanding of their disease, and limited motivation to preserve fertility, even though they are at the beginning of their reproductive years. Finally, the economic implications of hospitalization of all adolescents with PID would be staggering, although it is the standard of care in other countries such as Sweden.

A very strong case can, however, be made for hospitalizing all adolescents with PID. Admission can be argued from medical as well as social and economic grounds.[7] The clinical diagnosis of PID is highly inaccurate, and significant surgical disease can masquerade as PID. In addition, automatic admission prevents the clinician from succumbing to the temptation to discharge those with "mild" clinical disease, which we know is often associated with the more significant morbidity. Economically, if the societal costs of infertility, chronic pain, surgery for ectopic pregnancy, and other complications are included in the calculations, the cost-benefit arguments against admitting adolescents with PID are less persuasive.

The social or societal rationale for admission of all patients with PID is also compelling. The adolescent is relatively unsophisticated about her sexuality, her future fertility plans, her awareness and knowledge of her disease, and its epidemiologic implications. To admit such a patient is to show her that this is a disease that physicians take seriously. In the hospital, there is more time to establish the kind of rapport with the patient that will result in better contact tracing, better compliance with subsequent outpatient therapy, and a chance to teach birth control and other aspects of responsible sexual behavior.

CONCLUSION

PID is epidemic among adolescents. Serious complications of persistent pain, infertility, recurrent infection, and ectopic pregnancy become more evident with time. The diagnosis of pelvic infection is difficult clinically and antibiotic treatment must be directed at a wide range of potential organisms. Admission of adolescents is strongly recommended to assure optimal treatment and enhance patient understanding of this potentially devastating disease.

REFERENCES

1. Westrom L, Mardh PA: Salpingitis, in Holmes KK, Mardh PA, Sparling PF, et al (eds): *Sexually Transmitted Diseases.* New York, McGraw-Hill Book Co, 1984, pp 615–632.

2. Westrom L: Effect of acute pelvic inflammatory disease on fertility. *Am J Obstet Gynecol* 1975;121:707–13.

3. Farrell RG (ed): *Ob/Gyn Emergencies: The First 60 Minutes.* Rockville, Md, Aspen Publishers, 1986, pp 168–194.

4. Ledger W: Diagnosis and treatment of salpingitis. *J Reprod Med* 1983;28:709–711.

5. Shafer MB, Irwin CE, Sweet RL: Acute salpingitis in the adolescent female. *J Pediatr* 1982;100:339–350.

6. Chinn DH, Callen PW: Ultrasound of the acutely ill obstetrics and gynecology patient. *Radiol Clin North Am* 1983;21:585–594.

7. Washington AE, Sweet RL, Shafer MB: Pelvic inflammatory disease and its sequelae in adolescents. *J Adoles Health Care* 1985;6:298–310.

8. Sweet RL, Schachter J, Robbie MO: Failure of beta-lactam antibiotics to eradicate *Chlamydia trachomatis* in the endometrium despite apparent clinical cure of acute salpingitis. *JAMA* 1983;250:2541–2545.

9. Eschenbach DA: Acute pelvic inflammatory disease. *Urol Clin North Am* 1984;11:65–81.

10. *Sexually Transmitted Diseases: Treatment Guidelines, 1985.* Atlanta, Centers for Disease Control, 1985.

Appendix 14-A

Acute Pelvic Inflammatory Disease: Treatment Guidelines

AMBULATORY REGIMENS

1. Cefoxitin sodium 2 g IM plus probenecid 1 g PO, followed by doxycycline 100 mg PO BID for 10 to 14 days; *or*
2. Ceftriaxone sodium 250 mg IM, followed by doxycycline 100 mg PO BID for 10 to 14 days; *or*
3. Amoxicillin 3.0 g PO *or* ampicillin 3.5 g PO *plus* probenecid 1.0 g PO, followed by doxycycline 100 mg PO BID for 10 to 14 days.

INPATIENT REGIMENS

1. Cefoxitin sodium 2 g IV QID *plus* doxycycline 100 mg IV BID. Continue for at least 4 days, followed by doxycycline 100 mg PO BID on discharge for a total of 10 to 14 days of therapy. Clindamycin or metronidazole therapy should be *added* for patients with severe toxicity or toxic patients with possible anaerobic infection.
2. Alternatively, clindamycin 600 mg IV QID *plus* gentamicin sulfate 2 mg/kg IV (load), followed by 1.5 mg/kg TID if renal function is normal. Upon discharge, clindamycin 450 mg PO QID should be administered for a total of 10 to 14 days of therapy.

PREPUBERTAL REGIMEN

1. Cefuroxime sodium 150 mg/kg/24 hr IV *or* ceftriaxone sodium 100 mg/kg/24 hr IV; *plus* erythromycin 40 mg/kg/24 hr q 6 hr IV *or* sulfisoxazole 100 mg/kg/24 hr q 6 hr IV. In children over 8 years of age, tetracycline

106

30 mg/kg/24 hr q 8 hr IV may be used. Continue the IV regimen for at least 4 days. Thereafter, continue the erythromycin, sulfisoxazole, *or* tetracycline orally to complete at least 14 days of therapy.

NOTES

- All patients receiving outpatient treatment should be re-examined after 48 to 72 hours of therapy to evaluate their response. If a poor response is noted, hospitalization may be necessary.
- Male sexual partners should be examined and treated with therapy directed against presumptive *Chlamydia* and gonococcal infection.
- If an IUD is in place, it should be removed at the onset of therapy, and the patient treated as an inpatient with therapy directed against anaerobes also.

Source: Adapted from *Sexually Transmitted Diseases: Treatment Guidelines, 1985.* Centers for Disease Control, Atlanta, 1985.

15. Pelvic Inflammatory Disease: Diagnosis and Management of the Adolescent

Henry E. Cooper, Jr, MD

The incidence of sexually transmitted disease in adolescents is high because of the increasing prevalence of sexual behaviors that put them at risk. They tend to have more sexual partners and use contraceptives and prophylactic measures less frequently than adults, leading to vaginitis, cervicitis, uterine infection, salpingitis, and concurrent complications.

Pelvic inflammatory disease (PID) is increasing at an alarming rate. The reported incidence in adolescents and women in their early twenties is 20 cases per 1,000 women. Among adolescents alone, one study[1-3] reported 12.5% of sexually active teenagers to be at risk.

The risks of PID are significant to the adolescent. Infertility rates as high as 75% after three episodes, and ectopic pregnancy rates of 15 cases per thousand pregnancies with a 10 fold increase in risk in patients with salpingitis are noted.[4]

ETIOLOGY

PID is polymicrobial. *Neisseria gonorrhoeae, Chlamydia trachomatis,* and other aerobic and anaerobic bacteria ascend the endocervix and infect the tubes and ovaries. In contrast, genital mycoplasma ascends the lympathics of the broad ligament to the parametrium and produces an infection that secondarily invades the tubes and ovaries. How bacteria reach the pelvic organs is poorly understood except when foreign bodies are present or invasive diagnostic procedures have been performed, disturbing the cervical mucous barrier.[5]

Gonorrhea is frequently associated with PID. Approximately 15% of women who acquire gonococcal cervicitis will develop PID. An estimated 35% to 50% of PID cases are associated with gonorrhea. Identifying host immunity factors and the strain of *N gonorrhoeae* helps determine the likelihood of PID developing.

Chlamydia infection is responsible for increasing numbers of genital tract infections. It may be asymptomatic or subacute, with a more subtle onset. Many patients have no fever, only minimal cervical purulent discharge, and mild leukocytosis; infection may occur at any time during the menstrual cycle. Although specimens are difficult to culture, a fluorescent antibody test for cervical and vaginal specimens is available.

Coliforms and anaerobes have been isolated and are usually bowel flora.

DIAGNOSTIC TOOLS

The diagnosis is based on clinical evidence and laboratory support. Classically, fever, adnexal mass or tenderness, and cervical motion tenderness are present, associated with an elevated sedimentation rate (particularly in chronic cases) and leukocytosis, the latter being noted in 30% to 50% of patients.

Laparoscopy or pelvic ultrasonography may be useful in further differentiating PID from other considerations including ruptured ovarian cysts, appendicitis, ectopic pregnancy, and endometriosis.

Results of cultures of cervical mucus do not correlate with those for fallopian tube aspirates.

TREATMENT

Considering the potential harm of PID, "overdiagnosis" and aggressive treatment may be the most judicious approach with adolescents with upper genital tract infections. The aim of treatment is to relieve symptoms, preserve tubal and reproductive functions, and educate patients to promote early detection of lower genital tract infections.

The treatment is determined by whether the patient will be treated in the inpatient or ambulatory setting. Many clinicians feel that the nulliparous young patient, which includes most adolescents, are best treated by hospitalization and parenteral antibiotics to ensure maximal drug levels and minimize tubal damage. Other indications for hospitalization are:

- uncertain diagnosis
- gastrointestinal symptoms limiting usefulness of oral medications
- any prepubertal child
- presence of an abscess

- pregnancy
- peritonitis
- intrauterine device present
- acute infection after vaginal diagnostic procedure
- poor response to ambulatory treatment including poor compliance and symptoms unchanged or worse after 48 hours of treatment.

Guidelines[6,7] for antibiotic management reflect the polymicrobial etiology of PID (organisms ascending from the lower genital tract), and are summarized in Appendix 14-A.

Another aspect of management, especially for adolescents, is the early treatment of lower genital tract infections and other sexually transmitted diseases. Further, counseling and education are essential. In some adolescent girls who are sexually active, periodic screening may be necessary to ensure early detection of lower genital tract infection. These periodic visits may also allow the clinician to do contraceptive counseling including methods to reduce the incidence of lower genital tract infections.

REFERENCES

1. Westrom L: Incidence, prevalence, and trends of acute pelvic inflammatory disease and its consequences in industrialized countries. *Am J Obstet Gynecol* 1980;138:880–892.

2. Sweet RL: Pelvic inflammatory disease: Etiology, diagnosis, and treatment. *Sex Transm Dis* 1981;8(suppl):508–515.

3. Eschenbach DA: Epidemiology and diagnosis of acute pelvic inflammatory disease. *Obstet Gynecol* 1980;55:142S–153S.

4. Svensson L, Mardh P, Westrom L: Infertility after acute salpingitis: With special reference to *Chlamydia trachomatis* associated infection. *Fertil Steril* 1983;40:322–329.

5. Toth A: Alternative causes of pelvic inflammatory diseases. *J Reprod Med* 1983; 28(suppl):699–702.

6. US Department of Health and Human Services, Centers for Disease Control: Sexually transmitted disease treatment guidelines. *MMWR* 1985;34:19–21.

7. Brunham RC: Therapy for acute pelvic inflammatory disease: A critique of recent treatment trials. *Am J Obstet Gynecol* 1984;148:235–240.

PART II

Respiratory Disease

Section 7

Asthma

The examination and management of children with asthma have evolved rapidly in recent years with greater analysis of the value of traditional assessment tools and the growing recognition of the importance of aggressive beta-agonist therapy in the initial management of the severely ill child.

Radiographs have a clear role in the child with severe exacerbation of wheezing that is unresponsive to conventional therapy as well as in patients with signs suggestive of an air leak or foreign body. Pulmonary function testing is useful for defining the contribution of bronchoconstriction to pulmonary symptoms such as cough, or in measuring response to therapy. Unresponsive patients should also be assessed using arterial blood gas measurements; oximetry potentially provides an alternative, noninvasive measure of arterial oxygenation.

Aggressive pharmacologic management of wheezing should include the systematic use of beta-agonist agents after oxygen is administered. Nebulized terbutaline sulfate and other newer agents may soon replace older drugs and routes; further studies are still required. Anticholinergics may have an as yet undefined benefit when combined with adrenergic agents.

High dose corticosteroids reduce the duration of hypoxemia. Theophylline is an important component of treatment once the initial beta-agonist therapy has been initiated. Serum levels should be monitored.

16. Assessment of the Child with Asthma

Diana J. Becker Cutts, MD
Patrick L. Carolan, MD
Martin D. Klatzko, MD

Assessment of children with an acute episode of wheezing has traditionally depended on the physician's clinical expertise. While this continues to be the mainstay of management, objective assessment of the patient's respiratory status can provide important information. Chest radiographs, pulmonary function testing, and noninvasive measures of blood gas exchange have central roles in the evaluation of the child with asthma.

RADIOGRAPHS

The role of the chest radiograph in the evaluation of asthma has been the subject of much controversy. Older studies[1,2] report a high incidence of radiographic abnormalities in hospitalized asthmatics, and conclude that all such patients should undergo chest radiography.[2] Others[3-6] question the usefulness of chest x-ray studies in the management of the vast majority of both hospitalized and ambulatory asthmatics.

Chest x-rays are generally ordered during the acute episode for two reasons: (1) to detect associated disease processes (pneumothorax, pneumomediastinum, pneumonia, atelectasis) that may require specific treatment measures; and (2) to exclude etiologies other than asthma in the child with new onset wheezing, such as foreign body aspiration, congestive heart failure, and external airway compression.

Much information has been accumulated regarding the incidence and clinical significance of disease processes associated with asthma. Pneumothorax, which can be life threatening and usually requires placement of a chest tube, is exceedingly uncommon. In five studies, comprising a total of 1,581 patients who were initially treated as outpatients, only one (0.06%) had a pneumothorax.[3-7] Pneumomediastinum is also quite uncommon. Although one study[3] reported an incidence of 5.4% in 479 hospitalized asthmatics, the five studies noted above reported an incidence of only 0.4%. Pneumomediastinum rarely requires treatment other than that required for uncomplicated asthma. However, since it may presage the development of a pneumothorax, it probably warrants inpatient observation until it begins to resolve.

The incidence of pneumonia documented by chest x-rays taken during acute episodes of asthma ranges from 3.2% to 10.0%.[2-6] The well-established association of acute exacerbations of asthma with viral respiratory infections and the lack of documentation of such an association with bacterial infections [8] suggest that many of these pneumonias are viral in etiology. Indeed, in actual practice, many of these pneumonias are not treated with antibiotics, apparently without sequelae.[4]

Small, subsegmental areas of atelectasis are seen in up to 19% of chest x-rays taken during episodes of acute asthma.[4] These atelectatic areas virtually always re-expand with improvement in the clinical condition. Larger areas of atelectasis, comprising entire bronchopulmonary segments, occur less frequently (2% to 4%).[4,6] In rare cases, the presence of segmental atelectasis might necessitate the use of bronchoscopy should the collapsed segment not re-expand spontaneously, or if the patient's clinical condition requires immediate re-expansion.

Attempts have been made to correlate clinical parameters (pulse, respiratory rate, auscultatory findings, etc) with the likelihood of finding radiographic abnormalities. Severity of the asthmatic episode, as assessed by the need for hospitalization did not correlate with x-ray findings of abnormalities in some studies, but did in others.[3,5,6] Many studies[3,4,6,7] have demonstrated that febrile asthmatic children do not have an increased incidence of chest x-ray abnormalities when compared with their afebrile counterparts. The presence of rales, however, has been shown to correlate with an increased incidence of pneumonia or atelectasis.[3,7]

The issue of whether routine chest radiography is indicated to rule out causes other than asthma in a child presenting with a first episode of wheezing was evaluated in a 1983 study.[6] All children presenting to a pediatric emergency room with an initial episode of wheezing after their first birthday were enrolled in the study. For each child, a complete history was obtained (including questions regarding foreign body aspiration), physical examination was performed, and chest radiographs were taken. All children were clinically suspected of having asthma. Chest x-ray examination did not disclose a cause other than asthma in any of the 371 study patients.

Thus, the literature suggests that in the vast majority of children with asthma, chest x-rays do not provide information that alters their management. Most chest x-rays taken during acute episodes of asthma are normal or show minor abnormalities like hyperinflation, increased central lung markings, and peribronchial thickening. Even x-rays showing abnormalities (atelectasis, pneumonia, pneumomediastinum, pneumothorax) often do not alter treatment.

Standard chest x-ray examination of all children over 1 year of age with an initial episode of wheezing rarely reveals a cause other than asthma. Furthermore, foreign body aspiration, one of the most important causes of wheezing other than asthma, cannot be reliably diagnosed with the standard posteroanterior and lateral views of the chest. If one suspects a patient has aspirated a foreign body, inspiratory-expiratory chest films, decubitus films, or fluoroscopy should be obtained.[6]

What then is the role of chest radiography in the management of acute episodes of asthma? In the child who is developing increasing respiratory distress or failing to respond as expected to conventional therapy, a chest x-ray may identify an associated disease process that requires specific treatment or provide reassurance that such a process is not being overlooked. A chest x-ray is indicated in a patient in whom a complication is suspected clinically. For example, in a child with palpable subcutaneous air, a chest x-ray to document the presence of a pneumomediastinum should be obtained. Although chest radiography in a child with an initial episode of wheezing is not routinely indicated, it is helpful in patients for whom other causes of wheezing are suspected clinically or in whom the diagnosis of asthma is questionable.

PULMONARY FUNCTION TESTING

Pulmonary function measurements in the child with respiratory symptoms provide objective data upon which to base treatment decisions. Peak expiratory flow can be measured simply and inexpensively in children as young as 5 years of age. Peak flow measurements are obtained in the first tenth of a second after initiation of maximal expiration. Therefore, children require little coaching beyond simple instructions to "blow out the candle."

The more difficult and expensive spirometer measurements of forced vital capacity (FVC) and its derivatives FEV_1 (forced expiratory volume in the first second) and FEF 25-75 (mean flow rate between 25% and 75% of FVC, which is least dependent upon effort) require complete exhalation and the maintenance of expiratory effort as long as flow continues.[9,10]

Standard peak flow values are a function of size, sex, and effort. Normative tables are available, based on height and sex. Race is also an important variable; predicted values for white, black, hispanic, and native-American populations are available.[11,12]

Peak expiratory flow reflects the caliber of larger central airways; FVC derivatives reflect the smaller peripheral airways. If there is a greater degree of small airway disease relative to the larger central airways, peak expiratory flow may not indicate the total extent of disease. Values less than 80% of the predicted norm are considered abnormal.[8] However, individual baseline values may vary, and a trial yielding an 80% of predicted value may represent a significant impairment.

Pulmonary function testing is useful in the evaluation of patients with nonspecific symptoms of cough or shortness of breath on exertion, but are wheeze-free on examination. If flow rates before and after bronchodilator therapy demonstrate reversibility of the obstructive airway disease, cough variant asthma should be suspected. Exercise-induced asthma may be confirmed by comparison of testing of pulmonary function at rest and after exertion. Inhaled and injectable bronchodilators should be available during testing, which require physician monitoring. An increase in heart rate to 170 beats per minute indicates an adequate exercise trial. Pulmonary function testing should be delayed 3 to 7 minutes following exercise to ensure monitoring of peak effects.

During acute exacerbations of asthma, pulmonary function testing can objectively measure the patient's response to aerosolized bronchodilator therapy. Lack of improvement may indicate the need for steroids, alternative bronchodilators, or more intensive inpatient care.[6]

Assessment of peak flow at home can help motivated patients maximize home therapy. Equipment can include either a Mini-Wright Peak Flow Meter or Assess, the latter being limited by its inability to measure high flows. When monitored at frequent intervals, deterioration in pulmonary function can be detected before clinical symptoms appear.[8] Decisions for initiating or changing medications, documenting relative efficacy of various regimens, and determining the optimal duration of therapy can thus be done at home in cooperation with the treating physician.

NONINVASIVE MEASURES OF BLOOD GAS EXCHANGE

Arterial hypoxemia is a universal finding in childhood status asthmaticus.[13–15] This results from alveolar hypoventilation and pulmonary arteriovenous shunting. It has been estimated that from 7% to 13% of pulmonary blood flow is directed to nonventilated areas of lung, contributing to the observed hypoxemia in asthmatic children.[13]

The magnitude of changes in blood gas tension has been assessed in several studies. The mean PaO_2 value at the initial evaluation of a group of hospitalized children with status asthmaticus while breathing room air was 58 mmHg.[14] Weng et al[15] noted that all patients with acute exacerbations of asthma and 50% of asymptomatic children with asthma breathing room air had PaO_2 values below normal.

Assessment of the adequacy of blood gas exchange may be essential to the management of patients experiencing acute exacerbations of asthma, particularly when they are unresponsive to initial care. Noninvasive measures include determinations of transcutaneous oxygen ($TcPO_2$) and carbon dioxide ($TcPCO_2$) tensions as well as oxygen saturation by pulse oximetry.[16]

Skin surface electrodes, which monitor transcutaneous oxygen or carbon dioxide tension, have been correlated with arterial PaO_2 and $PaCO_2$ sampling. These correlations, however, depend on adequate arterialization of cutaneous blood flow. Factors altering local circulation include hypotension, acidosis, hypothermia, peripheral edema, and severe anemia.[16] A poor correlation between cutaneous and arterial oxygen tension was demonstrated for a group of asthmatic children experiencing an acute exacerbation of their asthma, possibly caused by significant peripheral vasoconstriction.[17,18]

Pulse oximetry is an alternative noninvasive measure of arterial oxygenation. A single sensor placed on a finger or toe, or mounted on the palm of the hand or dorsum of the foot, measures heart rate and hemoglobin oxygen saturation (SaO_2) simultaneously. This peripheral sensor functions by positioning a pulsatile arterial vascular bed between a diode that passes red and infrared light (660 nm and 960 nm) through this bed to a photocell detector. Changes in light absorption produced by pulsation of blood through this vascular bed are recorded and integrated by a microprocessor. Factors that alter vascular pulsation such as low cardiac output or hypothermia may produce a poor correlation between directly measured and calculated SaO_2. However, pulse oximeter SaO_2 correlated highly when compared with directly measured SaO_2 in infants and children with a variety of life-threatening disorders.[19,20] These studies demonstrated the accuracy and reliability of the pulse oximeter over a wide range of hemodynamic variables and measured SaO_2 values. Pulse oximetry offers the technical advantages of a peripheral sensor that is easily mounted. In addition, no site preparation or instrument calibration is necessary.

The precise role of noninvasive measures of blood gas exchange has yet to be determined. Transcutaneous monitoring may be limited by the cutaneous vasoconstriction associated with asthma. Pulse oximetry offers many technical advantages, and future studies should confirm its potential usefulness.

CONCLUSION

Physicians managing patients with either first episodes of wheezing or acute exacerbations of bronchial asthma are confronted with an extensive array of evaluation strategies. Routine chest x-ray studies are probably not indicated. Radiographs may provide useful information about associated disease processes or alternative diagnoses associated with wheezing. Valuable objective data using peak flow measurements can be obtained simply and inexpensively. The severity of an attack and response to therapy can thus be measured. Pulse oximetry may be a useful adjunct to the management of asthmatic patients.

REFERENCES

1. Dworetzky M, Philson AD: Review of asthmatic patients hospitalized in pavilion service of the New York Hospital from 1948–1963 with emphasis on mortality rate. *J Allergy* 1968;41:181–194.

2. Eggleston PA, Ward BH, Pierson WE, et al: Radiographic abnormalities in acute asthma in children. *Pediatrics* 1974;54:422–449.

3. Rushton AR: The role of the chest radiograph in the management of childhood asthma. *Clin Pediatr* 1982;21:325–328.

4. Brooks LJ, Cloutier MM, Afshani E: Significance of roentgenographic abnormalities in children hospitalized for asthma. *Chest* 1982;82:315–318.

5. Press S, Tamer MA, Cogan J, Duncan RC: Chest x-rays and asthma (letter). *Clin Pediatr* 1982;21:744.

6. Gerschel JC, Goldman HS, Stein REK, et al: The usefulness of chest radiographs in first asthma attacks. *N Engl J Med* 1983;309:336–339.

7. Zieverink SE, Harper AP, Holden RW, et al: Emergency room radiography of asthma: An efficacy study. *Radiology* 1982;145:27–29.

8. McIntosh K, Ellis EF, Hoffman LS, et al: The association of viral and bacterial respiratory infections with exacerbations of wheezing in young asthmatic children. *J Pediatr* 1973;82: 578–590.

9. Wall MA: Office pulmonary function testing. *Pediatr Clin North Am* 1984;31:773–783.

10. Ganeshananthan M, Fink JR: Pulmonary function testing in the pediatric outpatient. *Pediatr Ann* 1986;15:323–339.

11. Hsu KTK, Jenkins DE, Hsi BP, et al: Ventilatory functions of normal children and young adults: Mexican-American, white, and black: I. Spirometry. *J Pediatr* 1979;95:14–23.

12. Wall MA, Olson D, Bonn BA, et al: Lung function in North American Indian children: Reference standards for spirometry, maximal expiratory flow volume curves, and peak expiratory flow. *Am Rev Respir Dis* 1982;125:158–162.

13. Ledbetter MK, Bruck E, Farhi LE: Perfusion of the underventilated compartment of the lungs in asthmatic children. *J Clin Invest* 1964;43:2233.

14. Downes JJ, Wood DM, Striker TW: Arterial blood gas and acid-base disorders in infants and children with status asthmaticus. *Pediatrics* 1968;238–242.

15. Weng TR, Langer HM, Featherby EA, et al: Arterial blood gas tensions and acid-base balance in symptomatic and asymptomatic asthma in childhood. *Am Rev Respir Dis* 1970; 101:274–282.

16. Pasnick M, Lucey JF: Practical uses of continuous transcutaneous oxygen monitoring. *Pediatr Rev* 1983;5:5–12.

17. Bourchier D, Dawson KP: Transcutaneous oxygen monitoring in acute asthma. *Aust Paediatr J* 1984;20:213–216.

18. Henderson WR, Shelhamer JH, Reingold DB, et al: Alpha-adrenergic hyper-responsiveness in asthma: Analysis of vascular and pupillary responses. *N Engl J Med* 1979; 300:642–647.

19. Yelderman M, New W: Evaluation of pulse oximetry. *Anesthesiology* 1983;59:349–352.

20. Fanconi S, Doherty P, Edmonds JF, et al: Pulse oximetry in pediatric intensive care. *J Pediatr* 1985;107:362–366.

17. Utility of the Chest X-Ray in Evaluating Wheezing in Children

Kim A. Ogle, MD

The emergency evaluation of the first episode of wheezing in a child, or an acute exacerbation in a known asthmatic patient, frequently includes antero-posterior and lateral chest x-ray studies. The chest radiograph is useful for determining the presence of complications with an exacerbation in the asthmatic patient and for identifying causes of wheezing other than asthma in the new onset wheezing patient. However, the recent literature[1-4] has questioned the utility of the chest x-ray study in evaluating wheezing. The studies suggest that most abnormal chest x-ray findings neither guide nor alter emergency treatment, nor do they aid in predicting the need for hospital admission.

RADIOLOGIC FINDINGS

The majority of wheezing children have normal chest radiographic findings. Simon et al[5] reported normal chest x-ray findings in 73% of 218 asthmatic children seen as outpatients. The other 27% had x-ray findings compatible with hyperinflation only. Hyperaeration is defined as a lung length the same or greater than lung width, or a large retrosternal area in lateral chest x-ray views.[6] The degree of hyperinflation shown in x-ray films has not been shown to correlate with the severity of the patient's disease.[6] Of 129 asthmatic children admitted because of exacerbation, the three children admitted to the intensive care unit did not show hyperinflation on their initial chest x-ray film.[3] Other typical x-ray findings in an asthmatic patient's radiograph include peribronchial cuffing or thickening, increased central lung markings, and subsegmental atelectasis (see Figure 17-1). The presence of these radiographic signs rarely alters the patient's treatment.

The incidence of other abnormal radiographic findings ranges from 5% to 20%.[7] The higher percentages are for studies of hospitalized patients only.

Segmental atelectasis, pneumonia, pneumomediastinum, and pneumothorax are the other major abnormal findings in an asthmatic patient's chest x-ray film. Segmental atelectasis and infiltrate are often hard to distinguish in a single x-ray study; they often necessitate serial x-ray studies hours to days apart. Atelectasis is associated with a lobar distribution, loss of lung volume, and a lack of pleural fluid (see Table 17-1). Atelectasis and infiltrate occur more often in children under 5 years of age and in children with rales, fever, tachypnea, and tachycardia at the time of presentation (see Figure 17-2).[1]

Pneumomediastinum occurs in fewer than 5% of asthmatic patients radiographed in the emergency department.[1,2] The incidence of pneumomediastinum is slightly higher in hospitalized asthmatic children, reflecting its association with more severe disease.[3,7] The classic signs and symptoms of pneumomediastinum are sharp chest or neck pain, a harsh brassy cough, no cardiac dullness, crepitus, and Homans' sign.[8] However, in a study by Eggleston et al,[7] 10 of 26 patients with radiologic evidence of pneumomediastinum had no signs on examination suggestive of this diagnosis. The mediastinal air initially appears as thin radiolucent streaks around the roots of the great vessels and mainstem bronchi (see Figure 17-3). In older children it often dissects into the axillary and cervical areas. Spontaneous pneumothorax is a very rare complication of asthma.[9] Pneumothorax usually follows therapy with either mechanical ventilation or positive-pressure devices.

THERAPEUTIC IMPLICATIONS

Knowing that a wheezing patient has atelectasis, an infiltrate, or a pneumomediastinum may not be clinically useful. In several studies,[1–4] both outpatient and hospitalized asthmatic patients did not benefit from such knowledge. Eggleston et al[7] found no correlation between the severity of the asthmatic episode and the presence or absence of infiltrates. A second study[3] of inpatients could not show any relationship between x-ray findings and the physician's clinical assessment of the patient. Rushton[2] studied x-ray films and clinical records of 391 pediatric emergency department visits for asthma. He found the same frequency of infiltrates and atelectasis in patients who were sent home and those admitted. He also could not show that the x-ray findings were useful in predicting the need for treatment and response to treatment.

Sixty-eight percent of the children who showed infiltrates on their radiographs in the study by Eggleston et al[7] received antibiotics, perhaps providing a justification for ordering a chest x-ray film.[7] However, in light of the current view that wheezing exacerbations are almost never associated with bacterial lower respiratory tract infections, the presence of an infiltrate on an x-ray film should not be the only criterion for putting a patient on antibiotics.[10]

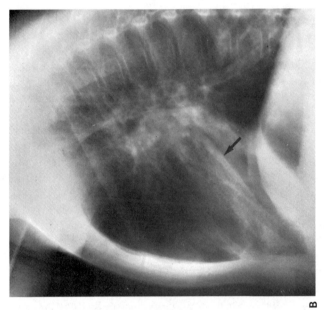

B

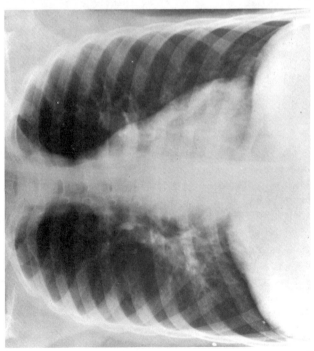

A

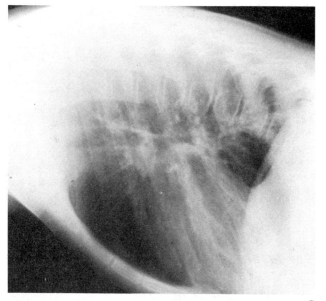

C

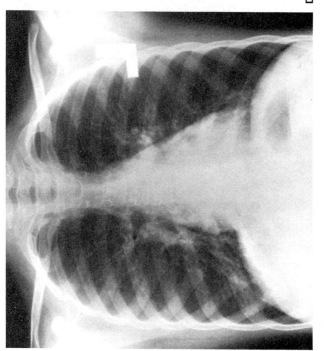

D

Figure 17-1 Asthma. (**A**) Frontal view shows diffuse, patchy densities, hilar cobweb, and indistinct pulmonary vessels. The silhouette of the right side of the heart is partially obscured. (**B**) Lateral view (simultaneous with A) shows increased anteroposterior diameter, anterior bowing of the sternum, patchy hilar densities, and a streaky density overlying the heart that represents partial atelectasis of the right middle lobe. (**C**) Four days later, the lungs still contain some increased densities but are clearer than previously. The border of the right side of the heart is now well defined. (**D**) Simultaneous lateral view shows less overaeration and a clear right middle lobe region (compare with **B**). *Source:* Reprinted from *Radiology of the Pediatric Chest* (p 213) by AH Felman with permission of McGraw-Hill Book Company, © 1987.

Table 17-1 Atelectasis v Infiltrate

	Infiltrate or Consolidation	Atelectasis or Collapse
Opacification	+	+
Shift of mediastinum	−	Toward lesion
Diaphragm position	NL or depressed	Elevated
Fissure position	NL or away from lesion	Toward lesion
Air bronchograms	+	±

+ = present
− = absent
NL = normal
± = may or may not be present

Source: Reprinted with permission from *Pediatric Clinics of North America* (1984;31:896), Copyright © 1984, WB Saunders Company.

The regimen asthmatic children receive as outpatients is not altered by atelectasis shown on their chest radiographs. The majority of atelectasis in asthmatic children will resolve quickly and spontaneously. Asthmatic children do not seem to acquire associated complications of atelectasis, ie, bronchiectasis, hemoptysis, lung abscess, and pulmonary fibrosis.[11]

The presence of a pneumomediastinum altered the therapy given to asthmatic children 10 to 15 years ago because positive-pressure devices were used to deliver adrenergic aerosols. There are reports[8] of pneumothoraces after such therapy. As these devices are no longer used to administer aerosols, this complication is much less common.

Widely accepted indications for chest x-ray studies for a wheezing patient include: first episode of wheezing, suspicion of foreign body aspiration, hospital admission, poor response to therapy, chest pain, and fever and rales. With our present knowledge, these indications may not all be valid.

Many feel that patients with an initial episode of wheezing should undergo x-ray studies for disease entities other than asthma that are associated with wheezing. Examples of such diagnoses are cystic fibrosis, congestive heart failure, external compression of the lower airway, bronchiolitis, immunodeficiency diseases, and aspirated foreign bodies. Gershel et al[4] looked at radiographs of 350 children over 1 year of age during their first episode of wheezing. No x-ray finding suggested a diagnosis other than reversible obstructive pulmonary disease. They conceded that their 12-month study may not have been of sufficient duration to have ensured that a child with an alternative diagnosis had been seen. However, they concluded that such cases are very rare in comparison with new cases of asthma. A chest x-ray is not the best screening study for many of these diseases. Thorough clinical examination of children

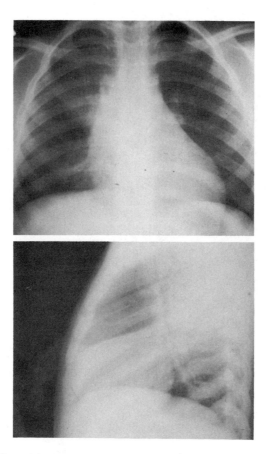

Figure 17-2 Radiographic appearance of right middle lobe atelectasis. Note the relatively normal appearance of the anteroposterior projection compared with the lateral projection. *Source:* Reprinted with permission from *Pediatric Clinics of North America* (1984;31:896), Copyright © 1984, WB Saunders Company.

with their first episode of wheezing should enable the physician to identify the child in whom chest radiography would aid in the diagnosis.

The child who aspirates a foreign body may have localized or diffuse wheezing depending on the location of the foreign body. These children usually have a history of a coughing or choking episode and abrupt onset of wheezing and respiratory distress. The anteroposterior and lateral chest x-ray findings of these children are often normal or may be so subtle as to be overlooked. Very few aspirated foreign bodies are radiopaque. Unilateral hyperexpansion, atelectasis, and an infiltrate may all be seen after aspiration.[12] Inspiratory/expiratory films or decubitus films are better for documenting a foreign body aspiration (see Figure 17-4). Any child with a history suggestive of a foreign

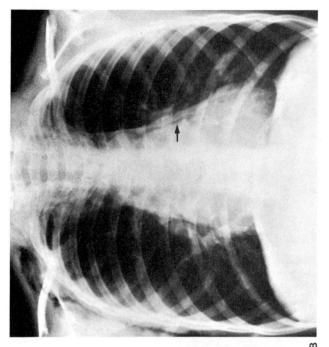

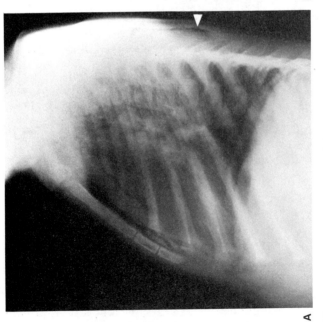

Figure 17-3 Pneumomediastinum. **(A)** The lucent shadows outlining the aortic knob and upper mediastinal tissues (arrows) indicate the presence of mediastinal air. Subcutaneous emphysema is present in the supraclavicular soft tissue and that of the right side of the chest. **(B)** The dark substernal lucencies represent mediastinal air. *Source:* Reprinted from *Radiology of the Pediatric Chest* (p 216) by AH Felman with permission of McGraw-Hill Book Company, © 1987.

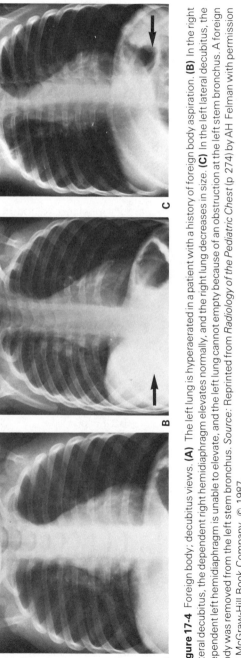

Figure 17-4 Foreign body; decubitus views. **(A)** The left lung is hyperaerated in a patient with a history of foreign body aspiration. **(B)** In the right lateral decubitus, the dependent right hemidiaphragm elevates normally, and the right lung decreases in size. **(C)** In the left lateral decubitus, the dependent left hemidiaphragm is unable to elevate, and the left lung cannot empty because of an obstruction at the left stem bronchus. A foreign body was removed from the left stem bronchus. *Source:* Reprinted from *Radiology of the Pediatric Chest* (p 274) by AH Felman with permission of McGraw-Hill Book Company, © 1987.

body aspiration or who has persistently unequal breath sounds after beta-adrenergic therapy in the emergency room should have radiologic studies done.

The information obtained from the radiograph of admitted patients is probably not helpful in their management unless their attack is severe and unresponsive to emergency therapy. The presence of atelectasis or an infiltrate does not alter the standard inpatient treatment of a child. Pneumothorax occurs more often among the subset of admitted patients with severe disease. These patients are more likely to have a pneumomediastinum. Since this is probably the group of patients that may require mechanical ventilation, it is important to document the presence of an air leak. A child with severe chest pain after emergency treatment may have a large air leak and should be radiographed.

Rushton[2] and others[1,4] found a higher incidence of abnormal chest radiographic findings (atelectasis and infiltrate) in children who had fever and rales with their wheezing. However, the x-ray findings were not useful in predicting the children's response to treatment or admission to the hospital. Treatment with beta-agonists is not influenced by x-ray findings nor is the decision to start antibiotic therapy based solely on the presence of an infiltrate on the chest x-ray film. The information obtained from x-ray studies of children who have rales, fever, and wheezing will probably not alter their management.

CONCLUSION

The indications for obtaining radiographs for wheezing children are controversial. The child with a severe exacerbation unresponsive to therapy or the child with any sign suggestive of an air leak or foreign body aspiration should undergo x-ray studies. The other indications are less clear, but with careful clinical examination and selection of the patients, the number of x-ray films obtained can be decreased, and the usefulness of the studies obtained increased.

REFERENCES

1. Zieverink SE, Harper AP, Holden RW, et al: Emergency room radiography of asthma: An efficacy study. *Radiology* 1982;145:27–29.

2. Rushton AR: The role of the chest radiograph in the management of childhood asthma. *Clin Pediatr* 1982;21:325–328.

3. Brooks LJ, Cloutier MM, Atshani E: Significance of roentgenographic abnormalities in children hospitalized for asthma. *Chest* 1982;3:315–318.

4. Gershel JC, Goldman HS, Stein RE, et al: The usefulness of chest radiographs in first asthma attacks. *N Engl J Med* 1983;309:336–339.

5. Simon G, Connolly N, Littlejohns DW: Radiological abnormalities in children with asthma and their relation to the clinical findings and some respiratory function tests. *Thorax* 1973; 28:115–123.

6. Gilles JD, Reed MH, Simons FER: Radiologic findings in acute childhood asthma. *J Can Assoc Radiol* 1978;29:28–33.

7. Eggleston PA, Ward BH, Pierson WE, et al: Radiographic abnormalities in acute asthma in children. *Pediatrics* 1974;54:442–449.

8. Bierman CW: Pneumomediastinum and pneumothorax complicating asthma in children. *Am J Dis Child* 1967;114:42–50.

9. Kravis LP: The complications of acute asthma in children. *Clin Pediatr* 1973;12:538–549.

10. Ellis EF: Asthma in childhood. *J Allergy Clin Immunol* 1983;72:526–539.

11. Redding GJ: Atelectasis in childhood. *Pediatr Clin North Am* 1984;31:891–905.

12. Cotton EC, Yasuda K: Foreign body aspiration. *Pediatr Clin North Am* 1984;31: 937–941.

18. Pharmacologic Management of Status Asthmaticus

Jeffrey H. Hill, MD, PhD

Although asthma is one of the most common presenting problems in the pediatric population, many aspects of its pharmacologic management remain controversial. Several factors contribute to this controversy. The first is common to all of medicine and is that significant new knowledge of the pathophysiology of asthma has been defined in the last 15 years. The second relates to the proliferation of pharmacologic agents with application to the treatment of asthma. Finally, there is the question of the importance of the lack of labeled indications for use of many pharmacologic agents in children, including many drugs useful in the management of asthma.

FDA-APPROVED INDICATIONS FOR USE

Unfortunately, in our highly litigatious times, the confusion surrounding FDA approval of a drug "for use in humans" versus "labeling" for indications continues to cause anxiety, particularly for physicians caring for children. Fortunately, FDA approval of a drug for any use makes that drug legal and available for use in any patient in the United States. Although package inserts list specific "indications for use" (labeled indications), they do not and are not intended to medicolegally limit drug use to those indications. Labeling is regulated by the FDA to the extent that indications for use must be supported by enough research to satisfy the FDA that in fact the claims of drug efficacy are reasonable. There is no requirement for labeling to include all indications for use even if massive amounts of medical literature support the safety and efficacy of a particular usage.

We are frequently faced with the alternative of employing a drug that is not labeled for use in children or by not using the drug in question, potentially increasing morbidity and mortality. Although articles are published about their efficacy and safety, many drugs commonly used in pediatric patients are not labeled for use in children, (e.g., dopamine hydrochloride, metaproterenol sulfate [Alupent Inhalant Solution] in children under 12 years old, etc). In fact, when the medicolegal issue has arisen concerning appropriate use of pharmacologic interventions, use of any drug, whether for its labeled indication or another indication, must be supported by "common practice" as defined by medical literature review, expert testimony, and clinical experience.

Each physician must personally come to terms with this issue, and it is not the intent of this article to resolve this problem. Without further regard to the misnomer of "FDA approval," the aggressive approach to pharmacologic management of asthma outlined herein is supported by medical literature, is safe, and is in daily use.

PATHOPHYSIOLOGY

The underlying defect in asthma is unknown, but abnormal neural control of airways, first proposed in the 1920s as the etiology of asthma, has recently gained new proponents.[1] Normal airways are enervated by parasympathetic efferent nerves that, when stimulated, release acetylcholine, which mediates bronchospasm and increased mucous production. Circulating epinephrine and, to some extent, sympathetic (adrenergic) stimulation of airways cause bronchodilation. In a person with asthma, the balance between these two systems is upset in favor of bronchospasm. This disequilibrium may reflect primary increased parasympathetic secretion, increased airway sensitivity to irritants resulting in increased efferent parasympathetic discharge, increased end organ (airway) sensitivity to parasympathetic stimulation, or any combination of these factors. Alternatively, airway sensitivity or response to adrenergic (beta$_2$) stimulation may be inadequate. In any given individual with asthma, perhaps all or only one of these mechanisms is present; however, the resultant imbalance in favor of bronchospasm results in clinically notable symptoms.[1]

Pharmacologic observations consistent with this theory of imbalance include the following in asthmatic persons:

- Beta-adrenergic blockade can precipitate wheezing.
- Beta$_2$-agonists can reverse bronchospasm.
- Methacholine (muscarinic agonist) can precipitate wheezing.
- Atropine (a muscarinic antagonist) can reverse bronchospasm.

Clinically, irritants such as cold or dry air, cigarette smoke, sulfur dioxide, or ozone can precipitate bronchospasm. These symptoms appear to result from stimulation of sensory afferent nerves in the bronchial epithelium that stimulate release of acetylcholine from efferent postsynaptic parasympathetic vagal nerve endings onto airway smooth muscle and into airway mucous glands. This release causes both bronchospasm and increased mucous production, which lead to airway obstruction.

Increased airway mucus, allergenic stimulation, and airway irritants also lead to increased production and release of inflammatory mediators that further exacerbate the clinical symptoms.[2] Not only do allergens and irritants cause lung mast cells to release leukotrienes and prostaglandins, but as resident macrophages attempt to perform their "house-cleaning" function and remove excess mucus from the airways by phagocytosis, they also release leukotrienes and prostaglandins. Leukotrienes and prostaglandins not only directly stimulate bronchospasm and increased mucous production, but also stimulate additional macrophage and granulocyte activation and influx into the lung, which results in release of additional inflammatory mediators. This ever-increasing inflammatory response also acts directly as an airway irritant to stimulate parasympathetic discharge in the airway. If not reversed, inflammation and inflammatory mediators can result in massive, overwhelming, self-perpetuating bronchospasm that is refractory to the bronchodilating effects of beta$_2$ agonists.

Various points of interference with this cycle of mediator release, inflammation, and parasympathetic discharge can be identified. In the early stages of the cycle, one can attempt to reverse bronchospasm directly with beta$_2$-adrenergic agonists or intravenous or oral theophylline and depend on the intrinsic host control mechanisms to prevent significant inflammation from developing. One can also attempt to block directly the effects of acetylcholine through use of inhaled anticholinergic drugs such as atropine sulfate or ipratropium bromide. Once the inflammatory mediator cycle is established, steroids are frequently required as adjunctive therapy to break that cycle and relieve bronchospasm. Prophylactic, long-term cromolyn sodium administration can reduce mast cell degranulation and bronchospasm caused by irritants or allergen exposure.

The challenge in the emergency management of asthma is to determine which specific agent(s) to use in any given patient, and how to administer safely and effectively the appropriate pharmacologic agent(s) in the shortest possible time.

BETA$_2$-AGONIST THERAPY

Bronchodilator therapy has come a long way since the discovery that epinephrine caused more bronchodilation than norepinephrine. That observation began the search for the class of specific bronchodilator drugs that we now call beta$_2$-adrenergic agonists.

The first drug to show real beta-receptor specificity was isoproterenol hydrochloride. Unfortunately, isoproterenol is a significant beta$_1$-adrenergic agonist at very low doses. Although it is also a potent beta$_2$-agonist, the beta$_1$ side effects of tachycardia, increased myocardial oxygen consumption, and dysrhythmogenicity predominate. In addition, the duration of bronchodilation obtained with isoproterenol is only approximately 1 hour.

The next sympathomimetic bronchodilator to be successfully marketed in the United States was isoetharine (Bronkosol). Isoetharine is a more pure beta$_2$-agonist than isoproterenol, but it has two drawbacks: The duration of action is still only 1 to 2 hours, and the nebulizer solution contains clinically significant amounts of metabisulfites that can cause bronchospasm in some asthmatic patients.[3]

Metaproterenol sulfate (Alupent) was developed as a relatively specific beta$_2$-agonist with a long duration of action.[4] Unfortunately, although its duration of action may be as long as 6 hours, its usefulness is limited by its alpha- and beta$_1$-agonistic side effects.

Many of the limitations of these agents were overcome in terbutaline and albuterol.[5,6] These drugs are essentially pure beta$_2$-agonists with primary side effects of tremor and reflex tachycardia (in response to beta$_2$ stimulation of peripheral vasodilatation). The bronchodilator effect of terbutaline is equipotent on a microgram per microgram basis with epinephrine hydrochloride and is of much longer duration (4 to 8 hours).[6,7] Since these agents are nearly pure beta$_2$-agonists, their use and maximum dose are limited only by beta$_2$ side effects, and therefore they have much higher therapeutic indexes than less beta$_2$-specific sympathomimetic agents.

The real limitation of the use of terbutaline or albuterol in the United States has been the limited availability of formulations. Albuterol has been available only as an oral liquid, a tablet, and in a metered-dose inhaler (MDI). In March 1987, albuterol became available in an inhalant solution form. Terbutaline is available as a tablet, an MDI, and a subcutaneous (SC) solution that can also be safely administered by nebulization.

ROUTE OF BETA$_2$-AGONIST ADMINISTRATION

One of the major questions surrounding beta$_2$-agonist use is which route of administration is most effective with the least associated side effects. Theoretically, one would like to obtain a maximal beta$_2$-agonist concentration at the bronchial smooth muscle beta$_2$ receptors that mediate bronchodilation, and minimal concentration at beta$_2$-agonist receptor sites that mediate systemic side effects. Three major routes of administration have been studied extensively, and although each is feasible with the currently available formulations of terbutaline and albuterol, one has distinct advantages.[8]

Orally administered beta$_2$-agonists are distributed throughout the body with no apparent selectivity for bronchial smooth muscle beta$_2$-agonist receptors and, therefore, have significant systemic side effects at therapeutic doses. In addition, beta$_2$-agonists are variably absorbed from the gastrointestinal tract, and the onset of clinically significant bronchodilation occurs between 30 and 120 minutes after oral administration. Although this may be acceptable for long-term asthma control, it is clearly not acceptable during therapy for an acute bronchospastic episode.

Although subcutaneous beta$_2$-agonist administration is also associated with notable systemic side effects, SC administration at 10% of the oral dose achieves comparable bronchodilation and has an onset of action of less than 5 minutes. Maximal bronchodilatory effect of SC terbutaline may not be reached for more than 30 minutes, but its bronchodilatory effect is equivalent to that of SC epinephrine within 5 minutes of administration and lasts up to 4 hours after administration.[7]

Subcutaneous terbutaline also seems to cause less vomiting, headache, tachycardia, and injection site pain than epinephrine. Unfortunately, the pain associated with even SC terbutaline administration may stimulate more wheezing in an already anxious child with severe respiratory compromise. This pain, coupled with the systemic side effects, makes SC terbutaline less than ideal although still of use in patients with respiratory patterns that do not facilitate delivery of inhaled drug.

Beta$_2$-agonist applied directly to the pulmonary epithelium by inhalation is locally absorbed and slowly translocated into the blood over 2 to 3 hours. The local concentration of bronchodilating drug appears to exceed the systemic concentration and be associated with relatively more bronchodilation. A number of studies[9-11] have shown equivalent bronchodilation in most asthmatic patients after inhaled or SC administration of terbutaline, and far fewer systemic side effects after inhaled versus SC administration.

Several techniques for the administration of inhaled beta$_2$-agonists are available.[11] Metered-dose inhalers are very popular because of their convenience of administration and portability, but adequate drug delivery requires good hand-breath coordination. Twenty to forty percent of adults, and most children under 5 years of age, attain less than maximal bronchodilation from such beta$_2$-agonist administration because of poor hand-breath coordination. Although a number of conflicting studies are published, drug delivery is probably improved in younger children and in other patients with poor hand-breath coordination by an MDI with an attached spacer device.

Airway drug deposition depends not only on hand-breath coordination but also on the rate and depth of inspiration. Slow, larger than normal breaths result in better airway deposition. In well patients, an MDI with a spacer device may result in better drug delivery than nebulization in single-dose studies. However, airway deposition of drug may be severely compromised during active bronchospasm, particularly if the drug is administered either by an MDI alone or with a spacer device. Most authors recommend nebulized administration of drug during active wheezing, which results in better, although not completely normal, airway deposition of drug.

Until recently, the only solution of terbutaline or albuterol available for nebulization in the United States was the parenteral terbutaline solution. Although this solution is safe and effective as a nebulized inhalant, it is relatively expensive. A nebulizer solution of albuterol is now available in the United States, and will reduce the cost of therapy considerably.

ANTICHOLINERGICS

Herbalists of the 1400s knew of the asthma "healing" effects of inhaling the fumes of burning weeds that we now know contained atropine. The more efficacious anticholinergic agent ipratropium bromide (formerly SCH 1000) is now available in the United States, and the bronchodilating efficacy and safety of other properly used anticholinergic drugs such as inhaled atropine is well documented both in adults and children.[12,13] Atropine can be safely used at a dosage of 100 µg/kg/dose by nebulization every 4 hours. Since the bronchodilator effects of anticholinergic drugs are somewhat additive to beta$_2$-agonist effects, and the systemic beta$_2$ side effects do not seem to be exacerbated by anticholinergics,[12,14,15] both can be administered concurrently. Anticholinergics may also greatly contribute to relieving airway obstruction in asthma by decreasing overall mucus production without altering the viscosity of the mucus.

STEROIDS

Inflammation has a major role in prolonging and exacerbating episodes of bronchospasm.[2] Inflammatory mediators such as leukotrienes, prostaglandins, and activated complement components increase airway edema and stimulate bronchospasm and mucous production. Once an inflammatory response is established, it can cause prolonged status asthmaticus, independent of the original precipitating event.

The general anti-inflammatory effects of glucocorticoids are well known, but it is worth mentioning that glucocorticoids also directly reduce mast cell and inflammatory cell release of mediators and directly inhibit mucous secretion. Although routine use of steroids in all outpatients with asthma is controversial,[16] any patient admitted to the hospital should be treated with appropriate steroids. Intravenous (IV) steroids are preferred during status asthmaticus not only because of decreased airway delivery of inhalant steroids, but also because steroids administered with MDIs are in a powdered form and may further irritate the airway. Methylprednisolone sodium succinate has fewer mineralocorticoid side effects than hydrocortisone and is given at a dosage of 1 to 2 mg/kg IV q 4–6 hours. Outpatient management with prednisone 2 mg/kg/day divided BID to a maximum dosage of 60 mg/day for 3 to 5 days is an adequate oral regimen. It is important to initiate appropriate steroid therapy early, as it may take 6 to 12 hours to achieve major reduction in inflammation.

THEOPHYLLINE

Outpatient management of theophylline therapy is complex at best; however, several comments about theophylline administration are in order. Because of the narrow therapeutic index of theophylline, no theophylline derivative should be administered to anyone who has received theophylline/aminophylline in the previous 24 hours until the serum theophylline level has been measured. Once the serum level is known, and assuming that no sustained-release preparation is still potentially being dissolved in the gastrointestinal tract, one can raise the serum level into the high therapeutic range (15 to 20 µg/mL) by administering an IV bolus of aminophylline over 30 to 45 minutes. Administration of aminophylline 1.1 mg/kg will raise the serum theophylline level approximately 2 µg/mL.

Theophylline metabolism is very variable in children and is affected by many factors including age, variable liver metabolism, viral infection, and drug-drug interactions. Unfortunately, 5 to 10 fold changes in clearance rate can occur in the same individual over a 24-hour period. In general, infants and senior citizens have the slowest clearance rates, and young adolescents the highest. A child 6 months of age may only require aminophylline 0.2 to 0.3 mg/kg/hr to maintain therapeutic levels, while in extreme cases an adolescent patient may require more than 2.0 mg/kg/hr. Obviously, rates of IV aminophylline administration must be individualized, and serum theophylline levels monitored closely. A safe starting maintenance IV dosage of aminophylline in children 6 to 12 months of age is 0.5 mg/kg/hr, and greater than 12 months of age is

1.1 mg/kg/hr. Frequent measurement of serum theophylline levels and adjustment of dose on an individual basis are critical.

CROMOLYN SODIUM

Cromolyn sodium is a drug without a well-defined mechanism of action (although many have been proposed). Cromolyn is as effective in long-term outpatient management of asthma as theophylline derivatives. Since cromolyn is not a sympathomimetic, it is particularly useful in small children in whom sympathomimetic side effects may be unacceptable.[17] No clear-cut episodes of clinically important drug toxicity have been described except for rare drug hypersensitivity and severe bronchospasm that can occur in response to powder deposition in the airway when cromolyn is administered by Spinhaler or MDI. Although cromolyn is very effective and safe when administered long-term, it can take as long as 6 weeks from the initiation of therapy to detect major therapeutic benefit. Initiation of cromolyn therapy during an episode of status asthmaticus will probably not benefit the patient during that episode. However, if a patient who has been on long-term cromolyn therapy comes with status asthmaticus to the emergency department, then cromolyn should be continued by nebulization, not by MDI or Spinhaler.

CONCLUSION

The goal of initial aggressive management is to shift the spectrum of disease toward a more mild course. Perhaps not all patients need aggressive therapy, but any patient with more than minimal symptoms might benefit from an organized aggressive approach. Over the last several years, I have developed the following approach, which depends heavily on administration of inhaled drugs:

Initially, administer oxygen and treat significantly ill patients with a single dose of SC terbutaline 10 μg/kg (maximum 0.5 mg) to ensure immediate delivery of an adequate dose in the face of severely compromised pulmonary function. Immediately thereafter, begin nebulization of terbutaline 100 μg/kg (maximum 5.0 mg) or 150 μg of albuterol inhalant solution mixed with atropine 100 μg/kg (maximum 5.0 mg). Place an IV catheter, draw a sample to determine the theophylline level (if indicated) from the catheter as soon as IV access is obtained, and immediately push solumedrol 2 mg/kg IV. If no history of theophylline use is present, begin an IV loading dosage of aminophylline 8 to 9 mg/kg over 30 to 45 minutes to attain a serum level of theophylline 15 to 20 μg/mL. When the first nebulization is completed, immediately re-examine the patient clinically and unless the lung exam is completely clear and air exchange normal, begin another nebulization of terbutaline 100 μg/kg or albuterol 150 μg/kg. If theophylline was administered in the previous 24 hours, wait for the serum theophylline level to be determined (ideally 30 minutes or less) and give a loading dose, if necessary, to raise the serum level to 16 to 18 μg/mL.

$$\text{Loading dose in mg/kg} = \frac{\text{desired serum level} - \text{measured serum level}}{2}$$

After either aminophylline loading scenario, immediately begin a constant IV infusion of aminophylline 1.1 mg/kg/hr in children over 12 months of age or aminophylline 0.5 mg/kg/hr in infants between 6 and 12 months of age. A repeat theophylline level is determined in 2 hours and thereafter as needed to fine-tune the rate of IV aminophylline administration.

This entire initial treatment sequence can be completed in 60 to 75 minutes from the time of presentation. Evaluation of ward versus intensive care unit (ICU) admission can be addressed and arterial blood gases measured to assist in the evaluation.

Occasionally, after aggressive initial management, a patient can be discharged to home. However, discharge to home is rare if the initial assessment of severity has been correct. Many patients will go to a ward; those who are admitted to an ICU will have received ICU-level pharmacologic management from the time of presentation. Side effects, pain, and anxiety are far less with this approach than with a more leisurely approach extending over several hours and depending primarily on multiple SC injections of epinephrine as the mainstay of therapy. This aggressive approach results in more rapid relief of symptoms and reduced overall morbidity.

REFERENCES

1. Barnes PJ: Neural control of human airways in health and disease. *Am Rev Respir Dis* 1986;134:1289–1314.

2. Sly RM: Pathogenesis of asthma. *Ann Allergy* 1982;49:16–19.

3. Koepke JW, Selner JC, Dunhill AL: Presence of sulfur dioxide in commonly used bronchodilator solutions. *J Allergy Clin Immunol* 1983;72:504–508.

4. Garra B, Shapiro GG, Dorsett CS, et al: A double-blind evaluation of the use of nebulized metaproterenol and isoproterenol in hospitalized asthmatic children and adolescents. *J Allergy Clin Immunol* 1977;60:63–68.

5. Kemp JP, Orgel A, Meltzer EO, et al: Terbutaline sulfate and isoproterenol sulfate (metered dose aerosols) in the treatment of asthma. *Ann Allergy* 1983;51:436–440.

6. Ahrens RC, Smith GD: Albuterol: An adrenergic agent for use in the treatment of asthma: Pharmacology, pharmacokinetics and clinical use. *Pharmacotherapy* 1984;4:105–121.

7. Simons FER, Gillies JD: Dose response of subcutaneous terbutaline and epinephrine in children with acute asthma. *Am J Dis Child* 1981;135:214–217.

8. Dulfano MJ, Glass P: The bronchodilator effects of terbutaline: Route of administration and patterns of response. *Ann Allergy* 1976;37:357–366.

9. Tinkelman DG, Vanderpool GE, Carroll MS, et al: Comparison of nebulized terbutaline and subcutaneous epinephrine in the treatment of acute asthma. *Ann Allergy* 1983;50:398–401.

10. Baughman RP, Ploysongsang Y, James W: A comparative study of aerosolized terbutaline and subcutaneously administered epinephrine in the treatment of acute bronchial asthma. *Ann Allergy* 1984;53:131–134.

11. Newhouse MT, Dolovich MB: Control of asthma by aerosols. *N Engl J Med* 1986;315:870–874.

12. Gross NJ, Skorodin MS: Anticholinergic, antimuscarinic bronchodilators. *Am Rev Respir Dis* 1984;129:856–870.

13. Hemstreet MPB: Atropine nebulization: Simple and safe. *Ann Allergy* 1980;44:138–141.

14. Beck R, Robertson C, Galdes-Sebaldt M, et al: Combined salbutamol and ipratropium bromide by inhalation in the treatment of severe acute asthma. *J Pediatr* 1985;107:605–608.

15. Rebuck AS, Gent M, Chapman KR: Anticholinergic and sympathomimetic combination therapy. *J Allergy Clin Immunol* 1983;71:317–323.

16. Littenberg B, Gluck EH: A controlled trial of methylprednisolone in the emergency treatment of acute asthma. *N Engl J Med* 1986;314:150–152.

17. Lenny W, Milner AD: Nebulized sodium cromoglycate in the preschool wheezy child. *Arch Dis Child* 1978;53:474–476.

19. Pharmacologic Approach to Acute Asthma

David Elkayam, MD

Asthma is one of the most commonly encountered childhood conditions. Asthma is characterized by an increased responsiveness of the airways to various stimuli and manifested by reversible obstruction to airflow. This presents clinically as episodic periods of wheezing and dyspnea. Chronic cough without associated wheezing or dyspnea has been found as well to represent a milder form of asthma, especially in childhood.

The sine qua non of asthma is the ability to show *reversibility* of the heightened resistance to airflow and concomitant airway obstruction. This change is effected by bronchoconstricting provocation or specific bronchodilating medications. When airflow is measured, a reversible change of at least 15% of the predicted FEV_1 from baseline must be achieved.

In clinical practice, however, most physicians are confronted with a patient who has had an acute or subacute deterioration in respiratory status and is in significant distress. A rapid, coordinated, and cohesive therapeutic program must be initiated.

Should the child be treated aggressively with one type of bronchodilator or are multiple medications of greater benefit? Should therapy be administered orally, parenterally, by nebulizer, or a combination of these? Are corticosteroids beneficial in all cases of severe bronchospasm?

The number of medications for the treatment of asthma is large and is growing rapidly: beta-adrenergic agonists, theophylline, cholinergic antagonists, cromolyn sodium, and corticosteroids. There are distinct advantages to using specific agents, although combination therapy with two or more is commonly employed.

BETA-ADRENERGIC AGENTS

Highly selective beta-adrenergic agents offer rapid relief from bronchospasm. They are the primary drugs for management of acute exacerbation of reactive airways, whether caused by chronic asthma, exercise-induced bronchospasm, or bronchospasm secondary to viral upper respiratory tract infection (URI), allergen exposure, smoke, or other specific triggers.

Patients with mild or intermittent asthma may often be maintained relatively symptom-free using beta-agonists alone. Of the medications currently licensed for use in the United States, the most efficacious seem to be terbutaline sulfate and albuterol; although both are widely used, only albuterol is FDA-approved for use in children under 12 years of age.[1]

Comparisons of routine doses of terbutaline administered by oral, subcutaneous (SC), and inhaled routes demonstrated greater effectiveness of the *inhaled route*. The inhaled aerosol induced the most rapid, substantial, and sustained response. Subcutaneous therapy had a rapid onset of effect, but even maximal doses of 0.50 mg of terbutaline sulfate injected SC produced significantly less bronchodilation than 0.375 mg of inhaled terbutaline sulfate aerosol; the duration of action was significantly less with the SC route. Administration of 5.0 mg of terbutaline sulfate orally was notable for a 2-hour delay in achieving maximal bronchodilation, and the peak effect was less by the oral route than by aerosol inhalation.[2–6] Skeletal muscle tremor and cardiovascular effects, including tachycardia and widening of the pulse pressure, although commonly seen after oral administration, are rarely seen with inhalation therapy except at high supratherapeutic doses.

Intravenous (IV) administration of albuterol or terbutaline causes substantial adverse reactions, even at doses which achieve submaximal therapeutic effects. Use of intravenous $beta_2$-selective agents is limited by unavoidable side effects.[3,4,7] Although continuous isoproterenol infusion is used extensively in severe status asthmaticus for impending respiratory failure and as an adjunct to mechanical ventilation, this approach is complicated by evidence of iatrogenically-induced ischemic myocardial damage; its continued use is therefore questioned.[8] Frequent parenteral doses of terbutaline may be safer and more efficacious.[1]

The differential effect of inhalational and parenteral administration of beta-agonists on proximal and distal airways is the subject of controversy. Relatively equivalent doses of albuterol were administered intravenously or by inhalation to a group of severely asthmatic patients (mean peak expiratory flow rate of 102 L/min). Two inhaled doses produced bronchodilation equivalent to IV administration followed by inhalational treatment. A similar study comparing inhaled or injected terbutaline in patients with severe obstruction (FEV_1 less than 25% predicted) showed relatively equal degrees of bronchodilation. Studies[9] using sophisticated pulmonary function assessments showed no differential effect upon distal airways by parenteral administration of beta-adrenergic agents.

Although it is clear that inhaled beta-adrenergic agonists are best in achieving rapid bronchodilation, this approach may be compromised by several factors. During severe exacerbations of asthma, high inspiratory flow rates, low tidal volumes, and narrowed, obstructed airways reduce effective delivery of the medication to peripheral airways. Additionally, dyspneic patients are often unable to coordinate the discharge and inhalation of medication from a metered-dose inhaler (MDI). This is one reason why patients with exacerbation of asthma may need much greater amounts of inhaled medication to achieve maximal bronchodilatory response, sometimes 5 to 10 times the patient's regular dose.[10] The wide therapeutic indices of terbutaline and albuterol allow for the safe administration of even these large doses.[10]

Young children are especially prone to improper use of MDIs. Pressure-driven nebulizers are recommended for those under six years old for delivery of inhalational treatments.[1] Even young and uncooperative children may be given inhalational treatments successfully if a mask is attached to a continuous nebulizer. The approach of the caregiver (often the mother) must be firm and consistent in these situations. Much of the medication may be lost to the surrounding environment under these circumstances, and dosage and adjustments may be indicated. Relatively high dosages of beta-agonists have been used successfully and safely even in small children, owing to the high safety margin of these agents.

The current manufacturer's instructions regarding MDI administration may be suboptimal. The best method is to discharge the MDI toward an open mouth from a distance of 3 to 4 cm. The MDI should be activated simultaneously with the beginning of a slow inspiration (lasting approximately 5 seconds) from functional residual capacity (the end of a normal exhalation) to total lung capacity. This procedure should be followed by 10 seconds of breathholding. This method administers up to twice as much medication to the lower respiratory tract as the closed mouth technique. The toxicity of inhaled fluorinated hydrocarbons seems to be minimal. The use of spacer devices, especially those with large reservoirs (greater than 700 mL), has been shown to improve lung penetration of active drug without the need for "appropriate" technique, even in the face of severe obstruction.[10]

In summary, parenteral administration of beta-adrenergic agonists is associated with substantial adverse side effects, while producing no greater (and usually less) benefit than inhalational therapy. To achieve maximal response, therapeutic doses may be repeated at 20 to 30 minute intervals over the first 2 hours of treatment. Giving an initial SC injection of a bronchodilating agent to a patient with moderately severe bronchospasm is not supported by current evidence, except when the patient's respiratory compromise does not permit adequate inhalational therapy.

THEOPHYLLINE

Should acute exacerbations of asthma be treated with intravenous theophylline? The different intracellular effects of beta-agonists and methylxanthines should lead to an additive or synergistic bronchodilatory effect. Combination therapy with beta-adrenergic agonists and theophylline has been shown to be effective, both in vitro and in clinical studies of stable asthmatic patients.[11–14] However, treatment of severe acute exacerbations of asthma with combination therapy of IV aminophylline and beta-agonists was shown not to produce a statistically significant difference in the rate of improvement or the absolute improvement at 60 or 90 minutes after initiation of therapy when compared with sympathomimetic therapy alone.[11,15] Moreover, there is a greater likelihood of adverse effects such as tremor, nausea, vomiting, headache, and palpitations when combination therapy is used.[16] Additionally, young children are often unreliable historians, possibly leading to incorrect theophylline loading dosage estimates and potential iatrogenic toxicity.[15]

In conclusion, beta-agonists have a pre-eminent role in the initial management of acute exacerbations of asthma. Intravenous aminophylline should be reserved for severe exacerbations that do not respond to maximal sympathomimetic therapy.[11]

Based on the current state of our knowledge, it is recommended that initiation of IV aminophylline therapy *not* be routinely instituted during the first hour of aggressive therapy. This mode of therapy is indicated when it is apparent that sustained hospital-based treatment will be necessary.

Despite its lack of demonstrable benefit in the initial management of bronchospastic episodes, theophylline is an important component of the therapeutic program, whether a patient is to be admitted or discharged. Whether oral or IV loading is more efficacious depends on the particular patient. Careful consideration must be given to recent dosing and current serum theophylline levels. It should be remembered, however, that institution of theophylline therapy in no way offsets the importance of continued beta-agonist therapy.

ANTICHOLINERGICS

The role of anticholinergic medications in the treatment of acute asthma is unresolved. Inhaled anticholinergic medications such as atropine sulfate and the newly-released ipratropium bromide (Atrovent) have been shown to produce substantial bronchodilation in patients with asthma. However, studies[17] of patients with severe, acute exacerbations of asthma have yielded conflicting results as to the efficacy of combined adrenoreceptor agonist and anticholinergic therapy. When adrenergic agonists are given in relatively large doses, no additive effect is gained from additional treatment with ipratropium or atropine.[18,19] However, when adrenergic agonists are delivered in smaller or less frequent doses, there does seem to be an additive response to the addition of anticholinergic treatments.[20,21] At the current time, therefore, routine administration of cholinergic antagonists in the treatment of acute asthma does not seem warranted, especially if sympathomimetic therapy is maximized.

CORTICOSTEROIDS

The role of corticosteroids in the treatment of acute exacerbations of asthma is no longer debated. Their beneficial effects are multifold but are primarily related to their anti-inflammatory properties as well as reversing beta-receptor down-regulation, a phenomenon recognized clinically as "subsensitivity." A single dose of IV hydrocortisone will counteract the chronic desensitizing effects of beta-agonists in as little as 3 hours.[22] When compared with placebo, administration of corticosteroid medications to patients with severe acute asthma results in very beneficial responses. Serial spirometric measurements of forced expiratory volume showed more rapid and greater improvements in steroid-treated patients than nonsteroid-treated patients when all other bronchodilator treatments were identical.[23]

Controversy persists in the appropriate dosing, choice of drug, and route of administration. In the treatment of status asthmaticus, evidence has accumulated that moderate-to-high–dosage corticosteroid therapy, eg, methylprednisolone 2 to 5 mg/kg/day, gives more rapid and significant relief from bronchospasm than a low-dose regimen of approximately 1 mg/kg/day of the same medication.[24] However, very high doses, eg, 10 mg/kg/day, do not seem more beneficial than medium-high dosages and would unnecessarily increase the risk of sodium retention, glycosuria, hypertension, and other adverse side effects of steroids, which are uncommon except at very high dosages.[25] The choice of corticosteroid for treatment of asthma is not critical; maximal glucocorticoid activity and minimal mineralocorticoid activity are the most important criteria. Perhaps the most commonly used parenteral preparation is methylprednisolone sodium succinate (Solu-Medrol), but equipotent doses of hydrocortisone or dexamethasone may be substituted. Corticosteroid treatment for status asthmaticus is usually initiated IV. The advantages are more rapid and complete delivery of the drug with an earlier peak effect.[24] However, in less severe exacerbations of asthma, oral corticosteroids such as prednisone and methylprednisolone are very efficacious. In an oral dose–response study[25] with prednisolone (Medrol), in a group of chronic asthmatic patients experiencing subacute exacerbations, the highest dosage regimen (0.6 mg/kg/day) produced greater response than medium (0.4 mg/kg/day) or low (0.2 mg/kg/day) dosage regimens.[26] Aerosolized corticosteroids such as beclomethasone dipropionate (Beclovent, Vanceril), triamcinolone acetonide (Azmacort), and flunisolide (AeroBid) have proven to be very useful adjuncts in the treatment of chronic asthma. Although few authorities advocate their use in severe, life-threatening asthma, minor deteriorations in pulmonary status may be treated with increased doses of aerosolized corticosteroids. Although adrenal suppression is minimized by administration of inhaled steroids, patients using them must still be considered at risk for sudden death secondary to adrenal insufficiency at times of traumatic, infectious, or surgical stress as well as acute severe exacerbations of their asthma.[10]

In summary, corticosteroids have a central role in the management of asthma and are a cornerstone for the treatment of status asthmaticus.[26] In the former instance, aerosolized steroids delivered by MDIs may well help optimize control of all but the mildest asthma. In the latter circumstance, systemic therapy, usually IV, is preferred. Relatively high, supraphysiologic doses appear to offer the greatest benefit, whereas megadoses do not produce additional bronchodilation.

CONCLUSION

The physician treating a child with acute exacerbation of asthma must employ a comprehensive, yet individualized approach. Oxygen therapy should never be overlooked. Beta-adrenergic agonistic therapy should be used in all patients.

Sympathomimetic drugs, such as the selective beta-adrenergic agonists, seem to be the most highly efficacious therapeutic agents for the relief of acute bronchospasm. Aerosolized preparations, delivered either via compressed-air nebulizer or MDI, offer unsurpassed efficacy in relieving bronchospasm. The need for injected sympathomimetic medications is therefore mitigated, except in exceptional circumstances. Intravenous aminophylline appears to offer little added benefit and substantial adverse side effects when used concomitantly with beta-selective agonists in the initial treatment of severe bronchospasm. However, in cases refractory to maximal beta-agonist therapy, eg, status asthmaticus, it still has an important role. Most authorities feel theophylline medications are still quite important for management of moderate-to-severe chronic asthma. The role of inhaled cholinergic antagonists in management of acute exacerbations of asthma is not fully defined, but they may provide additional bronchodilation in certain circumstances. Corticosteroids are essential for the treatment of status asthmaticus. Oral steroids are useful for treating subacute exacerbations of chronic asthma and inhaled steroids have become very useful in the management of chronic asthma.

REFERENCES

1. Nelson HS: Adrenergic therapy of bronchial asthma. *J Allergy Clin Immunol* 1986; 77:771–785.

2. Dulfano MS, Glass P: The bronchodilator effects of terbutaline: Route of administration and patterns of response. *Ann Allergy* 1976;37:357–366.

3. Pierce RJ, Payne CR, Williams SJ, et al: Comparison of intravenous and inhaled terbutaline in the treatment of asthma. *Chest* 1981;79:506–511.

4. Thuringer G, Svedmyr N: Comparison of infused and inhaled terbutaline in patients with asthma. *Scand J Respir Dis* 1976;57:17–24.

5. Weber RW, Petty WE, Nelson HS: Aerosolized terbutaline in asthmatics: Comparison of dosage strength, schedule and method of administration. *J Allergy Clin Immunol* 1979; 63:116–121.

6. Weber RW, Smith JA, Nelson HS: Aerosolized terbutaline in asthmatics: Development of subsensitivity with long-term administration. *J Allergy Clin Immunol* 1982;70:417–422.

7. Williams SJ, Winner SJ, Clark TJH: Comparison of inhaled and intravenous terbutaline in acute severe asthma. *Thorax* 1981;36:629–631.

8. Reed CE: Aerosols in chronic airway disease, editorial. *N Engl J Med* 1986;315:888–889.

9. Shaw RJS, Waller JF, Hetzel MR, et al: Do oral and inhaled terbutaline have different effects on the lung? *Br J Dis Chest* 1982;76:171–176.

10. Newhouse MT, Dolovich MB: Control of asthma by aerosols. *N Engl J Med* 1986; 315:870–874.

11. Fanta CH, Rossing TH, McFadden ER: Treatment of acute asthma: Is combination therapy with sympathomimetics and methylxanthines indicated? *Am J Med* 1986;80:5–10.

12. Smith JA, Weber RW, Nelson HS: Theophylline and aerosolized terbutaline in the treatment of bronchial asthma. Double blind comparison of optimal doses. *Chest* 1980; 78:816–818.

13. Vandewalker ML, Kray KT, Weber RW, et al: Addition of terbutaline to optimal theophylline therapy. Double blind crossover study in asthmatic patients. *Chest* 1986;90:198–203.

14. Wolfe JD, Tashkin DP, Calvarese B, et al: Bronchodilator effects of terbutaline and aminophylline alone and in combination in asthmatic patients. *N Engl J Med* 1978;298:363–367.

15. Josephson GW, MacKenzie EJ, Lietman PS, et al: Emergency treatment of asthma, a comparison of two treatment regimens. *JAMA* 1979;242:639–643.

16. Siegel D, Sheppard D, Gelb A, et al: Aminophylline increases the toxicity but not the efficacy of an inhaled beta-adrenergic agonist in the treatment of acute exacerbations of asthma. *Am Rev Resp Dis* 1985;132:282–286.

17. Sly RM, Anderson JA, Bierman CW, et al: Adverse effects and complications of treatment with beta-adrenergic agonist drugs. *J Allergy Clin Immunol* 1985;75:443–449.

18. Easton PA: A comparison of the bronchodilating effects of a beta-2 adrenergic agent (albuterol) and an anticholinergic agent (ipratropium bromide) given by aerosol alone or in sequence. *N Engl J Med* 1986;315:735–739.

19. Karpel JP, Appel D, Breidbart D, et al: A comparison of atropine sulfate and meta-proterenol sulfate in the emergency treatment of asthma. *Am Rev Respir Dis* 1986;133:727–729.

20. Beck R, Robertson C, Galdes-Sebaldt M, et al: Combined salbutamol and ipratropium bromide by inhalation in the treatment of severe acute asthma. *J Pediatr* 1985;107:605–608.

21. Bryant DH: Nebulized ipratropium bromide in the treatment of acute asthma. *Chest* 1985;88:24–29.

22. Holgate ST, Baldwin CJ, Tattersfield AE: Beta-adrenergic agonist resistance in normal human airways. *Lancet* 1977;1:375–377.

23. Fanta CH, Rossing TH, McFadden ER: Glucocorticoids in acute asthma. *Am J Med* 1983;74:845–851.

24. Haskell RJ, Wong BM, Hansen JE: A double-blind, randomized clinical trial of methyl-prednisolone in status asthmaticus. *Arch Intern Med* 1983;143:1324–1327.

25. Raimondi A, Figueroa-Casas JC, Roncoroni AJ, et al: Comparison between high and moderate doses of hydrocortisone in the treatment of status asthmaticus. *Chest* 1986; 89:832–835.

26. Webb JR: Dose response of patients to oral corticosteroid treatment during exacerbations of asthma. *Br Med J* 1986;292:1045–1047.

Section 8

Croup

Croup is a common cause of upper airway obstruction in children. It requires prompt recognition, careful differentiation from epiglottitis and bacterial tracheitis, and aggressive early management. A variety of objective scoring systems and pulse oximetry may assist in the clinical assessment of the child.

Racemic epinephrine provides transient resolution of the relative obstruction but is associated with a "rebound" phenomenon after administration; hospitalization is therefore required. Although steroids remain controversial because of the lack of consistent prospective data, most clinicians have observed a beneficial effect in the management of viral croup.

20. Croup: Management Controversies

Jeffrey S. Schiff, MD

Acute upper airway obstruction in children is among the most emergent of problems. It is imperative that the correct diagnosis is made promptly and appropriate management initiated to ensure a favorable outcome. Croup, bacterial tracheitis, epiglottitis, and aspirated foreign body are the most common conditions causing obstruction. Croup and bacterial tracheitis are the focus of this discussion.

The terminology of acute upper airway obstruction is somewhat confusing. Appropriate terminology should accurately describe both etiology and anatomic location. Croup was originally used to describe all forms of obstruction including epiglottitis and diphtheria. Currently it is commonly used to describe only viral and spasmodic types of upper airway obstruction. The term "laryngotracheobronchitis" (LTB) commonly used to describe upper airway obstruction caused by viral agents, will be used only when preceded by the appropriate causal agent.[1]

CLINICAL PRESENTATION

Viral laryngotracheobronchitis describes an acute upper airway obstruction preceded by an upper respiratory tract infection (URI) with an associated fever. It has little or no response to inhaled mist and has an onset of symptoms at any time of the day. The entity occurs more frequently in the winter months.[2]

The term *"virus" croup* was first used in 1948. Subsequently the condition was shown to have a viral etiology.[3-6] Denny et al[2] isolated viral agents in 360 of 951 episodes of croup. The majority were parainfluenza (48% type 1, 17.5% type 3 and 8.6% type 2). Additional causal agents include respiratory syncytial virus, *Hemophilus influenzae* types A and B, and *Mycoplasma pneumoniae*.

Spasmodic croup describes an acute subglottic obstruction, usually nocturnal in onset. Davison[7] observed pale-water edema of the conus elasticus, the area immediately below the vocal cords. There is little or no prodrome of respiratory tract infection or associated fever. An IgE mediated allergenic response to viral agents is currently implied but not proven to be associated with recurrences.[8] Nebulized mist is the mainstay of treatment. A response to mist is assumed but not proven to indicate spasmodic rather than viral croup. This observation was used in some studies[9,10] as a distinguishing factor.

In contrast, purulent upper airway drainage that is culture positive for bacteria has been "rediscovered." *Bacterial tracheitis* is characterized by a 1- to 6-day prodrome of URI with croup symptoms. Fever, toxicity, and acute progressive upper airway obstruction develop acutely.[11] Patients do not attempt to splint open their airways. This observation along with the relatively long prodrome distinguishes bacterial tracheitis from epiglottitis. Radiologic evaluation of the upper airway identifies "membranes" in 32% of cases.[12] Pneumonia is present in 53% to 100% of patients.[11,12] The total white blood cell count is relatively normal; there is a significant increase in bands (average 34.6%).[11]

The diagnosis of bacterial tracheitis is confirmed by endoscopic examination showing acute inflammation of the subglottic tracheal mucosa often with more distal extension to involve the trachea and bronchial tree. Copious purulent or mucopurulent exudate (34 of 71 cases) or a pseudomembrane easily separable from the mucosa (37 of 71 cases) is present.[13] Gram's stain shows many neutrophils and most often a predominant organism. *Staphylococcus aureus* has been cultured from the tracheal exudate in 74% of patients.[14] Other organisms found include *Hemophilus influenzae*, alpha streptococcus, *Streptococcus pyrogenes, Streptococcus pneumoniae*, and *Pseudomonas aeruginosa*.[14–16] Blood cultures are uniformly negative. Viral cultures have been positive for parainfluenza and influenza, underlining the observation that bacterial tracheitis may represent a superinfection in patients with viral LTB.[12,14,17]

Patients with bacterial tracheitis virtually always need aggressive airway management to permit vigorous tracheobronchial suctioning. The duration of intubation is much longer than that required for epiglottitis because of the persistence of copious purulent secretions. Antibiotic therapy is directed toward *S aureus* and common respiratory pathogens. In two reports,[11,16] 4 of 12 patients suffered cardiopulmonary arrests because the diagnosis was initially missed. In three studies,[11,15,16] a total of 18 cases of bacterial tracheitis were diagnosed during an interval in which 35 cases of epiglottitis were diagnosed and 436 patients with croup were hospitalized.

ASSESSING THE CROUP PATIENT

Evaluating the course and response to therapy of upper airway obstruction is the source of much controversy. Most studies[5,6,18] used subjective scoring systems and some objective data (respiratory rate, PaO_2).

The scoring systems, using arbitrary units and subjective variables, are the subject of much criticism. They assign increasing point values to increasing levels of respiratory distress. Variables assessed include color, cyanosis, stridor, retractions, air entry, level of consciousness, cough, anxiety, heart rate, and respiratory rate. The units assigned to each variable are arbitrary and vary greatly among studies, as shown in Table 20-1. These scales, however, serve to assign a numerical value to the same variables used to judge the clinical severity of upper airway obstruction. A score that gives weight only to clinical features relatively specific for upper airway obstruction is a useful tool for examining patients (Table 20-2).[19]

Other more objective measurements have not correlated as well with clinical improvement. Respiratory rate, which is frequently used along with the croup score, is a less sensitive but more objective assessment of changes in the clinical course.[20,21] Arterial blood gas determinations of hypoxemia and hypercapnea have not correlated reliably with clinical variables.[22] Total respiratory resistance, measured by frequency oscillation, is an objective measure of airway obstruction.[23] Unfortunately, it is technically complicated and its original use is described only in cooperative older children.

Table 20-1 Croup Score Variables

Variable	No. of Studies	Range of Maximum Point Value	Range of Score (%)
Color/cyanosis	5	2-5	20-29
Stridor	5	2-3	12-21
Retractions	5	1-3	9-19
Air entry	3	2-3	12-21
Level of consciousness	3	2-5	14-29
Anxiety/air hunger	1	2	20
Cough	1	2	20
Respiratory rate	1	3	27
Heart rate	1	3	27
Total	25	10-17	

Sources: British Medical Journal (1965;1:614), Copyright © 1965, British Medical Association; *New England Journal of Medicine* (1959;261:1–9), Copyright © 1959, Massachusetts Medical Society; *Pediatrics* (1973;52:68–71), Copyright © 1973, American Academy of Pediatrics.

Table 20-2 Croup Score Ratings

Clinical Variables	0	1	2
Inspiratory breath sounds	Normal	Harsh	Delayed
Stridor	None	Inspiratory	Inspiratory and expiratory
Cough	None	Hoarse cry	Bark
Retractions and flaring	None	Flaring and supersternal retractions	As under 1 plus subcostal, intercostal retractions
Cyanosis	None	In room air	In 40% O_2
Total croup score points (0 = normal; 10 = most severe)			

Source: Reprinted with permission from *Anesthesiology* (1975;43:242–250), Copyright © 1975, JB Lippincott Company.

Pulse oximetry is a noninvasive tool for the assessment of hypoxemia during upper airway obstruction. To date, pulse oximetry data have not been correlated with any other measure of croup severity. For the present, croup must be recognized as a clinical entity for which use of clinical variables to assess outcome of therapeutic intervention is appropriate.

THERAPEUTIC INTERVENTION

Two therapeutic interventions, the use of inhaled epinephrine and the use of steroids, are subjects of much controversy.

Racemic Epinephrine

The use of inhaled racemic epinephrine by intermittent positive pressure breathing (IPPB) for the treatment of laryngotracheobronchitis was introduced by Jordan et al.[24] Adair et al[25] in a large retrospective study (N = 780) showed that tracheostomy could be prevented by delivery of racemic epinephrine via IPPB. Subsequent prospective double-blind studies[5,6,18,26] reported generally positive results. Clinical symptoms lessened immediately after the use of racemic epinephrine. These studies were criticized because viral LTB was inadequately differentiated from spasmodic croup, and because sample sizes were small.[27]

Lenny and Milner[23] avoided the use of croup scores by measuring total respiratory resistance. This variable fell 30% in eight patients after the use of aerosolized phenylephrine hydrochloride, a potent alpha agonist, delivered by IPPB. The total respiratory resistance rose 7.6% after use of water as control. Fogel et al[9] subsequently showed nebulization alone was as effective as the more complicated delivery via IPPB.

The relief of airway obstruction after administration of racemic epinephrine or phenylephrine is transient and does not affect the total duration of illness. Symptoms, as judged by croup scores, return to pretreatment severity within 2 hours of epinephrine nebulization.[9,10] This is termed the "rebound" phenomenon. No studies have documented a worsening of clinical symptoms after the epinephrine is metabolized. In some patients the "rebound" may actually reflect the course of the disease. Because of the transient duration of improvement, all children treated with racemic epinephrine must be hospitalized or observed for a minimum of 8 hours in an outpatient holding area to assess the course of their airway obstruction. Further objective studies should separate viral LTB from spasmodic croup, include an appropriate croup score, and measure respiratory rate and oxygenation by pulse oximetry during racemic epinephrine therapy and the "rebound" period.

Steroids

The uses of corticosteroids for the treatment of croup was first suggested 30 years ago.[28] An episode of viral LTB or spasmodic croup is thought to be caused by an inflammatory response involving increased permeability of the capillary endothelium. This increased capillary permeability is responsible for edematous formation and hence symptoms of upper respiratory tract obstruction. Corticosteroids block the inflammatory response at the cellular level, thereby modulating the increased capillary permeability. After a large parenteral dosage, the onset of action is considered to be approximately 2 hours. In contrast to racemic epinephrine, steroids are purported to decrease the duration of illness. No rebound has been suggested.

Since their introduction in 1954, many studies have addressed the use of steroids for croup. The conclusions of these reports are controversial.[1,29,30] The controversy centers on three major criticisms: (1) Patient selection protocols did not until recently distinguish viral LTB from spasmodic croup. As mentioned previously, it is not known, but is generally assumed, that these are unique entities. Furthermore, pretreatment severity was often not addressed. (2) The dosage, schedule, and route of administration varied widely, and the dosages varied 50 fold. (3) Clinical criteria were generally used for assessing outcome.[24,30] Fewer of these studies[31,32] used a "croup score" to measure relief of obstructive symptoms than did those evaluating racemic epinephrine therapy.

Several studies have addressed the use of steroids with appropriate methodology. The conclusions of these studies are not uniform. Koren et al[21] showed no decrease in respiratory rate in 22 patients *v* 27 controls with acute laryngotracheitis (viral LTB) after a single large intramuscular dose of dexamethasone sodium. In contrast, two studies of patients with viral LTB showed improved symptoms as measured by clinical scores recorded by blinded examiners. Massicottee and Tétreault[32] reported an improvement in 25 study *v* 17 control patients at 4 hours of 80% *v* 41% and at 8 hours of 96% *v* 47% on a protocol of 4 mg/kg of methylprednisolone every 4 hours for three doses. Similar positive findings in patients with viral LTB were reported by Tunnessen.[33] Overall these data promise a role for corticosteroids in the treatment of viral LTB.

The efficacy of steroids in the treatment of spasmodic croup is also unclear. Well-controlled studies measuring respiratory rate or clinical scores have shown conflicting results. Two studies reported significant improvement after treatment with dexamethasone,[21,33] but another[32] did not. Because abrupt onset and rapid resolution is the natural history of spasmodic croup, interpretation of these data is difficult.

Resolution of the steroid controversy awaits further well-controlled prospective studies. These should distinguish LTB from spasmodic croup and use both clinical scores and objective assessments of severity (respiratory rate and pulse oximetry).

CONCLUSION

The efficacy of racemic epinephrine is well established in the management of the child with upper airway obstruction secondary to croup. Steroids have a less well-established role but are commonly used.

REFERENCES

1. Cherry JD: The treatment of croup: Continued controversy due to failure of recognition of historic, ecologic, etiologic and clinical perspectives. *J Pediatr* 1979;94:352–354.

2. Denny FW, Muraphy TF, Clyde WA, et al: Croup: An 11-year study in a pediatric practice. *Pediatrics* 1983;71:871–876.

3. Rabe EF: Infectious Croup: I. Etiology. *Pediatrics* 1948;2:255–265.

4. Rabe EF: Infectious Croup: II. "Virus" croup. *Pediatrics* 1948;2:415–427.

5. Halzel A: Virus isolations from throats of children admitted to hospital with respiratory and other diseases, Manchester 1962-64. *Br Med J* 1965;1:614.

6. Vargosko AJ, Chanock RM, Huebner RJ, et al: Association of type 2 hemadsorption (parainfluenza 1) virus and Asian influenza A virus with infectious croup. *New Engl J Med* 1959;261:1–9.

7. Davison FW: Acute laryngeal obstruction in children. *JAMA* 1959:171:1301–1305.

8. Welliver RC: Advances in the understanding of the croup. *Pediatr Virology* 1987;2:1–5.

9. Fogel JM, Berg IJ, Gerber MA, Sherter CB: Racemic epinephrine in the treatment of croup: Nebulization alone versus nebulization with intermittent positive pressure breathing. *J Pediatr* 1982;101:1028–1031.

10. Westley CR, Cotton EK, Brooks JG: Nebulized racemic epinephrine by IPPB for the treatment of croup. *Am J Dis Child* 1978;132:484–487.

11. Sofer S, Duncan P, Chernick V: Bacterial tracheitis: An old disease rediscovered. *Clin Pediatr* 1983;22:407–411.

12. Han BK, Dunbar JS, Striker TW: Membranous laryngotracheobronchitis (membranous croup). *AJR* 1979;133:53–58.

13. Nelson WE: Bacterial croup: A historical perspective, editor's column. *J Pediatr* 1984;105:52–55.

14. Henry RL, Mellis CM, Benjamin B: Pseudomembraneous croup. *Arch Dis Child* 1983;58:180–183.

15. Jones R, Santos JI, Overall JC: Bacterial tracheitis. *JAMA* 1979;242:721–726.

16. Mahajan A, Alvear D, Chang C, et al: Bacterial tracheitis, diagnosis and treatment. *Int J Pediatr Otorhinolaryngol* 1985;10:271–277.

17. Edwards KM, Dundon MC, Altemeier WA: Bacterial tracheitis as a complication of viral croup. *Pediatr Infect Dis* 1983;2:390.

18. Gardner G, Powell K, Roden V, et al: The evaluation of racemic epinephrine in the treatment of infectious croup. *Pediatr* 1973;52:68–71.

19. Downes JJ, Raphaely R: Pediatric intensive care. *Anesthesiology* 1975;43:242–250.

20. Skowron PN, Turner JA, McNaughton GA: The use of corticosteroid (dexamethasone) in the treatment of acute laryngotracheitis. *Can Med Assoc J* 1966;94:528–531.

21. Koren G, Frand M, Barzilay Z, et al: Corticosteroid treatment of laryngotracheitis v spasmodic croup in children. *Am J Dis Child* 1983;137:941–944.

22. Newth CJ, Levison CB, Bryan AC: The respiratory status of children with croup. *J Pediatr* 1972;81:1068–1073.

23. Lenny W, Milner AD: Treatment of acute viral croup. *Arch Dis Child* 1978;53:704–706.

24. Jordan WS, Graves CL, Elwyn RA: New therapy for postintubation laryngeal edema and tracheitis in children. *JAMA* 1970;212:585–588.

25. Adair JC, Ring WH, Jordan WS, et al: Ten-year experience with IPPB in the treatment of acute laryngotracheobronchitis. *Anesth Analg* 1971;50:649–654.

26. Taussig LM, Castro O, Beaudry PH, et al: Treatment of laryngotracheobronchitis (croup). *Am J Dis Child* 1975;129:790–793.

27. Koran G: Efficacy of racemic epinephrine in croup, letter to editor. *J Pediatr* 1983;103:661–662.

28. Martensson B, Nilsson G, Torbjar JE: The effect of corticosteroids in the treatment of pseudo-croup. *Acta Otolaryngol* 1960;158(suppl):62–71.

29. Tunnessen WW, Feinstein AR: The steroid-croup controversy: An analytic review of methodologic problems. *J Pediatr* 1980;96:751–756.

30. Hawkins DB: Corticosteroids in the management of laryngotracheobronchitis. *Otolaryngol Head Neck Surg* 1980;88:207–210.

31. Leipzig B, Oski FA, Cummings CW, et al: A prospective randomized study to determine the efficacy of steroids in treatment of croup. *J Pediatr* 1979;94:194–196.

32. Massicottee P, Tétreault L: Evaluation of methylprednisolone in the treatment of acute laryngitis in children. *Union Med Can* 1973;102:2064–2089.

33. Tunnessen WW: Croup and corticosteroid therapy, letter to editor. *J Pediatr* 1981; 98:506–507.

Section 9

Epiglottitis

Clearly, the approach to the child with upper airway obstruction is controversial and partially based on personal and institutional experience. However, irrespective of the approach selected, it is imperative that a plan for stabilization and management be clearly delineated in advance.

Management alternatives focus on the initial diagnostic test selected and on stabilizing the airway. The relative benefits of the lateral neck x-ray study must be contrasted with direct visualization of the epiglottis. Lateral neck x-ray films provide a noninvasive evaluation of the epiglottis, but false-negatives and false-positives are reported. Furthermore, lateral neck films may require moving the patient to the radiology department unless portable films can be taken, or there is equipment in the emergency department. Once the lateral neck film is completed, direct visualization may still be required.

The technique of direct visualization is relatively safe if safety measures and all precautions are taken to ensure proper equipment and personnel. Preoxygenation is essential, and visualization is best done with the child in the upright position.

Ideally, patients who clinically show an illness consistent with epiglottitis should be visualized in the operating room with appropriate equipment and personnel. The lateral neck x-ray study adds little to the management of such patients since direct visualization is required irrespective of the findings on the radiograph. Patients are generally intubated when the diagnosis is confirmed.

Under all circumstances, the child must be observed closely and with immediate capability to initiate active airway intervention. Although ampicillin and chloramphenicol sodium are the traditional antibiotics of choice, recent evidence supports the efficacy of third generation cephalosporins.

The choice of approach must reflect institutional discussions and evaluation of personnel and equipment, and should be discussed before such a patient arrives.

21. Epiglottitis: Diagnostic and Management Considerations

Steven M. Selbst, MD

Epiglottitis was first described as a clinical entity in the early 1940s. Since then, numerous articles have described the bacteriology, epidemiology, clinical manifestations, and management of this life-threatening infection. Most authors seem to agree that epiglottitis is almost always caused by *Hemophilus influenzae* type B. Most authors agree that the infection can occur at any time of the year, and can affect children of all ages (from infancy to adulthood). Most authors seem to agree that fever and respiratory distress are the most common features of this disease, whereas stridor, drooling, and croupy cough are found less consistently. Most authors agree that the infection can progress rapidly and will cause airway obstruction and death if not properly treated.

Despite this seeming unanimity, there remains considerable controversy about the management of children who are presumed to have epiglottitis. Most of this controversy concerns confirming the diagnosis and preventing morbidity and mortality from the disease. Epiglottitis is managed differently in various parts of the country; treatment is often dependent on the experiences of an individual institution or the particular specialty service managing the patient.

There are two possible reasons for the variations in management of this infection. First, many children with epiglottitis are not in extreme respiratory distress when they initially come for treatment. Many respond very quickly (within hours) to intravenous (IV) ampicillin and IV chloramphenicol sodium, and never develop respiratory distress. However, some will have sudden and complete airway obstruction, and there is no way to predict when this will occur or who is at greatest risk for this outcome.

Second, the pathophysiology of this infection is not completely understood. Despite 40 years of experience with epiglottitis, no one is sure what actually causes some patients to have sudden airway obstruction and death. Some authors[1] believe that respiratory arrest is caused by a swollen, floppy epiglottis that drops into the glottis to cause airway obstruction. Others[2] insist that the epiglottis is rigid when it is inflamed, and that pooled saliva accumulates because of impaired swallowing, which leads to aspiration of oropharyngeal secretions. Fatigue from breathing against a closed glottis may cause respiratory arrest; sudden death from epiglottitis may be caused by hypoxia.[3] Finally, many hypothesize that patients with this infection can have laryngospasm at any time, which rapidly causes airway obstruction and death.

CONFIRMING THE DIAGNOSIS

Visualizing the Epiglottis

There seems to be agreement that the epiglottis should be directly visualized to confirm the diagnosis of epiglottitis, but there is disagreement as to where or when to do so. It has long been believed that it is dangerous to depress a child's tongue forcibly in the emergency department to visualize the epiglottis. This may precipitate laryngospasm and cause sudden death. In fact, many believe that even when this examination is performed, it remains difficult to see the epiglottis. Johnson et al[4] reported that 36 of the 50 patients in their study of children with respiratory distress showed the epiglottis poorly or not at all when a tongue blade was used to examine the pharynx. This study included three patients with epiglottitis. Selbst[5] reported that when an attempt was made to examine the oropharynx in four of eight patients with epiglottitis, the epiglottis was not seen well or was erroneously thought to be normal. Patients have become cyanotic when they were restrained in a supine position to have their pharynx examined with a tongue depressor.[6]

Despite these fears of precipitating laryngospasm, Milko et al[7] reported that the diagnosis of all 41 cases of epiglottitis in their study was safely confirmed by examining the oropharynx with a tongue depressor. Others[3,8,9] believe this examination should be performed only once, because it may be dangerous, and that preoxygenation is the key to preventing complications from this maneuver.

It may be that the real danger to patients involves putting them in a supine position rather than depressing the tongue. However, several reports[2,3,10] indicate that any painful stimulus, such as starting an IV line, can cause a child to cry and precipitate respiratory arrest. Therefore, in view of the potential dangers, and misleading or nonhelpful findings, it does not seem justified to subject a child to direct visualization of the epiglottis in the emergency department. If children are cooperative and can easily open their mouth, the physician may attempt to visualize the epiglottis without putting instruments into the mouth. Otherwise, the diagnosis can be confirmed in a more safe environment, such as the operating room, or with an x-ray film of the lateral neck in lieu of direct visualization.

Lateral Neck Radiograph

The lateral neck radiograph is in itself a controversial point in the management of epiglottitis. Rapkin[11] reported in the early 1970s that such a film was easy to obtain and interpret, and that it reliably confirmed the presence or absence of epiglottitis. It can be obtained without agitating the child. Despite this, many feel that x-ray films are misleading and often waste time in confirming the diagnosis. Certainly, there is a risk involved in transporting any patient with respiratory disease out of the emergency department for radiographs or other procedures. Therefore, some specialists recommend that the x-ray study be eliminated altogether, and that suspected cases be proven in the operating room with direct laryngoscopy in the presence of personnel prepared to manage respiratory complications.

This controversy can be muffled if the lateral neck radiograph is reserved for selected cases of airway obstruction. First, it should be noted that this study is highly sensitive and reliable only if interpreted by an experienced person. If there is no one present who can read such radiographs, the study should not be ordered. Second, the risks of transport can be eliminated if a portable film is obtained in the emergency department. If patients must leave the department for a radiograph, airway equipment and skilled personnel must accompany them for the entire procedure. This will make it possible to deal with a sudden deterioration. The accompanying physicians can also assure that the radiology technicians do not manipulate or aggravate the child such that the airway is compromised while the film is obtained. If the trip seems to be a long one, or the delay in obtaining the x-ray film is unreasonable, the film should not be obtained.

Radiographs should be used only for children for whom the diagnosis of epiglottitis is in doubt. Certainly, the radiograph is not necessary if the child is in moderate or severe distress, if the child has classic clinical findings of epiglottitis, or if the epiglottis is easily visualized when the child opens the mouth. In such cases, the child should be transported directly to the operating room for airway management. Once epiglottitis is noted on the x-ray film, there should be no attempt to obtain blood samples or start an IV line in the emergency department.

MANAGEMENT

The management of the airway is another point of controversy in epiglottitis. Cantrell et al[2] reviewed the literature and found that 16% of 749 patients with epiglottitis, in combined series, developed sudden airway obstruction and required emergency tracheostomies. The mortality rate was 6% when patients were observed for signs of distress before an airway was placed. Similarly, Johnson et al[4] noted that 12 of 41 "observed" patients with epiglottitis developed obstruction; three had complete arrest and one died. Rapkin[12] reported retrospectively a 20% mortality rate with one additional patient left irreversibly brain damaged when artificial airways were not routinely placed in children with this infection.

During the early 1970s, it became apparent that it was safer to place an artificial airway in all patients as soon as the diagnosis of epiglottitis was made. Baxter and Pashley[13] reported a mortality rate of 0.5% in a large series in which all patients with epiglottitis had an artificial airway placed upon their arrival at the hospital.

Despite these statistics, some centers still prefer to observe children with epiglottitis to see if they will improve rapidly. The use of steroids, antibiotics, and even bag-mask ventilation when needed, was used as part of a "noninstrumentation" protocol.[8,14] One study[14] reported 40 cases managed by observation without a death; however, morbidity was not discussed. This approach seems risky since many case reports in the literature describe sudden death when the patient with epiglottitis was closely monitored with physicians nearby. Certainly, an intensive care unit (ICU) physician could be involved with another critically ill patient when the "stable" child with epiglottitis obstructs. Resuscitation of a child with a completely obstructed airway is technically difficult, and failure could cause permanent brain damage or death.

Finally, another useful protocol for airway management describes intubation of the child with epiglottitis in the emergency department with ketamine hydrochloride anesthesia.[15] This protocol safely avoided transport to the operating room and the associated costs.

Which type of artificial airway to choose for a child with epiglottitis is less controversial. Fifteen years ago it was thought to be impossible to intubate the trachea of a child with epiglottitis. Tracheostomy was believed to be the method of choice to establish an airway in such patients. However, with the development of soft, flexible, polyvinyl tubes, it has become possible to intubate a child even with a very inflamed and swollen epiglottis. Several authors have noted that this is a safe and effective way to manage this infection, and that tracheostomy should be performed only in those rare cases in which intubation is impossible. There are surgical risks involved with tracheostomy including possible pneumothorax. A surgical scar is inevitable and hospital stay is prolonged with this procedure. On the other hand, the tracheostomy provides for easier suctioning, and it makes displacement of the artificial airway less likely.

Nasotracheal intubation avoids surgery and scarring. It poses a risk of subglottic stenosis, but this is minimal because the endotracheal tube is rarely needed for more than a few days. This risk is further minimized if a smaller diameter tube is used than one would ordinarily choose for the particular child. Suctioning may be difficult with smaller tubes, and it is necessary for someone to be nearby at all times who could reintubate the patient should the tube become dislodged. Nasal intubation is preferred, but oral tracheal intubation may suffice if the former cannot be accomplished.

Thus, the choice between tracheostomy and endotracheal intubation depends on the preference of the individual center, and the skills and workload of the nursing and medical staffs who care for the child.

Antibiotics

There is little controversy about the choice of antibiotics used to treat this infection. Since it is almost always caused by *H influenzae* type B, which is often resistant to ampicillin, it is wise to treat with IV ampicillin and IV chloramphenicol. The duration of such treatment, however, is debatable. Although most physicians prefer to treat *H influenzae* bacteremia conservatively with 10 days of IV antibiotics, children with epiglottitis are often dramatically improved after only a few days of medications. Faden[16] reported success with the use of 3 to 5 days of parenteral antibiotics followed by oral therapy. Many other institutions have had similar good results with brief courses of IV medications, but there are no controlled data regarding duration of therapy.

The use of steroids to treat epiglottitis is, of course, controversial. Gross[17] reported that steroids are advantageous and described a regimen of 5 mg of dexamethasone given intravenously for the first 5 kg of body weight and 1 mg for each additional 5 kg. This dose was repeated every 15 minutes until a response was noted, or was discontinued after 2 hours if there was no response. Strome and Jaffee[8] recommended similar steroid therapy. However, no controlled studies show steroids to be of value in treating epiglottitis. On the contrary, Johnson et al[4] reported no substantial difference in the duration of hospital stay or need for tracheostomy when 34 patients with epiglottitis who received steroids were compared with 21 who did not. Likewise, a retrospective study[18] of 64 children with epiglottitis at the Children's Hospital of Philadelphia failed to reveal any difference in the duration of intubation or tracheostomy or hospital stay when use or omission of steroids was compared. Despite this, some physicians at that institution still feel steroids help reduce the edema of epiglottitis.

The use of racemic epinephrine in epiglottitis is *not* controversial. It may increase oxygen demands or precipitate laryngospasm, and it should not be used in this disease.

Transport

Another dilemma involves the difficult questions of when and how to transport a child with epiglottitis to another facility. Most would agree that children with this infection should be managed at a hospital capable of handling complete airway obstruction. Certainly, an office or emergency department physician who is not skilled in pediatric airway management should arrange to transport the child to another facility. This should be done by ambulance, instead of the parents' car. The physician or person most adept at airway management should stay with the child at all times. There is some disagreement about the need to establish an artificial airway under less than ideal conditions before transport. Ideally, a transport team from the admitting hospital should come to pick up the patient and, if possible, establish an artificial airway before the return trip to the admitting hospital. Even a short ride back to the hospital can be a long nightmare if the child has a respiratory arrest en route. As noted previously, the intubation of a patient with epiglottitis is challenging under ideal circumstances, let alone in the back of an ambulance. However, this becomes a more difficult problem if there is not an equipped operating room at the transferring hospital or personnel capable of performing a tracheostomy should intubation attempts fail. Also, there is debate about how to manage the patient while awaiting help, especially if the transport team must come a long distance.

It seems reasonable that no attempts be made by unskilled personnel to establish an airway unless the patient is completely obstructed. Even then, it should be remembered that such children can sometimes be resuscitated by mouth-to-mouth or bag-mask ventilation. The benefits of starting antibiotic therapy while waiting for help are even less clear. Breviak and Klaastad[3] recommended oral ampicillin if the patient could still swallow and if there would be a long delay in transport. However, the effectiveness of this approach seems doubtful. Intravenous or intramuscular antibiotics would be more useful. Their administration is not without risk, as noted earlier, but waiting several hours for help to arrive may be even more dangerous.

CONCLUSION

Epiglottitis is a life-threatening condition requiring prompt recognition and diagnosis, the latter being accomplished by lateral neck x-ray studies or direct visualization under controlled conditions. Airway stabilization can best be done in the operating room, followed by antibiotic treatment.

REFERENCES

1. Vetto RR: Epiglottitis, report of thirty-seven cases. *JAMA* 1960;173:990–995.

2. Cantrell RW, Bell RA, Morioka WI: Acute epiglottitis: Intubation versus tracheostomy. *Laryngoscope* 1978;88:994–1004.

3. Breviak H, Klaastad O: Acute epiglottitis in children, review of 27 patients. *Br J Anaesthesiol* 1978;50:505–510.

4. Johnson GK, Sullivan JL, Bishop LA: Acute epiglottitis. *Arch Otolaryngol* 1974; 100:333–337.

5. Selbst SM: Epiglottitis: A review of 13 cases and a suggested protocol for management. *J Fam Pract* 1984;19:333–337.

6. Bass JW, Fajardo JE, Brien JE, et al: Sudden death due to acute epiglottitis. *Pediatr Infect Dis* 1985;4:447–449.

7. Milko DA, Marshak G, Striker TW: Nasotracheal intubation in the treatment of acute epiglottitis. *Pediatrics* 1974;53:674–677.

8. Strome M, Jaffee B: Epiglottitis: Individualized management with steroids. *Laryngoscope* 1974;84:921–928.

9. Benjamin B, O'Reilly B: Acute epiglottitis in infants and children. *Ann Otolaryngol* 1976; 85:565–572.

10. Tarnow-Mordi WO, Berrill AM, Darby CW, et al: Precipitation of laryngeal obstruction in acute epiglottitis. *Br Med J* 1985;290:629.

11. Rapkin RH: The diagnosis of epiglottitis: Simplicity and reliability of radiographs of the neck in the differential diagnosis of the croup syndrome. *J Pediatr* 1972;80:96–98.

12. Rapkin RH: Tracheostomy in epiglottitis. *Pediatrics* 1973;52:426–429.

13. Baxter JD, Pashley NRT: Acute epiglottitis: 25 years experience in management, the Montreal Children's Hospital. *J Otolaryngol* 1977;6:473–476.

14. Glicklich M, Cohen RD, Jona JZ: Steroids and bag and mask ventilation in the treatment of acute epiglottitis. *J Pediatr Surg* 1979;14:247–251.

15. Adler E, Gibbons PA, Striker TW, et al: Ketamine: An alternative for the anesthetic management of acute epiglottitis. *Anesth Analg* 1986;65:53.

16. Faden HS: Treatment of *Haemophilus influenzae* type B epiglottitis. *Pediatrics* 1979; 63:402–407.

17. Gross CW: Upper airway obstruction in children. *Otolaryngol Clin North Am* 1977; 10:156–157.

18. Wetmore RF, Handler SD: Epiglottitis: Evolution in management during the last decade. *Ann Otol Rhino Laryngol* 1979;88:822–829.

22. Visualization of the Child with Suspected Epiglottitis

Frank J. Martorano, MD

Children do not read books describing classic signs and symptoms associated with specific clinical problems. A patient may have croup with drooling,
epiglottitis with a barky cough, or bacterial laryngotracheitis and suffocate on
his own mobilized bronchial concretions during convalescence from what
clinically appeared to be a mild case of viral croup. This emphasizes the need
for definitive diagnostic tests, because failing to recognize and manage epiglottitis or laryngotracheitis aggressively can cause substantial morbidity and even
mortality.

Several illustrations may be helpful:

Case 1: JW, a 3-year-old boy, awoke suddenly in the early morning and
went to his parents in obvious respiratory distress. There had been no prodromal illness, and he had been put to bed just 5 hours earlier apparently well.

On examination in the emergency department his color was ashen, and he
refused to swallow or do anything but sit up and lean forward. A lateral neck
film was ordered, and during the process of positioning him a respiratory arrest
occurred.

Case 2: TR, a 4-year-old girl, complained to her parents late in the evening
of a sore throat. She was given acetaminophen and a decongestant for
accompanying fever and rhinitis. After having been in bed for several hours,
she awoke her parents stating in a hoarse voice that she couldn't breathe.

Upon examination in the emergency department she was noted to be in
substantial respiratory distress and a lateral neck radiograph was ordered. The
x-ray film was interpreted by the primary physician and the radiologist as being
suggestive of epiglottitis. The operating room staff, anesthesiologist, and
otolaryngologist took her to the operating room for visualization.
Laryngoscopy showed a normal epiglottis without evidence of purulent
drainage. Nebulized racemic epinephrine and intravenous steroids were
administered. Subsequent hospitalization for viral croup was uneventful.

Case 3: JR, an 8-month-old boy, developed a substantial barky cough and stridor at rest after several days of an upper respiratory tract infection. He was admitted to the pediatric unit for presumed viral croup. The lateral neck film was interpreted as showing a normal epiglottis. No throat examination was performed to avoid precipitating laryngospasm. He was treated with high humidity, corticosteroids, and inhaled racemic epinephrine, but over the next 6 hours he worsened, requiring emergent airway intervention. In the operating room, a cherry red swollen epiglottis was noted. Blood cultures were obtained and he was started on third generation cephalosporin therapy. *Hemophilus influenzae* was recovered.

The preceding cases illustrate the variability of the reliability of using the lateral neck x-ray for definitive diagnosis. Since the clinical picture can be blatantly deceptive, an approach must be developed that gives an unequivocal answer. This has led to our use of direct laryngoscopy rather than the lateral neck x-ray study.

Lateral neck x-ray films are noted to be problematic as the diagnostically preferred test. Diaz[1] noted that radiologic evaluation "cannot be recommended as the initial diagnostic procedure in suspected epiglottitis. Lateral neck films may prove time-consuming, non-diagnostic, or even harmful in some children with acute epiglottitis." Stankiewiez and Bowes[2] concluded in a lengthy discussion that lateral neck and chest x-ray films "do not add significantly to the clinical diagnosis [of croup or epiglottitis] and indeed may be dangerous and unwarranted." Constant mention is made of the problem of false-negatives and false-positives in the interpretation of the radiographs.

APPROACHING THE PATIENT

If the lateral neck film is not useful diagnostically, what tools are available to differentiate croup, epiglottitis, and bacterial laryngotracheitis? Certainly, the variant prodromal picture and clinical presentation may be helpful but not definitive. Careful, atraumatic visualization of the epiglottis may be quickly and safely performed providing therapeutically valuable information in a timely fashion.

A given child's presentation may be so classic for epiglottitis that any maneuver other than transportation to the operating room for intubation under controlled conditions and general anesthesia would be superfluous. In less obvious or extremely early cases, however, visualization of the epiglottis is a high yield procedure.

To visualize the epiglottis, the child is kept in a sitting position on the lap of a person trained and experienced in gentle, but unequivocal, restraining of children. The head is held with a hand on the forehead; the adult's other arm encircles the child's chest and upper extremities. This will hold the child's occiput and back firmly against the restrainer's chest. The legs may be tucked in between the holder's thighs.

The examiner, positioned in front of the restrained child, gently slides a straight laryngoscopic blade about two thirds of the way back on the child's tongue, depressing the tongue. This maneuver usually brings the epiglottis located at the level of C2-3 into view. Care is taken not to hit the epiglottis.

Many suggest preoxygenating the child before initiating this procedure. *Airway management equipment must be available and ready for use. Do not agitate the child unnecessarily.*

The inflamed swollen epiglottis is not a subtle finding. If the epiglottis is normal, tenacious purulent secretions may be present, indicating bacterial laryngotracheitis. This latter condition may occur in children who initially had croup that subsequently "relapsed." A normal epiglottis and no unusual secretions suggest viral croup.

CONCLUSION

Our practice has used this technique in lieu of lateral neck films for the last 12 years with no adverse experience.

We are frequently referred children for admission with suspected epiglottitis on lateral neck x-ray films, only to find a normal epiglottis on admission examination. One such child had the following report forwarded: "The epiglottis cannot be well seen on this film. Whether this is due to faulty positioning or because the epiglottis itself is swollen cannot be ascertained. Indeed epiglottitis cannot be excluded by this examination."

REFERENCES

1. Diaz JH: Croup and epiglottitis in children. The anesthesiologist as diagnostician. *Anesth Anal* 1985;64:621-633.

2. Stankiewicz JA, Bowes AK: Croup and epiglottitis: A radiologic study. *Laryngoscope* 1985;95:1159-1160.

Section 10

Bronchiolitis

Traditionally, after careful examination to exclude respiratory failure, bronchiolitis is managed with watchful waiting and support. Bronchodilators are thought to have a minimal role with children under 6 months of age because of their relatively poor smooth muscles development in the bronchioles. However, with older children, bronchodilators have a beneficial effect, and it is in this group that further studies must document their role before more widespread use can be justified.

Ribavirin is an effective pharmacologic agent in the seriously ill inpatient.

23. Treatment Dilemmas in Bronchiolitis

Esequiel C. Guevara, MD

Bronchiolitis is an acute small airway infection, usually caused by a virus that may be associated with respiratory distress. The primary pathologic process is inflammatory with necrosis of the respiratory epithelium. Bronchoconstriction is secondary, in marked contrast to asthma.

The most common viral cause is respiratory syncytial virus, implicated in 50% to 75% of cases,[1,2] Other causal viruses include parainfluenza types 1, 2, and 3; adenovirus types 3, 7, and 21; mumps; and influenza. *Mycoplasma pneumoniae* and *Chlamydia trachomatis* may be rare causes.[1,3]

Bronchiolitis occurs primarily in epidemics, with a peak incidence between November and March. It occurs primarily in children under 2 years of age, with a peak incidence in children 6 months old. Adults have rarely been reported to contract this illness.[1] The reported mortality is 4% to 7%.

Children typically present with rhinorrhea and low-grade fever. The illness progresses to include cough, marked tachypnea (often disproportionate to the degree of distress), diffuse wheezing, and dyspnea. Perioral cyanosis may develop, and feeding may become difficult. Infants commonly have apnea as an initial sign of infection; those at greatest risk are premature infants and those under 44 weeks of age (from the time of conception).

Severely affected children often have respiratory rates of 60 to 80 breaths per minute, flaring of nasal alae, and retractions. Wheezing and rales are heard if air exchange is adequate.

The chest roentgenogram commonly shows hyperinflation and peribronchial thickening. Desaturation and mild hypoxia may be shown by arterial blood gas measurements or oximetry.

MANAGEMENT

Pharmacologic management of children with bronchiolitis is in flux. Previously, treatment was solely supportive and consisted of hydration, oxygena-

169

tion, monitoring, and nursing care. Rarely, endotracheal intubation and mechanical ventilation were required. More recently, a number of therapeutic modalities have become increasingly important.

Bronchodilators

The efficacy of bronchodilators with bronchiolitic children is undefined. Many authors[4-6] do not support their use; others[7,8] are advocates. Part of the inconsistency may relate to the patient populations. One group of children has an obstructive pattern secondary to inflammatory changes, and a second group develops obstruction from a combination of inflammation and bronchospasm.

How much does bronchospasm accompanying smooth muscle constriction contribute to the pathology? The smooth muscle that surrounds the bronchioles is poorly developed in children under 3 years of age.[1] The quantity of smooth muscles in the bronchioles is disproportionately small in infancy.[9] The primary mode of obstruction is therefore not bronchospasm but mucous formation and edema.

A retrospective study[10] of hospitalized bronchiolitic children noted no beneficial effect of theophylline. However, the study employed bolus rather than continuous therapy. Earlier studies[4-6,9] documented a similar lack of efficacy.

Others showed that bronchodilators may be effective in older children. Hogg and Williams[11] found improved airway conductance in those over 4 years of age. A study[12] of children aged 7 months to 3 years, 7 months with a history of wheezing noted that children over 18 months of age benefitted from nebulized bronchodilators.

A marked increase in tidal volume, decrease in total airway resistance, and improvement in $PaCO_2$ was shown with continuous intravenous aminophylline therapy.[13-15] A loading dose of aminophylline followed by a constant infusion was used. Two of these studies[13,14] focused on children 2 to 12 weeks old.

CORTICOSTEROIDS

Steroids do not provide significant benefit. A prospective double-blind study[16] of 297 infants and children revealed no improvement over controls.

Ribavirin

Ribavirin is a synthetic nucleoside possessing significant antiviral efficacy in the management of respiratory syncytial viral infection. It is administered by aerosol and absorbed systemically. Studies[17,18] of hospitalized children documented that treated children improved more rapidly than those given aerosolized placebo. Severe respiratory syncytial viral infections of the lower respiratory tract should be treated if the hospitalization is anticipated to be more than 3 days; the vast majority of patients with mild, self-limited disease do not require hospitalization or antiviral therapy.

Treatment is carried out for 12 to 18 hours per day for at least 3 and no more than 7 days as part of the treatment and support program. A Viratek Small Particle Aerosol Generator is used to administer the course of therapy, which is relatively expensive.

Pulmonary Function Tests

Measuring and interpreting normal and abnormal pediatric lung functions are problematic in the child with bronchiolitis. The absence of standards poses substantial problems in determining the beneficial effect of bronchodilators on pulmonary dysfunction. Studies[19,20] have attempted to measure physiologic responses to single-dose treatments with nebulized bronchodilators with limited success.

CONCLUSIONS

Although many clinicians continue to doubt the efficacy of bronchodilators, some have expressed increasing enthusiasm for their use in ameliorating bronchospasm caused by an allergic predisposition or infectious response.

Initial therapy for children with significant respiratory distress is oxygen delivered by mask or nasal cannula. Although controversial, bronchodilators can be used in the child with tachypnea, severe wheezing, and dyspnea; our preference is either metaproterenol (0.01 mg/kg/dose to a maximum of 0.30 mg/dose) or terbutaline sulfate (0.1 mg/kg/dose to a maximum of 3.0 mg/dose). These are mixed in 2 mL of normal saline and administered by a nebulizer. (See Chapters 18 and 19.)

If the patient responds well to the nebulized bronchodilator with decreasing respiratory effort, subsequent therapy may include oral theophylline and, occasionally, epinephrine (Sus-Phrine) given subcutaneously (0.005 mL/kg/dose using a single-dose vial). Theophylline is loaded orally at 6 mg/kg/dose. If the patient is not on bronchodilators, a sustained long-acting theophylline is continued for two weeks at a dose of 16 mg/kg/24 hours in two divided doses every 12 hours.

Children with marked respiratory distress may be started on IV aminophylline therapy. Patients not already receiving medications are loaded with 6 mg/kg over 20 to 30 minutes and then continued at 1 mg/kg/hr; theophylline levels should be monitored. If the patient remains tachypneic and in respiratory distress 1 hour after this therapy is initiated, a second nebulized treatment is warranted, using terbutaline. A chest roentgenogram may be indicated. Ribavirin is generally initiated in severely ill children.

Children who are not markedly tachypneic, have no evidence of respiratory distress or dehydration, and can be easily followed, may be considered for ambulatory management. Strict follow-up instructions should be provided, making certain that there is telephone contact in 8 to 12 hours to check on respiratory and hydration status and an appointment for re-evaluation in 12 to 24 hours. The parents must be specifically instructed to bring the child back if there is any evidence of respiratory distress or progression.

As greater sophistication becomes available for the management of emergent pulmonary functions in the emergency department or office setting, the role of bronchodilators will be further clarified.

REFERENCES

1. Wohl MEB, Chernick V: Bronchiolitis. *Am Rev Respir Dis,* 1978;118:759–781.

2. Nelson W (ed): *Textbook of Pediatrics,* ed 11. Philadelphia, WB Saunders Co, 1979, pp 1203–1205.

3. *Report of the Committee on Infectious Diseases,* ed 19. Evanston, Ill, American Academy of Pediatrics, 1982, pp 59, 326.

4. Cook CD, Reynolds EOR: The treatment of bronchiolitis. *J Pediatr* 1963;63:1205–1207.

5. Phelan PD, Williams HE: Sympathomimetic drugs in acute viral bronchiolitis. *Pediatrics* 1969;44:493–497.

6. Rutter N, Milner AD, Hiller EJ: Effect of bronchodilators on respiratory resistance in infants and young children with bronchiolitis and wheezy bronchitis. *Arch Dis Child* 1975;50:719–722.

7. Holland WW, Colley JRT: Measurement of respiratory effort and assessment of a method of treating lower-respiratory-tract infections in small children. *Lancet* 1960;2:1166–1167.

8. Milner AD, Henry RL: Acute airways obstruction in children under 5, editorial. *Thorax* 1982;37:641–645.

9. Matsuba K, Thurlbeck WM: Amorphometric study of bronchial and bronchiolar walls in children. *Am Rev Respir Dis* 1972;105:908–913.

10. Brooks LJ, Cropp GJA: Theophylline therapy in bronchiolitis. *Am J Dis Child* 1981;135:934–936.

11. Hogg JC, Williams J: Age as a factor in the distribution of lower-airway conductance and in the pathologic anatomy of obstructive lung disease. *N Engl J Med* 1970;282:1283–1287.

12. Lenny W, Milner AD: At what age do bronchodilator drugs work? *Arch Dis Child* 1978;53:532–535.

13. Schena JA, Crone RK: The use of aminophylline in severe bronchiolitis, abstract. *Crit Care Med* 1984;12:225.

14. Outwater KM, Crone RK: Management of respiratory failure in infants with acute viral bronchiolitis. *Am J Dis Child* 1984;138:1071–1075.

15. Motoyama E, Lister G, Mallory G, Mestad P, Rothstein P, Weng T: Evidence of bronchial hyperactivity in infants with acute bronchiolitis, abstract. *Anesthesiology* 1982;57:A100.

16. Leer JA, Green JL, et al: Corticosteroid treatment in bronchiolitis: A controlled collaborative study in 297 infants and children. *Am J Dis Child* 1969;117:495–503.

17. Hall CM, McBride JT, Walsh EE, Bell DM, Gala CL, Hildreth S, Tengyck LG, Hall WJ: Aerosolized ribavirin treatment of infants with respiratory syncytial viral infection. *N Engl J Med* 1983; 308:1443–1447.

18. Taber LH, Knight V, Gilbert BE, McClung HW, Wilson SZ, Norton HS, Thurson JM, Gordon WH, Atmar RL, Schlaudt WR: Ribavirin aerosol treatment of bronchiolitis associated with respiratory syncytial virus infection in infants. *Pediatrics* 1983;72:613–618.

19. Wohl MEB: Present capacity to evaluate pulmonary function relevant to bronchiolitis. *Pediatr Res* 1977;11:252–253.

20. Silverman M: Bronchodilators for wheezy infants? *Arch Dis Child* 1984;59:84–87.

Section 11

Foreign Bodies in Airway

Foreign body aspiration may be a difficult diagnosis based solely on history and physical findings if the object is in the tracheobronchial tree; those in the upper airway cause life-threatening respiratory distress. Inspiratory and expiratory chest radiographs may substantiate the presence of a tracheobronchial foreign body, but definitive evaluation may require bronchoscopy.

Management of the choking child is in transition, the goal being to generate positive intrathoracic pressure and thereby expel the object. Current recommendations are that the child under 1 year of age initially receive back blows in a head-down position followed by chest thrusts. Older children are treated initially with abdominal thrusts.

Definitive management may require rigid bronchoscopy.

24. Foreign Bodies in the Airway

Madolin K. Witte, MD

The dangers associated with foreign body aspiration in children have been chronicled in the medical literature for more than 350 years, and airway foreign bodies continue to be a problem frequently encountered by pediatric practitioners today. Although the vast majority of children who aspirate foreign bodies are effectively treated and survive without sequelae, fatalities can occur, especially in young children. Children under 4 years of age account for 20% of all deaths caused by inhaled foreign materials, and foreign body aspiration is the most common cause of accidental death in children under 1 year of age.[1] Despite wide recognition of the scope and magnitude of this health problem, a consensus does not exist with respect to the initial and definitive management of airway foreign bodies.

PRESENTATION

Foreign body aspiration is most frequent in the 1 to 2 year age group, with 85% of cases occurring in children under 3 years of age.[2] Food items, including nuts, shells, candies, and hot dogs, account for the vast majority of aspirated substances. Three fourths of inhaled foreign bodies lodge in a mainstem or lobar bronchus, with less than 5% finding their way to more distal portions of the tracheobronchial tree.[2] The extrathoracic airway (larynx and proximal trachea) is the site of obstruction in approximately 20% of cases, with laryngeal foreign bodies being especially common in infants under 1 year of age.[2] In almost all cases, a history suggestive of foreign body aspiration can be elicited, and most patients present within 48 hours of the incident. Clinical symptoms and physical findings depend on the site of obstruction: Laryngo-tracheal foreign bodies most commonly cause dyspnea, cough, stridor, and hoarseness or aphonia. Bronchial foreign bodies produce cough, wheezing, and decreased air entry in the involved area of the lung. Approximately 5% of patients, in whom the aspiration of foreign material is not initially recognized, will present 2 or more weeks after the event with atelectasis, pneumonia, or hemoptysis.

The diagnosis is usually made on the basis of a suggestive history and physical findings consistent with airway obstruction. Although most aspirated foreign bodies are radiolucent, chest radiography may corroborate the diagnosis by demonstrating the secondary effects of airway foreign bodies on lung mechanics. Chest radiographs taken during both phases of respiration will reveal obstructive emphysema with hyperinflation in approximately 60% of children with a bronchial foreign body.[2,3] Fluoroscopy, demonstrating inspiratory shift of the mediastinal shadow characteristic of unilateral bronchial obstruction, may improve the diagnostic yield to as high as 90%.[2] Radiography is less useful in diagnosing laryngotracheal foreign bodies; inspiratory and expiratory chest radiographic findings are normal in most patients. Fluoroscopy is only slightly more helpful, and was reported[2] to show inspiratory widening of the mediastinal shadow, characteristic of laryngeal or tracheal obstruction, in one third of children with foreign bodies in these areas. Other radiographic modalities that expose the child to higher levels of radiation, such as xeroradiography or tomography, are not definitive and seldom have roles in the diagnosis of airway foreign bodies. Thus, although radiography may be useful in substantiating the diagnosis in some patients, the presence of airway foreign bodies cannot be excluded based on normal radiographic findings. Therefore, definitive treatment should not be delayed for the purpose of an extensive diagnostic workup in any child with a history and physical findings suggesting foreign body inhalation.

In patients for whom the history, physical findings, and radiographic findings are equivocal, flexible fiberoptic bronchoscopy may be an extremely helpful diagnostic tool. In experienced hands, this procedure affords a thorough and rapid examination of the airways and allows a definitive diagnosis in virtually all cases of foreign body aspiration. Because flexible bronchoscopy can be comfortably performed with light sedation and topical airway anesthesia, the risks inherent to general anesthesia and rigid bronchoscopy are avoided. However, this procedure should be used for diagnostic purposes only. Although some authors have advocated foreign body extraction via the flexible bronchoscope in selected patients, to do so introduces unnecessary risks. There are not sufficiently reliable instruments that can be used through the flexible pediatric bronchoscope to ensure controlled extraction, and attempts at removal may result in dislodging the foreign body from a relatively benign location, such as a lobar bronchus, to a more dangerous position in the trachea or glottis. In addition, since patients cannot be ventilated through a flexible bronchoscope, hypoxemia or hypercarbia may result during the prolonged procedure an attempted extraction could entail. For these reasons, flexible bronchoscopy should not be routinely employed in the management of foreign body aspiration, but should be reserved to establish the diagnosis before rigid bronchoscopy in patients with equivocal presentations.

MANAGEMENT OF FOREIGN BODY ASPIRATION

Emergency Treatment of the Choking Child

Few issues pertaining to the management of medical emergencies in children have generated as much controversy as has first aid of the choking victim. The goal of any treatment of choking is to simulate the body's natural defense mechanism for expelling foreign material from the airway, namely the cough. Thus, the intent of all maneuvers advocated for treatment of choking is to generate positive intrathoracic pressure by compressing the intrathoracic gas volume to expel the foreign substance from the airway.

Although there is general agreement regarding the goal of first aid maneuvers applied to a choking victim, the method of treatment that most successfully meets this goal is hotly debated. The techniques which have been most widely advocated and used for the treatment of obstructing foreign bodies include back blows, chest thrusts, and abdominal thrusts (Heimlich maneuver). In experimental studies,[1] back blows produced a large but brief intrathoracic pressure spike and vibratory movements in the airway, which would theoretically dislodge a foreign body wedged in the airway. Chest and abdominal thrust maneuvers produce a lower but more sustained elevation in intrathoracic pressure, which will ideally propel a foreign body out of the airway.

In 1981, the Committee on Accident and Poison Prevention of the American Academy of Pediatrics (AAP) issued their recommendations for first aid for the choking child. The treatment measures advised in this statement, which conformed with those recommended by the American Heart Association (AHA) and the National Academy of Sciences–National Research Council, were the delivery of a series of blows to the area of the back between the shoulder blades. If this maneuver was unsuccessful in relieving airway obstruction, the rescuer was to perform a series of chest thrusts in the same manner as that used for external cardiac compression.[4] The use of the abdominal thrust (Heimlich maneuver), which had been introduced in the medical and lay literature several years earlier, was cautioned against because of purported potential for injury to abdominal organs in infants and young children. After the publication of these recommendations, a spirited debate took place, which unfortunately generated much more heat than light. Proponents of the Heimlich maneuver claimed that back blows were ineffective at best, and may worsen airway obstruction. Proponents of the recommendations of the AAP argued that back blows were effective in generating the pressure needed to expel a foreign body from the airway and were safer than abdominal thrusts. Perhaps the most scientific and enlightening of these communications is the work of Day et al.[5] These investigators showed that back blows failed to move various types of foreign bodies placed on the vocal cords of a model of an infant's upper airway. In addition, using accelerometers attached to human subjects, they showed ballistic forces in response to back blows that would result in displacement of supraglottic foreign bodies further down into the airway. These same investigators, using body plethysmography and pressure measurements recorded at the mouth, showed greater airway pressure generation with abdominal thrusts than with back blows. In addition to these experimental data, analysis of anecdotal reports of 225 choking incidents collected by the AHA revealed that abdominal thrusts were more successful in relieving airway obstruction than were back blows.[6] Furthermore, a separate survey[7] of nearly 1,400 choking incidents found that victims were 4 times more likely to lose consciousness or die when back blows preceded abdominal thrusts than when abdominal thrusts were used alone.

Because of the continued controversy surrounding the treatment of choking, a panel on Management of Foreign Body Airway Obstruction was convened in July 1985 by the AHA, American College of Cardiology, and the American Red Cross. This panel reviewed the available data and now recommends the abdominal thrust (Heimlich maneuver) as the exclusive method to treat airway obstruction in choking victims over 1 year of age. In July 1986 the Committee on Accident and Poison Prevention of the AAP issued their statement "Revised First Aid for the Choking Child."[8] This recommends abdominal thrusts for treatment of obstructing airway foreign bodies in children over 1 year of age, and back blows in a head-down position followed by chest thrusts in infants. Abdominal thrusts are not recommended in children under 1 year of age because of the purported high risk for injuries to abdominal organs in this age group. Although much attention has been given to the potential for organ damage during abdominal thrusts in infants, cases of such trauma have not been documented. Chest and abdominal organ injuries after external cardiac compression (using the same techniques as recommended for chest thrusts in the treatment of choking) are well documented in both adults and children. One must question the wisdom of trading a treatment with potential complications for one in which the complications are well established. There is also a danger that the existence of vastly different treatment recommendations for different pediatric age groups will substantially reduce the chance of either method being used appropriately by rescuers. One suspects that the controversy over treatment of the pediatric choking victim has not been laid to rest.

Nonemergent Management of Foreign Body Aspiration

Although not nearly so controversial as the treatment of choking, opinions differ regarding the best approach to the nonemergent removal of foreign bodies from the lower airways. As previously mentioned, rigid bronchoscopy is the most widely used and widely accepted method of foreign body extraction. This procedure is performed using general anesthesia and a hollow tube through which the patient can be ventilated and instruments passed to allow extraction of the foreign body. Because almost all lower airway foreign body removals can be postponed long enough to ensure adequate gastric emptying, anesthetic complications are minimized, and transient airway edema is the only complication that occurs with any frequency. Rigid bronchoscopy is effective in foreign body removal in more than 90% of patients.[2,3,8] Endoscopic failures necessitating thoracotomy are virtually always associated with a prolonged interval between the time of aspiration and rigid bronchoscopy.[3,8]

Because most airway foreign bodies produce unilateral bronchial obstruction, the majority of children with this diagnosis experience little or no respiratory distress. This fact has led some authors to suggest initial nonsurgical management of lower airway foreign bodies in an attempt to obviate the small but real risks involved with general anesthesia and rigid bronchoscopy. Cotton et al[9] treated 24 children with suspected endobronchial foreign bodies with bronchodilator aerosol therapy followed by postural drainage. They reported successful removal of the foreign bodies in 80% of cases after 1 to 70 treatments. Despite the occurrence of one respiratory and one cardiorespiratory arrest with residual cortical blindness in their small patient population, these authors advocated inhalation and postural drainage therapy for at least 4 days before bronchoscopic removal was attempted. From the same institution, Law and Kosloske[8] reported only a 25% success rate for inhalation–postural drainage therapy for documented foreign body aspiration compared with a greater than 90% successful removal rate with rigid bronchoscopy. In no case of long-standing foreign body aspiration was postural drainage effective. Although no complication of postural drainage treatment was seen in this series, migration of the foreign body within the tracheobronchial tube occurred in nearly one half of the children. Based on their experience, these authors recommended a limited trial of chest physiotherapy in a hospital setting, with rigid bronchoscopy if postural drainage was not successful within 24 hours. One month after their article was published, the authors cared for a child who suffered a cardiopulmonary arrest when an aspirated nut moved from the right mainstem bronchus into the trachea after a postural drainage treatment. Based on its poor efficacy and risk for serious complications, Dr. Kosloske[10] withdrew her previous recommendation for inhalation–postural drainage therapy for airway foreign bodies. O'Neill et al[3] found postural drainage successful in only 1 of 30 patients, with foreign bodies successfully removed via rigid bronchoscopy from all postural drainage failures.

Because of its low success rate and formidable risks, postural drainage is not an acceptable method for treatment of aspirated foreign bodies. Today, rigid bronchoscopic removal is the standard of care for all airway foreign bodies in pediatric patients. Regardless of how minimal their symptoms are, all children with aspirated foreign bodies should be closely monitored in a hospital until foreign body removal is achieved.

CONCLUSION

Foreign body aspiration is a relatively common and potentially tragic occurrence in children. Current recommendations for the emergency treatment of the choking child include abdominal thrusts (the Heimlich maneuver) for children over 1 year of age, and back blows and chest thrusts for infants. The definitive management of all airway foreign bodies is removal via rigid bronchoscopy.

REFERENCES

1. Mofenson HC, Greensher J: Management of the choking child. *Pediatr Clin North Am* 1985;32:183–192.

2. Blazer S, Naveh Y, Friedman A: Foreign body in the airway. A review of 200 cases. *Am J Dis Child* 1980;134:68–71.

3. O'Neill JA Jr, Holcomb GW, Neblitt WW: Management of tracheobronchial and esophageal foreign bodies in childhood. *J Pediatr Surg* 1983;18:475–479.

4. Greensher J, Mofenson HC: Emergency treatment of the choking child. *Pediatrics* 1982; 70:110–112.

5. Day RL, Crelin ES, DuBois AB: Choking: The Heimlich abdominal thrust vs. back blows: An approach to measurement of inertial and aerodynamic forces. *Pediatrics* 1982;70:113–119.

6. Redding JJ: The choking controversy: Critique of evidence of the Heimlich maneuver. *Crit Care Med* 1979;7:475–479.

7. Patrick EA: Choking: A questionnaire to find the most effective treatment. *Emergency* 1980;12:59–62.

8. Law D, Kosloske AM: Management of tracheobronchial foreign bodies in children: A reevaluation of postural drainage and bronchoscopy. *Pediatrics* 1976;58:361–367.

9. Cotton EK, Abrams G, VanHoritte J, et al: Removal of aspirated foreign bodies by inhalation and postural drainage. *Clin Pediatr* 1973;12:270–276.

10. Kosloske AM: Tracheobronchial foreign bodies in children: Back to the bronchoscope and a balloon. *Pediatrics* 1980;66:321–323.

25. Management of Upper Airway Foreign Body Obstruction in Young Children

LeRoy M. Graham, MD
Steven H. Abman, MD

In the United States alone, an estimated 3,000 deaths result annually from acute upper airway obstruction by foreign body aspiration, including nearly 500 children under 5 years of age.[1] Sixty-five percent of deaths by foreign body aspiration in the pediatric population occur in young infants.[2] Since most of these episodes occur away from hospital emergency departments and trained medical personnel, health care practitioners must provide clear, simple, and effective public guidelines for the rapid management of the choking child. However, because of the inherent difficulties in performing controlled clinical trials and collecting reliable descriptive information from witnessed events, the volume of experimental data is small. Thus the treatment of foreign body obstruction of the upper airway is controversial. Much of the controversy revolves around the appropriate sequence or relative merits of abdominal thrusts (the Heimlich maneuver), back blows, and chest thrusts to dislodge the foreign body.

CLINICAL SIGNS

Statistically, a foreign body more commonly enters the esophagus than the respiratory tract.[3] It may lodge in the supraglottic airway or larynx, triggering protective reflexes to dislodge the object. Subsequent impaction in the supraglottic airway may also stimulate laryngospasm. This life-threatening condition can lead to anoxia and death.

Note: This article was supported in part by the American Heart Association [AHA-Squibb Clinician Scientist Award (SHA)]. The authors are grateful to Mrs. Shirley McKenzie for her secretarial assistance.

Upper airway obstruction by foreign body aspiration is abrupt. Aspiration often occurs while a child is eating, or running with food or other objects in the mouth, and is associated with the sudden onset of coughing or gagging. An infant or toddler may have been observed playing with coins or other small objects before choking. One of the most common reports is of an older sibling "feeding" age-inappropriate food (such as peanuts, hard candies, hot dogs, apple or carrot slices) or small objects to the younger child. Similarly, poor household "child proofing" contributes to the availability of similar items to the exploring young child.

Obstruction may be only partial, with the child able to maintain air exchange as evidenced by coughing, perhaps stridor, vocalizing, and breath sounds (if auscultation were to be performed). In such cases, attempts at removal are unnecessary and potentially dangerous. The child's natural attempts to expel the foreign body should be allowed to continue without intervention. Profound respiratory distress accompanies more complete obstruction. Typically, children are initially tachypneic, with suprasternal retractions and an inability to cough or vocalize, and will not tolerate lying down. Without successful intervention, hypoxia leads to marked cyanosis, increasing respiratory distress, and panic, followed by bradycardia, apnea, loss of consciousness or seizures, and cardiopulmonary arrest.

MANAGEMENT

The emergency treatment of upper airway obstruction by foreign body aspiration is the subject of strident debate.[4–12] Redding[13] reviewed 225 cases of food choking reported to the AHA's Emergency Cardiac Care Committee. Of these cases, 116 used only one method, 29 used several methods, and 75 used multiple methods but reported that only one was successful. As the initial procedure, back blows, chest thrusts, and abdominal thrusts had success rates of 50%, 64%, and 78%. Each technique was reported as successful in cases where another had failed. The skill of the rescuer and hence the appropriate performance of any method could not be assessed. Similarly, the relation of the "failure" of one technique to the subsequent success of another was equally unclear. Redding concluded there was insufficient evidence to condemn or recommend strongly one technique over another. The nonhospital setting of such episodes, as well as ethical considerations, prohibits adequate prospective clinical study.[13,14]

Several experimental studies have attempted to clarify the issue. The experimental approaches, findings, and conclusions from five major studies of methods employed in treating foreign body upper airway obstruction are outlined in Table 25-1. Overall, the findings are inconclusive. Interpretation of the data

Table 25-1 Summary of Experimental Data

Study	Subjects	Experimental Model	Results	Recommendations
Heimlich[18]	Dogs	Four animals anesthetized, intubated; ET tube obstructed; CT and AT performed.	AT but not CT successful in relieving obstruction.	AT best technique.
Guildner et al[9]	Humans	Anesthetized volunteers; measured flow, volumes, and pressure with CT, AT, and BB.	BB ineffective; CT developed greater airway pressure, volume, and flow than AT.	CT best procedure; BB should be performed, then CT.
Gordon et al[15]	Dogs, baboons, humans	Animal studies; meat placed above and below epiglottis; BB, CT, and AT compared. Human studies: conscious and anesthetized; pressure, flow, and volume measured.	BB best with meat above epiglottis; none successful if below epiglottis; normal cough with highest pressures; BB created highest, more rapid rise in pressure; CT and AT expelled greater volume than AT.	High and rapid rise in pressure from BB best in dislodging impacted foreign object; combination of BB plus CT or AT better than single maneuver.
Ruben and MacNaughton[16]	Cadavers, humans	Silicone rubber casts of larynx attached to ET tubes of humans and cadavers; occluded, then BB, CT, and AT performed.	BB > CT > AT in generating airway pressure; tightly impacted foreign body not removed by any technique.	BB best.
Day et al[17]	Humans, model of infant airway	Body plethysmography, accelerometers, and strain gauges used; ball bearing placed in model of infant airway.	AT generated greater pressure than BB (15–27 v 7–13 mm Hg); BB caused straightening of spine, forward neck movement; BB with infant model caused downward movement of ball bearing.	AT best; BB may be dangerous.

Note: ET, endotracheal; AT, abdominal thrust; CT, chest thrust; BB, back blow.

is problematic because of differences in experimental design (human *v* animal *v* artificial models; sedated *v* nonsedated) and difficulty in simulating the actual clinical problem. However, some limited conclusions can be drawn. Gordon and co-workers measured air flow, volume, and pressure following the administration of back blows, chest thrusts, and abdominal thrusts to human volunteers, and compared these measurements with those generated by normal coughing.[15] In six conscious subjects, normal coughing produced mean pressures of 72 and 115 mm Hg at resting lung volume and total lung capacity, respectively. With anesthesia, back blows generated higher pressures than did chest or abdominal thrusts (35 *v* 19 *v* 15 mm Hg) but none of these maneuvers approached the pressures achieved by coughing in awake subjects. Thus, based on the ability to generate much higher pressure than with any of the maneuvers, a natural cough is superior to an artificial one. Accordingly, one should allow a child with a partially obstructed airway to cough without interference.

Although back blows generate higher and more rapid rises in pressure than the other techniques,[15,16] pressure is less sustained with back blows than abdominal or chest thrusts (0.5 second [abdominal thrusts] *v* 0.02 second [back blows]). This results in the expulsion of less air. In addition, some feel that back blows may be "death blows."[5,17] Using body plethysmography, chest strain gauges and accelerometers attached to the subjects' necks, Day et al[17] found that delivery of back blows caused the forward movement of the neck and straightening of the spine. Back blows of seated patients further accelerated the neck upward, thereby forcing the foreign body downward at three times the pull of gravity, potentially leading to impaction or converting a partially obstructed airway to complete obstruction. Further studies of volunteers with curved tubes involving ball bearings placed in their mouths actually suggested that abdominal thrusts generated greater pressures than back blows (15–27 *v* 7–13 mm Hg). There were several criticisms of this study. First, some[7] believed that the accelerometer should have been attached to the foreign body, not the neck. Second, were a foreign body to favor downward motion, this force would be counterbalanced by a rise in intrathoracic pressure induced by the back blow.[10] Third, a foreign body would not accelerate downward in an airway if it were not "structurally connected to elements of the neck itself;" that is, a foreign body would be expected to maintain its position in the larynx during movement of the neck.[8,10]

In a study of four anesthetized, intubated dogs, Heimlich[18] observed that abdominal thrusts, but not chest thrusts, were successful in relieving obstruction. Conversely, Reuben[16] concluded that back blows generated higher airway pressures than abdominal or chest thrusts in a study involving cadavers and laryngeal casts of live subjects. Interestingly, tightly impacted foreign bodies were not expelled by any of these methods.

The potential for complications is an additional factor in selecting the optimal approach. Ruptured stomach, lacerated spleen, retinal detachment, aortic thrombosis, and pneumoperitoneum were reported after abdominal thrusts.[19] Although unproven, many feel that back blows may worsen an obstruction. Possible complications from chest thrusts include fractured ribs, pneumothorax, myocardial contusion, and abdominal trauma, as based on experience with cardiopulmonary resuscitation (CPR). The actual frequency and relative risks for these injuries with each intervention remain unknown. Whether or not infants or small children are at relatively greater risk than adults from abdominal thrusts is unclear. The AHA's[2] continued support of the combination of back blows with chest thrusts rather than abdominal thrusts is based on the assumption that infants under 1 year of age are at greater risk for intra-abdominal injuries with abdominal thrusts than with complications from back blows and chest thrusts. Although there are few data available to answer this question, a study[20] of complications after CPR in young infants found that rib fractures secondary to chest compressions (thrusts) are rare. However, as seen occasionally in child abuse cases, chest compressions can injure the retina (Purtscher retinopathy).[21]

If a synthesis of these findings is possible, one may conclude that the rapid rise in pressures with back blows may be effective in dislodging the impacted foreign body, and subsequent chest or abdominal thrusts may further facilitate its removal by expelling greater volumes of air.

RECOMMENDATIONS

In summary, if obstruction is partial, the child's cough reflex should be allowed to extrude the foreign body. If, after a brief observation period, obstruction persists or the child is unconscious or apneic, then intervention is required. Current recommendations from the AAP and the AHA distinguish between children under and over 1 year of age with regard to the optimal management.

Choking infants under 1 year of age should be treated with a combination of back blows and chest thrusts. The infant should be placed face down over the rescuer's arm, with the head positioned lower than the trunk. Four measured back blows should be delivered rapidly between the infant's shoulder blades (midthorax) with the heel of the rescuer's hand. If adequate breathing is not resumed, the infant should be rolled over and four rapid compressions of the chest performed, as is done with CPR. This sequence should be repeated until the obstruction is relieved.

The AHA advises that abdominal thrusts be performed in children over 1 year of age. Their caveat that "in small children the maneuver must be applied gently"[2] reflects some uncertainty regarding potential risks in this age group.

In both age groups, blind probing of the airway to dislodge a foreign body is discouraged. The airway may be opened by the jaw thrust maneuver. If a foreign body is seen, it can be removed with the fingers or available instruments (Magill forceps or Kelly clamps). With persistent apnea and the inability to achieve adequate ventilation, emergency intubation, tracheostomy, or needle cricothyroidectomy may be performed, depending on the setting and rescuer's skills.

CONCLUSIONS

The controversy over whether abdominal thrusts, back blows, or chest thrusts should be used to treat infants and young children remains unresolved. Neither experimental studies employing various (and highly creative) models of upper airway obstruction nor retrospective "field" studies provide conclusive evidence supporting the application of one technique over another. However, despite persistent controversy and the need for further study, clear and uniform instructions are necessary to provide the public with adequate guidelines to allow for more rapid and successful interventions. Further investigation, especially of age-related differences in the pathophysiology of airway obstruction and the effects of the various therapeutic options, is required before any approach becomes etched in stone.

REFERENCES

1. *Accident Facts.* Chicago, National Safety Council, 1978.

2. American Heart Association: Standard guideline for CPR and emergency cardiac care. *JAMA* 1986;255:2959.

3. Blazer S, Davek Y, Friedman A: Foreign body in the airway. *Am J Dis Child* 1980;34:68.

4. Committee on Accident and Poison Prevention, American Academy of Pediatrics: First aid for the choking child. *Pediatrics* 1981;67:744.

5. Heimlich JH: First aid for choking children: Back blows and chest thrusts cause complications and death. *Pediatrics* 1982;70:120–124.

6. Day RL: Differing opinions on the emergency treatment of choking. *Pediatrics* 1983;71:976–977.

7. Greensher J, Mofenson HC: Emergency treatment of the choking child. *Pediatrics* 1982;70:110–112.

8. Greensher J, Mofenson HC: Treatment of the choking child. *Pediatrics* 1983;71:468–469.

9. Guildner C, Williams D, Subitch T: Airway obstruction by foreign material: The Heimlich maneuver. *Ann Emerg Med* 1972;5:675–677.

10. Montgomery WH: Back blows and choking. *Pediatrics* 1983;71:982–983.

11. Heimlich HJ: Letter. *Pediatrics* 1983;71:983–984.

12. Abman SH, Fan LL, Cotton EK: Emergency treatment of foreign body obstruction of the upper airway in children. *J Emerg Med* 1984;2:7–12.

13. Redding JS: The choking controversy: Critique of evidence on the Heimlich maneuver. *Crit Care Med* 1979;7:475–479.

14. Day RL: Comments on first aid for victims of choking. *Pediatr Res* 1986;20:1013.

15. Gordon AS, Belton MK, Ridolpho PF: Emergency management of foreign body airway obstruction, in Safar PJ, Elam JO (eds): *Advances in Cardiopulmonary Resuscitation.* New York, Springer-Verlag, 1977, pp 39–50.

16. Ruben H, MacNaughton FI: The treatment of food choking. *Practitioner* 1978;221:725–729.

17. Day RL, Crelin ES, Dubois AB: Choking: The Heimlich abdominal thrust versus back blows: An approach to measurement of inertial and aerodynamic forces. *Pediatrics* 1982;70:113–119.

18. Heimlich HJ: Life saving maneuver to prevent food choking. *JAMA* 1975;234:398–401.

19. Hoffman JR: Treatment of foreign body obstruction of the upper airway. *West J Med* 1982;136:11–22.

20. Feldman KW, Brewer DK: Child abuse, cardiopulmonary resuscitation and rib fractures. *Pediatrics* 1984;339–342.

21. Tomasi LG: Purtscher retinopathy in the battered-child syndrome. *Am J Dis Child* 1975;129:335.

Section 12

Infantile Apnea

The apneic infant, often following an episode of near-miss sudden infant death syndrome, is both a diagnostic and management challenge. Diagnostic considerations include a variety of infectious, metabolic, and traumatic conditions. Management should be based primarily on the clinical history and physical examination. Rational home monitoring and ongoing support and counseling must reflect the clinical picture and the home environment.

26. Infantile Apnea: Evaluation and Management in the Acute Care Setting

Jeffrey L. Goldhagen, MD, MPH

Clinicians are often confronted with infants with a history of a recent life-threatening event who otherwise look and act healthy. The oftentimes normal examination provides little solace to the parent who witnessed the event. The usually unspoken but universal concern among these parents is whether the child was a victim of a "near miss/aborted" sudden infant death syndrome (SIDS) episode and whether the event will recur. This anxiety is well founded as SIDS is the most common cause of death in children during infancy. From medical, psychosocial, and legal perspectives, it behooves clinicians to develop a rational approach to the evaluation and management of these infants and their families. The importance of the development of a consistent approach is magnified by the controversy concerning the etiology and prevention of SIDS.

GENERAL APPROACH TO EVALUATION

The parent who seeks examination of a child after a real or perceived life-threatening event does so with a great deal of anxiety and stress. Obtaining a reliable history is difficult, and the often normal clinical appearance of the child may belie the seriousness of the preceding event. Hospital admission is therefore indicated for both emotional and medical reasons. Five clinical precepts are offered to the reader to facilitate an empathetic and complete evaluation of such children:

1. SIDS is the major cause of death in children under the age of 1 year. The incidence varies among racial and socioeconomic groups, with increasing risk from whites, to blacks, and native Americans. The incidence of SIDS in the general population is 2 to 5 per 1,000 live births. The risk is

7 to 20 per 1,000 in subsequent siblings of SIDS victims and 45 per 1,000 in the surviving twin of a SIDS victim. Ninety percent of deaths occur in children between 1 and 6 months of age.[1]

2. Parental observations are valid. Initial management plans and clinical decisions must be based on parental descriptions of events.

3. Children who are at risk for apnea of infancy or SIDS may have underlying physiologic differences that may be detected when they are compared with a similar population not at risk.[2-6]

4. The observed event is not a disease in itself but a symptom of a pathologic process that may be delineated. The evaluation must therefore attempt to diagnose the underlying problem so that primary management and prevention can ensue.

5. If a diagnosis cannot be made and the underlying disorder cannot be effectively corrected or treated, the event may recur.

All management decisions should be based primarily on the clinical and family histories; inconsistent or normal laboratory data should not override the historical perspective. The medical history should include the location of the observer; the state of consciousness of the child during the event; the position of the child; the child's tone, color changes, and respiratory effort; and any history consistent with seizures, gastroesophageal reflux, or airway obstruction. Historical risk factors for SIDS include prematurity, fetal growth abnormalities, increasing birth order, male sex, black and native-American race, lower socioeconomic status, young maternal age, smoking, maternal drug addiction, and maternal anemia and low blood pressure during pregnancy. A family history of SIDS, apnea, seizures, dysrhythmias, etc, should also be obtained. A thorough physical examination should be documented including evidence of neurodevelopmental abnormalities.

The medical history should include a detailed description of the event, the environment in which the child lives, and an in-depth perinatal and family history. Special attention should be given to the psychosocial milieu in which the child lives. The differential diagnosis of near-miss SIDS includes child abuse and Munchausen syndrome by proxy, and the history must specifically attempt to evaluate these possibilities. We have also evaluated several infants caught in the midst of parental discord whose apneic events were fabricated in order to influence other family members. Parents under stress or with borderline intellectual abilities may also use a history of apnea to gain attention and access to medical and other resources in the community.

The laboratory evaluation should be tailored to a rational differential diagnosis of the event. A recent study[7] found that only 0.5% of 1,278 laboratory measurements in 163 patients hospitalized for a presumed near-miss SIDS event were useful in diagnosing or treating the apnea episodes. Therefore, recognition of the infrequency of determination of a specific underlying cause should temper the extent of the initial evaluation. A pneumocardiogram to evaluate central apnea, or polysomnography if obstructive apnea is considered a possibility, may be included in the evaluation. Although the predictive validity of these studies for subsequent apnea or SIDS is controversial, respiratory control abnormalities and cardiac dysrhythmias can be identified. These abnormalities include prolonged apnea, periodic breathing, shallow breathing potentially associated with O_2 desaturation, bradycardia, cardiac dysrhythmias, obstructive apnea with or without gastroesophageal reflux, and seizures. A normal pneumocardiogram or polysomnogram, however, does not negate the parental history, or the potential for a subsequent life-threatening event.

DIFFERENTIAL DIAGNOSIS

In evaluating and managing the child with near-miss SIDS episode, several considerations must be excluded.

Cardiac Abnormalities

Case reports of dysrhythmias in victims of SIDS and near-miss SIDS episodes resulting from Wolff-Parkinson-White syndrome, prolonged QT syndrome, and ventricular tachydysrhythmias appear in the literature.[8,9] Epidemiologic studies also show cardiac conduction abnormalities in 2% to 5% of young infants.[10,11] Other investigators fail to document dysrhythmias in children dying or at risk for SIDS. Therefore, although the association of cardiac dysrhythmias with SIDS is controversial, an electrocardiogram (ECG) should be part of the initial evaluation.

Seizures

Apnea is a well-documented symptom of seizure activity and may be the sole symptom of a seizure disorder. Early postictal electroencephalograms (EEGs) may disclose paroxysmal activity, but later findings are usually negative. This emphasizes the need to obtain EEGs soon after presentation if seizures are considered a likely cause for the event.

Status epilepticus may also be a consequence of an anoxic ischemic episode secondary to a near-miss SIDS event, and not its cause.

Infections

Apnea may occur early in septic neonates and infants. Although older infants usually appear symptomatic, neonatal sepsis may progress rapidly from apnea to cardiovascular collapse in a recently normal-appearing newborn.

Infants with respiratory syncytial viral (RSV) infections often have a history of recurrent apnea without other marked symptoms. Younger infants and those with a history of prematurity are at increased risk and should be admitted to an intensive care unit if apnea is one of the clinical symptoms. There is little correlation between the occurrence of apnea and the severity of the other symptoms of this infection. Controversy exists as to the necessity of home monitoring after discharge, as there may be a higher incidence of SIDS among these children. A diagnosis of RSV can be made rapidly by fluorescent antibody studies and confirmed by viral culture.

Metabolic Abnormalities

Although metabolic abnormalities were initially postulated to be associated with SIDS, few have thus far been defined. Biochemical thiamine deficiency (erythrocyte transketolase), hypertriiodothyroninemia, magnesium deficiency, hypocalcemia, and increased lead burdens have been reported, but their roles in the pathogenesis of SIDS are still unclear. Information concerning exposure to toxic minerals should be obtained, but the initial metabolic evaluation should be limited to glucose, electrolyte, and calcium determinations.

Toxins

Carbon monoxide poisoning has also been linked to SIDS. Use of a wood burning stove should alert the clinician to a possible environmental toxin.

Infantile botulism has caused the sudden death of infants. The association was first reported in California in 1970 and is thought to be caused by ingestion of honey contaminated by *Clostridium botulinum* spores. Reports[12] have documented *C botulinum* contamination of the gut in 43% of SIDS victims as compared with none in controls.

Immunizations

No causal link exists between DTP immunization and SIDS, near-miss SIDS, or ventilatory abnormalities.[13,14] Parental concerns will continue to persist despite these data, and it is the responsibility of the emergency department physician to deal empathetically with these issues during the initial assessment of the child and family.

Child Abuse

The differentiation of SIDS and near-miss SIDS and child abuse in individual cases is often difficult. The primary role of the emergency department physician is not to make a diagnosis of either entity, but rather not to make a misdiagnosis. There are multiple reports of child abuse simulating near-miss SIDS as well as accusations of child abuse in infants dying from classic SIDS. *There is no necessity to establish either diagnosis definitively during the assessment in the emergency department.* Unsubstantiated accusations of child abuse can have devastating effects on parents and families with a child who has died of SIDS or who had a perceived life-threatening event. They may result in further morbidity or mortality if the child is discharged with a diagnosis of child abuse and a subsequent episode of apnea occurs. Conversely, the misdiagnosis of near-miss SIDS may result in the return of a child to an environment in which further injury or death may occur. Hospital admission, close monitoring, and support by a multidisciplinary team should be the minimum resources offered to the child and family if the diagnosis is unclear. Kirschner and Stein's recent report[15] of the death of 11 children by potentially treatable illnesses or SIDS who were misdiagnosed as victims of child abuse highlights the necessity of this aggressive approach.

Anatomic Abnormalities

Anatomic and functional abnormalities resulting in central and obstructive apnea include gastroesophageal reflux, tracheomalacia, laryngomalacia, mass lesions, and dysynchronous neuromuscular activity of oropharyngeal structures. Reflux of gastric contents can precipitate central apnea and bradycardia by stimulating afferent fibers in the superior laryngeal nerve.[16] The association of gastroesophageal reflux and SIDS awaits better definition. A history of reflux may be vague; apnea and aspiration can occur without frank emesis. Subtle clues of mild weight loss; irritability during and after feedings; symptoms of esophagitis, chronic cough, or wheeze; and improvement after therapeutic intervention should alert the clinician to the potential contribution of reflux to the apnea episodes. The definitive diagnosis is made by documenting apnea occurring simultaneously with reflux. This documentation is obtained using polysomnography, a multichannel recording of esophageal pH, nasal and oral air flow, chest wall excursion, ECG, O_2 saturation, and end title CO_2. The overall evaluation may also include a barium swallow and radiolabeled milk scintography to evaluate potential gastric outlet obstruction, delayed gastric emptying, or pulmonary aspiration.

Tracheomalacia and laryngomalacia can cause collapse of the extrathoracic airway during inspiration, resulting in obstructive apnea. Both occur frequently in children with a history of prematurity or intubation. Inspiratory and expiratory stridor are classic symptoms that may worsen with viral URI or improve during sleep. Tracheomalacia can be diagnosed with fluoroscopy of the airway, but bronchoscopy is required to diagnose laryngomalacia.

Symptoms associated with mass lesions resulting in airway obstruction include noisy breathing, retractions, and cyanosis. More subtle symptoms of daytime lethargy and somnolence, behavior disorders, nocturnal enuresis, failure to thrive, cardiorespiratory failure, hypertension, frequent upper airway infections, learning disabilities, and attentional deficit disorders may also be consequences of frequent episodes of nocturnal obstructive apnea resulting in disordered sleep. Clinical entities include macroglossia, Down's syndrome, congenitally small airways, tonsillar and adenoid hypertrophy, cerebral palsy, myopathies, micrognathia, and generalized facial abnormalities. Diagnosis is made using polysomnography. Therapy is usually surgical correction of the abnormality or tracheostomy, although medical intervention may occasionally be successful.

A DECISION-MAKING ALGORITHM

A decision-making algorithm to help guide the clinician is presented in Figure 26-1.

If a diagnosis cannot be made and the underlying disorder effectively corrected or treated, a repeat near-miss event can be expected to recur in up to 60% of term and 80% of pre-term infants.[17] This is the basis for the rationale of home monitoring. The efficacy of home monitoring in the prevention of subsequent SIDS remains controversial. However, although home monitoring should not be considered a cure for SIDS, a subset of children who experience apnea will have episodes that could be fatal if parents are not alerted by a monitor alarm.

Although the bulk of the assessment of children with a perceived life-threatening event will be performed after hospitalization, parental anxiety and confusion will be at their peak during the initial emergency department evaluation. Questions commonly asked by parents include:

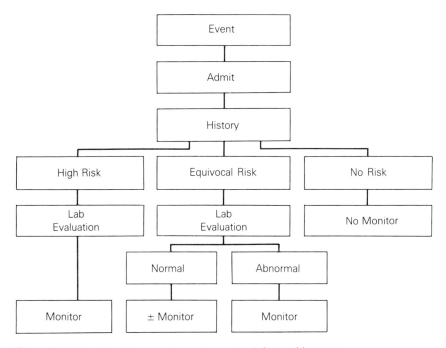

Figure 26-1 Algorithm for assessing and managing infants with apnea.

Question: Can SIDS be prevented?

Answer: SIDS probably has multiple causes, none of which have been well defined; therefore, we do not presently know in which children SIDS could have been prevented.

Question: Can a child with SIDS be resuscitated to prevent death?

Answer: Investigators anticipate that apnea of infancy will prove to be one of the causes of SIDS. Only a small number of children who experience apnea of infancy have life-threatening events. In some of these cases, parents who are appropriately trained and alerted to these events may be able to intervene to prevent their child's death.

Question: Does home monitoring prevent SIDS?

Answer: Home monitoring, by alerting parents to the occurrence of a potentially life-threatening event, can prevent death in some children with apnea of infancy. The impact of home monitoring on the overall incidence of SIDS has not been determined.

Question: Are subsequent children in families who had a SIDS death also at risk?

Answer: The risk of SIDS in subsequent siblings is controversial, and the relative risk of an individual subsequent sibling cannot be determined. Therefore, the benefit of home monitoring for an individual infant cannot be predicted and the decision to conduct home monitoring should include both psychosocial and medical considerations.

Every parent whose child experiences a perceived life-threatening event should become involved in an infant apnea program. If monitoring is instituted, the program can provide discharge planning and parental instruction, monitor management, infant CPR training for parents and babysitters, 24-hour consultation, periodic phone follow-up, parent and sibling support groups, information on community resources, etc. If home monitoring is not considered, parental questions can be answered, and the definition and risks of apnea of infancy and its relationship to SIDS better understood.

CONCLUSION

The emergency department physician has a pivotal role in the initial evaluation and management of a near-miss SIDS event. The special needs of each child and family should be considered. Management is made more complex by the lack of laboratory tools to aid in evaluation and the fears and psychosocial stresses that often accompany the diagnosis. A successful multidisciplinary approach to evaluation and management includes identification of those at risk, comprehensive diagnostic evaluation, home monitoring instruction, support services, re-evaluation, and support after discontinuation of home monitoring. Consideration of a differential diagnosis based on a detailed history of the event should facilitate a rational and cost-effective evaluation and management plan.

REFERENCES

1. Peterson DR, Chinn NM, Fisher LD: The sudden infant death syndrome: Repetitions in families. *J Pediatr* 1980;97:265–267.

2. Guilleminault C, Ariagno R, Souquet M, et al: Abnormal polygraphic findings in near-miss sudden infant death. *Lancet* 1976;1:1326–1327.

3. Steinschneider A: Prolonged sleep apnea and respiratory instability: A discriminative study. *Pediatrics* 1977;59(suppl):962–970.

4. Shannon DC, Kelly DH, O'Connell K: Abnormal regulation of ventilation in infants at risk for sudden-infant-death syndrome. *N Engl J Med* 1977;297:747–750.

5. Shannon DC, Kelly DH: Impaired regulation of alveolar ventilation and the sudden infant death syndrome. *Science* 1977;1974:367–368.

6. Kelly DH, Shannon DC: Periodic breathing in infants with near-miss sudden infant death syndrome. *Pediatrics* 1979;63:355–360.

7. Lewis J, Ganick D: Initial laboratory evaluations of infants with presumed 'near-miss' sudden infant death syndrome. *Am J Dis Child* 1986;140:484–486.

8. Haddad G, Epstein M, Epstein R, et al: The Q-T interval in aborted sudden infant death syndrome infants. *Pediatr Res* 1979;13:136.

9. Steinschneider A: Sudden infant death syndrome and prolongation of the Q-T interval. *Am J Dis Child* 1978;132:688–692.

10. Jones R, Sharp C, Rabb L, et al: 1028 neonatal electrocardiograms. *Arch Dis Child* 1979;54:427–432.

11. Southall D, Orrell M, Talbot J, et al: Study of cardiac arrhythmias and other forms of conduction abnormality in newborn infants. *Br Med J* 1977;2:597–600.

12. Arnon S, Damus K, Midura T, et al: Intestinal infection and toxin production by *Clostridium botulinum* as one cause of sudden infant death syndrome. *Lancet* 1978;1:1273–1277.

13. Bernier R, Frank J, Pondero T, et al: Diphtheria-tetanus toxoid-pertussis vaccination and sudden infant deaths in Tennessee. *J Pediatr* 1982;101:419–421.

14. Keens T, Davidson S, Ward S, et al: Ventilatory pattern following DPT immunization in infants at risk for sudden infant death syndrome. *Am J Dis Child* 1985;139:991–993.

15. Kirschner R, Stein R: The mistaken diagnosis of child abuse: A form of medical abuse? *Am J Dis Child* 1985;139:873–875.

16. Boggs D, Bartlett D: Chemical specificity of a laryngeal apneic reflex in puppies. *J Appl Physiol* 1982;53:455–462.

17. Ariagno R, Guilleminault C, Korobkin R, et al: Near-miss for sudden infant death syndrome infants: A clinical problem. *Pediatrics* 1983;71:726–730.

PART III

Seizures

Section 13

Febrile Seizures

Febrile seizures occur in up to 5% of the population between 5 months and 5 years of age. It is a problem to exclude meningitis yet not do diagnostic studies that have little historical or clinical indication. Increasing data have assisted in focusing the evaluation and initiating ongoing therapy for children who are truly at risk of ongoing seizure disorder.

27. Febrile Seizures: Evaluation and Management

Gary R. Strange, MD

In the mid-1970s, a survey of practicing pediatricians showed variable but frequent use of diagnostic tests in evaluating febrile seizures in children. More than one third of respondents routinely ordered serum chemistry tests and analyzed cerebrospinal fluid. Almost three fourths used skull radiographs in the workup. Admission to the hospital was customary, and most respondents advised prophylactic phenobarbital be given at the onset of any febrile illness. The cost of this management was estimated to be in the hundreds of millions of dollars annually.[1]

Since that time, the approach to this common problem has been considered more critically, leading many physicians to eliminate certain diagnostic tests and to reduce significantly the number of children treated with anticonvulsants.

THE NATURE OF FEBRILE SEIZURES

Febrile seizures occur in infants and children, usually between 3 months and 5 years of age, and are associated with fever but without evidence of intracranial infection or defined cause. They occur in 3% to 5% of children and are associated with a strong familial tendency but no definite pattern of inheritance. The great majority occur in children between the ages of 1 and 3 years and are associated with a temperature of 38.3 °C to 40.0 °C. The seizure is frequently the first indication of illness, tending to occur early in the illness as the temperature rises. Most are of short duration: 50% last less than 5 minutes, and 92% less than 15 minutes. The vast majority are generalized (85%). Recurrence in the same illness is rare (2% to 3%), but recurrence with future illness is common (30%).[2]

Table 27-1 Classification of Febrile Seizures

Simple	Complex
Generalized	Focal
Brief (less than 15 min)	Prolonged (more than 15 min)
Single	Recurrent (within 24 hr)

Febrile seizures are commonly divided into simple and complex (Table 27-1). This differentiation has prognostic significance as well as implications regarding appropriate workup and management.[3]

PROGNOSTIC CONSIDERATIONS

The parents of a child who has had a first febrile seizure are concerned not only about the immediate situation but also the long-term implications for the child's health and development. The National Collaborative Perinatal Project followed 1,700 children with febrile seizures: 30% had a second seizure, roughly 20% had two recurrences, and only 10% had three or more. It is clear that there is no increased risk of mental retardation, learning disability, or other neurologic or developmental sequelae.[4]

There is however a small increase in the chance of epilepsy developing in the child with febrile seizures. The incidence of epilepsy in the general population is 0.5%; it is increased to 2% to 3% in children with febrile seizures. In this latter group, specific risk factors increase the chances of developing epilepsy:

- previous abnormal neurologic status
- complex seizures
  - –Duration over 15 minutes
  - –Focal
  - –Recurrent within 24 hours
- first degree family history of epilepsy
- age at onset less than 6 months.

The chances increase from a base level of 2%, to 3% with one risk factor and up to 13% with two or more risk factors. If the initial seizure occurs in a child under 6 months of age, there is a 4 fold increase in the incidence of epilepsy.[3]

EVALUATION

Children who have a seizure during a febrile illness should be examined by a physician. With a simple febrile seizure, when the source of infection is obvious and there is no evidence of central nervous system infection (CNS), a complete history and physical examination are all that are necessary. Extensive laboratory evaluation is not necessary in this situation. If the source of infection is not apparent after history and physical examination or the child is not acting normally, a fever workup should be done and may include complete blood count (CBC), urinalysis, blood and urine cultures, chest x-ray studies, and lumbar puncture. It is imperative to be certain that despite an obvious focus, no more serious infection such as meningitis is present concurrently.

Table 27-2 lists diagnostic tests that may be considered and their indications. Calcium and magnesium levels are almost never helpful. The electroencephalogram (EEG) shows abnormal findings during and after a febrile seizure, but findings should be normal by 1 week postseizure. Some authors recommend an EEG 1 to 2 weeks after seizure for children with a first seizure or a complex event. A CBC is not always necessary; it has been shown to be most helpful in detecting occult bacteremia in children under 2 years of age with temperatures greater than 39.4 °C.

The indications for a lumbar puncture for a child with a febrile seizure remain controversial. Recommendations range from tapping all such children,

---

Table 27-2 Diagnostic Assessment of Children with a Febrile Seizure

History/physical	All cases
Fever workup	As indicated by history/physical
Electrolytes	Dehydration
	Vomiting
	Diarrhea
Blood glucose	History of diabetes, hypoglycemia, depressed consciousness; or abnormal mentation
Bedside glucose estimation	Persistent depression of level of consciousness
Calcium/phosphorus/magnesium	Neonatal seizures
Skull x-ray study	Evidence of trauma
CT scan	Evidence of trauma
	Progressive neurologic impairment
EEG	Complex seizure
CBC	Suspicion of occult bacteremia
Lumbar puncture	Age below 18 months
	Prior physician visit within 48 hr
	Seizure in emergency department
	Focal seizure
	Suspicious physical or neurologic examination

only those with a first episode, or employing greater selectivity. Using a decision analysis approach, investigators[5] at Johns Hopkins and the University of Pennsylvania defined five historical and physical examination findings that discriminate between children with and without meningitis who have had a febrile seizure (see Table 27-2). In the group with none of these risk factors, there was no meningitis. They recommend against lumbar puncture in this group, and in their population this would have spared 62% of the children without meningitis the need for this test.[5] Physical examination may be much less specific and sensitive in picking up evidence of CNS infection in very young children; therefore, a spinal puncture for children under 18 months of age was also recommended.

Nevertheless, controversy still abounds. Thirteen percent of children with meningitis are reported to have seizures, and these can closely resemble a simple febrile seizure. Children with an extracranial source of infection, such as otitis media, can also have intracranial infection. Children who have a history of febrile convulsions can develop meningitis and seizure. These arguments against limiting lumbar puncture to those with a first seizure or those without an obvious source of infection have theoretical validity but do not seem to be confirmed in statistical studies. One point that seems clear is that children with complex seizures are more likely to have an etiology other than fever alone and require more extensive investigation.

PHARMACOLOGIC MANAGEMENT

The child who comes to the emergency department with a febrile seizure may be treated with anticonvulsant agents acutely, chronically, intermittently, or not at all. In the great majority of cases, the latter option is probably the best.

Intermittent therapy with various medications during febrile episodes has been suggested. It would seem that aggressive fever control with antipyretics would help reduce recurrences, but this does not seem to be true. This is probably because the seizure occurs early in the illness, frequently before the parents become aware of the fever and the slow decline of the fever after treatment. Similarly, intermittent use of phenobarbital is ineffective. The time required to reach a therapeutic level is far too long.

Interestingly, intermittent therapy with rectally-administered diazepam was found to be effective. Reduction of recurrence from 39% without treatment to 12% with rectal diazepam is reported. Refinement of this study shows that children at low risk of recurrence do not benefit from intermittent prophylaxis. Risk factors for recurrence are:

- onset at 15 months of age or less
- epilepsy in first degree relative
- febrile seizures in first degree relative
- complex seizure
- day nursery care.

Children with two or more risk factors should be considered for prophylaxis.[6]

Administration of rectal diazepam will provide therapeutic plasma levels within 30 minutes, which can be maintained for the first 24 hours with repeated dosing with 0.5 mg/kg at 8-hour intervals. A suppository form of diazepam is not currently available in this country.

Continuous daily administration of phenobarbital is also very effective, reducing recurrence from 25% to 5% in one study. However, compliance with regular dosing in a healthy child is difficult, and undesirable side effects (hyperactivity, insomnia, and behavioral changes) occur in 40% of children.[7]

Other anticonvulsants may also prevent recurrent febrile seizures. Valproic acid, which has been studied extensively in Europe, is effective, reducing recurrence from 35% with placebo to 4% with treatment. Side effects are a concern but occur in significantly fewer cases than with phenobarbital, requiring a change in treatment in only 14%.[8] Phenytoin sodium and carbamazepine appear ineffective. In general, prophylactic treatment of children with febrile seizures is not recommended unless children have two or more risk factors. It may be considered for those children with atypical seizures, family history of febrile seizures, abnormal neurologic examination, first seizure occurring under 1 year of age, and recurrent seizures. Children whose parents are emotionally or intellectually unable to handle a recurrent seizure may be added to this list.

CONCLUSION

Since febrile seizures are not generally associated with adverse neurologic consequences; since there is minimal increased risk for development of epilepsy and this risk is unchanged by treatment; since simple history and physical examination can differentiate those children needing extensive diagnostic tests; and since medications used in this setting have significant side effects; the following four recommendations can be made for children suffering a simple febrile seizure:

1. Laboratory and radiologic tests should be ordered only as specifically indicated by the history and physical examination.
2. The source of infection should be determined and adequately treated.
3. Lumbar puncture should be reserved for children who by history or physical examination are at increased risk for meningitis, or who by virtue of age are less likely to show obvious signs of meningitis.
4. Prophylactic treatment should generally be reserved for children at high risk of recurrence, and a regimen should be selected that is effective, produces few side effects, and is easy to administer.

REFERENCES

1. Guraraj V: Febrile seizures: Current concepts. *Clin Pediatr* 1980;19:731–738.

2. Vining E, Freeman J: Seizures which are not epilepsy. *Pediatr Ann* 1985;14:711–722.

3. Nelson K, Ellenberg J: Predictors of epilepsy in children who have experienced febrile seizures. *N Engl J Med* 1976;295:1029–1033.

4. Nelson K, Ellenberg J: Prognosis in children with febrile seizures. *Pediatrics* 1978; 61:720–727.

5. Joffe A, McCormick M, DeAngelis C: Which children with febrile seizures need lumbar puncture? *Am J Dis Child* 1983;137:1153–1156.

6. Knudsen F: Recurrence risk after first febrile seizure and effect of short term diazepam prophylaxis. *Arch Dis Child* 1985;60:1045–1049.

7. Camfield P, Camfield C, Shapiro S, et al: The first febrile seizure: Antipyretic instruction plus either phenobarbital or placebo to prevent recurrence. *J Pediatr* 1980;97:16–21.

8. Herrany J, Armijo J, Arteaga R: Effectiveness and toxicity of phenobarbital, primidone and sodium valproate in the prevention of febrile convulsions, controlled by plasma levels. *Epilepsia* 1984;25:89–95.

Section 14

Status Epilepticus

Initial intervention must focus on airway protection and ventilation control.

A broad range of pharmacologic agents are available. The early administration of diazepam combined with ongoing therapy with phenobarbital or phenytoin sodium provides rapid control but increases the risk of respiratory depression. Others argue that immediate control is clinically less important than the risk of respiratory arrest, and use only phenobarbital or phenytoin. This group stresses that few sequelae occur if the seizure is controlled within the initial 10 minutes, provided that hypoxia is prevented. Lorazepam may be a promising new agent for initial control.

The routes of administration for anticonvulsants have broadened. Although experience is very limited, and the intravenous route is still preferred, the intraosseous route has been used with diazepam, phenytoin, and phenobarbital. Diazepam has also been given via the endotracheal route as well as rectally and intramuscularly when intravenous access is not achieved in a timely fashion.

28. Management of Status Epilepticus in Children

Ronald A. Dieckmann, MD, MPH

Status epilepticus in children requires rapid, definitive management. The duration of seizure activity is closely correlated with outcome: The longer the time interval between onset of seizures and effective treatment, the worse the prognosis.

It is a condition of the very young. About 85% of pediatric cases occur before 5 years of age.[1] In approximately three fourths of cases, the child has no prior history of seizures or neurologic or developmental abnormalities. The younger the child, the more likely an etiology will be found.

Continuous seizure activity or recurrent seizures without return to consciousness for more than 30 minutes are characteristic. Status epilepticus may be either *generalized* or *focal* (Table 28-1). Generalized tonic-clonic, tonic, or clonic seizures are most frequent, although generalized myoclonic and petit mal epilepticus may also occur. Unilateral seizures are not uncommon in childhood. The clonic form is most likely in focal status epilepticus.

Multiple causes exist (see Table 28-1). Central nervous system (CNS) infection, fever without primary CNS involvement, fluid and electrolyte disturbances, poisoning, and poor compliance with anticonvulsant therapy are the most frequent. In approximately one half of all children with status epilepticus, no organic cause is ever identified.

PATHOPHYSIOLOGY

The approach to treatment of status epilepticus must encompass an understanding of the pathophysiology and the critical time frame of neuronal injury. Molecular events leading to neuronal death probably begin within minutes after the onset of the convulsion. Calcium, free radicals, and other toxic substances accumulate and ultimately mediate brain edema and cell death.

Table 28-1 Conditions Associated with Status Epilepticus in Children

Acute Conditions
Poor Compliance with Anticonvulsants
Fever
CNS Infection
   Bacterial meningitis
   Aseptic meningitis
   Encephalitis
Fluid and Electrolyte Disturbances
   Hypoglycemia
   Hyponatremia
   Hypocalcemia
Poisoning
   Lead
   Aspirin
   Theophylline
   Antidepressants
   Isoniazid
   Phenothiazines
   Hydrocarbons
   Sympathomimetics (phencyclidine, cocaine, LSD, amphetamine)
Closed Head Trauma

Chronic Conditions
Posthypoxic
Posthemorrhagic
Postinfectious
Post-traumatic
Degenerative disease

Idiopathic

As convulsive status epilepticus continues, lactic acidosis, hyperthermia, respiratory acidosis, hyperkalemia, and dehydration further compromise cellular function. Neurologic sequelae are frequent. A recent series[2] of 239 pediatric patients noted neurologic deficits in 67% who survived an episode of convulsive status epilepticus; in 36%, neuronal injury was directly attributed to the seizure itself.

Neurologic outcome is related to the duration of status epilepticus. Seizures lasting more than 60 minutes, or more than 30 minutes in association with fever, are correlated almost universally with high morbidity and mortality. Permanent sequelae may, however, begin after only 10 to 15 minutes, especially in patients who are already jeopardized by hypoxia, hypercarbia, infection, intoxication or other metabolic derangements.

MANAGEMENT APPROACHES

Adequacy of the airway and ventilation is essential, focusing on routine measures for positioning the head, clearing the airway, providing oxygen, and assisting ventilation. Hypoventilation is common; one study reported a respiratory acidosis in 43% of patients, 19% having a $PaCO_2$ greater than 60 mm Hg. Acidosis does not seem to affect ultimate mortality or neurologic functioning.[3] However, until there is further substantiation of this finding, in children, airway protection and ventilation must be a primary focus of management.

Intubation for airway protection or mechanical ventilation, or both, can generally be withheld until failure of initial medical therapy. Obviously, this decision must be individualized and constantly re-evaluated.

Next, vascular access must be established. Gaining venous access for drug administration is frequently the rate-limiting step in successful management of status epilepticus.[4] When conventional intravenous (IV) access cannot be expeditiously achieved, alternative routes for drug administration should be used (see Chapter 46).

ALTERNATIVE ROUTES FOR DRUG DELIVERY

Experience with these routes is limited, so they should be used only when venous access is not readily achieved. Nonetheless, they have been shown to be efficacious.

The *intraosseous (IO) route* offers an effective conduit for anticonvulsant drug therapy. Although pharmacokinetics in children are not well established, several agents important to seizure management have been effectively delivered IO: dextrose, diazepam (Valium), phenytoin sodium, and phenobarbital. Cumulative experience at San Francisco General Hospital and elsewhere indicates a complication rate of less than 1%.[5]

A second option, when venous access is not achieved in the actively convulsing child, is *rectal administration* of diazepam. Rectal solutions of diazepam are rapidly absorbed with anticonvulsant plasma concentrations obtained within 4 ($\pm$1) minutes. A prospective study[6] of 44 children given rectal diazepam, aged 6 months to 5 years, showed clinical efficacy in more than 80% of patients after a single dose. Successful termination of seizure activity was closely linked to speed of administration.[6]

A rectal dose of 0.5 mg/kg of diazepam may be administered. The IV dose form, without dilution, is instilled into the rectum through a 5 FR plastic tube with a blunt tip. After instillation of the drug, the tube is squeezed, withdrawn, and the buttocks held together. The rectal route, however, is somewhat unpredictable with respect to absorption, and serum peak drug levels occur later than with intravenous use. Dextrose, phenytoin, phenobarbital, and other agents have no demonstrated effectiveness via the rectal route.

A third alternative is the *endotracheal route*. If the child is already intubated, an infant feeding tube or umbilical artery catheter should be inserted past the distal tip of the endotracheal tube. Diazepam may then be instilled after dilution to 3 mL with distilled water or normal saline. Bag ventilation disperses the drug distally. Anecdotal experience suggests an effective dose of 0.3 mg/kg. One complication of endotracheal diazepam is pneumonitis, although the incidence is unknown. Arterial PO_2 and PCO_2 do not appear to be affected. Other anticonvulsants cannot be administered using this route.

ANTICONVULSANT AGENTS

The primary focus must be on airway and ventilatory adequacy. Possible metabolic or toxic causes require early consideration, since such conditions respond poorly to anticonvulsant therapy, but are often readily reversible with specific antidotes or metabolic correction.

It is essential to individualize the use of anticonvulsants, to accommodate individual patient status, prior efficacy of drugs, availability, and clinical experience of the practitioner.

The pharmacologic approach to management of status epilepticus in children at San Francisco General Hospital is outlined in Table 28-2.[7]

Diazepam

Diazepam, 0.3 mg/kg, is our best agent for immediate seizure control. Approximately 79% of generalized tonic-clonic and 88% of partial status epilepticus cases will respond in less than 5 minutes.[8] Diazepam is less effective in children suffering from extensive acute brain injury, major toxic insults, or prolonged status epilepticus.

The choice of diazepam as an initial anticonvulsant derives from two of its properties. First, its rapid brain penetration allows expeditious control of the convulsive event. Phenytoin, while equally effective in terminating status epilepticus, is slower, usually requiring 20 minutes. Phenobarbital may take 30 minutes or more. Since morbidity and mortality are closely tied to seizure duration, early control is a therapeutic axiom.

The second major attribute of diazepam is ease of administration. Dosing at 1 mg/min is completed in several minutes. Although rapid bolus injection may terminate the convulsion more promptly, since the rate of increase of plasma

Table 28-2 Drug Therapy for Status Epilepticus

Drug	Dose	Route	Rate	Complication
First-Line Agents				
Oxygen	100%	Nasal cannula Mask Endotracheal		Possible free radical formation
Dextrose	$D_{25}W$ 2 mL/kg	Intravenous Intraosseous*	Bolus	Hyperosmolality Increased lactate
Diazepam	0.3 mg/kg	Intravenous Intraosseous* Endotracheal* Rectal*	1 mg/min	Respiratory arrest Hypotension Sedation
	0.5 mg/kg		Bolus	
Phenytoin sodium	15–20 mg/kg load	Intravenous Intraosseous*	0.5 mg/kg/min (infants) 1 mg/kg/min (children)	Heart block Bradycardia Hypotension
Secondary Agent				
Phenobarbital	15–20 mg/kg load	Intravenous Intraosseous*	1 mg/kg/min (infants) 2 mg/kg/min (children)	Respiratory arrest Hypotension Sedation
Tertiary Agents				
Paraldehyde	0.25 mL/kg	Rectal Intramuscular	1:2 in mineral oil Bolus	Pulmonary edema Metabolic acidosis
Lidocaine, 1%	1 mg/kg load	Intravenous Intraosseous* Endotracheal*	20-50 µg/kg/min continuous infusion	Seizures
Pentobarbital	5 mg/kg/hr for 2 hr	Intravenous Intramuscular* Intraosseous*	1-2 mg/kg/hr	Respiratory arrest Hypotension

*Indicates limited experience.

drug concentration influences therapeutic effect, delivery that is too speedy probably increases the risk of adverse effects. Diazepam can be infused more quickly than other major anticonvulsants. Furthermore, alternative routes for its administration are potentially available: IV, IO (limited experience), endotracheal (limited experience), or rectal. Oral or intramuscular (IM) use is contraindicated in status epilepticus.

Limitations of diazepam include its short duration of action and the potential for sudden and unpredictable respiratory depression and hypotension. Because of its brief anticonvulsant effect (15 minutes), a second drug with a longer half-life must be given for lasting seizure control. Multiple administrations of diazepam should be avoided to avert apnea and hypotension, complications potentiated by phenobarbital. Immediate capabilities for endotracheal intubation and airway support must be available.

Lorazepam

Lorazepam is a newer benzodiazepine with well-documented effectiveness in status epilepticus.[9] Its capacity to enter the CNS rapidly, and terminate seizures promptly compares favorably with diazepam. Possible advantages include a longer duration of action and fewer cardiopulmonary complications. However, data with children are inconclusive. The drug probably equals diazepam in initial effectiveness and may have a more prolonged action. On the other hand, sedation seems more profound, and major side effects are no less frequent than with diazepam. We have found no advantage in using lorazepam instead of tandem therapy with diazepam and phenytoin.

Phenytoin

Our pharmacologic sequence in status epilepticus requires phenytoin administration, after diazepam, *in every case*. If status epilepticus is terminated by diazepam, phenytoin provides lasting control because of its longer half-life. If diazepam fails to stop the convulsion, phenytoin may succeed. Furthermore, phenytoin does not potentiate diazepam's adverse cardiopulmonary effects, or further depress the level of consciousness.

Monotherapy of status epilepticus with phenytoin is favored by some authors. It is as equally effective as diazepam in stopping seizures, but slower; and administration is more problematic. The drug is poorly soluble and must be infused in normal saline. The rate of administration in young children is 1 mg/kg/min (20 mg/min maximum).

The child receiving phenytoin must be followed by cardiac monitoring and measurement of blood pressure on an ongoing basis. The infusion should be slowed or stopped for systolic blood pressure dips of 10 mm Hg, second or third degree heart block, or bradycardia. Hypotension occurs most commonly with rapid administration.

Brain concentrations of phenytoin peak at the end of the drug dosing. Therefore, if status epilepticus continues after the infusion is finished, a secondary long-acting anticonvulsant should be added *immediately* to avoid a therapeutic gap.

Phenobarbital

When status epilepticus persists after phenytoin administration, phenobarbital should be used next. The dosage is 20 mg/kg, given at 1 to 2 mg/kg/min (100 mg/min maximum). Phenobarbital does not have the difficulties of administration associated with phenytoin. It is an excellent alternative for the phenytoin-allergic child. However, its peak brain level is usually at 30 to 60 minutes.

Phenobarbital has an extended and variable half-life, up to 4 days. An important side effect of the drug is sedation. Occasionally, hypotension and respiratory depression occur; the risk is highest in patients who previously received diazepam.

We wait 30 minutes after completion of phenobarbital dosing before advancing to a tertiary agent.

Other Agents

Rarely, status epilepticus continues after maximum doses of diazepam, phenytoin, and phenobarbital. Paraldehyde or lidocaine are therapeutic alternatives. Paraldehyde may be given at 0.25 mL/kg, diluted 1:2 in mineral oil, rectally. As with diazepam, the solution should be administered by tube, high in the rectum. The buttocks should be taped after withdrawal of the tube. Severe pulmonary complications have limited its IV use. The drug may also be administered IM, at 0.25 mL/kg; absorption is rapid by this route.

Lidocaine may be useful in refractory status epilepticus. The loading dose is 1 mg/kg of the 1% solution, followed by a continuous infusion of 20 to 50 μg/kg/min. Status epilepticus may be exacerbated with lidocaine as the initial therapy. The value of lidocaine is familiarity of use, rapid peak serum level, and short half-life. If effective, lidocaine will terminate seizure activity within minutes. The drug should be discontinued if status epilepticus is not terminated in 5 minutes.

When paraldehyde and lidocaine are unsuccessful in the treatment of status epilepticus, and resources for intensive cardiopulmonary support of children are present, pentobarbital coma may be indicated. Pentobarbital dosages are 5 mg/kg/hr for 2 hours, then 1 to 2 mg/kg/hr thereafter. Such therapy requires ongoing intensive care monitoring, intubation, and careful cardiovascular observation. Pentobarbital doses should be adjusted to produce burst suppression on the electroencephalogram (EEG). Hypotension is typically the limiting factor in effective pentobarbital therapy of status epilepticus.

ADDITIONAL CONSIDERATIONS

Hyperpyrexia

Seventy-seven of 90 patients (86%) studied by Aminoff and Simon[3] had elevations in rectal temperature; only three were infected. Hyperpyrexia occurred from increased motor activity during the convulsive period.

Hyperpyrexia is a significant risk factor for increased morbidity in status epilepticus. It is also easily preventable. Recognition and treatment of hyperthermia are essential to early therapy for status epilepticus.

Acidosis

Acidosis is common in status epilepticus, and may be metabolic, respiratory, or mixed. Clinical and experimental data do not correlate acidosis with neurologic outcome.

Therapy with sodium bicarbonate during status epilepticus is discouraged. It is usually unnecessary and possibly harmful. Metabolic alkalosis, hyperosmolality, decreased ionized calcium, hypokalemia, lowered fibrillation threshold, and leftward shift of the oxyhemoglobin dissociation curve may all result from alkalosis. Bicarbonate therapy of lactic acidosis is usually unsuccessful during active convulsions. The acidosis of seizures will reverse itself within 30 minutes of the cessation of seizure activity.

An intriguing unsubstantiated theory is that acidosis in status epilepticus is potentially helpful. Acidosis increases the production of the inhibitory neurotransmitter gamma-aminobutyric acid (GABA), which may be protective during acute seizure activity. Alkalosis increases metabolism of GABA.

Neonatal Seizures

Therapy in neonatal status epilepticus varies slightly in the infant and older child. After $D_{10}W$, at 2 mL/kg, we prefer phenobarbital as the first-line anticonvulsant, then phenytoin. Drug doses are both 20 mg/kg. We do not use diazepam in this age group because of problems with drug metabolism.[10] Pyridoxine hydrochloride, 100 mg IV, is indicated for neonatal seizures; a deficiency in pyridoxine-dependent GABA synthesis may present as neonatal status epilepticus.

CONCLUSION

Status epilepticus requires immediate attention to the airway and ventilation and a systematic, rational choice of drugs based on the patient's condition and the clinician's experience. New agents and new routes are available.

REFERENCES

1. Aicardi J, Chevrie JJ: Convulsive status epilepticus in infants and children: A study of 239 cases. *Epilepsia* 1970;11:187–197.

2. Aicardi J, Chevrie JJ: Consequences of status epilepticus in infants and children, in Delgado-Escueta AV, Wasterlain CG, Treiman DM, Porter RJ (eds): *Advances in Neurology*, vol 34. New York, Raven Press, 1983, pp 115–124.

3. Aminoff MJ, Simon RP: Status epilepticus: Causes, clinical features and consequences in 98 patients. *Am J Med* 1980;69:657–666.

4. Rosetti VA, Thompson BM, Aprahamian C, et al: Difficulty and delay in intravascular access in pediatric arrests, abstracted. *Ann Emerg Med* 1984;13:406.

5. Rosetti VA, Thompson BM, Miller J, et al: Intraosseous infusion: An alternative route of pediatric intravascular access. *Ann Emerg Medicine* 1985;14:885–888.

6. Knudsen U: Rectal administration of diazepam solution in the acute treatment of convulsions in infants and children. *Am J Dis Child* 1979;54:855–857.

7. Dieckmann R: Seizures in children, in Callaham M (ed): *Current Therapy in Emergency Medicine*. BC Decker, Inc., New York, 1986, pp 1017–1020.

8. Schmidt D: Benzodiazepines: An update, in Pedley TA, Beldrum BS (eds): *Recent Advances in Epilepsy*. New York, Churchill Livingstone, Inc., 1985, pp 125–134.

9. Levy RJ, Krall RL: Treatment of status epilepticus with lorazepam. *Arch Neurol* 1984;41:605–611.

10. Painter MJ: General principles of treatment: Status epilepticus in neonates, in Delgado-Escueta AV, Wasterlain CG, Treiman DM, Porter RJ (eds): *Advances in Neurology*, vol 34. New York, Raven Press, 1983, pp 385–393.

PART IV

Poisoning and Ingestion

Section 15

Alternatives to Ipecac

Syrup of ipecac is effective in inducing vomiting, but its efficacy in removing poisons from the gastrointestinal tract is undefined. Activated charcoal may be more effective in reducing drug absorption.

Administering activated charcoal, often combined with gastric lavage, may be the best approach in children with potentially dangerous ingestions. Others suggest administering only activated charcoal for ingestions treated 1 to 2 hours after the event that do not involve drugs that impair gastrointestinal motility. Further studies are required to define ipecac's role in the treatment of pediatric ingestions.

29. Is Ipecac Overused in Acute Childhood Poisoning?

Kenneth W. Kulig, MD

In 1978, the Commissioner of the United States Food and Drug Administration concluded that syrup of ipecac should be readily available over the counter without a prescription. Since that time, millions of doses have been sold or given away in a nationwide attempt to provide a readily accessible home remedy for acute childhood poisonings. The use of ipecac in emergency departments has simultaneously become commonplace, even with adults, although many patients receiving it do so many hours after an ingestion has occurred.

The concept that inducing emesis is effective treatment of an acute poisoning has become popular among both health care professionals and consumers. Induction of emesis with ipecac is relatively rapid, reasonably safe, and provides physical evidence that *some* treatment (as opposed to doing nothing) has been rendered. Widely overlooked, however, is a mounting evidence that syrup of ipecac:

- probably does not remove a substantial amount of ingested poison in most cases;
- is probably not as effective as gastric lavage;
- is probably not as effective as a single oral dose of activated charcoal; and
- may cause morbidity and even mortality with therapeutic dosing.

Given the currently available data, one may conclude that ipecac is overused in acute childhood poisoning.

PHARMACOLOGY OF IPECAC

Ipecac is the material obtained from drying the roots of the plants *Cephaelis ipecacuanha* or *C acuminata*. It is indigenous to Brazil and Central America,

219

and is also cultivated in India and Malaysia. The alkaloids contained in this material include emetine, cephaeline, cykotrine, hydroipecamine, and ipecamine. Most of these are amebicidal; ipecac has been used for centuries to treat dysentery.

A 30-mL dose of syrup of ipecac contains various amounts and percentages of the two major alkaloids, but generally has approximately 12 mg of emetine and 23 mg of cephaeline. Cephaeline is probably a demethylated metabolite of emetine (Figure 29-1) that retains some pharmacologic activity. Both act to cause vomiting by local gastric irritation and by stimulating the chemoreceptor trigger zone in the medulla. For the latter to occur, the alkaloids must be absorbed into the blood. This was documented in actual overdose patients.[1]

SAFETY

Syrup of ipecac is reasonably safe for use in children over the age of 6 months. The vast majority of patients who receive a therapeutic dose will vomit within 30 minutes; some may require a second dose. Cardiotoxicity[2] and cardiomyopathy[3,4] were shown in patients with eating disorders who chronically abused ipecac. Cardiotoxicity was associated with the old fluid extract,[5,6] but should not be a concern after one or two therapeutic doses of syrup of ipecac, even if the patient does not vomit.

Worrisome side effects of a therapeutic dose of ipecac in children include lethargy, protracted emesis, and diarrhea. In one study, 11.6% of the 146 children receiving ipecac at home developed "atypical lethargy" related to the ipecac and not the ingested substance.[7] In 21 patients aged 9 to 12 months, drowsiness after receiving ipecac was described in 43%.[8]

Protracted emesis (more than 1 hour of vomiting or more than six episodes noted) occurred in 17% of 146 patients after receiving ipecac.[7] The emetic effect continued for 4.2 hours (range 2 to 8 hours) in adult volunteers given

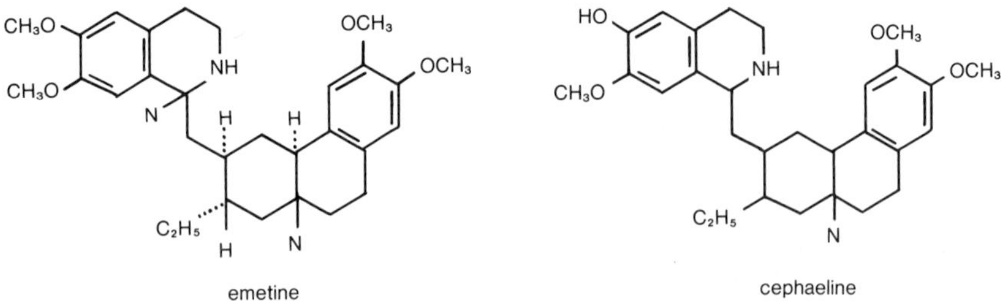

emetine   cephaeline

Figure 29-1 Molecular structures of emetine and cephaeline, the two principal alkaloids in syrup of ipecac.

one therapeutic dose.[9] Diarrhea was also reported in 13% of 146 patients after receiving ipecac.[7]

Rare case reports of major morbidity or mortality after a single dose of ipecac include:

- ruptured diaphragm and death in a 2-year-old[10]
- Mallory-Weiss tear of the esophagus[11]
- cerebrovascular accident in an elderly patient[12]
- pneumomediastinum and retroperitoneum[13]
- aspiration of gastric contents.[14,15]

EFFICACY

Ever since the study by Boxer et al in 1969,[16] it has been assumed that ipecac in children is more effective than lavage. In that study, 17 children with a history of salicylate ingestion were given either ipecac then lavage, or lavage then ipecac, and salicylates were subsequently measured in emesis and lavage fluid. Emesis contained significantly more salicylate. However, the mean quantity of salicylate removed by emesis was only 144 mg (less than two baby aspirins), and by lavage was only 84 mg (about one baby aspirin). Therefore, rather than showing superior efficacy of ipecac, the study actually showed that neither technique was very effective. These children probably could have been as effectively and much less traumatically managed had they been observed and supported only, or been given oral activated charcoal only.

In another pediatric study, magnesium hydroxide was given orally as a marker immediately before ipecac, and magnesium in the emesis was measured. Although there was essentially no delay between giving marker and ipecac, as opposed to the more common clinical scenario of delay between ingestion of toxin and ipecac, ipecac removed a mean of only 28% of the marker (range 0% to 78%).[17]

Recent studies in adults have concluded the superiority of gastric lavage over ipecac using thiamine[18] or cyanocobalamin[19] as markers. Both studies used large-bore orogastric hoses instead of small nasogastric tubes, perhaps accounting for the discrepancy with the study by Boxer et al.[16]

A single dose of activated charcoal was also shown to be superior to ipecac-induced emesis in preventing drug absorption in two volunteer models[9,20] of acute poisoning. Activated charcoal did not induce emesis unless ipecac had been previously administered; charcoal itself was not an emetic agent. Failing to administer ipecac before or concurrently with activated charcoal may allow the charcoal to remain in the gastrointestinal tract where it can continue to "catch up" with drugs distal to the stomach.

ALTERNATIVES TO IPECAC

In the home setting, there are two alternatives to the use of ipecac in the asymptomatic child: (1) to observe only, or (2) to administer activated charcoal. Both options mandate that a responsible adult be present who knows what symptoms and signs to look for, and who can get appropriate medical care promptly if necessary. Frequent follow-up telephone contacts should be made by the regional poison center. Whenever the appropriateness of the decision for home observation is in doubt, the child should be seen in a health care facility.

The second option is not presently possible in most homes, but as activated charcoal becomes more widely available for home use, administering it instead of ipecac will become possible. Charcoal currently can be purchased without a prescription.[21] It might initially seem to be nearly impossible to get a child to swallow charcoal in the home. However, one recent study[22] found that 30 of 50 (60%) children between the ages of 8 months and 5 years were able to drink the total dose of charcoal at home that had been recommended by the regional poison center.

If the child is sent to a health care facility, two additional options are available: (1) gastric lavage, then charcoal or (2) administration of activated charcoal down a small nasogastric tube without lavage. Gastric lavage with a large-bore orogastric hose empties the stomach immediately without the 20 to 30 minute delay of ipecac, allows activated charcoal to be administered hours sooner, and thereby maximally reduces absorption of the poison.[14] Gastric lavage, however, is more traumatic for the child than the other modalities, and therefore should probably be reserved for truly life-threatening exposures.

Administering charcoal down a small nasogastric tube with or without preceding lavage is another alternative to giving ipecac. This technique is less traumatic in children than orogastric lavage with a large tube, and allows immediate rather than delayed administration of charcoal.

It would be inappropriate without additional data to outline which of these four options should be generally used (Table 29-1). A "cookbook approach" to the management of the acutely poisoned patient is what caused the nearly universal acceptance of ipecac 20 years ago. What is needed in all cases of pediatric poisoning is the use of clinical judgment based on a thorough knowledge of the expected toxicity.

Table 29-1 Alternatives to Ipecac

Home setting*
　Observe only
　Administer activated charcoal

Health care facility
　Gastric lavage
　Activated charcoal using NG tube without lavage

*Can be done at health care facility as well.

CONCLUSION

Syrup of ipecac is an effective agent at inducing vomiting but not at removing poisons from the gastrointestinal tract. Not every child who has accidentally ingested a possibly toxic material needs to be given syrup of ipecac, as there are better methods of treating the acutely poisoned child. As ipecac's substantial limitations become more widely recognized, its use will, we hope, be put into proper perspective.

REFERENCES

1. Moran DM, Crouch DJ, Finkle BS: Absorption of ipecac alkaloids in emergency patients. *Ann Emerg Med* 1984;13:1100–1102.

2. Adler AG, Walinsky P, Krall RA, et al: Death resulting from ipecac syrup poisoning. *JAMA* 1980;243:1927–1928.

3. Palmer EP, Guay AT: Reversible myopathy secondary to abuse of ipecac in patients with major eating disorders. *N Engl J Med* 1985;313:1457–1459.

4. Bennett HS, Spiro AJ, Pollack MA, et al: Ipecac-induced myopathy simulating dermatomyositis. *Neurology* 1982;32:91–94.

5. Allport RB: Ipecac is not innocuous. *Am J Dis Child* 1959;98:786–789.

6. Miser JS, Robertson WO: Ipecac poisoning. *West J Med* 1978;128:440–443.

7. Czajka PA, Russell SL: Nonemetic effects of ipecac syrup. *Pediatrics* 1985;75:1101–1104.

8. Gaudreault P, McCormick MA, Lacouture PG, et al: Poisoning exposures and use of ipecac in children less than 1 year old. *Ann Emerg Med* 1986;15:808–810.

9. Neuvonen PJ, Vartiainen M, Tokola O: Comparison of activated charcoal and ipecac syrup in prevention of drug absorption. *Eur J Clin Pharmacol* 1983;24:557–562.

10. Robertson WO: Syrup of ipecac associated fatality: A case report. *Vet Hum Toxicol* 1979;21:87–89.

11. Tandberg D, Liechty EJ, Fishbein D: Mallory-Weiss syndrome: An unusual complication of ipecac-induced emesis. *Ann Emerg Med* 1981;10:521–523.

12. Klein-Schwartz W, Gorman RL, Oderda GM, et al: Ipecac use in the elderly: The unanswered question. *Ann Emerg Med* 1984;13:1152–1154.

13. Wolowodiuk LJ, McMicken DB, O'Brien P: Pneumomediastinum and retropneumoperitoneum: An unusual complication of syrup-of-ipecac-induced emesis. *Ann Emerg Med* 1984;13:1148–1151.

14. Kulig K, Bar-Or D, Cantrill SV, et al: Management of acutely poisoned patients without gastric emptying. *Ann Emerg Med* 1985;14:562–567.

15. Kurt TL, Bost R, Gilliland M, et al: Accidental Kwell (lindane) ingestions. *Vet Hum Toxicol* 1986;28:569–571.

16. Boxer L, Anderson FP, Rowe DS: Comparison of ipecac-induced emesis with gastric lavage in the treatment of acute salicylate ingestion. *J Pediatr* 1969;74:800–803.

17. Corby DG, Decker WJ: Clinical comparison of pharmacologic emetics in children. *Pediatrics* 1968;42:361–364.

18. Auerbach PS, Osterloh J, Braun O, et al: Efficacy of gastric emptying: Gastric lavage versus emesis induced with ipecac. *Ann Emerg Md* 1986;15:692–698.

19. Tandberg D, Diven BG, McLeod JW: Ipecac-induced emesis versus gastric lavage: A controlled study in normal adults. *Am J Emerg Med* 1986;4:205–209.

20. Curtis RA, Barone J, Giacona N: Efficacy of ipecac and activated charcoal/cathartic: Prevention of salicylate absorption in a simulated overdose. *Arch Int Med* 1984;144:48–52.

21. Federal Register: Drug products for over-the-counter human use for the treatment of acute toxic ingestion; establishment of a monograph. 21 CFR Part 357, Jan 15, 1985.

22. Dockstader LL, Lawrence RA, Bresnick HL: Home administration of activated charcoal: Feasibility and acceptance. *Vet Hum Toxicol* 1986;28:471.

Section 16

Gastrointestinal Foreign Body Ingestion

The appropriate assessment of the child with a definite or potential history of foreign body ingestion varies with the symptoms, time since ingestion, and nature of the object. Initial radiologic evaluation must include plain films, using two projections with one perpendicular to the other. Contrast studies or endoscopy may on occasion be required.

Asymptomatic patients ingesting benign objects can probably be observed and monitored for passage. Those smooth, inert objects above the gastro-esophageal junction that do not pass within 24 hours should generally undergo Foley catheter extraction; fiberoptic endoscopy is another alternative. The esophagus presents a unique danger with retention of even a smooth, inert object because it has no serosa, and the potential for mediastinitis exists.

Symptomatic patients and those ingesting sharp or potentially dangerous objects, such as an alkaline battery, should undergo immediate assessment and removal of the object.

30. Foreign Body Ingestion

Martin J. Smilkstein, MD

Every pediatrician, family physician, and emergency physician will manage children with ingested foreign bodies (IFBs). Despite a wealth of experience with IFBs, several strategies for the best management remain controversial:

- the role of radiographic evaluation in the initial assessment
- observation *v* early removal of esophageal foreign bodies (EFBs) in the asymptomatic patient
- endoscopy *v* Foley catheter extraction for removal of EFBs
- observation *v* early removal of "high-risk" foreign bodies (ie, alkaline button batteries) below the esophageal junction
- the optimum method of surveillance and appropriate timing of intervention for IFBs below the gastroesophageal junction.

INGESTION

Ingested foreign bodies are common occurrences, with more than 1,000 cases reported since 1970. Although a higher incidence and risk of IFBs are reported for children with developmental delay or underlying gastrointestinal disorders, IFBs are more commonly associated with normal developmental exploring. The majority occur between 6 months and 4 years of age.[1-4] Coins are consistently the most common offender,[2,3] followed by chicken and fish bones, and then a long list of objects reflecting the scope of children's curiosity, exploration, and willingness to put any object in their mouths.

Foreign body aspiration, with or without airway compromise, occurs in the same developmental stages and must always be considered when assessing patients with a history of IFB. In one 10-year review, the ratio of IFBs to airway foreign bodies was 116 to 45, indicating that aspiration is also a frequent problem.[3]

Foreign bodies in the gastrointestinal tract may produce a wide range of symptoms. Eighteen to sixty-five percent of children are asymptomatic.[2,4,5] Symptoms may include hoarseness, stridor, cough, gagging, or wheezing as the IFB is in transit through the hypopharynx, or can result from extrinsic airway compression from an IFB in the esophagus. Pain on swallowing, refusal to eat, drooling, or vomiting can occur from IFB impaction or from mucosal or submucosal injury after IFB passage.[2,6]

INITIAL EXAMINATION

When a history of an IFB is present or there are signs or symptoms consistent with an IFB, it is essential to obtain as much information as possible regarding the nature and number of IFBs, the incidence and severity of initial symptoms, and the progression of symptoms since ingestion. Subsequent strategies vary with the type of foreign body, presence of symptoms, and the reliability of follow-up.

Symptomatic Patients

All symptomatic patients should be examined immediately. Telephone management has no role for such patients. After stabilizing the child and obtaining the initial history, the examiner should look for signs of airway involvement, oropharyngeal and posterior pharyngeal trauma, and abdominal findings. Patients who remain symptomatic must undergo further assessment and treatment, often requiring removal of the IFB.

Radiolucent IFBs (ie, fish and chicken bones) commonly cause morbidity.[1,6] Symptoms of impaction or penetration may be indistinguishable from symptoms of residual mucosal or submucosal injury after IFB passage. Unless rapid symptom resolution occurs, the IFB should be assumed to be still present.

With radiolucent IFBs, plain radiographs will detect only major abnormalities (ie, retropharyngeal free air or increased soft tissue swelling), which are rarely present. When available, xeroradiography may be able to locate otherwise radiolucent IFBs. Barium or other contrast studies, including swallowing a cotton pledget soaked in contrast medium, can assess esophageal patency or show extravasation.[3]

Most mucosal lesions are not evident radiographically. Direct visualization must be done in the symptomatic patient to assess the injury and locate and remove the IFB if still present. This will usually require laryngoscopy and endoscopy; an aggressive approach is warranted to avoid missing a potential perforation that may become lethal.

All symptomatic patients with possible radio-opaque IFBs (ie, coins, pins) should undergo radiography. To locate the IFB, views should include all possible sites, from the nasopharynx to the anus in at least one projection, using the minimum number of exposures needed.[7] Once located, a second view of the involved area is useful in determining position and orientation. Direct endoscopic visualization is indicated for IFB removal in some cases or if upper gastrointestinal symptoms persist without a radiographically demonstrable IFB to account for them.

Asymptomatic Patients

The initial approach to asymptomatic patients with a history of IFB is controversial. At issue is whether or not esophageal perforation can occur in an asymptomatic patient, and if so, how quickly. The absence of data has led to widely disparate approaches ranging from home management without physician contact to immediate examination, radiography, and removal of the IFB if located in the esophagus.

In one study[4] of 80 children with a history of coin ingestion, 16% of asymptomatic children were found to have an EFB, suggesting that an immediate x-ray study is indicated for all such patients, irrespective of symptoms. Of patients with an EFB, 44% were asymptomatic; 18% of the 80 patients underwent removal of the coins.[4]

In contrast, many clinicians merely observe asymptomatic patients. Since 1818, only 25 to 30 cases of esophageal perforation in children by coin ingestion have been reported.[1] The total number of ingestions in the same period is unknown, but more than 300 pediatric coin ingestions have been reported since 1970, and the risk of perforation would thus appear to be very small.

Impacted IFBs can cause injury; patients managed by observation must have follow-up to exclude a retained IFB. Commonly, stool may be strained or nonemergent x-ray studies obtained at follow-up. If symptoms ensue or the object is not passed in 72 to 96 hours, the condition must be fully evaluated, including x-ray studies when appropriate.

Ingestion of intrinsically harmful objects should not be managed solely by observation. Button batteries (synonyms: disk, alkaline, or miniature batteries) with potential for causing alkaline corrosive injury, large objects, open safety pins and straight pins, needles, or other sharp objects require a more active and aggressive approach.[1,8,9] They must be localized, usually by x-ray films, and evaluated for possible removal.

FOREIGN BODIES ABOVE THE GASTROESOPHAGEAL JUNCTION

If an EFB is allowed to remain in place, esophageal perforation can occur. The risk is greatest for destructive objects (ie, button batteries) and for sharp objects, such as pins and bones, but coins and buttons can also lead to perforation.[1,6] Substantial morbidity and mortality has resulted from complications including abscess, mediastinitis, aortoesophageal fistula, and extrinsic airway compression.[1]

In symptomatic patients, perforation has been reported on the day of ingestion of many sharp EFBs and, in one case, after a coin.[1] Button batteries have produced marked esophageal injury in as little as 4 hours.[8] There are no reports of early perforation in asymptomatic children; often perforation is discovered weeks after ingestion and, in one child, a fatal aortoesophageal fistula occurred 4 years after ingestion.[1] Because of the unpredictable timing and the devastating nature of the complications, resolution of all EFBs must be aggressively pursued.

Symptomatic Patients

The EFB should be removed as soon as possible. In the case of button batteries, a delay of even a few hours may allow serious change to occur.

Asymptomatic Patients

The management of such patients is controversial. Advocates of early removal emphasize that a fraction of these EFBs will not pass into the stomach spontaneously, and therefore pose a risk of perforation. Proponents of observation note that the vast majority will pass without difficulty, and that removal entails iatrogenic risks.

Button batteries and sharp objects have an increased propensity to cause early perforation and should be removed immediately, regardless of symptoms. This approach should probably also apply to large EFBs.

Asymptomatic patients who present early with less hazardous EFBs may be watched. Ironically, some of the only data supporting observation are derived from a study that advocated early removal. On initial x-ray studies, 25 patients in the study had EFBs. All were scheduled for removal, but by the time of removal (1 to 5 hours delay), only 14 remained. Of the 10 that passed into the stomach (one was vomited), the majority were in the asymptomatic patients. The high rate of spontaneous passage in 5 hours suggests that if given enough time, the remaining asymptomatic patients might not have required EFB removal.[4] Others[5] have advocated 24 hours as a safe observation period.

After an observation trial, repeat x-ray studies must be done and if the EFB has not progressed, removal should be undertaken. If the object is to be removed, an x-ray study should be repeated immediately before the procedure to make certain the object has not passed beyond the gastroesophageal junction in the interim.

Method of Removal

Endoscopic removal and Foley catheter extraction have both been used for EFB removal with excellent results. These techniques are highly successful in experienced hands, but entail risks. Often the most appropriate method is the one most familiar to the clinician.

Endoscopy has traditionally been used and offers the advantage of direct visualization.[3,6,10] This allows control, and is therefore the method of choice for any large, sharp, or irregularly shaped EFB. Endoscopy also allows evaluation of mucosal injury.

Foley catheter extraction has gained recent popularity.[2,4,5] It can be done quickly in the radiology suite under fluoroscopic control and does not require general anesthesia. It is a "blind" technique and should be used only when fine control of the EFB is not critical. Foley extraction should not be used for EFBs in place over 24 hours, or when there is evidence of perforation, because of the risk of adding to possible pre-existing injury. Furthermore, this technique does not permit inspection of the mucosa.

In adults, glucagon has been used to alter esophageal smooth muscle tone. It can be hazardous and should not be used in children.

FOREIGN BODIES BELOW THE GASTROESOPHAGEAL JUNCTION

Between 80% and 100% of IFBs in children that reach the stomach will pass spontaneously without intervention.[11] Although this dictates a less aggressive approach than for EFBs, injury can still occur. The degree of symptoms and the nature of the IFB guide the treatment.

Symptomatic Patients

Children with persistent abdominal pain or vomiting, evidence of an acute abdomen, or signs of active bleeding from the rectum should undergo immediate IFB removal.

Patients with less significant symptoms should undergo serial evaluation and serial x-ray studies.[2,7,9,10] Failure of the IFB to progress over 72 hours with persistence of symptoms, or any significant worsening of signs or symptoms, should lead to IFB removal.[10] For "high-risk" IFBs (button batteries, sharp or large objects), the threshold for removal must be lower, and even minor persistent or developing symptoms should probably be treated with intervention without a 72-hour trial of observation.

Asymptomatic Patients

These children should be observed and their stools strained to detect IFB passage. If symptoms develop, patients should be managed as previously outlined. If they remain asymptomatic and fail to pass the IFB, optimum follow-up and timing of intervention are speculative.

Based upon the pathophysiology of injury caused by various IFBs, stationary IFBs clearly present the greatest risk. Even slow progress appears to be well tolerated for coins and other objects that injure by causing pressure necrosis. Button batteries can cause severe injury when stationary for even a few hours, but have been well tolerated during a week of slow passage once they are below the gastroesophageal junction.[8]

Serial outpatient evaluation is sufficient in most cases.[7] Radiography is indicated after any change in patient condition and at arbitrary intervals to assess progress. Although some authors[9] arbitrarily removed IFBs after 4 weeks,[9] objects such as coins can probably be observed indefinitely and "high-risk" objects should probably be removed earlier. Unfortunately, data do not exist to allow more specific recommendations.

Method of Removal

Endoscopy has been used with variable success to remove accessible IFBs below the gastroesophageal junction.[9] Sigmoidoscopy and colonoscopy have been used in adults, but lower gastrointestinal IFBs have not been problematic in children. Laparotomy has been used in most cases. The choice of method must be individualized, based on the position and type of IFB, and the skill and experience of the clinician.

CONCLUSION

The optimum management strategy for a child with an IFB remains controversial, partially stemming from attempts to view IFBs as a single entity. Ideal management must be based on features that vary on a case-by-case basis. The type and location of the IFB, the degree of symptoms, and the adequacy of follow-up must be considered in formulating a rational approach to this common problem.

REFERENCES

1. Remsen K, Lawson W, Biller HF, et al: Unusual presentations of penetrating foreign bodies of the upper aerodigestive tract. *Ann Otol Rhinol Laryngol* 1983;105(suppl):32–44.

2. Binder L, Anderson WA: Pediatric gastrointestinal foreign body ingestions. *Ann Emerg Med* 1984;13:112–117.

3. Brooks JW: Foreign bodies in the air and food passages. *Ann Surg* 1972;175:720–731.

4. Hodge D, Tecklenberg F, Fleisher G: Coin ingestion: Does every child need a radiograph? *Ann Emerg Med* 1985;14:443–446.

5. Chaikhouni A, Kratz JM, Crawford FA: Foreign bodies of the esophagus. *Am Surgeon* 1985;51:173–179.

6. Nandi P, Ong GB: Foreign body in the oesophagus: Review of 2394 cases. *Br J Surg* 1978; 65:5–9.

7. Rumack BH, Rumack CM: Disk battery ingestion. *JAMA* 1983;249:2509–2511.

8. Litovits TL: Button battery ingestions: A review of 56 cases. *JAMA* 1983;249:2495–2500.

9. Gracia C, Frey CF, Bodai BI: Diagnosis and management of ingested foreign bodies: A ten-year experience. *Ann Emerg Med* 1984;13:30–34.

10. Selivanov V, Sheldon GF, Cello JP, et al: Management of foreign body ingestion. *Ann Surg* 1984;199:187–191.

11. Pellerin D, Fortier-Beaulieu M, Gueguen J: The fate of swallowed foreign bodies: Experience of 1250 instances of sub-diaphragmaic foreign bodies in children. *Prog Pediatr Radiol* 1969; 2:286–302.

31. Foreign Bodies in the Gastrointestinal Tract

Deborah M. Lince, MD
Joel D. Blumhagen, MD

The natural inclination of infants and toddlers to explore their environments is reflected by the observation that the majority of foreign bodies are swallowed by children between 6 months and 3 years of age.[1] Mentally retarded older children are also prone to swallow foreign bodies. A positive history is conveyed by the patient or parent in fewer than half the cases[1,2]; the presence of a swallowed foreign body may be suspected on the basis of signs and symptoms or discovered incidentally.

The clinical picture depends on: a) characteristics of the foreign material including the size, shape, quantity, and chemical composition; b) time since ingestion; c) location of objects within the alimentary tract; and d) the patient's age. Dysphagia or chest and abdominal pain may occur. Signs include excessive drooling, refusal to eat or drink, regurgitation, stridor, wheezing, and irritability. Complications may result in fever, recurrent pneumonia, progressive chest pain, gastrointestinal hemorrhage, obstruction, or peritonitis.

RADIOLOGIC EVALUATION

Radiography is an essential part of the diagnostic evaluation; many foreign bodies—coins and pins, some buttons and toys—are easily recognized on plain radiographs by their radiodensity and shape. Frontal and lateral views of the neck and chest and a frontal view of the abdomen are the routine initial radiographs when there is a clinical suspicion of foreign body ingestion (Figure 31-1 (A, B)). Omission of the frontal view or the lateral view of the chest and neck is a dubious saving of cost and radiation exposure in view of the crucial role of alignment of the x-ray beam in visualization of many flat nonmetallic objects (see Figure 31-2).

233

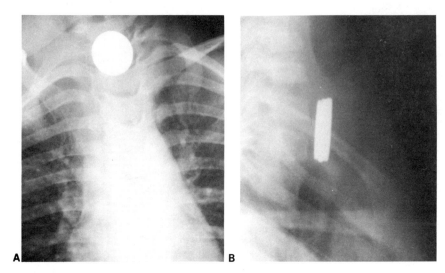

Figure 31-1(A) Frontal view of chest and neck shows round metallic foreign body, probably a coin, oriented in the sagittal plane, indicating esophageal position. **(B)** Lateral view shows the "coin" is actually three coins stacked together, a fact the person removing the objects might appreciate knowing in advance.

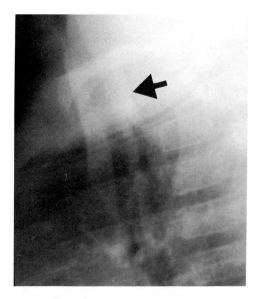

Figure 31-2 Lateral radiograph of upper thorax and neck in a 15-month-old boy shows a plastic button lodged at the thoracic inlet. The AP view was normal.

For metallic objects, the particular combination of views is less important than the necessity of including the entire alimentary canal and the respiratory system on the radiographs. A second radiograph at right angles to the first view is usually helpful in localizing the object (Figure 31-1 (A, B)). If the clinical presentation suggests foreign body ingestion, but plain radiographs are normal, a contrast study of the esophagus and upper gastrointestinal tract may be diagnostic, especially for esophageal foreign bodies (EFBs).

ESOPHAGEAL FOREIGN BODIES

In a series of 660 children with alimentary tract foreign bodies, the object was in the esophagus at the time of diagnosis in 231 (35%) of the cases. Of those, 66% were lodged in the upper esophagus at the thoracic inlet; 20% in the midesophagus above the crossing of the aortic arch and left main bronchus; and 14% in the distal esophagus near the gastroesophageal junction.[1] Campbell et al[3] observed a similar distribution.

Chest and neck radiographs are usually diagnostic of radio-opaque objects. When a coin or other smooth, flat object lies in the coronal plane, it is usually located in the esophagus (Figure 31-1 (A, B), and Figure 31-2); whereas sagittal orientation indicates tracheal or laryngeal location, because the membranous posterior portion of the trachea allows one edge of the object to protrude posteriorly. Food is unlikely to lodge in a child's esophagus unless a predisposing cause, ie, congenital anomaly, postsurgical stricture, reflux esophagitis, or previous caustic agent ingestion, has led to stricture or muscle dysfunction.[1,2]

Radiolucent objects, such as plastic toys, are best delineated by a contrast esophagram (Figure 31-3). However, many can be perceived or strongly suspected on well-positioned and collimated plain films (Figure 31-2).

Esophageal foreign bodies frequently cause complications because the esophageal wall is relatively thin and is close to vital thoracic structures such as the aorta and trachea. Regurgitation and aspiration can lead to asphyxiation. Foreign bodies may remain lodged in the esophagus for a period of time, producing an inflammatory response and stricture or perforation; abscess, mediastinitis, tracheoesophageal fistula, or even esophagoaortic fistula can result.[4] Perforation is more likely with sharp than blunt objects, particularly those that remain in place for an extended period. Even coins may cause perforation if retained for a long time.[5]

Management

If a recently swallowed, smooth and inert object is located in the distal esophagus, where the threat of aspiration is minimal, a "wait-and-see"

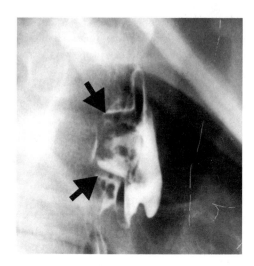

Figure 31-3 Lateral view of esophagram showing a plastic toy, a cowboy hat (arrows), lodged in the proximal esophagus above the aortic arch. The object was not visible on plain films.

approach for 12 to 24 hours may be justifiable. Most objects that reach the gastroesophageal junction will pass through the remainder of the gastrointestinal tract uneventfully.

Esophageal foreign bodies were most often removed by rigid endoscopes during the first half of this century. In the 1970s, the flexible fiberoptic endoscope was used with great success; other tools for foreign body extraction were also described, including the Foley catheter, a magnetic-tipped catheter, and, recently, wire-mesh baskets designed for biliary stone removal.[6–8]

Foley Catheter Extraction

Current controversy centers on management of the smooth radio-opaque foreign body that has been in the esophagus for a short period of time. When the object is sharp, pointed, radiolucent, or present for an extensive period of time, most physicians agree that it should be extracted endoscopically. Others argue that all EFBs should be removed endoscopically.[9,10]

Foley catheter removal of smooth, radiodense objects has been advocated[3,9,11] since Bigler[6] described the Foley catheter technique in 1966. Details of the Foley catheter technique for foreign body extraction vary according to individual experience. After plain films establish that a smooth, radiodense object lies in the esophagus, it is important to elicit any history of esophageal disease (eg, reflux esophagitis), anomaly (eg, tracheoesophageal fistula), prior surgery, or alkali ingestion, and to establish the length of time the object has been in place. Most physicians who use catheter extraction prefer that objects be in place no longer than 72 hours[9]; others[3,11] use Foley extraction up to 2 weeks postingestion, having found no difference in the ease of extraction compared to objects in place for known, shorter durations.

A 12 to 16 Fr Foley catheter is used for the procedure. Airway support equipment and personnel must be immediately available. The child is kept in Trendelenburg's position to minimize aspiration. The Foley catheter is inflated and inspected before insertion: asymmetric or leaky balloons and balloons that cannot be deflated are discarded. Although some early reports described blind removal with the Foley catheter,[12] authors with extensive experience insist that direct fluoroscopic visualization is essential for the child's safety. Some authors perform a limited esophagram with a small amount of barium to exclude underlying esophageal pathology and multiple radiolucent objects. Others perform the contrast study only for objects in unusual locations or for patients who have a history suggestive of esophageal disease.[3]

After appropriate restraints are applied, the child is placed in a lateral position. The catheter is inserted orally to avoid conversion of esophageal to nasal foreign bodies and to reduce the risk of aspiration. Lidocaine spray may be applied to the oropharynx in limited amounts; the gag reflex should not be eliminated. A bite block is placed in the "down" side of the mouth, and the lubricated catheter is passed beyond the foreign body under fluoroscopic guidance. In order to avoid overdistension of the esophagus, the balloon is partially inflated with 3 to 7 mL of contrast material, depending on the size of the patient. The child is changed to a prone oblique position facing the physician, and the table is tilted into a steep head-down position.

Once the balloon engages the object, the operator applies smooth, continuous traction while observing the object's course fluoroscopically. When it reaches the mouth, some people allow the child to spit the object out unaided; others sweep a finger through the mouth to catch the object and diminish the risk of aspiration. If the balloon pops past the foreign body, it should be deflated and then repositioned for the next attempt. Multiple attempts and greater balloon distension may be required.

When the foreign body cannot be retrieved and is small enough to pose no risk of gastric or small bowel obstruction, it may be pushed with the balloon until it passes the esophagogastric junction. After the procedure, the child is observed for 2 to 3 hours. Admission to the hospital is usually unnecessary.

The success rate of the Foley catheter technique for EFB extraction was estimated to be 85% to 90%.[9] Among 100 patients in one study,[3] foreign bodies were successfully retrieved in 91; the object was pushed into the stomach in 7; and the technique failed in 2. Of 66 cases reported from Vanderbilt University,[11] 52 foreign bodies were extracted and 10 advanced across the esophagogastric junction. Four of the five patients with failures in these two series had underlying esophageal disease. A nationwide survey described 1,512 cases with only 25 complications, including 19 nosebleeds, 4 coins displaced into the nose, 1 fever, 1 case of laryngospasm, and no deaths.[9]

Physicians experienced in the balloon catheter technique note that it is safe when applied to recently ingested, radiodense, smooth foreign bodies if all recommended safety precautions are observed. Equipment and personnel to initiate airway intervention must be present, and the patient kept in steep Trendelenburg's position. Furthermore, sedation is minimized to maintain an intact gag reflex, and hospitalization is not generally required.

In view of the excellent success rate and low complication rate, why does controversy surround the use of Foley catheters in foreign body removal? Proponents of endoscopy state that it protects the airway and has been proven effective in thousands of cases. They worry that the inflated balloon might cause pressure on the trachea[13]; but this concern has not been supported in major series,[3,9,11] and fluoroscopy enables the physician to confirm that the balloon is not overinflated.[14]

Because children may swallow multiple objects, some of which may be radiolucent, endoscopists argue that sharp or ragged objects, invisible to the fluoroscopist, could perforate the esophagus, when moved by the balloon.[13,15] They also state that without direct mucosal visualization by endoscopy, perforation may occur, yet go undetected.

Radiologists who use the catheter extraction technique usually perform a barium swallow in any child with a history of prior foreign body ingestion or any other unusual history. In one series about 10% of the patients had multiple objects, but most of these were similar objects, usually coins.[14] Many believe that mucosal reaction probably takes longer than 2 weeks to develop, and that this technique may be used safely without direct internal visualization unless the time of ingestion is thought to be remote.[11]

A recent report from the University of Virginia[8] describes basket extraction of EFBs using catheters initially designed for removal of biliary tract stones. The use of catheters with "grasping" capabilities may become incorporated in this technique to protect the airway even further.

In conclusion, there are two camps divided over the management of smooth, radiodense, recently ingested EFBs, and in any particular institution, the procedure of choice depends on the experience and prejudices of the emergency physician, pediatrician, pediatric surgeon, otolaryngologist, and radiologist involved. Based on the evidence, the Foley catheter technique can be a safe and cost-effective alternative to endoscopic foreign body retrieval when the physicians involved adhere to the specific indications and techniques described above.

GASTRIC AND INTESTINAL FOREIGN BODIES

Once a foreign body successfully negotiates the lower esophageal sphincter, it usually progresses through the gut without complication, exiting per rectum days to weeks after ingestion. Unlike EFBs, 90% to 95% of gastric foreign bodies safely pass; therefore invasive procedures are usually not necessary.[16]

Foreign bodies tend to lodge in certain locations beyond the esophagus: the pylorus, duodenum, ileocecal valve, and appendix. Chronic retention may result in perforation at these sites. The sigmoid colon may also be perforated, but much less commonly. Alterations of the gut by prior trauma or surgery and anomalies of the gastrointestinal tract such as antral web, annular pancreas, duplication cyst, and Meckel's diverticulum may interfere with passage and lead to obstruction or perforation in atypical locations.

Management

Placing the patient in the right decubitus position may aid in passage out of the stomach. For objects that have reached the small or large intestine, some authors have recommended the use of cathartics and enemas; however, these interventions could be hazardous in the case of sharp objects.

Serial radiographs can monitor for the passage of a foreign body. Daily stool examination can eliminate the need for further radiography if the foreign object is passed and identified. In asymptomatic patients, serial radiographs may be obtained once a week or less often.

Endoscopy is appropriate for removal of a gastric or duodenal foreign body if symptoms (eg, progressive pain, vomiting, or hematemesis) occur or if passage is delayed.

Certain foreign bodies, such as alkaline disk batteries, wood or bone fragments, and sharp, ragged, or long, slender objects, pose a greater risk of complications. For these higher risk objects the length of time one waits for spontaneous passage of the object should be shortened. Surgery is necessary for failure of endoscopic removal, for objects in the distal small intestine, or if complications arise such as embedded objects or perforation.

ALKALINE DISK BATTERY INGESTION

Alkaline disk batteries used in hearing aids, cameras, watches, calculators, and other household items pose a unique risk when ingested. The first reported case of complications caused by disk battery ingestion appeared in 1977.[17]

The ingestion was unsuspected until a chest radiograph revealed a radiodense esophageal foreign body. Despite endoscopic removal of the battery, the esophageal injury progressed to perforation with tracheoesophageal fistula and arterial erosion resulting in death. Since that time, other reports[4,18–20] have substantiated the potential danger of these small, smooth, foreign bodies.

If lodged in one spot, a battery may cause pressure necrosis just as any other foreign body. KOH or NaOH may leak from the battery and burn surrounding tissue, just as lye ingestion causes burns. Production of low-voltage current may be another source of injury. Further, as gastrointestinal secretions erode the external casing, heavy metals such as mercury, silver, and cadmium are released. Rising serum and urine levels of these metals have been detected, although no definite ill effects have been described as a result of systemic absorption.[19]

Battery ingestion can be easily established by plain radiography.

Management

The current controversy centers on management of the alkaline disk battery once it has been identified in the alimentary tract.

Early intervention is favored by many because injury can occur as early as 1 hour after the onset of mucosal contact. Esophageal batteries must be removed promptly. Gastric batteries can be removed endoscopically. If endoscopy is not successful or feasible, gastrotomy should be considered if the battery has remained in the stomach for more than 8 hours. Once in the small bowel, a battery should be followed with serial radiographs every 8 hours: if it appears lodged in the same location, surgical or endoscopic intervention should be considered.

Other authors believe that less emergent intervention is advisable for batteries that have reached the stomach although early removal is advisable for esophageal ones. Close follow-up is essential. Litovitz[21] estimates there are more than 500 alkaline battery ingestions per year in the United States. Most of these cases go unreported because of few significant symptoms or complications.

In a review of 56 alkaline disk battery ingestions, Litovitz[21] found only six cases with significant complications. In five of these, the battery was lodged in the esophagus. Two patients died; one survived a cardiac arrest but eventually required a colonic interposition; another acquired second degree burns of the distal esophagus; and the last child had an esophageal perforation that resolved without sequelae.

Of the 51 patients in whom the batteries had passed the gastroesophageal junction, only 4 were symptomatic, and only 1 had a major complication:

perforation by lodgement of the battery in a Meckel's diverticulum.[20] One of the other symptomatic children underwent gastrotomy; the other two were kept under close observation until the batteries passed per rectum without complication.

All but 14 of the asymptomatic patients passed the batteries without complication or intervention. Seven of the 14 who had either surgery or endoscopy had detectable mucosal erosions, but no ulceration, perforation, or evidence of peritonitis.[21]

Rumack and Rumack[22] argued against excessively frequent radiography, ie, every 6 to 8 hours because the natural course of foreign body passage could take several days to 2 weeks or longer. More frequent examinations, of course, should be obtained in the child with persistent vomiting, abdominal pain, bleeding, or other symptoms or signs of intestinal injury.[22]

In conclusion, ingested alkaline disk batteries are of special concern because retention may lead to severe injury or death. Roentgenographic examination of the entire gastrointestinal tract, including the nasopharynx, should be done to locate the battery. If it is lodged in the esophagus, it should be removed immediately, whereas those lying beyond the gastroesophageal junction may be observed for passage and signs of complications. An esophagram performed 2 to 3 weeks later is useful to exclude persistent problems, ie, residual mucosal irregularity or stricture.

REFERENCES

1. Spitz L: Management of ingested foreign bodies in childhood. *Br Med J* 1971;4:469–472.

2. Turtz MG, Stool SE: Foreign bodies of the pharynx and esophagus, in Bluestone CD, Stool SE (eds): *Pediatric Otolaryngology*. Philadelphia, WB Saunders Co, 1983, pp 1095–1110.

3. Campbell JB, Quattromani FL, Foley LC: Foley catheter removal of blunt esophageal foreign bodies. Experience with 100 consecutive children. *Pediatr Radiol* 1983;13:116–119.

4. Shabino CL, Feinberg AN: Esophageal perforation secondary to alkaline battery ingestion. *Ann Emerg Med* 1979;8:360–362.

5. Janik JS, Bailey WC, Burrington JD: Occult coin perforation of the esophagus. *J Pediatr Surg* 1986;21:794–797.

6. Bigler FC: The use of a Foley catheter for removal of blunt foreign bodies from the esophagus. *J Thorac Cardiovasc Surg* 1966;51:759–760.

7. Volle E, Hanel D, Beyer P, et al: Ingested foreign bodies: Removal by magnet. *Radiology* 1986;160:407–409.

8. Shaffer HA Jr, Alford BA, de Lange EE, et al: Basket extraction of esophageal foreign bodies. *AJR* 1986;147:1010–1013.

9. McGuirt WF: Use of Foley catheter for removal of esophageal foreign bodies: A survey. *Ann Otol Rhinol Laryngol* 1982;91:599–601.

10. Berdon WE: Editorial comment on the preceding paper. *Pediatr Radiol* 1983;13:119.

11. O'Neill JA Jr, Holcomb GW Jr, Neblett WW: Management of tracheobronchial and esophageal foreign bodies in childhood. *J Pediatr Surg* 1983;18:475–479.

12. Brown LP: Blind esophageal coin removal using a Foley catheter. *Arch Surg* 1968; 96:931–932.

13. Zonakis PM: Foley catheter technique. *Arch Otolaryngol* 1984;110:63.

14. Campbell JB, Foley LC: In reply to Foley catheter technique. *Arch Otolaryngol* 1984; 110:63.

15. Stool SE, Deitch M: Potential danger of catheter removal of foreign body. *Pediatrics* 1973;51:313–314.

16. Christie DL, Ament ME: Removal of foreign bodies from esophagus and stomach with flexible fiberoptic panendoscopes. *Pediatrics* 1976;57:931–934.

17. Blatnik DS, Toohill RJ, Lehman RH: Fatal complications from an alkaline battery foreign body in the esophagus. *Ann Otolaryngol* 1977;86:611–615.

18. Votteler TP, Nash JC, Rutledge JC: The hazard of ingested alkaline disk batteries in children. *JAMA* 1983;249:2504–2506.

19. Kulig K, Rumack CM, Rumack BH, et al: Disk battery ingestion: (Elevated urine mercury levels and enema removal of battery fragments). *JAMA* 1983;249:2502–2504.

20. Willis GA, Ho WC: Perforation of Meckel's diverticulum by an alkaline hearing aid battery. *Can Med Assoc J* 1982;126:497–498.

21. Litovitz TL: Button battery ingestions. *JAMA* 1983;249:2495–2500.

22. Rumack BH, Rumack CM: Disk battery ingestion. *JAMA* 1983;249:2509–2511.

PART V

Other Medical Dilemmas

Section 17

Rehydration

Oral rehydration therapy may evolve as a safe, efficacious alternative to intravenous hydration of the child with mild to moderate dehydration. Fluids should generally contain 50 to 90 mmol/L sodium in a 2% glucose solution. Careful monitoring of intake and output and clinical status is essential. The success of this technique depends on the cooperation of the child and parent as well as the experience of the treating clinician.

Although intravenous fluids (20–40 mL/kg of normal saline or lactated Ringer's solution) are traditionally used for initial therapy of the moderately dehydrated child, oral rehydration may be tried in the stable child who can be monitored closely in a hospital setting. Increasingly parenteral or oral rehydration of moderately dehydrated children is being done in emergency department observation or short-stay units. The role of oral rehydration in severe dehydration remains controversial.

32. Oral Rehydration Therapy

Dawn L. Martin, MD

Among the major contemporary medical advances is the development of oral glucose-electrolyte solutions for the treatment of acute dehydrating diarrhea. Diarrheal disease persists as a cause of significant morbidity and mortality in the developing world and access to a therapy that is inexpensive, simple to administer, and does not require sterile conditions has had widespread impact.[1] Despite the recently documented success of oral rehydration therapy (ORT) in well-nourished children, the implementation of ORT in the United States has been slow and controversial. Debate has focused on the composition of the rehydrating salts, especially the sodium content, and the method of administration.

PATHOPHYSIOLOGY OF DEHYDRATING DIARRHEAL AGENTS

The pathophysiology and epidemiology of various diarrheal pathogens are important in understanding the basis for ORT. In the developing world, toxigenic *Escherichia coli* and rotavirus are major causes of diarrhea, although *Vibrio cholera* may be a significant pathogen in certain areas. The predominant pathogens in the developed world are viral, especially rotavirus.

Agents such as *E coli* or cholera are ingested in large numbers in contaminated food or water, bind to a receptor on the mucosal surface of the jejunum, and produce an enterotoxin. The toxin migrates to the inner plasma membrane where it increases production of cAMP and decreases the active absorption of

Note: The assistance of R. Bradley Sack, MD, Professor of International Health, Director, Division of Geographic Medicine, Johns Hopkins School of Public Health, is gratefully acknowledged.

sodium; isotonic fluid is hypersecreted at a rate that exceeds the bowel's absorptive capacity (Table 32-1). There is no inflammatory response; the epithelium remains intact and glucose-stimulated sodium absorption remains functional.

Viral agents invade the mucosal cell and interfere with electrolyte transport via an inflammatory response that disrupts the normal absorptive capacity of the small bowel epithelium. An increased flow of solute, carbohydrate, and amino acids into the colon results in watery diarrhea. Stool electrolyte losses vary, but are generally less than that seen with toxigenic diarrheas (Table 32-1).[2]

Water absorption in the small bowel is linked to sodium transport across the gut mucosa. Thus, absorption occurs via passive diffusion, an active sodium pump, and glucose-facilitated sodium transport. Intraluminal glucose enhances sodium and water absorption forming the basis for ORT. Thus, a physiologic mechanism persists, in a secretory diarrhea such as with cholera or toxigenic E coli or in an inflammatory viral diarrhea, enabling the intestinal mucosa to absorb sodium and water and provide for effective rehydration.

COMPOSITION OF THE WHO REHYDRATING SOLUTION

The World Health Organization (WHO) recommends a rehydrating solution with 90 mmol/L sodium, 20 mmol/L potassium, 30 mmol/L citrate, and 110 mmol/L (2%) glucose with a resulting osmolarity of 330 mOsm (Table 32-2). The WHO formulation is the standard against which other rehydrating solutions are compared. (For monovalent ions and cations, mmol/L is equivalent to mEq/L.) The solution contains enough sodium to optimize fluid absorption. This eliminates the need for excessive fluid intake to replace ongoing fluid losses. The equimolar content of the sodium and glucose is significant because sodium and glucose are optimally absorbed at a 1:1 or 1:2

Table 32-1 Stool Electrolyte Losses in Diarrheal States (mmol/L)[2]

	Sodium	Potassium	Bicarbonate	Osmolality
Cholera				
Adult	124	16	48	
Pediatric	88	30	32	300
Toxigenic E coli	53	37	18	300
Rotavirus	37	38	6	300

Source: Journal of Pediatrics (1981;98:835–838), Copyright © 1981, CV Mosby Company.

Table 32-2 WHO Oral Rehydration Solution (mmol/L)

Sodium	90	
Potassium	20	
Chloride	80	
Citrate	30	
Glucose	111	(2%)
Total Osmolality	330	

ratio in the intestinal mucosa. The optimal concentration of glucose is 60 to 140 mmol/L (1% to 2%). At concentrations greater than 2.5% (160 mmol/L) there is decreased absorption of sodium and water, and at concentrations greater than 4% the high carbohydrate load produces an osmotic diarrhea.[1] In the past, commercial glucose-electrolyte solutions in the United States have contained at least 5% glucose, an amount well above the optimal range for sodium absorption.

Potassium is necessary to replace known losses during diarrheal disease, which tend to be greater in children than in adults. Base is also required to replace diarrheal losses and to help correct the acidosis present with moderate to severe dehydration.

ORT IN THE DEVELOPING WORLD

Oral rehydration therapy has had a dramatic impact on the morbidity and mortality of children and adults in the developing world. Children with a variety of diarrheal pathogens, including rotavirus, have been successfully rehydrated with the WHO salts. Hypernatremia has not been a problem with the 90 mmol/L solution when used in the rehydration phase of fluid replacement. The solution has been used in all pediatric age groups. Because of the higher risk for hypernatremia in neonates, a 2:1 ratio of the WHO solution with solute-free liquids such as breast milk (7 mEq/L sodium) or formula (12 mEq/L sodium) has been used.[3]

ORAL REHYDRATION IN DEVELOPED NATIONS

There has been less acceptance of oral rehydration therapy as the primary treatment for dehydrating diarrhea in the developed world. Attention has focused on the potential exacerbation of hypernatremic dehydration with the 90 mmol/L sodium content of the WHO salts. Physicians have noted the lower stool sodium content of the predominant viral diarrheas encountered in the developed world as compared to the toxigenic bacterial diarrheas found in developing nations. There has also been concern about its use in young infants who have an increased susceptibility to hypernatremic dehydration. Until recently, oral rehydration solutions with 50 to 90 mmol/L sodium had not been studied in the developed world. As a result of these concerns, dehydrating diarrhea in the developed world has been managed primarily with parenteral therapy, or hypotonic/hyperosmolar commercial solutions (Table 32-3) and "clear liquids" (Table 32-4).

A landmark article by Santosham et al[4] in 1982 documented the success of ORT in well-nourished children in this country and in Panama. Solutions containing 50 to 90 mmol/L sodium were compared with traditional intravenous (IV) therapy and found to be equally effective in treating dehydrating noncholera diarrhea even with associated vomiting. Given the current evidence that oral rehydration is effective in the treatment of mild to severe dehydration in well-nourished children of all ages, the availability of appropriate rehydrating solutions, and increasing economic constraints, more attention is needed to develop guidelines for ORT.

ASSESSMENT AND MANAGEMENT OF DEHYDRATION

Oral management of diarrhea, including selection of a rehydrating solution, is dependent on the severity of dehydration, the availability of a committed caretaker to administer the rehydrating solution, and the capacity to monitor the child's progress.

Vomiting is not a contraindication to initiating ORT. Retention is enhanced by administering the solution slowly and in small amounts. In situations in which IV fluids are clinically indicated and IV access is a problem, oral or nasogastric fluids should be administered until an IV site is obtained (see also Chapters 46 and 47). Care must be taken in these circumstances to protect the airway and prevent aspiration.

Table 32-3 Contents of Commercial Oral Rehydration Solutions (mmol/L)

	Sodium	Potassium	Base	Carbohydrate
Lytren	30	25	36	7.7% glucose + corn syrup
Pedialyte	30	20	28	5% glucose
Reosol	50	20	34	2% glucose
Infalyte	50	20	30	2% glucose
Pedialyte RS	75	20	30	2.5% dextrose
WHO salts	90	20	30	2% glucose

Table 32-4 Contents of Frequently Used Clear Liquids (mmol/L)

	Sodium	Potassium	Base	CHO	OSM
Apple juice	2.0	28	—	10.7%	730
Jello water (0.5 strength)	12.0	.5	—	10.0%	320
Gatorade	20	3.0	3.0	4.6%	330
Ginger Ale	2.7	.8	4.0	5.3%	540
7-Up	5.2	1.5	—	7.4%	530

Mild Dehydration

There is considerable latitude in the type of rehydrating solution administered to the child with mild dehydration. Several available solutions containing 30 to 90 mmol/L sodium are equally effective.[5] Although many studies have documented good results with ORT given ad libitum, specific guidelines should be given to caretakers administering the fluids. The most appropriate solution for mild dehydration is one with 50 to 75 mmol/L sodium given at a rate of 100 to 150 mL/kg/day to replace fluid deficits and ongoing losses. It is important to *continue* solute-free liquids such as breast milk (7 mEq/L Na^+), or 0.5 strength formula for maintenance requirements. Total daily volumes of fluids administered should be in the range of 200 to 250 mL/kg for the first 24 hours. Infants and children with mild dehydration can be treated at home if the caretaker is reliable and willing to administer the fluids. Careful instructions should be given and should include signs of worsening dehydration for which the infant or child should be re-evaluated.

After 24 hours, fluid intake should be in the range of 150 mL/kg/day to accommodate moderate ongoing stool losses and maintenance requirements. This can be accomplished with formula or breast milk alone or in combination with an ORT solution. Rehydrating solutions should not be used exclusively for more than 24 hours and can usually be discontinued after 48 hours. If oral solutions are to be used for a prolonged period of time, the child should be reassessed. Lactose-free formulas have traditionally been used for the child recovering from diarrhea. The value of this approach is currently under investigation.[6]

Moderate Dehydration

If an infant or child is more than 5% dehydrated, a 50 to 90 mmol/L sodium rehydration fluid with 2% glucose should *definitely* be used. Patients receiving hypotonic solutions with 30 mmol/L sodium are at risk of developing hyponatremia.[7] Commercial preparations (Table 32-3) with more than 2.5% glucose may aggravate the dehydration by causing an osmotic diarrhea, and conventional clear liquids (Table 32-4) are often hyperosmolar and contain inadequate amounts of sodium, potassium, and base.

Oral rehydration therapy permits rapid replacement of the fluid electrolyte deficit over 4 to 8 hours.[5,8] Many studies have noted the success of this approach to rehydration in contrast to the traditional 24 to 48 hour parenteral rehydration and fast. Ad libitum rehydration has been successful, but the goal of therapy should be 75 to 90 mL/kg of a 50 to 90 mmol/L sodium solution over the first 4 to 8 hours. The WHO solution given in a 2:1 ratio with solute-free liquids has been used successfully in neonates during the rehydration phase. Patients should be observed in a holding area or short-stay unit during the rehydration phase. If rehydration is performed in the home, re-evaluation in 4 to 8 hours is mandatory.

After the initial rehydration phase, therapy for the first 24 hours should continue with a rehydrating solution either alone or preferably in combination with breast milk or 0.5 strength formula. Most studies of ORT have administered formula or breast milk after the initial rehydration phase. Total fluid intake in the first 24 hours should usually be in the range of 250 to 300 mL/kg. Therapy at this point should replace ongoing losses (stool, vomitus) and supply maintenance fluid requirements.

As the stool output diminishes, ORT should be gradually discontinued and the regular diet resumed. This can usually be accomplished in the second 24-hour period. However, in the face of continuing diarrhea, therapy should continue as a combination of the rehydrating solution and solute-free liquids (breast milk or formula). The original rehydrating solution can usually be used in this setting. However, others[9] advocate the use of a lower sodium content (40–50 mmol/L) maintenance solution during the second phase of therapy. Total volumes administered should be in the range of 200 mL/kg/24 hr. If ongoing stool losses are excessive, one should calculate specific maintenance requirements and replace stool losses one to one.

Severe Dehydration

Infants and children with greater than 8% dehydration have been successfully rehydrated with ORT.[8] Contraindications to ORT include shock, extreme fatigue, stupor, or coma resulting in inability to drink and severe, sustained vomiting. In children with underlying nutritional deficits and protracted severe diarrhea (> 10 mL/kg/hr of stool), ORT is also contraindicated. Serum electrolytes are indicated with patients with severe dehydration as well as those with a prolonged course of dehydrating diarrhea. However, electrolyte disturbances such as hypo- or hypernatremia or acidosis are not contraindications to ORT.

Infants and children receiving ORT for severe dehydration should be observed by medical personnel throughout the rehydration phase. Closer monitoring and early consideration of parenteral fluids are required. As with moderate dehydration, the initial rehydration phase should attempt to replace losses over 4 to 8 hours with fluid intakes of 90 to 130 mL/kg. A 75 or 90 mmol/L sodium solution is mandatory. A 90 mmol/L sodium solution may also be used in neonates, but it should be rotated on a 2:1 basis with solute-free liquids. Maintenance and prevention therapy should be provided as described for moderate dehydration.

Hypernatremic Dehydration

Infants and children with hypernatremic (serum sodium > 150 mmol/L) diarrheal dehydration have been successfully managed with ORT. Hypernatremic dehydration is especially concerning because it is often associated with seizure activity and intracranial hemorrhage because of rapid changes in serum sodium and plasma osmolarity. Infants managed with oral rehydration show rates of seizure activity less than that seen with IV management of hypernatremic dehydration.[3] Intestinal and renal regulatory mechanisms may provide a safer and more physiologic correction of the disturbance.[10,11]

Hypernatremic infants and children may require a slower initial rehydration phase.[11] Replacement of the fluid deficit over 12 hours may decrease risk of seizure activity. Slow rehydration is accompanied by a more gradual fall in the serum sodium. A 90 mmol/L sodium solution should be used alone in the rehydration phase. It should not be offered in combination with solute-free liquids.

Refeeding

The traditional 24 to 48 hour fast may be detrimental. Delayed feeding resulted from a desire to avoid the consequences of malabsorption, such as depletion of the bile acid pool, fluid loss secondary to the osmotic effect of unabsorbed carbohydrates, and mucosal injury creating possible problems in protein absorption. Early refeeding helps maintain the level of intestinal disaccharidases, which are inducible, and stimulates pancreatic secretions, which are potent stimuli for intestinal repair, prevents protein and energy deficits, and allows for sustained breastfeeding.

Breast or formula feeding should be continued throughout ORT. After the initial rehydration phase, solids such as rice, cereal, wheat noodles, potatoes, saltines, and bananas may be started. Solids have the added benefit of delaying gastric emptying and thus improve absorption of the substrate delivered to the small bowel.[12]

CONCLUSION

Oral rehydration therapy has distinguished itself as a safe and effective treatment for dehydrating diarrheal disease in both the developing and developed world. The current availability of appropriate rehydration solutions should make widespread use of this approach more feasible. Hospitalization and medical costs will be reduced as will morbidity secondary to dehydrating diarrheal disease.

REFERENCES

1. Hirschhorn N: The treatment of acute diarrhea in children: An historical and physiological perspective. *Am J Clin Nutr* 1980;33:637–663.

2. Molla AM, Rahman M, Sarker SA, et al: Stool electrolyte content and purging rates in diarrhea caused by rotavirus, enterotoxigenic *E coli*, and *V cholerae* in children. *J Pediatr* 1981;98:835–838.

3. Pizarro D, Posada G, Mata L: Treatment of 242 neonates with dehydrating diarrhea with an oral glucose-electrolyte solution. *J Pediatr* 1983;102:153–156.

4. Santosham M, et al: Oral rehydration therapy of infantile diarrhea. *N Engl J Med* 1982;306:1070–1076.

5. Santosham M, et al: Oral rehydration therapy for acute diarrhea in ambulatory children in the United States: A double-blind comparison of four different solutions. *Pediatrics* 1985;76:159–165.

6. Groothuis JR, Berman S, Chapman J: Effect of carbohydrate ingested on outcome in infants with mild gastroenteritis. *J Pediatr* 1986;108:903–906.

7. Finberg L: The role of oral electrolyte-glucose solutions in hydration for children: International and domestic aspects. *J Pedatr* 1980;96:51–54.

8. Tamer AM, et al: Oral rehydration of infants in a large urban US medical center. *J Pediatr* 1984;107:14–19.

9. Finberg L, Harper PA, Harrison HE, et al: Oral rehydration for diarrhea. *J Pediatr* 1982;101:497–499.

10. Aperia A, Marin L, Zetterstrom R, et al: Salt and water homeostasis during oral rehydration therapy. *J Pediatr* 1983;103:364–369.

11. Pizarro D, Posada G, Levine MM: Hypernatremic diarrheal dehydration treated with "slow" (12-hour) oral rehydration therapy: A preliminary report. *J Pediatr* 1984;104:316–320.

12. Brown KH, MacLean WC: Nutritional management of acute diarrhea: An appraisal of the alternatives. *Pediatrics* 1984;73:119–125.

33. Parenteral Versus Oral Therapy for the Moderately Dehydrated Child

M. Douglas Baker, MD

Dehydration is the leading cause of infant death worldwide and is second only to respiratory illness as a cause of nonsurgical pediatric hospital admissions.[1] As with many other common medical disorders, dehydration may occur in varying degrees of severity, and may involve a wide range of associated metabolic derangements. The clinical estimation of these variables markedly affects most physicians' management plans.

GAUGING THE SEVERITY OF DEHYDRATION

Dehydration in children may be gauged as mild (up to 5% loss of body weight), moderate (10% loss of body weight), or severe (15% loss of body weight) (see Table 33-1).[2,3] An estimate of the degree of dehydration is based on a number of historical, physical, and laboratory factors.

Most cases of clinically marked dehydration occur with both increased fluid losses and decreased intake. The history should focus on both; losses through the skin and respiratory, urinary, as well as the gastrointestinal tracts, are important. Children with illnesses causing anorexia, stomatitis, pharyngitis, nausea, or vomiting may have diminished intake. Burns, fever, tachypnea, and hyperglycemia may result in increased fluid losses in the absence of impressive gastrointestinal losses. Establishment of a recent weight, either from the child's medical record or from the parent's account, is extremely useful information.

The physical examination is instrumental in assessing hydration status regardless of the cause of dehydration. The single most important determination is the patient's weight. An accurate assessment of weight loss will properly identify the patient's degree of fluid deficit.

When a reliable estimate of weight loss is not possible, other physical findings may help establish severity of dehydration (Table 33-1).[2,3] Tachycar-

Table 33-1 Clinical Findings in Dehydration

Degree of Dehydration	Clinical Findings
5%	Dry mucous membranes Orthostatic increased heart rate Orthostatic decreased blood pressure Minimal loss of skin turgor
10%	Increased severity of above signs plus: Loss of skin elasticity (tenting) Depressed fontanelle (infants) Sunken eyes Mildly increased heart rate Mildly decreased blood pressure
15%	Marked increase of above signs plus: Markedly increased heart rate Markedly decreased blood pressure Cold, mottled, poorly perfused skin

Source: Adapted with permission from Pediatrics in Review (1982;3:113-120), Copyright © 1982, American Academy of Pediatrics.

dia is often the first sign of substantial dehydration, which underscores the importance of recording accurate vital signs. A sunken fontanelle or sunken eyes are also seen in the patient with at least moderate dehydration. Orthostatic blood pressure measurement tests the patient's cardiovascular reserve in maintaining perfusion with decreased intravascular volume.

The examination of the skin may be useful in determining the state of hydration, particularly in the child under 2 years of age. When dehydration is moderate to severe, pinched abdominal skin will remain standing in folds rather than snapping back promptly upon release, because elasticity has been lost. This sign may also be seen, however, in serious malnourishment without dehydration.

Decreased skin turgor is a sign of circulatory inadequacy and is seen in moderate to severe dehydration. Slowness of capillary refill in the absence of a local skin disorder or edema denotes a loss of turgor.

Although prospective studies[2,3] documenting need are lacking, certain laboratory studies are felt to be routinely indicated in the child who is clinically judged to be moderately to severely dehydrated. A routine urinalysis may be helpful in several ways. Keeping in mind the possible influence of glucose and protein on the result, determination of urine specific gravity gives an approximation of osmolality, which is a sensitive measure of renal function. The presence of glucose or ketones (as in diabetes mellitus), or cellular elements or protein (as in primary renal disease) may indicate a specific disorder.

Other useful studies include serum electrolytes, urea nitrogen, and hematocrit measurements. The latter two are often elevated in the dehydrated child, although either can deviate from the norm in a well-hydrated child. Abnormally high or low sodium levels require specific therapeutic measures. Bicarbonate concentrations are decreased with acidosis, which often has bearing upon the disposition of the child from the emergency department. Rapid glucose determinations (ie, Chemstrip or Dextrostix) can also yield useful information, particularly in newborns and infants. Additional laboratory tests, such as measuring blood gases, calcium, phosphorous, magnesium, and albumin, and chest roentgenograms are generally not needed. If ordered for other reasons, however, the chest roentgenogram will show a small cardiac shadow and decreased pulmonary vascular markings in the significantly dehydrated child.

MANAGEMENT IN THE EMERGENCY DEPARTMENT

Oral Rehydration

As is true for many other disorders, dehydration in children can be therapeutically approached in several different ways, yielding equally acceptable results. Although the initial mode of treatment of moderate dehydration in the emergency department is often parenterally focused, in the absence of impaired intake, oral methods of rehydration may also be considered. Oral rehydration with glucose-electrolyte solution was shown to be effective in the treatment of diarrhea with mild to moderate dehydration (< 8%), regardless of etiology, age of patient, or serum-sodium concentration.[4-6] Similar results were shown in trials of oral rehydration of severe diarrheal dehydration.[7] In a comparison of oral *v* intravenous (IV) rehydration in *well*-nourished children with diarrhea and moderate dehydration, no outcome differences were detected.[4] The cost of oral rehydration is lower, much of the treatment can be given by the parent, and the discomfort and potential complications of IV therapy, such as skin infiltrations, which rank among the most common causes of medical litigation, are avoided.[8]

Despite the potential for success of oral rehydration of children, it should be pointed out that in developed countries, trials of oral rehydration have taken place in a hospital setting, involving only mild to moderately (< 8%) dehydrated children, and have been guided by measurement of stool water losses.[4,5] Although the same management principles might apply to more seriously dehydrated children, in the emergency department, parenteral therapy should at this point remain the cornerstone of management. This is especially true in cases involving intractable vomiting, inability to drink, extreme fatigue, gastrointestinal distension, severe glucose malabsorption, or high rates of stool water loss, which are prone to failure by the oral route.[4-6]

Parenteral Rehydration

The safety and efficacy of emergency department outpatient IV rehydration was recently addressed in a large series of patients in a pediatric emergency department who were all judged to be moderately (5% to 10%) dehydrated secondary to a variety of causes.[9] Only 3 of the 58 patients in the study group failed their initial parenteral outpatient rehydration. Of these, one had been ill for 2 weeks before treatment and one had cerebral palsy and mental retardation. The remaining 55 children (95%) were efficiently and effectively rehydrated using a combination of parenteral administration of fluids in the emergency department, followed by continued oral rehydration at home.

Even though parenteral rehydration is an appropriate initial step in the management of dehydration in the emergency department, not all children so treated are candidates for continued rehydration at home. None of the patients in the previously cited series were considered to be more than 10% dehydrated, none had severe acidosis or electrolyte problems, and all showed sufficient clinical improvement (ie, return to normal of vital signs, peripheral vascular integrity, and neurologic status) after fluid administration to be discharged home.

The choice of initial parenteral hydrating solutions is open to some debate. Most of the fluid loss in isonatremic dehydration is from the extracellular fluid,[3] particularly in the acute phase. Normal saline (20 to 40 mL/kg), lactated Ringer's solution (20 to 40 mL/kg), single-donor plasma (20 mL/kg), or 5% albumin (20 mL/kg) are all acceptable choices for infusion during the initial phase of correction.

Subsequent parenteral fluid administration should be based on continued clinical needs. Persistent acidosis, significant electrolyte abnormalities, and lack of adequate oral intake or urine output are all legitimate reasons for continuation of rehydration by parenteral means. Exact electrolyte and fluid deficits should be calculated and corrected over the ensuing 24 hours. In general, either ⅓ normal or ½ normal saline containing between 5% and 10% dextrose and appropriate concentrations of potassium will be effective for correction of isotonic dehydration.

Disposition

Several factors to be considered when establishing the need for admission of a moderately dehydrated child were previously enumerated. In the presence of severe dehydration (> 10%), severe acidosis, marked electrolyte abnormalities, or inadequate or impaired intake, admission is recommended. Adequate provision of subsequent care is a prerequisite for continued treatment of the moderately dehydrated child at home. If the managing physician is not reasonably assured of parental or patient compliance with plans for continued outpatient management, then rehydration should be completed in the inpatient setting. When the decision is made to attempt home oral rehydration, it is incumbent upon the physician to provide specific, clearly written dietary instructions to the child's parents. Preprinted patient handouts are often helpful in this regard.

It is also important that the opportunity for subsequent medical care be made available to the patient, particularly if discharge home from the emergency department is to occur at night. Every effort should be made to arrange follow-up with the patient's primary physician. When follow-up by the primary physician is not an option, arrangements should be made for reassessment of the patient's condition within 24 hours in the emergency department. In certain circumstances, this might be accomplished by telephone. Regardless of the means, the reassessment should be documented in the patient's medical record.

Another practical point to be considered in the rehydration process is the availability of outpatient facilities. In a survey of 173 pediatric training programs,[9] 77 (44.5%) indicated that fewer than 5% of patients requiring IV rehydration were treated as outpatients, whereas only 20 (11.6%) used outpatient IV rehydration for the majority of patients requiring such therapy. Many programs indicated their use of outpatient IV rehydration was limited by lack of personnel and physical facilities. The provision of short-stay or holding units is one way to address this issue. In such a setting, either oral or parenteral rehydration could be attempted for a more prolonged period than is generally feasible in a busy emergency department.

CONCLUSION

The dehydrated child requires proper clinical and laboratory assessment to determine the severity of fluid loss and extent of metabolic derangement. In the child with moderate isonatremic dehydration, several therapeutic options exist. Careful consideration should be given to the individual's underlying disease process, intake capabilities, and availability of follow-up when formulating a plan of management. The answers to several issues await proper prospective investigation.

REFERENCES

1. Grant JP: The state of the world's children 1982–1983. New York, UNICEF, 1982.

2. Finberg L, Kravath RE, Fleischman AR: *Water and Electrolytes in Pediatrics*. Philadelphia, WB Saunders Co, 1982, pp 73–77, 115–128.

3. Finberg LF: Treatment of dehydration in infancy. *Pediatr Rev* 1982;3:113–120.

4. Santosham M, Daum RS, Dillman L, et al: Oral rehydration of infantile diarrhea. *N Engl J Med* 1982;306:1070–1076.

5. Hirschhorn N, McCarthy BJ, Ranney B, et al: Ad libitum oral glucose-electrolyte therapy for acute diarrhea in Apache children. *J Pediatr* 1973;83:562–571.

6. Hirschhorn N: The treatment of acute diarrhea in children: An historical and physiological perspective. *Am J Clin Nutr* 1980;33:637–663.

7. Sharifi J, Ghavami F: Oral rehydration therapy of severe diarrheal dehydration. *Clin Pediatr* 1984;23:87–90.

8. Mackenzie A, Barnes G: Oral rehydration. *Aust J Paediatr* 1984;20:7–8.

9. Rosenstein BJ, Baker MD: Pediatric outpatient intravenous rehydration. *Am J Emerg Med* In press.

Section 18

Limp or Altered Locomotion

Assessment of the child with a limp must be systematic to exclude those entities that require prompt recognition and immediate treatment. Although toxic synovitis or fracture is common, septic arthritis and osteomyelitis must also be considered along with several neurologic diseases.

Children with a normal examination and no evidence of acute infection may often be observed closely with frequent re-evaluation to assure improvement. Other children may require early laboratory and radiologic examination.

34. Altered Locomotion: An Approach to the Assessment of the Child with a Limp

Jonathan I. Singer, MD

The smooth succession of movement from a stance to a swing phase produces locomotion. The stance phase is initiated by the heel striking the ground and terminates with toeing-off. The swing phase begins with flexion of the knee and hip followed by extension of the knee and ends with dorsiflexion of the foot permitting heel contact.

Altered locomotion or gait disturbance occurs with any deviation from this rhythmic movement. Paralysis implies loss or impairment of neuromuscular mechanisms whereas pseudoparalysis occurs in children without an underlying organic pathologic condition who refuse to ambulate. Limp occurs when there is an abnormal rhythm of the swing and stance phases, generally caused by pain.[1]

About 15% of school-aged children without a history of chronic disease occasionally experience limb pain. More than 4% of children report either extra-articular limb pain of longer than 3 months duration or pain of sufficient severity to disturb normal activity. Pediatric patients with gait disturbances are a diagnostic and therapeutic challenge to the examining physician.[2] Prioritizing the evaluation and management is problematic: when, what, and how emergently!

ETIOLOGY

There are a multitude of causes of acutely altered gait (Table 34-1), of which ten are most common (Table 34-2). The differential considerations must include a number of disease processes including traumatic, inflammatory, infectious, neoplastic, metabolic, vascular, and idiopathic. These can derange a combination of bone, soft-tissue, intra-articular structures, intra-abdominal organs, and neural tissues.[3,4]

Table 34-1 Causes of Altered Childhood Locomotion

Osseous
- Toddler's fracture
- Stress fractures
- Child abuse
- Osgood-Schlatter disease
- Legg-Calvé-Perthes disease
- Slipped capital femoral epiphysis
- Meyer's dysplasia
- Köhler's bone disease
- Osteomyelitis
- Sacroiliac infection
- Intervertebral disk infection
- Pott's disease
- Paraspinal abscess
- Intervertebral disk herniation
- Tumors
- Sickle cell disease
- Bone marrow necrosis
- Hypervitaminosis A
- Rickets
- Caffey's disease
- Blount's disease

Soft Tissue
- Sprain, strain, hematoma
- Myositis ossificans
- Myositis, viral and trichinosis
- Myositis, pyogenic
- Imbedded foreign body
- Calluses, corns, ingrown toenails
- Cellulitis
- Thrombophlebitis
- Postimmunization diseases
- Injections
- Erythema nodosum
- Sexual abuse
- Erythromelalgia
- Baker's cyst
- Scurvy
- McArdle syndrome

Peripheral Nervous System
- Guillain-Barré syndrome
- Poliomyelitis
- Acute transverse myelopathy
- Diabetes mellitus
- Heavy metal intoxication
- Drug intoxication
- Tick paralysis
- Periodic paralysis
- Electrolyte imbalance
- Causalgia

Articular
- Pyarthrosis
- Transient synovitis
- Osteochondritis dissecans
- Chondromalacia patellae
- Systemic lupus erythematosus
- Dermatomyositis
- Scleroderma
- Childhood polyarteritis
- Juvenile rheumatoid arthritis
- Anaphylactoid purpura
- Inflammatory bowel disease
- Serum sickness
- Hemophilia
- Enteric pathogens
- Brucellosis
- Rat-bite fever
- Congenital syphilis
- Kawasaki disease
- Lyme disease
- Chronic meningococcemia
- Hepatitis
- Mumps arthritis
- Varicella arthritis
- Herpes simplex arthritis

Central Nervous System
- Cerebral vascular accident
- Cerebral abscess
- Meningitis, encephalitis
- Acute infantile hemiplegia
- Complicated migraine
- Acute cerebellar ataxia
- Drug intoxication
- Malingering
- Conversion reaction

Intra-Abdominal
- Appendicitis
- Appendiceal abscess
- Cervicitis
- Salpingitis
- Retroperitoneal abscess
- Iliac adenitis
- Retroperitoneal fibrosis

Source: Modified and reproduced with permission from JI Singer: "Evaluation of Acute and Insidious Gait Disturbance in Children Less Than 5 Years of Age," in LA Barness et al (Eds): *Advances in Pediatrics*, Vol 26. Copyright © 1979 by Year Book Medical Publishers, Inc., Chicago.

Table 34-2 Common Causes of Altered Childhood Locomotion

- Overt and occult trauma
- Cellulitis
- Osteomyelitis
- Pyarthrosis
- Sickle cell, vaso-occlusive crisis
- Drug intoxication
- Transient synovitis
- Legg-Calvé-Perthes disease
- Appendicitis
- Juvenile rheumatoid arthritis

Source: Adapted with permission from JI Singer, "The Cause of Gait Disturbance in 425 Pediatric Patients," *Pediatric Emergency Care* (1985;1:9), Copyright © by Williams & Wilkins Company, 1985.

Distinguishing those children with an altered gait who require hospitalization and acute intervention from those who have self-limited conditions is of paramount importance. The history, physical examination, and ancillary laboratory findings may be helpful.

HISTORY

Young children identify the site of pain poorly. They find it difficult to differentiate muscular or joint pain from bone pain. Observation is essential; focusing on altered sleeping patterns, discomfort with handling a specific body part, avoidance of a particular position, and nature of the altered gait may be useful.

The intensity and pattern of the pain may differentiate certain diseases. Prolonged intermittent discomfort in the hip or ipsilateral knee over several days to months is consistent with Legg-Calvé-Perthes disease or slipped capital femoral epiphysis. Hip pain is often referred to the knee. A sporadic, intense pain in the buttock, back, or hip that increases with standing, sitting, or walking suggests an intervertebral disk infection. Insidious low back pain after trauma that is aggravated by standing, coughing, and defecation and improved by resting requires evaluation to exclude an intervertebral disk herniation or intraspinal tumor.

Stress fractures may be associated with lower extremity pain that is exacerbated by physical exertion and improved with rest without total resolution. Fractures are associated with the acute onset of pain after a fall, twisting injury, or direct blow to the lower limbs. Less commonly, arthralgia accompanied by morning stiffness with decreased motor strength and agility suggests a collagen vascular disease. Deep, boring extremity pain relieved by aspirin, becoming worse with rest and severe at night, is characteristic of osteoid osteoma.

Preceding events may be useful. Two thirds of children with Guillain-Barré syndrome have a febrile respiratory or gastrointestinal prodrome. Short, symptom-free periods occur with metastatic infections, whereas antecedent or current infectious processes involving the respiratory tract or soft-tissue are present in patients who develop osteomyelitis, pyarthrosis, or paraspinal or retroperitoneal abscesses. Fever almost uniformly accompanies inflammatory and infectious problems.

The review of systems should emphasize cutaneous lesions. Kawasaki disease is accompanied by a scarlatiniform erythroderma. Erythema chronicum migrans and erythema marginatum are pathognomonic for Lyme disease or acute rheumatic fever, respectively. Maculopapular eruptions are seen with rat-bite fever and chronic meningococcemia. Urticarial lesions accompany or precede the joint manifestation of hepatitis; if fixed or purpuric, anaphylactoid purpura needs consideration. Erythema nodosum can be either primarily or secondarily associated with an altered gait.

Exposures to animals, ticks, and potential intoxicants such as arsenic, mercury, lead, insecticides, alcohol, hydantoin, isoniazid, antimetabolites, and corticosteroids should be excluded. Recent intramuscular injections must be delineated. Parental drug use should be explored.

Sickle hemoglobinopathy, diabetes mellitus, immunocompromised state, or recent acute illness are important differential considerations. Previous joint disease producing an effusion may alter the synovial lining and predispose to future septic complications. Prior lumbar punctures may predispose to infection or tumor formation.

PHYSICAL EXAMINATION

Inspection begins with observation of the position of the patient at rest. Those with paraspinal abscess, intervertebral disk infection, or intraspinal tumors prefer the prone position. Children with transient synovitis of the hip or a sacroiliac, retroperitoneal, or hip infection are most comfortable with the affected hip held flexed, abducted, and externally rotated while supine or seated upright. Rarely, a patient with transient synovitis will prefer to maintain the flexed hip adducted and internally rotated. Those with pyarthrosis of the ankle or myositis of the calf muscles maintain the foot plantar flexed at rest.

Observe the gait. A cautious, methodical, shuffling gait accompanied by flexion of the trunk should suggest an underlying salpingitis, cervicitis, or appendicitis. An unsteady, clumsy, broad-based gait with tremor may be caused by acute cerebellar ataxia, hydantoin intoxication, or tick paralysis.

Children with increased intra-articular pressure in the hip place the affected limb on the ground in the same position of comfort that existed when lying supine. All muscular forces acting on the involved hip are decreased. Thus, the abductor and extensor actions are decreased while walking so that the pelvis tips downward as the trunk swings toward the affected side. The foot is held in plantar flexion so that the toe, rather than the heel, meets the ground. The reduced swing phase is terminated with the affected extremity advanced in relation to the unaffected side. With pyarthrosis of the hip, pseudoparalysis is common when there is marked distension of the capsule; the child will refrain from placing the foot on the floor.

A fracture of the tibia results in toddlers refusing to place the foot completely on the floor, but they may crawl without difficulty.

Observe the method chosen to achieve the erect position. Children who stand by flexing their trunk at the hips, putting hands on knees, and pushing the trunk upward by working the hands up the thighs (Gower's maneuver) have either proximal muscular weakness or intervertebral disk disease or infection.

Inspection should focus on the skin, looking for evidence of hemorrhagic diathesis, occult trauma, and penetrating wounds. Pigmentary changes, a hairy patch, or a deep sacral dimple may be clues to neural lesions. Brawny edema or erythematous discoloration of the feet may suggest sickle cell dactylitis or Kawasaki disease.

Compare the presumed unaffected paired body parts with the affected side for soft-tissue swelling and erythema. Areas involved with cellulitis often have defined erythematous borders, and other septic processes have diffuse swelling. For instance, the gluteal fold may be obliterated or the hip and inner thigh may be enlarged diffusely from soft-tissue swelling from sacroiliac joint infection or osteomyelitis of the proximal femur, respectively.

Localization of pain is an important factor. Disease of the spine, sacroiliac joint, pelvis, ilium, or hip may produce referred pain to the lower extremity, often the hip. Painful direct pressure of the lower extremities suggests one of three diseases. Obviously, fractures cause direct pain; extensive subperiosteal reaction may extend the location of this pain. Direct pressure over the metaphysis in patients with osteomyelitis produces exquisite pain, and myositis associated with viral infections (influenza, etc); polyarteritis causes pain with compression of the gastrocnemius, quadriceps, or soleus muscle groups.

In contrast, compression over the spinous process at the level of subjective back pain may produce pain in the back or over the iliac crest, sacroiliac joint, or buttock when associated with intervertebral disk infection, sacroiliac infection, paraspinal abscess, or extradural tuberculous abscess. Typically, palpation in the midline over a herniated disk is not painful, although paraspinal muscle spasm and scoliosis are common. Back pain may be enhanced with valsalva, heel strike, or straight leg raising if there is intervertebral disk herniation as well as intervertebral disk infection, intraspinal tumor, paraspinal abscess, and sacroiliac infection. Only sacroiliac infection is aggravated by compression or rocking of the ileal wings.

Abdominal pain in gait disturbance unaccompanied by abdominal guarding should raise suspicion of cord involvement. There may be a palpable mass in the iliac fossa or in the pelvic floor with appendicitis, appendiceal abscess, retroperitoneal abscess, or iliac adenitis.

The range of motion should be systematically tested, often requiring distraction of the pediatric patient. Patients with transient synovitis may not guard against motion, but may show some discomfort with attempts to rotate internally or extend the hip. Up to one third of patients with toxic synovitis show no limitation of motion. Cellulitis produces minimal limitation of joint movement, whereas osteomyelitis associated with a sympathetic joint effusion has more reduction in movement. The protected hip associated with sacroiliac joint infection, intervertebral disk infection, retroperitoneal abscess, or appendicitis can be gently rotated and flexed but not extended because of irritation of the iliopsoas muscle. In contrast, all attempted motion of a septic hip will magnify the protective muscle spasm and pain.

Abnormal neurologic examinations and gait disturbances may be associated with tick paralysis, Guillain-Barré syndrome, acute transverse myelopathy, intradural tumors, extradural hematoma, osteomyelitis of the lumbar spine, intervertebral disk infection, intervertebral disk herniation, systemic lupus erythematosus, sickle cell vaso-occlusive crisis with segmental necrosis of the cord, and acute cerebellar ataxia. There may be a sensory disturbance, loss of sphincter tone, paresis of the lower extremities, or a broad-based gait. Hemiplegia may develop with cerebral vascular accident, cerebral abscess, infantile hemiplegia, or complicated migraine. Those with paraspinal abscess, cerebral abscess, meningitis, acute transverse myelopathy, and intraspinal tumor may have nuchal rigidity.

LABORATORY ADJUNCTS

A complete blood count and erythrocyte sedimentation rate (ESR) may support a presumptive diagnosis; plain radiographs, computed tomography, scintigraphy, and nuclear magnetic resonance imaging may further define the differential diagnosis.

The total white blood cell count, absolute neutrophil count, percentage of band forms, and their morphologic appearance may be useful but have not prospectively been studied. However, many clinicians use the quantitative and qualitative changes in the leukocyte series to facilitate the diagnosis of systemic infection and to differentiate bacterial from nonbacterial infections. The sensitivity, specificity, and predictive value of alterations in the leukocyte series is improved when combined with the ESR.

The ESR correctly identifies more than 75% of patients with limb pain and underlying inflammatory or infectious disease. Approximately 70% of patients with an ESR > 30 mm/hr have an infectious or inflammatory origin for arthralgia or arthritis, and those with an ESR ≥ 40 mm/hr have bacterial infections as a cause of their refusal to walk. In contrast, less than 10% of pediatric patients with arthralgia from functional or mechanical problems have an elevated ESR. Kawasaki disease and leukemia have characteristic hematologic patterns.[5]

Radiographs of the painful or involved areas have diagnostic value. Findings may include periostitis, osteochondroses, benign and malignant tumors, mechanical disturbances, metabolic derangements, and infectious diseases. However, films with negative findings may not exclude the hairline tibial fracture in the toddler, the septic hip in a child over 1 year old, osteomyelitis of a long bone or pelvis, sacroiliac joint infection, or intervertebral disk infection. Radiographs may be insensitive, especially early in the course of a condition.[6]

Radionuclide scans provide important confirmatory data. A technetium scan with abnormal findings indicates a condition in which there is increased bone formation or blood flow. Scans with normal findings do not definitively exclude an infectious process and may require follow-up with a gallium scan, the latter accumulating in leukocytes irrespective of the blood-flow pattern. A gallium scan with abnormal findings supports the provisional diagnosis of an infection; technetium and gallium scans with normal findings refute it. The diagnostic accuracy of these procedures is augmented only when both scans are performed sequentially.

Computed tomography may delineate tumors as well as inflammatory and infectious problems of the musculoskeletal system of children. Magnetic resonance imaging is superior for identifying soft-tissue detail and may be particularly useful in establishing the early diagnosis of Legg-Calvé-Perthes disease, differentiating bone infarction from osteomyelitis in a patient with sickle cell disease and differentiating benign from malignant bone tumors.

However, all of these imaging methods have only limited utility in the evaluation of altered locomotion by the emergency physician.

DIAGNOSTIC ACCURACY

Limp or refusal to walk may be a symptom of a variety of diseases. The initial examination should focus on distinguishing children who require immediate hospitalization and treatment from those who may be followed for better definition of the underlying condition. *Early diagnosis is required for the 11 diseases listed in Table 34-3.* These conditions must be promptly and appropriately treated to avoid deformity, functional disability, or death.[4]

Children with altered locomotion require examination, treatment, and close follow-up. Children with an indolent illness, especially if febrile in the preceding 2 weeks, should be considered to have a serious infectious cause of gait disturbance. Even in those with a seemingly benign intercurrent illness, marked musculoskeletal disease may develop.

Those febrile patients with nuchal rigidity, limitation of joint motion, lower-limb direct metaphyseal pain, compression tenderness over a spinal process, or back pain enhanced with valsalva movement, heel strike or straight leg raising should have vigorous pursuit of a definitive diagnosis. Those who have a gait disturbance with altered consciousness, cranial nerve weakness, subjective or objective sensory disturbance, ataxia, alteration of sphincter tone, urinary retention, or altered deep tendon reflexes must have an expeditious confirmation of their diagnosis.

A systematic, aggressive workup of the child with altered locomotion is essential to exclude rapidly progressive processes to minimize morbidity. The differential considerations are varied and the evaluation complex, but nonetheless of crucial importance.

Table 34-3 Disease States Requiring Prompt Recognition

- Osteomyelitis
- Pyarthrosis
- Appendicitis
- Retroperitoneal abscess
- Paraspinal abscess
- Cord tumor
- Guillain-Barré syndrome
- Tick paralysis
- Cerebral abscess
- Meningitis
- Encephalitis

Source: Modified and reproduced with permission from JI Singer: "Evaluation of Acute and Insidious Gait Disturbance in Children Less Than 5 Years of Age," in LA Barness et al (Eds): *Advances in Pediatrics,* Vol 26. Copyright © 1979 by Year Book Medical Publishers, Inc, Chicago.

REFERENCES

1. Callanan DL: Causes of refusal to walk in childhood. *South Med J* 1982;75:20–22.

2. Passo MH: Aches and limb pain. *Pediatr Clin North Am* 1982;29:209–219.

3. Singer JI: The cause of gait disturbance in 425 pediatric patients. *Pediatr Emerg Care* 1985; 1:7–10.

4. Singer JI: Evaluation of acute and insidious gait disturbance in children less than five years of age. *Adv Pediatr* 1979;26:209–273.

5. McCarthy PL, Wasserman D, Spiesel SZ, et al: Evaluation of arthritis and arthralgia in the pediatric patient. *Clin Pediatr* 1980;19:183–190.

6. Bowyer SL, Hollister JR: Limb pain in childhood. *Pediatr Clin North Am* 1984;31: 1053–1081.

Section 19

Pregnancy Testing

The increased sensitivity and specificity of pregnancy tests have facilitated the assessment of the female patient with lower abdominal pain and will, we hope, reduce the complications of pregnancy such as ectopic pregnancy. They may also permit earlier termination of unwanted pregnancies.

The beta subunit human chorionic gonadotropin (HCG) radioimmunoassay test and the monoclonal antibody tests are ideal to exclude ectopic pregnancy, whereas less expensive tests may be adequate to confirm a routine pregnancy.

35. Pregnancy Testing in the Emergency Department

Ann R. McGravey, MD

Pregnancy in adolescents is a not uncommon problem faced by pediatricians, family practitioners, and emergency physicians. Between 1971 and 1982 the estimated percentage of teens aged 15 to 19 years with premarital sexual experience increased from 26.8% to 42.8%.[1] Efforts have been made to promote sex education, but only 57% of adolescents can correctly identify the period of greatest risk of pregnancy.[2] Despite attempts to provide accessible birth control counseling, 27% of sexually active adolescents have never used contraceptives.[3]

Data show that 23% of teenagers under 15 years of age and 13% of teenagers 15 to 19 years of age obtain abortions after the first trimester, when the risk of death and major complications for the mother are significantly higher. Two thirds of teens under age 15 and one half of teens aged 15 to 17 years receive no prenatal care during the critical first 3 months of pregnancy.[4]

Accurate diagnosis of pregnancy soon after conception offers the option of terminating an unwanted pregnancy by safe, simple, effective, and inexpensive procedures or initiating early prenatal care to a population with high rates of perinatal mortality, low birth weight infants, toxemia, and anemia. Perhaps of even greater importance with the acutely ill girl with abdominal pain is the ability to diagnose pregnancy early and thereby reduce complications such as ruptured ectopic pregnancy.

DIAGNOSIS OF PREGNANCY

Adolescents often wait until the end of the first trimester or even well into the second trimester to seek care for a possible pregnancy. This may be because of deliberate delays by the adolescents, or because the diagnosis of pregnancy is

270

particularly elusive in adolescents as there is rarely a straightforward history or physical examination. Adolescents rarely give a true history of sexual activity. Their menstrual pattern is often irregular or simply unknown to the adolescent who pays no attention to the calendar. Variations in menses go unnoticed and thus spotting may be mistaken for a normal period. Occasionally, adolescents complain of amenorrhea or symptoms of pregnancy: dizziness, syncope, nausea, or breast tenderness. More often they are asymptomatic, have not missed a period, or present with totally unrelated complaints, assuming that the physician will diagnose pregnancy if it exists.

Adolescents can often hide changes in body image from parents, friends, and even physicians until 4 to 6 months into the pregnancy. Denial may be so extreme as to ascribe quickening, the perception of fetal movements, to stomach gurgling. Abdominal palpation alone will not be diagnostic until at least 10 to 12 weeks into gestation. The uterus is not enlarged until 7 to 8 weeks. Chadwick's sign, a bluish hue to the cervix and vaginal mucosa, is inconstant. Hegar's sign, softening of the cervix, does occur early but if an adolescent is difficult to examine, the physician will be reluctant to rely solely on this finding. Thus pregnancy tests are relied on for diagnosis.

PHYSIOLOGY

To understand the basis of pregnancy testing, one must review some physiology. Ovulation usually occurs about 14 days before the next expected menstruation triggered approximately 30 hours before by a surge of luteinizing hormone (LH). About 9 days later (1 to 2 days after implantation) human chorionic gonadotropin (HCG) produced by the syncytiotrophoblast becomes detectable. HCG maintains the corpus luteum of pregnancy, supporting the continued secretion of estrogen and progesterone until the placenta is sufficiently developed. HCG is a sialoglycoprotein with alpha and beta subunits. The alpha subunits are indistinguishable from those of follicle stimulating hormone (FSH), LH, and thyroid stimulating hormone (TSH). The beta subunits are biologically and immunologically specific. HCG initially increases 2 fold every 2 days so that by the expected day of menstruation it is 50 mIU/mL, 2 days later 100, a week later 400. By the sixth week of gestation (2 weeks after the first missed period) it is about 3,000 mIU/mL (Table 35-1). It peaks at 8 to 12 weeks reaching levels of 20,000 to 100,000 mIU/mL. Later in the third trimester the levels decline, reaching values sometimes lower than those at 8 weeks gestation (Figure 35-1).[5]

AVAILABLE TESTS

During the last century many different techniques for the detection of pregnancy have been used. Bioassays performed by injecting urine or serum

Table 35-1 Serum HCG Levels in Early and Ectopic Pregnancy[7]

Day of Cycle	Range of HCG (mIU/mL)	Median HCG (mIU/mL)
21–28	30–1,100	130
35–42	200–70,000	1,000
49–56	500–70,000	2,500
63–70	1,000–100,000	10,000
Ectopic pregnancy	150–800	

Source: Reprinted with permission from *Critical Reviews in Clinical Laboratory Sciences* (1984;19:354), Copyright © 1984, CRC Press Inc, Boca Raton, FL.

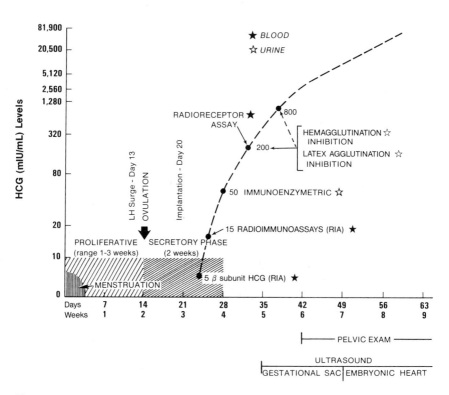

Figure 35-1 Average HCG levels in pregnancy after two typical 28-day menstrual cycles. Titers, gestational weeks, and times when available tests show positive results are indicated and compared with ultrasound and pelvic examination. *Source:* Reprinted with permission from *Journal of the National Medical Association* (1984;76:308), Copyright © 1984, Appleton & Lange.

samples into animals were initially used; these looked for ovarian hypertrophy, hyperemia, or hemorrhage. The agent responsible, at that time, was thought to be a hypophyseal hormone. Problems with this method included the care and handling of animals, animal fatality from urine toxicity, variations in animal sensitivity, and test performance time. The sensitivity of this method is 10,000 mIU HCG/mL, meaning that detection is possible only after day 39 of the cycle.

Hormonal tests done by injecting women intramuscularly with progesterone/estradiol or progesterone alone have been used to differentiate amenorrhea caused by pregnancy from amenorrhea of other causes. This has the serious disadvantage of teratogenic effects, ie, the VATER syndrome, masculinization of the female fetus, and thrombotic phenomenon in the mother.

With the knowledge that HCG is the hormone of pregnancy, assays measuring the immunologically active part of the molecule were developed in 1960. The first one developed was the direct hemagglutination assay in which antibodies directed against HCG are adsorbed onto sheep red blood cells (RBCs). When urine containing HCG is added, agglutination occurs. Indirect agglutination inhibition offers a more sensitive method. An HCG reagent is combined with the patient's urine and subsequently with RBCs or latex particles coated with HCG. If the patient's urine contains sufficient HCG, it binds the antiserum, and no agglutination with RBCs or latex particles occurs. Problems include drug interference (which cause increased urine excretion of LH, which has identical subunits) particularly by methadone and phenothiazines, protein interference (if $> 1g/24$ hr), instability of the lattice of agglutination, and reliance on subjective interpretation by the reader, which is further dependent on lighting and background interference. These agglutination tests are of two types: slide and tube. Improved methods now permit sensitivities of 200 mIU HCG/mL.

In the 1970s a radioimmunoassay (RIA) based on the ability of a limited quantity of antibody to bind a fixed amount of radiolabeled antigen and the inhibition of this reaction by an unlabeled antigen was formulated. A blood sample is mixed with a fixed amount of antibody to HCG and then with labeled HCG. If HCG is present, antiHCG binds to it and leaves labeled HCG free to be quantitated. This assay can detect levels of HCG of 25 to 50 mIU HCG/mL (day 20 of cycle), which occur just after fertilization. Initially the sensitivity had to be decreased somewhat since specimens collected close to the time of ovulation raise the potential of interference from the LH surge. The development of antiserum specific for the beta subunit of HCG excludes this crossreaction.

In 1977, attempts to measure the biologically active portion of HCG generated the radioreceptor assay. The patient's HCG and radioiodine-labeled

HCG compete for specific receptor sites on a cell membrane. After free and bound radiolabeled HCG are separated, the radioactivity is measured and compared with a reference. The reference control is predetermined to be greater than the LH surge, since LH is the only crossreacting hormone. The sensitivity of this test is 200 mIU HCG/mL and thus detects pregnancy after day 26 of the cycle. The radioreceptor assay has the sensitivity of the RIA and the specificity of the bioassay, measuring only biologically active HCG, not inactive fragments.

The 1980s have seen the development of the enzyme immunoassay. The patient's sample and horseradish peroxidase-labeled HCG compete for solid-phase antibody directed against the beta subunit of HCG. This is almost as sensitive as the RIA (ie, 40 mIU/mL) and offers advantages over the RIA in its greater shelf life, lack of radioactive hazard, and need for specialized disposal.

The most recent advances have been in the use of monoclonal antibodies. In one such assay, an immunoradiometric qualitative or quantitative assay employs a solid-phase monoclonal antibody directed against a remote portion of HCG, and a second monoclonal antibody is radiolabeled and directed against the beta subunit. Thus only biologically active HCG is measured, without crossreactivity and regardless of the reference preparation used. The second test is a qualitative immunoenzymetric assay. The first solid-phase monoclonal antibody reacts to the beta subunit and serves to capture and immobilize the HCG molecule. The second monoclonal antibody is chemically linked to an enzyme that will cause a color change in a developer solution. This binds to the beta subunit of the immobilized HCG molecule, thus "sandwiching" the HCG molecule between the membrane-linked antibody and the enzyme-linked antibody. Washing removes unbound enzyme-linked antibody, and bound enzyme can then be measured by a calibrated color change. The sensitivity is 40 to 50 mIU HCG/mL, and the test offers the advantages of a long shelf life, lack of instrumentation or isotopes, ability to perform batch or single tests, and increased specificity because of monoclonal antibodies. A review by Cartwright et al[6] recommends The Icon (Hybritech) as the easiest, fastest, and most reliable of these newer urine assays.

CHOOSING A TEST

How does one determine which test is best? Availability, specificity, sensitivity, requirements for specialized equipment, test time performance, and ease of acquisition of required specimen must be considered (Table 35-2). For a patient with simple uncomplicated intrauterine pregnancy presenting shortly after a missed menses, the immunologic agglutination inhibition tests available in most offices and hospitals are adequate.

However, for the detection of abnormal pregnancy or early pregnancy more specialized tests are justified. The case of abnormal pregnancy is clear. The diagnosis of unruptured ectopic pregnancy has been aided by ultrasonography, culdocentesis, and by more accurate pregnancy testing. A series from Los Angeles[8] reported sensitivities of 99.1% for quantitative beta subunit RIA, 90% for enzyme-linked urine assays, and 51% to 61% for urine slide hemagglutination. A modification of the enzyme-linked urine assay, using a larger volume of urine when the specific gravity is less than 1.015, increased the sensitivity to 96.3%.[9] Quantitative beta subunit RIA testing allows serial measurements so blighted ova, ectopics, and impending abortion may be diagnosed by falling or plateauing titers. Multiple gestations and molar pregnancies can be diagnosed by HCG titers that are much higher than normal.

With regard to the early detection of normal pregnancies, the issues are less clear. The fact that organogenesis, when the fetus is most susceptible to serious malformations, concludes by the eighth week (only 4 weeks after the first missed period) is frightening. If irradiation, drugs, vaccines, anesthesia, and surgery are to be avoided, early detection is necessary and thus beta subunit RIA testing has become a hospital admission screen for women of reproductive age, and should probably be performed before the use of any potentially teratogenic agents or procedures.

Rape victims who may be offered pregnancy prophylaxis need sensitive screening to rule out an ongoing early pregnancy that they might wish to carry to term. For women who wish to consider therapeutic abortion, the termination procedures are simpler and safer early in pregnancy. For adolescents who may require considerable counseling to arrive at a decision, earlier detection permits more time.

Prenatal care has become a specialized field and the earlier instituted the better. In adolescents, issues of poor nutritional habits, anemia, and use of cigarettes, alcohol, and drugs are common enough to make this prenatal care/counseling especially important. One other issue to consider is that adolescents may wait until well into the pregnancy (fifth or sixth month) to seek care. If they go to a walk-in clinic simply for a pregnancy test without an examination, the levels of HCG may have dropped to levels below the detection capability of standard urine slide tests.

But what about the woman who simply wants to know immediately if she is pregnant and is not willing to wait a few weeks? Does this warrant specialized testing? The adolescent population perhaps should be considered separately. As a whole, they often have immature mechanisms of coping with stress. Worry over the question of pregnancy can lead to depression, suicide attempts, or drug abuse. Noncompliance is also a problem. Asking an adolescent to return in a week or two for repeat testing is probably unreasonable. Thus a

Table 35-2 Comparison of Available Pregnancy Tests

Test (Brand Names)	Specimen	Test Time (Minutes)	Stated Sensitivity (mIU/mL)	Earliest* Detection (Day from LMP)	False (+)	False (−)	Cost†
Slide (Gravindex)	Urine	2	3,500	35	Protein, detergents, drugs	Ectopic 60%	$ 5
(Pregnosis)			1,500–2,500	33	None		
(UCG slide)			2,000	33	Protein, blood, bacteria		
Tube hemagglutination inhibition	Urine	60–120					$20
(Gravindex 90)			750–1,250	32–35	Protein, drugs	Ectopic 30%	
(Pregnosticon)			750–850	32	Detergents, drugs, protein, bacteria		
(UCG Lyphotest)			500–1,000	32	Blood, protein, bacteria		
Latex particle agglutination (Sensitex)			250	28	High level of protein		
(Placentex)			1,000	32			

Radioimmunoassay (beta subunit)						
Qualitative	Serum	60–120	6–50	20		Ectopic 1%	$20–30
Quantitative							$34–50
Radioreceptor (Biocept G)	Serum	60	200	26	Elevated LH		
Immunoenzymetric monoclonal antibody (Tandem Icon)	Urine	4	50	21	Prolonged reading time Temperature dependent	Ectopic 10%	$10–15
Home test	Urine		1,250–2,000	35–42	Contamination protein	Overall rate 24%	$ 5–15

*Assuming average cycle = 28 days

†Range of prices from three laboratories

sensitive test, yet one that can be performed while the adolescent waits, avoiding telephone calls that might break confidentiality, seems warranted.

One detrimental effect of highly sensitive early testing is the diagnosis of pregnancies that will result in early embryonic loss (only a little more than one third of all implantations are carried to term). Many of these were previously unknown to the women who considered the bleeding either normal or delayed menstruation. Receiving early confirmation by a sensitive test may cause emotional trauma when the loss occurs.

Ease of acquisition of the specimen should be a consideration. One needs to realize that HCG is more concentrated in urine than in serum and is not surrounded by many other proteins that act as interfering substances. In adolescents the incidence of proteinuria is rather low, but menstrual irregularity is common and crossreacting tests that would measure LH can present a problem. So, in fact, a urine test with beta subunit specificity might be ideal.

Cost probably needs to be considered separately for office *v* emergency department (hospital based) use. Clearly the high price of the quantitative beta subunit test would be hard to justify, but the increased cost of the urine enzyme assay (Tandem Icon) or qualitative beta subunit tests might be balanced by their increased sensitivity.

CONCLUSIONS

The 1980s have seen the generation of sensitive urine and serum pregnancy tests that have markedly increased our ability to evaluate vaginal bleeding, abdominal or pelvic pain, and the question of early pregnancy in the emergency department. It would seem that sensitivity and performance time should be the foremost considerations when dealing with an adolescent in an emergency setting. Thus the routine use of urine enzyme assay, a sensitive test performed on urine in approximately 4 minutes, should be strongly considered. The quantitative beta subunit RIA test, in association with ultrasonography, could serve as the backup when an abnormal pregnancy is suspected.

REFERENCES

1. Teenage pregnancy and fertility trends—United States, 1974 and 1980: Leads from the MMWR. *JAMA* 1985;253:3064–3065.

2. Zelnik M: Sexual knowledge and knowledge of pregnancy risk among US teenage women. *Fam Plan Perspect* 1979;11:355.

3. Zelnik M, Kantner JF: Sexual activity, contraceptive use and pregnancy among metropolitan area teenagers, 1971–1979. *Fam Plan Perspect* 1980;12:230.

4. *Teenage Pregnancy: The Problem That Hasn't Gone Away.* New York, Alan Guttmacher Institute, 1981, pp 55,59.

5. Pedro A: Early detection of pregnancy. *J Natl Med Assoc* 1984;76:308–314.

6. Cartwright PS, Victory DF, Wong SW, et al: Evaluation of the new generation of urinary pregnancy tests. *Am J Obstet Gynecol* 1985;153:730–731.

7. Rippey JH: Pregnancy tests: Evaluation and current status. *Crit Rev Clin Laboratory Sci* 1984;19:354–357.

8. Barnes RB, Roy S, Yee B, et al: Reliability of urinary pregnancy tests in the diagnosis of ectopic pregnancy. *J Reprod Med* 1985;30:827–831.

9. Cartwright PS, Victory DF, Moore RA, et al: Performance of a new enzyme-linked immunoassay urine pregnancy test for the detection of ectopic gestation. *Ann Emerg Med* 1986; 15:1198–1199.

PART VI

Trauma

Section 20

Head Trauma

Head trauma is common in children; the major unresolved issues focus on the nature of the appropriate diagnostic evaluation and the requirements for hospitalization and observation.

Further assessment of suggested scales to evaluate the traumatized child must be undertaken, focusing on cortical function of purposeful movement and brainstem function related to breathing.

The diagnostic procedure of choice after significant head trauma is computed tomography of the head. This is indicated in children with either generalized or focal neurologic deficits or a deteriorating status. In contrast, skull x-ray studies may be considered in children with a normal neurologic status and a risk of skull fracture based on the mechanism of injury.

36. Closed Head Injury in Children

Peter T. Pons, MD

Trauma remains the leading cause of death in the pediatric age group,[1] and head injuries are among the most common reasons for admission, accounting for approximately 200,000 to 250,000 hospitalizations annually.[2,3] The great diversity in symptoms and signs can test the ability of the physician to differentiate those patients with serious injury from those with minor head trauma. The decision regarding what to do with the child who is comatose is usually an easy one; the workup and management of the child who has sustained blunt head trauma and is not unconscious becomes a subject of great debate.

The majority of head injuries in pediatric patients occur as a result of falls or motor vehicle accidents (either auto-pedestrian or as passengers in the automobile). A smaller number of children sustain their injuries from direct blows to the head. These may be accidental as in sports-related trauma (for example, being struck with a baseball bat) or nonaccidental as in child abuse.[4]

PRESENTATION

A clear and concise history is invaluable in helping to decide the likelihood of a serious intracranial pathologic condition as well as an associated life-threatening injury. The mechanism of injury should be ascertained, with a special awareness of inconsistencies in the history that suggest child abuse. The presence, absence, or development of a neurologic deficit should be ascertained over time. For instance, a child who was initially unconscious and is now alert is much less worrisome than the child who was initially alert and is now unconscious. Nonlocalizing complaints such as vomiting, headache, and drowsiness should also be sought from the patient or relatives.

283

Before any consideration is given to the head injury, a complete physical examination must be performed for associated significant trauma that might be life-threatening. Only after excluding the possibility of other major injury should the head trauma be addressed.

The single most important observation is the level of consciousness and mental status over time. The terminology used should be descriptive; avoid using words such as lethargic, stuporous, or semicomatose since they mean different things to different observers. Instead, a more valuable description is the response of the patient to such things as verbal commands or other stimuli, including motor response and spontaneous movements. Most serious trauma-related neurosurgical problems are associated with an alteration in the level of consciousness, and it is at this point that the diagnosis must be made, before focal neurologic deficits are manifest. If one waits for the development of a dilated pupil and hemiparesis to consider the possibility of increased intra-cranial pressure, either from cerebral edema or a space-occupying hemorrhage, then it may well be too late for a satisfactory patient outcome.

A complete neurologic examination should be performed with careful attention to any focal deficits that may be detected. Age-related neurologic findings should also be noted, such as the startle response or plantar response of the infant. This portion of the examination should include looking at the ear canal and tympanic membrane for the presence of blood, hemotympanum, or cerebrospinal fluid, indicating a basilar skull fracture. The nose should also be carefully examined for possible cerebrospinal fluid leak, again pointing to basilar skull fracture. Additional physical findings include postauricular ecchymosis (Battle's sign) or bilateral orbital ecchymosis (raccoon eyes). Fun-duscopic examination of the eyes must also be performed looking for retinal hemorrhages, which suggest possible child abuse.

The Glasgow Coma Scale (GCS) has been used as a scoring system for the patient who has sustained a neurologic injury. This scale evaluates the best motor response, eye opening, and verbal response to stimuli. There are difficulties with a scale of this type for the injured infant. A variation of the GCS for infants and children in the preverbal stage, developed at Children's Ortho-pedic Hospital and Medical Center in Seattle, uses cortical and brainstem function as an alternative for these patients.[5]

DIAGNOSTICS

The nature and number of diagnostic studies depend on the mechanism of injury and the clinical condition of the patient. If the mechanism or condition of the patient is such that there is a potential for serious injury or, in fact, there are injuries present, then studies such as a hematocrit, type and cross-match for blood, chest and pelvic x-ray studies, and urinalysis are indicated. The workup for the neurosurgical injury follows these studies. If the patient has isolated cranial trauma, the evaluation can proceed immediately to address that concern.

Recognition and management of surgically correctable injuries must be accomplished as rapidly as possible. The diagnostic procedure of choice for the evaluation of any patient in whom a post-traumatic intracranial lesion is suspected is computed tomography (CT) of the head.[2,6] This is the only study that provides the definitive answer about the necessity for neurosurgical intervention. A CT scan is indicated for children who are in coma after head injury, show focal neurologic deficits, or have a deteriorating level of consciousness or neurologic status. This study should be obtained as rapidly as possible once other life threats have been excluded. It must be stressed that in the child who has any neurologic signs or symptoms a CT scan of the head should be obtained as expeditiously as possible and never delayed to perform skull radiography.

The issue of skull radiography has generated and continues to generate a great deal of discussion and controversy. Radiologic examination of the skull provides no information about the pathophysiology occurring in the cranial vault and, as such, does not assist in making the diagnosis of an acute neurosurgical emergency. Therefore, skull x-ray studies should never be considered a primary diagnostic study in a child with neurologic symptoms or signs.

Skull x-ray films may be obtained for a child who is awake, has no neurologic abnormalities, and who has a risk of skull fracture (especially depressed fracture). Finding a linear skull fracture mandates, at least, admission to the hospital for observation for 24 hours (and often a CT scan if the fracture crosses a vascular groove), whereas a depressed fracture may require surgical elevation of the fragment.

The primary issue has been the rather low yield of abnormal findings generated by skull x-ray studies. As a result, a number of investigators have proposed high-yield criteria for obtaining skull radiographs, thus improving the probability of finding an abnormality. These criteria are useful guidelines; however, it must be remembered that they must be individualized. Indications for radiography of the skull include:

- history of loss of consciousness
- mechanism of injury capable of producing a depressed fracture (all of the force dissipated over a small area, ie, struck with a hammer or fireplace poker)
- localized scalp hematoma[7]
- possible child abuse[8]

- penetrating trauma[7]
- a parent who insists on the study.

The child who falls and bumps his head usually does not need a skull x-ray film in the absence of other signs or symptoms. One management strategy for radiographic imaging is summarized in Table 36-1.

MANAGEMENT

The discussion will focus only on the treatment of the head-injured child and presupposes that other injuries are recognized and managed appropriately.

Therapy in the emergency department is aimed at control of increased intracranial pressure while definitive diagnosis of the intracranial pathology (cerebral edema v intracranial hematoma) is established. Intracranial pressure should be presumed to be elevated if the patient has a deteriorating level of consciousness, progressive neurologic deficits, or focal findings.

Hyperventilation is the most rapid method of reducing intracranial pressure in the emergency department. Reduction of the carbon dioxide tension to 20 to 25 mmHg, documented by arterial blood gas determination, is the desired goal.[3] In order to accomplish this, airway control is necessary, usually endotracheal intubation. If necessary, chemical paralysis, and rapid sequence induction should be performed.

Intubation and hyperventilation are indicated in any patient who has head trauma and is comatose, has deteriorating neurologic findings, an altered level of consciousness with focal deficits, or has penetrating cranial injury. Cervical spine injury must be excluded before oral endotracheal intubation. If the need for airway management is emergent and the cervical spine cannot be cleared, then nasotracheal intubation or cricothyroidotomy should be attempted. After tracheal intubation, nasogastric decompression should be accomplished.

Increased intracranial pressure can further be reduced via the use of diuretics, either osmotic or loop. Mannitol (0.25 mg/kg IV over 15 minutes) or furosemide (1 mg/kg IV) may be used. The use of mannitol has been associated with a number of potential complications that necessitate careful monitoring of the patient during and after the mannitol infusion. These problems include hyperosmolality, volume overload, or dehydration. In the past, larger doses of mannitol were used, and there was often a substantial problem with rebound edema of the brain after the effect of the drug had dissipated. The smaller doses now used have decreased the incidence of this side effect, but it is still a concern.

Table 36-1 Management Strategy for Radiographic Imaging in Patients with Head Trauma*

Low-Risk Group	Moderate-Risk Group	High-Risk Group

Possible findings
  Asymptomatic
  Headache
  Dizziness
  Scalp hematoma
  Scalp laceration
  Scalp contusion or
    abrasion
  Absence of moderate-risk
    or high-risk criteria
	Possible findings
	  History of change of
	    consciousness at the
	    time of injury or
	    subsequently
	  History of progressive
	    headache
	  Alcohol or drug
	    intoxication
	  Unreliable or inadequate
	    history of injury
	  Age less than 2 yr (unless
	    injury very trivial)
	  Post-traumatic seizure
	  Vomiting
	  Post-traumatic amnesia
	  Multiple trauma
	  Serious facial injury
	  Signs of basilar fracture†
	  Possible skull penetration
	    or depressed fracture‡
	  Suspected physical child
	    abuse
		Possible findings
		  Depressed level of
		    consciousness not clearly
		    due to alcohol, drugs, or
		    other cause (eg,
		    metabolic and seizure
		    disorders)
		  Focal neurologic signs
		  Decreasing level of
		    consciousness
		  Penetrating skull injury or
		    palpable depressed
		    fracture

Recommendations
  Observation alone:
    discharge patients with
    head-injury information
    sheet (listing subdural
    precautions) and a
    second person to
    observe them.
	Recommendations
	  Extended close
	    observation (watch for
	    signs of high-risk group).
	  Consider CT examination
	    and neurosurgical
	    consultation.
	  Skull series may (rarely) be
	    helpful, if positive, but do
	    not exclude intracranial
	    injury if normal.
		Recommendations
		  Patient is a candidate for
		    neurosurgical
		    consultation or
		    emergency CT
		    examination or both.

*Physician assessment of the severity of injury may warrant reassignment to a higher-risk group. Any single criterion from a higher-risk group warrants assignment of the patient to the highest risk group applicable.

†Signs of basilar fracture include drainage from ear, drainage of cerebrospinal fluid from nose, hematotympanum, Battle's sign, and "raccoon eyes."

‡Factors associated with open and depressed fracture include gunshot, missile or shrapnel wounds; scalp injury from firm, pointed object (including animal teeth); penetrating injury of eyelid or globe; object stuck in the head; assault (definite or suspected) with any object; leakage of cerebrospinal fluid; and sign of basilar fracture.

Barbiturates are also used for intracranial pressure control, particularly when other modalities fail to decrease pressure adequately. Barbiturates, however, should be used only after neurosurgical consultation has been obtained since they will render the patient comatose and will void the value of the physical examination.

Steroid administration continues to be a controversial therapy. Although they have never been shown to improve the edema associated with trauma, their use is widespread. Steroids have not been demonstrated to be efficacious. Certainly they should not be considered as a first-line drug, as any effect they might have will not be noted for hours. The decision to use steroids should be made in concert with the neurosurgical consultant.

Another controversy revolves around the use of systemic antibiotics in cases of basilar skull fracture. The issue is whether prophylactic administration prevents meningitis or selects for resistant organisms and is not consistently used. As with barbiturates and steroids, a joint decision with the neurosurgical consultant is appropriate.

Fluid administration should be kept to a minimum to decrease the possible development of increased intracranial pressure or cerebral edema. The desire to restrict fluids does not pertain to the patient who has multiple injuries or is in shock. In these instances, treatment of the head injury must be deferred in favor of adequate trauma resuscitation with appropriate fluid administration.

Elevation of the patient's head to 30° is thought to promote venous drainage from the cerebral circulation and thus decrease intracranial pressure.[3] This should be performed only after other injuries have been excluded.

The routine use of anticonvulsant medication remains controversial and is generally not recommended except when there is a high likelihood or documentation of brain injury. These cases include:

- penetrating injury
- documented structural brain lesion
- depressed skull fracture
- seizures.

The drug of choice for post-traumatic seizures is phenytoin sodium.[2] It has the primary advantage of not sedating the patient. Diazepam or phenobarbital are also excellent drugs for seizure control and may be used in this setting, but both have sedative actions and make neurologic evaluation more difficult. Dosages are as follows:

- phenytoin: load 10 to 20 mg/kg IV (< 50 mg/min); maintenance 5 to 10 mg/kg/day PO

- diazepam: 0.2 to 0.3 mg/kg up to 10 mg IV (< 1 mg/min)
- phenobarbital: load 10 mg/kg IV (< 25 mg/min); maintenance 3 to 5 mg/kg/day.

PATIENT DISPOSITION

The criteria for hospitalization can be summarized as follows: patients with altered mental status, neurologic deficits, suspected child abuse, persistent or progressive symptoms, prolonged unconsciousness, skull fracture, a poor home environment, or suspected nonaccidental trauma.[9]

Neurosurgical consultation should be obtained for any patient admitted to the hospital. Immediate consultation in the emergency department is indicated for children in coma or who have progressive or focal findings.

If discharge from the hospital is contemplated for the child, a responsible adult must be present, and explicit instructions must be given to that person regarding observation and care for the patient. The instructions should include the following:

- Awaken the patient every 2 to 4 hours (return immediately if unable to awaken child).
- Call or return immediately if the following are noted:

    change in equality of pupils
    increased sleepiness or lethargy
    stumbling or abnormal gait or crawl
    seizures
    change in personality or behavior
    persistent vomiting (more than two or three times)
    blood or clear discharge from nose or ears.

- Use acetaminophen for pain; do not use any narcotic.

REFERENCES

1. Committee on Trauma Research, Commission on Life Sciences, National Research Council, Institute of Medicine: *Injury in America: A Continuing Public Health Problem.* Washington, National Academy Press, 1985, p 18.

2. Rosman NP, Herskowitz J, Carter AP, et al: Acute head trauma in infancy and childhood: Clinical and radiologic aspects. *Pediatr Clin North Am* 1979;26:707–736.

3. Raphaely RC, Swedlow DB, Downes JJ, et al: Management of severe pediatric head trauma. *Pediatr Clin North Am* 1983;27:715–727.

4. Ivan LP, Choo SH, Ventureyra ECG: Head injuries in childhood: A 2-year survey. *Can Med Assoc J* 1983;128:281–284.

5. Morray JP, Tyler DC, Jones TK, et al: Coma scale for use in brain-injured children. *Crit Care Med* 1984;12:1018–1020.

6. Bruce DA, Schut L: The value of CAT scanning following pediatric head injury. *Clin Pediatr* 1980;19:719–725.

7. Leonidas JC, Ting W, Binkiewicz A, et al: Mild head trauma in children: When is a roentgenogram necessary. *Pediatrics* 1982;69:139–143.

8. Merten DF, Osborne DRS, Radkowski MA, et al: Craniocerebral trauma in the child abuse syndrome: Radiological observations. *Pediatr Radiol* 1984;14:272–277.

9. Dershewitz RA, Kaye BA, Swisher CN: Treatment of children with posttraumatic transient loss of consciousness. *Pediatrics* 1983;72:602–607.

Section 21

Blunt Abdominal Trauma

The child rarely suffers life-threatening abdominal injury requiring immediate surgical intervention. Therefore, a strategy for accurately assessing the patient with blunt abdominal trauma is essential.

Historically, diagnostic peritoneal lavage (DPL) was the procedure of choice; it is a rapid technique but is invasive, does not provide localization of the injury, and may be less sensitive for isolated visceral damage and diaphragmatic or retroperitoneal injuries. Newer guide wire techniques may simplify the procedure. Computed tomography (CT) technology has improved, allowing greater definition of the organ(s) involved and the nature of the injury. However, CT may be unable to identify gastrointestinal perforation, intraluminal hematoma, or pancreatic injury and is dependent on the equipment and expertise of those interpreting the results. Unstable patients should normally have DPL performed unless immediate laparotomy is obvious. The assessment of stable patients often combines both modalities along with the close observation of the patient depending on the mechanism of injury.

Ultrasonography, technetium scanning, and intravenous pyelography have more limited roles.

37. Evaluation of Blunt Abdominal Trauma in Childhood

Anthony J. Haftel, MD

Trauma is the leading cause of death in childhood. Blunt trauma is the major mode of injury, accounting for about 85% to 90% of occurrences. Boys are involved in blunt trauma approximately twice as frequently as girls, and the peak age of occurrence seems to be 6 to 8 years of age. Injury is usually done to the skeletal system, the brain, and the abdominal contents. The evaluation of blunt abdominal trauma (BAT) in pediatrics has certain controversial aspects.

The unstable child who has physical findings of serious intra-abdominal injury such as gross distension, marked tenderness, absent bowel sounds, tread marks across the abdomen, or gross hematuria presents little difficulty in terms of evaluation and management. They generally require oxygen supplementation and active ventilation management, multiple large-bore intravenous (IV) catheters, volume resuscitation, nasogastric and Foley intubation, consideration of a "one shot" intravenous pyelogram (IVP) to define renal status and function, and then a quick trip to the operating room for exploratory laparotomy. More sophisticated studies of the abdomen diagnostic peritoneal lavage (DPL), diagnostic ultrasound (DUS), CT scanning, or arteriography are dangerous because of the time needed to obtain them, and unnecessary because these children are *obvious* surgical candidates.

This situation, however, is a rarity in the practice of pediatric traumatology. A minority of children sustaining BAT cannot be stabilized in the trauma suite for more detailed studies. The object of further evaluation is the enumeration and identification of exact organs of injury, and an attempt to locate and quantitate intra- and extraperitoneal hemorrhage. The ideal management is to keep the child out of the operating room. The advantages of avoiding laparotomy are manifold and include avoiding anesthetic morbidity and mortality, preventing future postsplenectomy overwhelming sepsis, and forming intra-abdominal adhesions with subsequent bowel obstruction. Critical to this approach is the availability of diagnostic modalities that are both sensitive and specific to intra-abdominal injury and can locate and quantitate intra- or extra-peritoneal hemorrhage. The surgeon is best supported in the decision to operate or not by the child's inherent stability, knowledge with a high degree of certainty of the organs injured, pattern of ongoing hemorrhage, and ability to monitor the child closely and to intervene on an emergent basis.

The modalities most frequently used for these determinations are DUS, diagnostic peritoneal lavage, IVP, IV contrast-enhanced abdominal CT scanning (CECT), and selective arteriography.

DIAGNOSTIC PERITONEAL LAVAGE

Diagnostic peritoneal lavage has enjoyed a long period of popularity and is considered by some trauma specialists to be the "gold standard" of diagnostic modalities in adult blunt abdominal trauma.[1-3] The ability to enter the peritoneum directly and find gross blood, bile, feces, or succus entericus is compelling evidence of serious intra-abdominal injury. Subsequent laboratory determinations of lavage fluid revealing red cell or white cell counts in excess of 100,000 or 500 cells/mm^3, respectively, an amylase in excess of 200 IU/L, a Gram's stain positive for bacteria, or a dipstick positive for bile are each indicative of a positive tap.

The intrinsic advantage of using DPL in children is its ability to be done rapidly in the trauma suite without transfer to another location. The disadvantages relate to its invasiveness, with a potential for intestinal, uterine, and bladder perforation. Diagnostic peritoneal lavage is relatively contraindicated with prior abdominal surgery, pregnancy, or obesity.

However, the problem with DPL in the pediatric patient is its lack of organ and injury specificity, and its inability to locate or quantitate intraperitoneal hemorrhage (unless, of course, the bleed is massive). If ideal management in BAT of childhood is to keep the child out of surgery when appropriate, how then does the surgeon determine probabilities of visceral injury, or propensity to continue hemorrhage with the limited information of a DPL with positive findings? In the series of DuPriest et al,[4] 85% of patients with abnormal DPL findings had surgery. Engrav et al[5] operated on approximately 90% of their patients with abnormal DPL findings. The comparable rate in CECT-assessed patients seems to be in the range of 10% to 15%.[6,7] In the series of DuPriest et al[4] there was a high rate of unnecessary surgery, not found with CT-assessed patients.

Finally the inability of DPL to assess the retroperitoneum further reduces its usefulness, whereas DUS or CECT may be very useful in defining retroperitoneal injuries and hemorrhage.[8] Unless there is gross extravasation of urine into the abdominal cavity from a ruptured bladder (a very rare injury in childhood), the DPL is insensitive to renal, ureteral, or bladder injury.

INTRAVENOUS CONTRAST-ENHANCED COMPUTED TOMOGRAPHY

Intravenous contrast-enhanced CT (CECT) scanning of the abdomen offers many advantages in the evaluation of BAT of childhood. CECT may be emerging as the "gold standard" for evaluating BAT in childhood because of its high sensitivity and specificity in identifying organs of injury, as well as its ability to locate and quantitate intra- and retroperitoneal hemorrhage. Relative disadvantages are the partial invasiveness (contrast infusion reactions), and the need to transport the patient out of the trauma area of the emergency department to the scanning suite.

In a study by Mohamed et al,[6] there were no false-positive and no false-negative results in 60 children evaluated by CECT for BAT. In an unpublished study (AJ Haftel et al) from Children's Hospital of Los Angeles (CHLA), there were two false-negatives (one perforated jejunum and one traumatized pancreas) and one false-positive (pancreas) in 90 children similarly studied. In addition, the surgery rate for patients with abnormal results is much higher in DPL-evaluated cases, in contrast with those studied by CECT. The inference is that the lack of specific organ information derived from DPL studies (when used alone) seems to push the surgeon in the direction of surgery. In the studies of Mohamed et al,[6] Karp et al,[7] and the CHLA the operative rate for patients with abnormal CECT findings was consistently in the 10% to 15% range.

However, CECT seems to miss gastrointestinal perforation and intraluminal hematoma and to be unable to identify pancreatic transection and ductal disruption. Even when gastrointestinal contrast enhancement is used, it does not pick up all gastrointestinal perforations and intraluminal hematomas. Therefore, it is recommended that a follow-up gastrointestinal series with water-soluble contrast media be done if these diagnoses are under consideration. The pancreas is consistently cited as a relatively blind area to CECT evaluation, and serious acute pancreatic injuries with major ductal disruptions are frequently missed.[8,9,10] Definitive confirmation of these injuries requires endoscopic retrograde cholangiopancreatography (ERCP) or selective coeliac axis arteriography.[8]

Renal integrity, vascularity, and function can all be ascertained with CECT.[11] This makes CECT superior to DUS, DPL, and IVP in evaluating renal injury associated with BAT. Besides defining renal anatomy and the continuity of renal vascularity, by concentrating IV contrast medium in the renal collecting system, CECT affords the opportunity to show any marked extravasation from the renal pyramids or calyces, the continuity of the ureters, and a cystogram of the urinary bladder. CECT may be more reliable in picking up these lesions than IVP.[11] Disruption and extra- or intraperitoneal extravasation of bladder contents are shown. The quality of the cystogram obtained in CECT is comparable with that acquired with Foley-instilled contrast medium, making the latter usually unnecessary. CECT affords no help whatsoever in the evaluation of the injured urethra, and any clinical suspicion of urethral disruption necessitates a retrograde urethrogram. None of the modalities discussed, ie, DUS, DPL, CECT, IVP, afford an adequate evaluation of the injured urethra.

Another advantage of CECT in BAT is its ability to define bony anatomy, especially of the pelvis. Pelvic fractures are frequently missed in the initial physical examination of seriously injured children, and even if pelvic scout films are obtained in the trauma suite, as recommended,[12] some occult fractures are missed. CECT with pelvic cuts is extremely sensitive to smaller fractures of the bony pelvis. One series[13] nicely showed this use of abdominal CT scanning with "cuts of the pelvis." Besides fracture anatomy, the presence and size of associated pelvic hematomas can be ascertained, and this is crucial in explaining occult hypotension, or a falling hematocrit, in the child with pelvic fracture.

The issue of gastrointestinal CECT in the emergency evaluation of BAT is controversial, with objections to the lengthy delay in getting good enhancement (occasionally more than 1 hour) and the additional risk of pulmonary aspiration of gastrointestinal contrast medium.

DIAGNOSTIC ULTRASOUND

Diagnostic ultrasound enjoys some popularity in the evaluation of BAT.[14] One practical problem is the availability of ultrasonography technicians and radiologists capable of reading sonograms at all hours of the night and day. No regionalized trauma system insists on in-house ultrasound technician availability 24 hours a day.

Diagnostic ultrasound has good sensitivity and specificity with relation to solid visceral injury (both intra- and retroperitoneal), and location and quantitation of intra- and retroperitoneal hemorrhage. Injuries missed with DUS are hollow viscus perforation (unless intestinal spillage of air or fluid is massive) and renal vascular injury.[14] In the injured pancreas, DUS detects organ swelling and peripancreatic fluid, but cannot pick up early transection with ductal disruption, an injury that must be emergently corrected by surgery. This limitation is common with DPL, CECT, and IVPs as well.

INTRAVENOUS PYELOGRAPHY

Intravenous pyelography is important in the rapid evaluation of the persistently unstable patient who is an obvious surgical candidate. This study determines the presence and location of the kidneys, their respective function, and any gross anatomic abnormality. This is very helpful for the surgeon. Obviously all attempts would be made to save a traumatized, solitary kidney.

In the evaluation of the stable patient with BAT, the IVP offers limited information. Though it affords a reasonable look at the kidneys, ureters, and bladder, it offers nothing to the evaluation of other intra-abdominal organs. Significant renal disruptions with extravasation of urine have been missed with IVP. Similarly nonvisualization of a kidney on IVP demands some other study to ascertain if the kidney is there and, if not missing, its vascular integrity.

The IVP should probably be considered in the stable child with a strong mechanism of injury (eg, fall from a height, struck by auto, major decelerating injury), a marked finding on physical examination of an intra-abdominal pathologic condition, or with gross hematuria. There is even controversy about its utility in minor BAT with only microscopic hematuria (see Chapter 41).[15]

CONCLUSION

Various diagnostic modalities are available to the physician evaluating BAT in childhood. The appropriate modality is dependent on the child's inherent stability. Children needing immediate laparotomy for life-threatening hemorrhage should be stabilized and taken immediately to surgery. This situation is very uncommon in pediatric traumatology. Children needing immediate surgery for devastating head or thoracic conditions, who do not have obvious intra-abdominal abnormalities, or have obtundation or coma making abdominal evaluation impossible should have DPL done rapidly, and if findings are abnormal and indicative of laparotomy, then one-shot IVP should be done either in the trauma suite or immediately upon arrival to the operating suite.

The usual victim of BAT, though, will become stable enough for CECT, which affords the highest sensitivity and specificity for organ of injury identification, and quantitation of intra- or extraperitoneal hemorrhage. The areas of relative insensitivity of the CECT in BAT are intestinal perforation, intraluminal hematoma, and pancreatic disruption. A follow-up ureterogastrointestinal series may be required to evaluate the first two; ERCP or arteriography may be required for the latter. Diagnostic peritoneal lavage, DUS, and IVP are inferior to CECT in the overall evaluation of BAT in the stable child.

REFERENCES

1. Bivins BA, Sachatello CR: Diagnostic peritoneal lavage in blunt abdominal trauma. *Am Surg* 1978;44:637–641.

2. Fischer RP, Beverlin BC: Diagnostic peritoneal lavage: Fourteen years and 2586 patients later. *Am J Surg* 1978;136:701–704.

3. Soderstrom CA, DuPriest RW, Cowley RA: Pitfalls of diagnostic peritoneal lavage in blunt abdominal trauma. *Surg Gynecol Obstet* 1980;151:513–518.

4. DuPriest RW, Rodriguez A, Shatney CH: Peritoneal lavage in children and adolescents with blunt abdominal trauma. *Am Surg* 1982;48:460–462.

5. Engrav LH, Benjamin CI, Strate RG, et al: Diagnostic peritoneal lavage in blunt abdominal trauma. *J Trauma* 1975;15:854–859.

6. Mohamed G, Reyes HM, Fantus R, et al: Computed tomography in the assessment of pediatric abdominal trauma. *Arch Surg* 1986;121:703–707.

7. Karp MP, Cooney DR, Berger PE, et al: The role of computed tomography in the evaluation of blunt abdominal trauma in children. *J Pediatr Surg* 1981;16:316–323.

8. Peitzman AB, Makaroun MS, Slasky S, et al: Prospective study of computed tomography in initial management of blunt abdominal trauma. *J Trauma* 1986;26:593–601.

9. Baker LP, Wagner EJ: Transection of the pancreas. *J Comp Assist Tomogr* 1982; 6:411–412.

10. Jeffrey RB, Federle MP, Crass RA: Computed tomography of pancreatic trauma. *Radiology* 1983;147:491–494.

11. McAninch JW, Federle MP: Evaluation of renal injuries with computed tomography. *J Urol* 1982;128:456–460.

12. Eichelberger MR, Rudolph JG: Pediatric trauma algorithm. *J Trauma* 1983;23:91–97.

13. Dunn EL: Computed tomography of the pelvis in trauma. *J Urol* 1982;128:456–460.

14. Grumbach K, Mechlin MB, Mintz MB: Computed tomography and ultrasound of the traumatized and acutely ill patient. *Emerg Clin North Am* 1985;3:607–624.

15. Kisa E, Schenk WG: Indications for emergency IVP in blunt abdominal trauma. *J Trauma* 1986;26:1086–1089.

38. Blunt Abdominal Trauma: Diagnostic Triage and Management

Ronald P. Ruffing, MD
John A. Marx, MD

In the United States, accidental injuries are responsible for 9,000 childhood deaths each year[1] and for nearly half of all deaths in children aged 1 to 14 years. Automobiles are the most frequent agents involved. Motor vehicle occupants and auto-pedestrian accidents comprise 70% to 80% of all accident fatalities. Most accident victims sustain multiple trauma. Isolated blunt or penetrating injury is less common. Although the central nervous system (CNS) and extremities are injured more frequently than the abdomen,[2] intra-abdominal injuries must be considered in all multiply injured patients.

When subjected to similar impact, younger children sustain more serious injury than older children and adults.[3] Anatomic, physiologic, and developmental differences increase the risk of blunt abdominal trauma in children. The absence of significant adipose tissue and abdominal musculature makes the intra-abdominal contents more vulnerable. Additionally, the elastic thoracic cage and decreased trunk diameter of the child increase the transmission of impacting forces, compressing the abdominal contents against the rigid thoracic and lumbar spine.

PHYSICAL EXAMINATION

Children often have an unreliable abdominal examination. Age, poor cooperation, concomitant CNS injury, fear, and intoxication complicate the diagnostic process. Thrust into the chaotic environment of a busy emergency department, restrained, instrumented, and "abandoned," a child is unlikely to cooperate with the medical team. Under these circumstances, assessment of the abdomen is particularly difficult.

Richardson et al[4] retrospectively reviewed the initial physical examination of 80 children, 40 of whom underwent exploratory laparotomy for blunt

298

abdominal trauma and 40 of whom did not. Initial examination showed little difference between children who required surgery and those who did not with regard to abdominal tenderness, the presence of bowel sounds, or evidence of external trauma. They concluded that differences in the initial physical examination between children with severe abdominal injuries and those with relatively minor ones were subtle. Fifteen percent of the patients who underwent exploratory laparotomy on the basis of abnormal physical examination findings alone had no marked pathologic condition.

Bivins et al[5] reported a prospective study of 21 children with blunt abdominal trauma. Of eight patients with abnormal findings on initial physical examination, only four had significant intra-abdominal injury. In the 13 children with normal examination findings, two ultimately required celiotomy. In this study the overall accuracy of the physical examination was 71%.

Delayed or undetected abdominal injury is repeatedly identified as a major cause of preventable death in trauma victims.[6] Unnecessary laparotomy exposes the child to the risk of surgery, general anesthesia, and prolonged hospitalization. Peritoneal lavage and diagnostic radiographic imaging offer the clinician more accurate methods to manage children with blunt abdominal injury.

DIAGNOSTIC PERITONEAL LAVAGE

Diagnostic peritoneal lavage (DPL) was described by Root and co-workers in 1965.[7] Aspiration of free intraperitoneal blood is attempted and if unproductive, isotonic saline is infused into the peritoneal cavity. The fluid is returned by gravity, inspected, and sent for quantitative studies. In children, the sensitivity of peritoneal lavage ranges from 88% to 100%, and the specificity is greater than 99%.[5,8–10]

In the assessment of children with blunt abdominal trauma, lavage should be considered when the mechanism of injury is serious, when the physical examination is unreliable, when there is unexplained hypotension, or if prolonged general anesthesia is anticipated for repair of extra-abdominal injuries. Diagnostic peritoneal lavage can be performed rapidly in the emergency department. The procedure is relatively simple, safe, and inexpensive. Because of its high sensitivity for intra-abdominal hemorrhage, lavage can effectively eliminate the abdomen as the source of acute hypotension in patients with multiple blunt trauma.

In adults, DPL has a complication rate of 0.85% to 1.7%. Self-limited injuries to the liver and spleen may produce a positive DPL because of the ability of lavage to detect even small quantities of hemoperitoneum. This has been implicated in unnecessary laparotomies in 6% of lavages with abnormal findings.[11] Additionally, while DPL is accurate in predicting the need for operative intervention, it is not organ specific. Finally, certain visceral injuries are less readily diagnosed by lavage. Isolated hollow visceral and diaphragmatic injuries tend to produce minimal hemorrhage. Hollow viscus perforation causes an intraperitoneal leukocytosis, but this is typically delayed 3 hours or more. Because DPL does not sample the retroperitoneal space, abnormality of these structures is not detected.

COMPUTED TOMOGRAPHY

Computed tomography (CT) generates detailed images of intraperitoneal and retroperitoneal anatomy. Solid organ injuries appear as a lack of homogeneity or as a disruption in the cortex. Hematoma appears as a nonenhanced collection of fluid that displaces normal anatomic relationships. Hollow organ perforation may be identified by intra-abdominal free air or extravasation of contrast. Failure to enhance organs after the intravenous (IV) injection of contrast suggests vascular injury.

Computed tomography is organ specific. It provides three-dimensional images of intraperitoneal and retroperitoneal structures. Disadvantages of CT include the need for IV and oral contrast, radiation exposure, sedation for patient cooperation, skilled radiologic personnel, scanner availability on a round-the-clock basis, and the staff to continuously monitor critically injured patients away from the emergency department. The accuracy of a CT scan to identify abnormalities resulting from blunt abdominal trauma varies with the technical capabilities of the scanner and the experience of the radiologist.

OTHER IMAGING TECHNIQUES

Plain abdominal roentgenograms are rarely helpful in the evaluation of patients with blunt abdominal trauma. Ileus and gastric distension are common nonspecific findings. Perforations rarely acutely produce free air. Diaphragmatic injury may be associated with normal x-ray findings or various radiographic abnormalities. Contrast studies aid in the diagnosis of urinary tract injury and duodenal hematoma. The intravenous pyelogram (IVP) assesses the functional and anatomic integrity of the kidneys. Duodenal obstruction secondary to a hematoma is best identified by an upper gastrointestinal series.

Technetium scanning is an alternative means to evaluate the liver and spleen. Injury appears as a filling defect. Liver-spleen scanning is noninvasive and requires little patient cooperation. It can often be accomplished without sedation. The use of IV radioactive contrast material and the relative lack of anatomic detail are its major limitations. Only the liver, spleen, and kidneys are evaluated. Liver-spleen scans are most useful in assessing stable patients with focal abdominal injuries.

Ultrasonography is a noninvasive, relatively inexpensive, portable tool that images the abdomen without associated radiation exposure. It assesses solid visceral organs and can identify free peritoneal fluid. It has the distinct advantage of rarely requiring sedation. The major drawback of ultrasound is its inability to show anatomic detail. It is most useful in the follow-up of solid visceral injury managed nonoperatively.

Diagnostic imaging modalities have an ever-increasing role in the assessment of patients with blunt abdominal trauma. They add quantification and specific anatomic localization. This added information must be weighed against the delay required to perform the diagnostic test. Unstable or potentially unstable patients may benefit more from definitive care than from further diagnostic studies.

AN APPROACH TO BLUNT ABDOMINAL TRAUMA IN CHILDREN

Children present to the emergency department with a wide spectrum of blunt injury. Even minor mechanisms of injury may incur significant pathology.[12] Multiple organ system involvement occurs in up to two thirds of patients. In those requiring surgery for intra-abdominal injuries, 60% will have one and 50% will have two additional organ systems involved.[10]

Initial resuscitation of children with blunt abdominal trauma requires airway management, vertebral column immobilization and assessment, and volume replacement. Appropriately sized equipment must be readily available. Medications and fluids should be given per kilogram of body weight. Hypothermia should be prevented. Careful monitoring of the fluid delivered will help prevent volume overload (Figure 38-1).

As with adults, peritoneal lavage is the primary triage tool. Twenty years of experience has established DPL as a rapid, safe, and accurate method of detecting intraperitoneal hemorrhage. After catheter insertion, the peritoneal cavity is aspirated. In adults, if more than 10 mL of nonclotting blood is obtained, the lavage is positive. It is unknown whether this figure should be extrapolated for children. If aspiration is negative, 15 to 20 mL/kg of warmed normal saline is infused and then collected by gravity. Lavage fluid is sent for laboratory studies. Guide wire techniques for peritoneal lavage are currently being investigated. Criteria for a positive lavage are listed in Table 38-1.

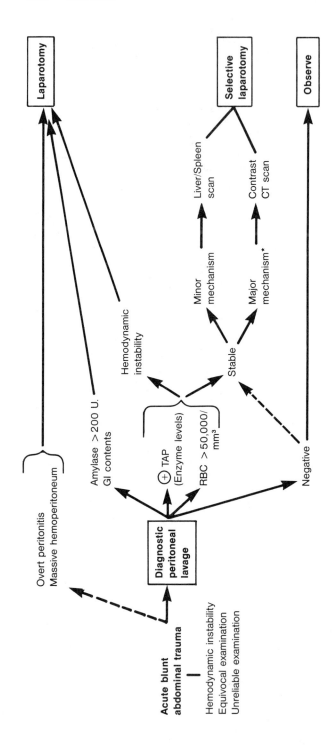

Figure 38-1 Selective management algorithm for suspected abdominal trauma in children. *Source:* S Rothenberg et al, "Selective Management of Blunt Abdominal Trauma in the Child: The Role of Peritoneal Lavage," presented at the 17th Annual Meeting of Western Trauma Association, Jackson Hole, Wyoming, February 23–27, 1987.

Table 38-1 Criteria for a Positive Diagnostic Peritoneal Lavage

Gross blood (aspirate) $\geq$ 10 mL *
RBC/mm³ > 100,000; 20,000–100,000 equivocal
WBC/mm³ > 500
Amylase > 175 µg/dL
Bile staining positive **
Gram's stain positive **

* Derived from adult studies. It is unknown if this figure requires specific adjustment for age or weight
** Rarely useful

In multiply blunt-injured children, numerous intraperitoneal and extra-peritoneal sources of hypotension exist. Therefore in unstable patients, unless an obvious indication for urgent laparotomy exists, DPL is performed. A negative lavage effectively eliminates the intraperitoneal cavity as the source of volume loss. A positive lavage in an unstable patient mandates laparotomy.

In hemodynamically stable patients with suspected blunt abdominal trauma, indications to perform DPL include unreliable examination because of coincidental CNS injury or intoxication, a history of unexplained hypotension, multiple organ system injuries, equivocal physical findings, or a major mechanism of injury. In patients with a positive or indeterminate lavage, who remain stable, CT scanning may identify specific solid visceral injuries that can be managed nonoperatively and thereby reduce the incidence of unnecessary surgery. This is particularly true when DPL is positive by red cell criteria. In cases of elevated levels of white blood cells or enzymes contained from lavage sample, operative management is more appropriate because of the likelihood of bowel or pancreatic injury. Computed tomography is permissible only if it can be performed in a safe, expeditious fashion under close supervision. In stable patients with isolated abdominal injuries, who lack a history of hypotension or a major mechanism of injury, or have a delayed (> 12 hours) presentation, CT scanning or liver-spleen scintigraphy may be used exclusive of DPL.

Computed tomography offers distinct advantages. However, prospective studies under level I trauma conditions comparing DPL and CT have failed to demonstrate the superiority of CT scanning in predicting the need for surgery in patients with blunt abdominal trauma.[13–16] Peritoneal lavage remains the most rapid and accurate means of determining the need for urgent celiotomy. It is exceptionally reliable in excluding intraperitoneal hemorrhage in the multiply injured child. Lavage can be rapidly performed in the resuscitation area with readily available equipment. Computed tomography complements peritoneal lavage by identifying self-limiting injuries to the liver and spleen, and by evaluating the retroperitoneal space, an anatomic location not investigated by peritoneal lavage.

The effective use of these diagnostic modalities depends largely on the personnel and the technical resources of the institution providing care for critically injured children.

REFERENCES

1. National Center For Health Statistics: *Vital Statistics of the United States,* DHHS publication No. (PHS) 83-1101. 1982, vol 2, Part A.

2. Eichelberger MR, Randolph JG: Progress in pediatric trauma. *World J Surg* 1985;9:222–235.

3. Karwacki JJ: Children in motor vehicles: Never too young to die. *JAMA* 1979;242:2848–2851.

4. Richardson JD, Berlin RP, Griffin WO: Blunt abdominal trauma in children. *Ann Surg* 1972;176:213–216.

5. Bivins BA, Jona JZ, Berlin RP: Diagnostic peritoneal lavage in pediatric trauma. *J Trauma* 1976;16:739–742.

6. Mckoy C, Bell MJ: Preventable traumatic deaths in children. *J Pediatr Surg* 1983;18:505–508.

7. Root HD, Hauser CW, McKinley CR, et al: Diagnostic peritoneal lavage. *Surgery* 1965;57:633–637.

8. Powell RW, Smith DE, Zarins CK, et al: Peritoneal lavage in children with blunt abdominal trauma. *J Pediatr Surg* 1976;11:973–977.

9. DuPriest BW, Rodriquez A, Shatney CH: Peritoneal lavage in children and adolescents with blunt abdominal trauma. *Am Surg* 1984;48:460–462.

10. Drew R, Perry JF, Fischer RP: The expediency of peritoneal lavage for blunt abdominal trauma in children. *Surg Gynecol Obstet* 1976;145:885–888.

11. Fischer RP, et al: Diagnostic peritoneal lavage: Fourteen years and 2586 patients later. *Am J Surg* 1978;136:701–704.

12. Haller JA Jr: Newer concepts in emergency care of children with major injuries. *Pediatrics* 1973;52:485–488.

13. Davis RA, Shayne JP, Max HM, et al: CT scan versus peritoneal lavage in blunt abdominal trauma: A prospective study. *Surgery* 1985;98:845–850.

14. Marx JA, Moore EE, Jorden RC, et al: Limitations of computed tomography in the evaluation of acute abdominal trauma: A prospective comparison with diagnostic peritoneal lavage. *J Trauma* 1985;25:933–937.

15. Fabian TC, Mangiante EC, White TJ, et al: A prospective study of 91 patients undergoing computed tomography and peritoneal lavage following blunt abdominal trauma. *J Trauma* 1986;26:602–607.

16. Peitzman AB, Makaroun MS, Slasky S, et al: Prospective study of computed tomography in initial management of blunt abdominal trauma. *J Trauma* 1986;26:585–590.

39. The Role of Peritoneal Lavage in the Pediatric Patient after Blunt Abdominal Trauma

Stephen K. Greenholz, MD
John R. Lilly, MD

Trauma is the leading cause of death in children in the United States. One third of the mortality is caused by blunt abdominal trauma.[1] The initial physical examination will be at variance with the ultimate intra-abdominal findings in 16% to 40% of cases.[1,2] Delay in identifying intra-abdominal injury has a profound impact on morbidity and mortality of blunt trauma; 12% of deaths are reportedly caused by unrecognized injuries.[1,3,4] Diagnostic maneuvers are designed to maximize early and accurate recognition of injury. However, the indications for selecting a diagnostic maneuver in the evaluation of the pediatric patient with blunt abdominal trauma are controversial. The relative roles of computed tomography (CT) and peritoneal lavage are undecided. Blind, steadfast reliance on one method should be avoided; the advantages and pitfalls of each technique in relation to specific potential injuries should be recognized and incorporated into the diagnostic and management plan.

PERITONEAL LAVAGE

Peritoneal lavage is accepted as the diagnostic procedure of choice after blunt abdominal trauma in adults. In a recent review[5] of 1,588 patients, lavage had an accuracy of 98.6% with a false-negative rate of 1.3%. The results of lavage have a similar accuracy in children, ie, 95.5%, 97.8%, and 98.6% were reported in three series[1,3,6] with only one false-negative noted. Accuracy is enhanced in the pediatric patient because of the underdeveloped omentum and shallow peritoneal recesses.

However, these high levels of accuracy may be deceptive. The extreme sensitivity of peritoneal lavage is for hemorrhagic injuries, most commonly the spleen and liver. The natural history of splenic and liver injuries in children

305

differs from that in adults.[7] Many such injuries stop bleeding spontaneously and can be successfully managed nonoperatively. For example, in separate reports,[8,9] 37 of 42 patients and 21 of 29 patients with splenic injuries were successfully managed nonoperatively. Selected hepatic injuries have also been managed nonoperatively.[10] Thus, identification of blood in the abdomen does not in itself indicate the need for surgery in children. Peritoneal lavage is also problematic in evaluating retroperitoneal injuries, being diagnostic in only 25% of patients.[11] For hollow viscus injuries without hemorrhage, several hours may be required to develop sufficient peritoneal findings to be noted on peritoneal lavage.[5] Furthermore, peritoneal lavage is an operative procedure with associated morbidity and a subsequent effect on the abdominal examination, rendering the examination unreliable.

In balance, however, when used appropriately, peritoneal lavage is a highly accurate, rapid, inexpensive, and, if adequate time has elapsed, sensitive test. Morbidity approximates only 1% and consists mainly of local wound complications.[12] The infraumbilical, totally open technique with free placement of the catheter improves the safety of the procedure.

COMPUTED TOMOGRAPHY

Computed tomography is championed as the alternative to peritoneal lavage.[13–15] When used with intravenous contrast (for vascular solid organs) or oral contrast (for stomach and intestine) it provides multiorgan information. It has been used successfully in the assessment and management of both adult and pediatric patients, frequently supporting nonoperative therapy (Figure 39-1).[13,14] In 46 pediatric patients, CT was reported to be 100% accurate for renal and liver injuries and 92% accurate for splenic injuries.[13]

However, there are drawbacks. The study often requires 47 to 70 minutes to perform, more than twice as long as peritoneal lavage (20 minutes).[16] Computed tomography costs eight times as much as lavage. Intensive monitoring is required during the study, frequently in a dark, ill-equipped environment.

Although helpful, CT has never been promoted as diagnostically sensitive for hollow viscus injuries, including the retroperitoneal duodenum.[13] Since minimal motion can produce an unreliable scan, sedation is often required in children, a factor that may distort subsequent clinical examination. Finally, not all institutions have comparable results. Marx and colleagues[17] reported an accuracy rate of 40% for CT in the evaluation of blunt trauma in all age groups with a false-negative rate of 60%, highlighting the dependence of the procedure on the quality of the machine.

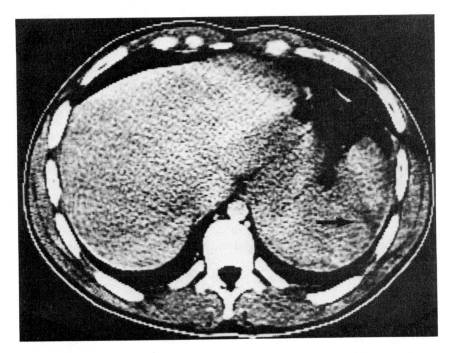

Figure 39-1 Abdominal CT showing splenic laceration (arrow) successfully managed non-operatively.

THE HOLLOW VISCUS INJURY

The hollow viscus injury deserves special consideration because of the diagnostic dilemma imposed by the initial occult manifestations and the high morbidity associated with delays in identification and repair.[18–20] The intestine is the third most commonly injured intra-abdominal organ, being injured in 6% to 16% of blunt trauma requiring operation. The initial examination in blunt trauma is unreliable, and plain radiographs are notoriously inaccurate, showing free air in only 20% to 30% of patients.[19,21]

Only sequential examinations and peritoneal lavage (with 70% to 95% accuracy) are diagnostically sensitive for intraperitoneal intestinal injury.[11,18–25] In the patient with an unreliable examination because of altered neurologic status, associated injuries, or a need for general anesthesia, peritoneal lavage is mandatory. The addition of CT (and occasionally barium intestinal studies) will further increase sensitivity, particularly for the retroperitoneal portion of the duodenum in the stable patient.

MANAGEMENT PROTOCOL

We recommend a management protocol (Figure 39-2) using a combination of diagnostic techniques reflecting the spectrum of injury and clinical status. The goal is to provide early identification of injury, aggressively exclude hollow viscus injury, and avoid unnecessary laparotomy, particularly for solid viscus lesions. Observation protocols reflecting the patient's clinical condition and previous workup are essential (Figure 39-3).

Children with a previous lavage or CT showing no abnormalities may often be observed unless clinical deterioration occurs. If there is a worsening abdominal examination, hemodynamic instability, or progressive transfusion requirement, a delayed or repeat peritoneal lavage should be performed (to confirm hollow viscus injury or progressive abdominal hemorrhage). If the patient has had a solid organ injury previously identified by CT, then deterioration would prompt immediate laparotomy.

In brief, a management protocol divides patients with three categories:

- *Unstable patient:* Peritoneal lavage is employed first because of its speed and sensitivity for intra-abdominal sources of shock. If positive criteria (RBC > 50,000/mm^3, WBC > 500/mm^3, or bacteria on Gram's stain) immediate laparotomy is performed.
- *Stable patient with reliable examination:* CT is used to identify solid and some hollow viscus injuries. The patient is followed by clinical course and serial abdominal examination.
- *Stable patient with unreliable examination:* Peritoneal lavage and CT scan are used. If the lavage is positive by RBC criterion only (> 50,000/mm^3), CT is done to attempt to localize the source of bleeding. If CT is negative for solid organ damage, laparotomy is required with suspicion of a mesenteric or bowel hemorrhagic injury in patients with a positive lavage. If CT is positive for a solid organ injury only, the patient is observed. A lavage positive for WBC (> 500/mm^3) or bacteria requires immediate laparotomy for hollow viscus injury.

A management protocol must also assure the availability of continuous intensive care monitoring (including in the radiology suite), high-quality CT equipment (scan time 1 to 5 seconds), experienced radiologists, and pediatric surgeons skilled in the use of peritoneal lavage. Ready availability of surgical and anesthesia expertise is essential; otherwise earlier laparotomy may be indicated.

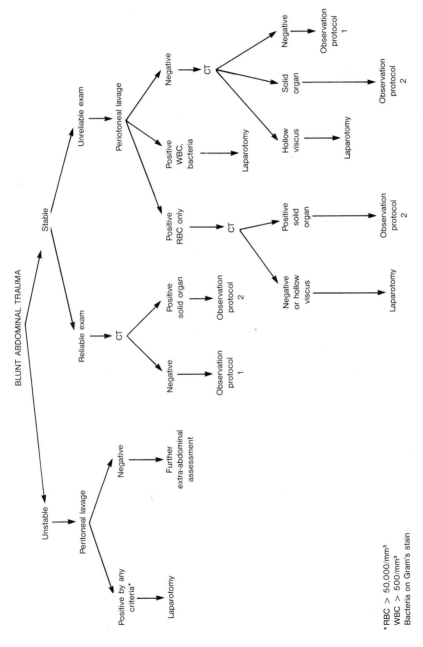

Figure 39-2 Diagnostic and management protocol for pediatric blunt abdominal trauma.

*RBC > 50,000/mm³
WBC > 500/mm³
Bacteria on Gram's stain

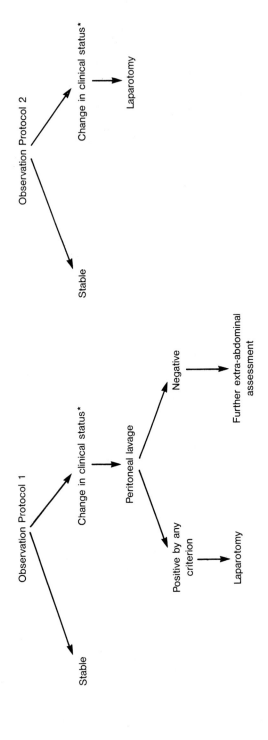

Figure 39-3 Observation protocols after initial diagnostic management of pediatric blunt abdominal trauma.

REFERENCES

1. DuPriest RW Jr, Rodriquez A, Shatney CH: Peritoneal lavage in children and adolescents with blunt abdominal trauma. *Am Surg* 1982;48:460–462.

2. Alyono D, Perry JF: Value of quantitative cell count and amylase activity of peritoneal lavage fluid. *J Trauma* 1981;21:345–348.

3. Drew R, Perry JF Jr, Fisher RP: The expediency of peritoneal lavage for blunt trauma in children. *Surg Gynecol Obstet* 1977;145:885–888.

4. Perry JF: A five-year survey of 152 acute abdominal injuries. *J Trauma* 1965;5:53–57.

5. Engrau LM, Benjamin CI, Strate RG, et al: Diagnostic peritoneal lavage in blunt abdominal trauma. *J Trauma* 1975;15:854–859.

6. Bivins BA, Jona JZ, Belin RP: Diagnostic peritoneal lavage in pediatric trauma. *J Trauma* 1976;16:739–742.

7. Ramenofsky ML: Abdominal trauma in children. *Curr Concepts Trauma Care,* Summer 1985, pp 4–9.

8. Eichelberger MR, Randolph JG: Progress in pediatric trauma. *World J Surg* 1985; 9:222–235.

9. Kakkasseril JS, Stewart D, Cox JA, et al: Changing treatment of pediatric splenic trauma. *Arch Surg* 1982;117:758–759.

10. Karp MD, Cooney DR, Pros GA, et al: The nonoperative management of pediatric hepatic trauma. *J Pediatr Surg* 1983;18:512–518.

11. Shuck JM, Lowe RJ: Intestinal disruption due to blunt abdominal trauma. *Am J Surg* 1978;136:668–673.

12. Powell RW, Smith DE, Zarns CK, et al: Peritoneal lavage in children with blunt abdominal trauma. *J Pediatr Surg* 1976;11:973–977.

13. Karp MP, Cooney DR, Berger PE, et al: The role of computed tomography in the evaluation of blunt abdominal trauma in children. *J Pediatr Surg* 1981;16:316–323.

14. Wing VW, Federle MP, Morris JA, et al: The clinical impact of CT for blunt abdominal trauma. *AJR* 1985;145:1191–1194.

15. Goldstein AS, Selafani SJ, Kupferstein NH: The diagnostic superiority of computerized tomography. *J Trauma* 1985;25:938–946.

16. Davis RA, Shayne JP, Max MH, et al: The use of computerized axial tomography versus peritoneal lavage in the evaluation of blunt abdominal trauma: A prospective study. *Surgery* 1985;98:845–849.

17. Marx JA, Moore EE, Jorden RC, et al: Limitations of computed tomography in the evaluation of acute abdominal trauma: A prospective comparison with diagnostic peritoneal lavage. *J Trauma* 1985;25:933–937.

18. Schenk WG III, Lonchyna V, Moylan JA: Perforation of the jejunum from blunt abdominal trauma. *J Trauma* 1983;23:54–56.

19. Maull KI, Reath DB: Impact of early recognition on outcome in nonpenetrating wounds of the small bowel. *South Med J* 1984;77:1075–1077.

20. Dauterive AH, Flanebaum L, Cox EF: Blunt intestinal trauma: A modern-day review. *Ann Surg* 1985;201:198–203.

21. Donohue JH, Crass RA, Tunkey DD: The management of duodenal and other small intestinal trauma. *World J Surg* 1985;9:904–913.

22. Talbot WA, Shuck JM: Retroperitoneal duodenal injury due to blunt abdominal trauma. *Am J Surg* 1975;130:659–666.

23. Reilley A, Marks M, Nance F, et al: Small bowel trauma in children and adolescents. *Am Surg* 1985;51:132–135.

24. Burney RE, Mueller GL, Coon WW, et al: Diagnosis of isolated small bowel injury following blunt abdominal trauma. *Ann Emerg Med* 1983;12:71–74.

25. Phillips TF, Brotman S, Cleveland S, et al: Perforating injuries of the small bowel from blunt abdominal trauma. *Ann Emerg Med* 1983;12:75–79.

Section 22

Renal Trauma

Renal trauma requires aggressive management after diagnostic evaluation based on physical examination, urinalysis, and radiologic assessment. Some injuries that may have previously required surgical repair are now treated conservatively.

Gross hematuria or microscopic hematuria with significant physical findings including hypotension, flank pain, tenderness or mass, ecchymoses, or pelvic injuries should generally be evaluated using an intravenous pyelogram (IVP). The necessity of evaluating an isolated finding of microscopic hematuria is controversial.

40. Renal Trauma

N.E. Peterson, MD
Ronald R. Pfister, MD

When a child comes to the emergency department after blunt abdominal trauma resulting in hematuria, the physician should identify the site and extent of injury in preparation of selecting appropriate therapeutic measures. Despite reports of significant renal injury unaccompanied by hematuria, such occurrences are rare, but still must be borne in mind. There is however, no reliable correlation between the extent of injury and the amount of bleeding. Evaluation for possible renal injury in the child may be provoked by indications other than hematuria, including flank or abdominal bruising, a flank mass or tenderness, lower rib or spinal fracture, and the coexistence of other injuries frequently associated with renal trauma (spleen, liver, colon). Although the degree of hematuria does not necessarily correlate well with the degree of injury, the rapidity of resolution of gross bleeding does correlate with the presence of injuries that are most likely to recover spontaneously; conversely, gross hematuria persisting for longer than a few hours makes spontaneous recovery less likely. In addition, bleeding recurring after a quiescent interval often indicates significant renal injury; expeditious management may include arteriographic identification combined with therapeutic embolization.

Having suspected renal trauma either by physical findings or by the presence of hematuria, one must verify the injury and assess its extent. There is an array of options. Surgical exploration may be necessary for acute intra-abdominal hemorrhage but is not optimal if time and stabilization allow other diagnostic measures.

Computed tomography (CT) is widely heralded as the recommended first and best study owing to its superior definition of anatomic detail.[1,2] However, its sensitivity in identifying minor parenchymal fractures and minimal degrees of extravasation is seldom critical to accurate therapeutic decisions. In addition, the expense and time involved detract from its routine use. At least one report[3] has documented the potential for erroneous exaggeration of renal trauma by CT scanning. However, it can simultaneously scan other vulnerable organs, which may constitute a critical advantage in the multitrauma patient.

Isotopic renal scanning has a similar limitation. Specifically, obligatory time requirements render these studies inappropriate to the life-threatening emergency, and the patient who may comfortably tolerate the delay will usually have sustained renal damage amenable to self-repair. An important exception is the rapidly performed isotopic flow scan for inspection of patency and integrity of the renal pedicle; the convenience and promptness of this specific application render it preferable to arteriography in many situations.

Renal arteriography has been largely supplanted by CT as the preferred method for appraising traumatic renal damage, and its indications have narrowed. However, to assess the nature of persistent fresh hemorrhage, or of delayed or intermittent hematuria, to evaluate renal shattering, and (occasionally) to support the acceptability of nonoperative management, arteriography remains a valuable and trustworthy maneuver.

Excretory urography and tomography is our preferred method for initial appraisal of suspected renal injury or traumatic hematuria. Easy availability and economy make the intravenous pyelogram (IVP) ideal as both an emergency maneuver and a screening examination, and the information provided is adequate for accurate therapeutic decisions or to indicate the need for further study. Reliance upon urography derives from the consistent experience that the mere presence or absence of urographic function constitutes a dependable index of the magnitude of renal damage. Any urographic function, regardless of delay or diminution, indicates injury amenable to self-repair. Parenchymal laceration or urinary extravasation is of secondary importance to assignment of severity, and will commonly resolve in patients uncompromised by hemorrhagic complications. A potential exception is the patient with apparent polar or hemirenal nonfunction in whom bleeding persists or recurs. This event suggests a parenchymal avulsion, and therapeutic options include partial nephrectomy (at laparotomy for other injuries) or selective embolization for control of hemorrhage. Defunctionalized segments are otherwise innocuous, with only rare development of subsequent hypertension.[4]

Until otherwise defined, persistent urographic nonfunction reflects either parenchymal shattering or pedicle interruption (avulsion, thrombosis). Clinical distinction is provided by severe and persistent bleeding (retroperitoneum, hematuria) in the former, and little of either in the latter. Shattered kidneys require removal.

Concurrent life-threatening conditions may prevent formal evaluation of renal injuries; these are best assessed by a bolus injection of contrast medium (1 mL/lb) whenever preoperatively possible, focusing on the presence or absence of urographic function. In circumstances prohibiting this process, or when evidence of renal injury is manifested intraoperatively, options include intraoperative urography (exposure 10 to 20 minutes after injection), intraoperative angiography (immediate exposure after 5 to 7 mL of contrast medium is injected into the renal artery), and operative exposure. Other considerations are the size and stability of the retroperitoneal hematoma, the status of the hematuria, and the known association of left renal injury with splenic trauma (25%), and right renal and liver injury (40%).[5]

STRATIFICATION OF RENAL INJURY

Most reviews of renal trauma note approximately 70% minor injuries, characterized by stable or acceptable vital signs, hemorrhage that tends to subside early post-trauma, and evidence of urographic function. Such injuries are typically contusions or superficial lacerations, and spontaneous resolution may be reliably anticipated. Approximately 10% will be major injuries, characterized by unstable or unacceptable vital signs, hematuria that is severe and unremitting (except with pedicle interruption), and urographic nonfunction. Such injuries will require further evaluation, and usually some form of active intervention.

Remaining is approximately 20% of the total that is not readily categorized, and therefore of intermediate degree.[6] Our experience has identified 100% of this group to have sustained significant renal laceration, and 60% to show urinary (contrast medium) extravasation. Before successful trials of conservative management, such injuries were frequently subjected to exploration and nephrectomy without other definitive preoperative evaluation (arteriography) that may well have modified management.

A reproducible feature of parenchymal laceration is its occurrence between and along vascular planes, resulting in sustained vascularization and function of the resulting fragments despite even broad separation. The diastasis is occupied by hematoma, which is slowly resorbed allowing the reapproximation of the renal fragments. Final resolution may occasionally be accompanied by minor distortions of intrarenal architecture, which are innocuous to function and drainage, and without sequelae.

Despite a common classification of traumatic extravasation as an unequivocal mandate for operative intervention, experience has shown that even extensive extravasation will commonly subside promptly and completely without incident. (Analogies are provided by nephrostomy and percutaneous endourological procedures.) Repeat urography at 48 to 72 hours will characteristically show substantial improvement in the volume of extravasation identified initially, and this improvement forecasts total resolution. In contrast, failure to show such improvement indicates a need to consider operative correction.

The relatively great risk of notable blood loss by hemorrhage, coupled with the lack of retroperitoneal fat in children resulting in the requirement for a larger hematoma to achieve tamponade, encourage a closer supervision and observation during early convalescence compared with similarly injured adults. The vulnerability of congenital renal disorders to traumatic injury, particularly from modest trauma, bears consideration. Congenital hydronephrosis, horseshoe kidney, and renal tumors assume predominance in these correlations.

PEDICLE AND VASCULAR INJURIES

Documented main renal artery thrombosis and pedicle avulsion are paradoxically associated with only modest retroperitoneal hemorrhage, owing to arterial retraction, and usually with brief periods of gross hematuria giving way to microhematuria. Therapeutic reactions to such injuries require consideration of the ischemic interval involved, and an appreciation that renal tolerances of warm ischemia rarely exceed 4 hours. Delay of revascularization beyond this interval commonly produces severely compromised results or sequelae requiring additional attention: often nephrectomy. A multitude of circumstances commonly intervene to prevent expeditious revascularization, and operative efforts in this setting may injudiciously prolong the operative exercise without benefit. Indeed, successful revascularizations are rarely documented.

Exceptions may include partial pedicle injury (usually venous), or polar vascular damage. The former injury is commonly identified at initial exploration and is successfully managed by simple ligation. The latter injury may require no intervention, and may be identified by subsequent renal hypertension requiring medication or partial nephrectomy. Asymptomatic polar atrophy may be identified at routine follow-up urography.

Patients sustaining deep parenchymal laceration identified by IVP, CT scan, or isotopic renal scan associated with persistent and significant hematuria, or with a flank mass and unstable vital signs, may be assumed to have sustained atypical parenchymal laceration with segmental vascular damage. Such injuries may be repaired (including partial nephrectomy) during laparotomy for other reasons, or may be confirmed by arteriography and corrected by selective embolization. Similarly, patients who return with fresh hematuria, usually after a satisfactory response to conservative management, will often show traumatic arteriovenous communication.[7,8] Embolization is advisable before primary attempts at correction.

Conservative (nonoperative) management of intermediate injuries has resulted in no incidence of deleterious consequences in our experience. No patient has required delayed exploration. No episode of chronic pain, stone formation, cyst, abscess, or pyelonephritis has been observed, despite published apprehensions.

CONSERVATIVE MANAGEMENT

Nonoperative management may occasionally be selected for patients whose injuries are likely to resolve without invasive management, and arteriography, isotopic scanning, or CT is available for more definitive staging and therapeutic definition. These studies are not commonly necessary, however; conservative care may usually be confidently selected. Such management includes bed rest until the subsidence of gross hematuria, restricted outpatient activity for the duration of microscopic hematuria (usually 1.5 to 3.0 weeks), and dismissal from follow-up thereafter. Patients sustaining renal contusion or superficial laceration require no follow-up urography, as these studies will merely confirm restoration of normal anatomy and function. More severe injuries (laceration with diastasis) are commonly characterized by stabilization of the healing process at 6 weeks; urography before this interval will disclose incomplete resolution, and therefore impose a need for subsequent study. Urography before a 6-week interval will be required only if mandated by unanticipated clinical events.

Isotopic scanning (DMSA) is a satisfactory modality for following patients with functionless renal segments, as well as documenting reapproximation of separated segments.

Significant delayed hemorrhage may be managed by a trial of bed rest. Such events are often transitory and innocuous. Failure to respond to bed rest, however, or the development of intermittent delayed fresh hemorrhage, dictates the advisability of angiography and preparation for selective therapeutic embolization.

AGGRESSIVE MANAGEMENT

Operative intervention, exclusively for the renal injury or incorporated into laparotomy mandated by coexisting injury, is sometimes imperative. Implicit is the performance of a preoperative urologic appraisal whenever permitted by prevailing events, including possible therapeutic embolization for renal hemorrhage. Urgent laparotomy is commonly warranted, however, thereby interdicting thorough preoperative evaluation.

Although there are frequent references to the desirability or necessity of suturing, debridement, and drainage for renal injuries, our experience has identified neither any advantage to these maneuvers nor any risk of compromise by their omission. Apprehension regarding infection, obstruction, stone, abscess, cyst, and hypertension has not been realized, and it is concluded that the attribution of operative success to these efforts may often assign credit unfairly for resolutions that commonly transpire spontaneously.

CONCLUSION

Traumatic renal injury may be reliably appraised by the status of hematuria and the information provided by IVP; abnormality of either dictates the requirement for additional diagnostic inquiry or operative intervention. Injuries previously considered worthy of repair or extirpation will commonly resolve spontaneously, including laceration with diastasis, extravasation, and a functionless segment. Many injuries characterized by persistent or delayed hemorrhage will respond to nonoperative selective embolization. These observations are not intended to suggest that retroperitoneal exposure and repair should be rigidly avoided during laparotomy for other reasons, but that many injuries previously routinely explored are uniquely amenable to spontaneous resolution without risk or deficit.

REFERENCES

1. McAninch JW, Federle MP: Evaluation of renal injuries with computerized tomography. *J Urol* 1982;128:456–59.

2. Bretan PN, McAninch JW, Federle MP, and Jeffrey RB: Computerized tomographic staging of renal trauma: 85 consecutive cases. *J Urol* 1986;136:561–565.

3. Karp MP, Jewett TC, Kunh FP, et al: The impact of computed tomography scanning on the child with renal trauma. *J Pediatr Surg* 1986;21:617–23.

4. Peterson NE: Fate of functionless post-traumatic renal segment. *Urology* 1986;27:237–42.

5. Peterson NE: Injuries associated with renal trauma. *J Urol* 1973;109:766–68.

6. Peterson NE: Intermediate-degree blunt renal trauma. *J Trauma* 1977;17:425–35.

7. Peterson NE: The significance of delayed post-traumatic renal hemorrhage. *J Urol* 1978;119:563–65.

8. Cosgrove MD, Mendez R, Morrow JW: Traumatic renal arteriovenous fistula: Report of 12 cases. *J Urol* 1973;110:627–31.

41. Hematuria after Blunt Trauma

Stephen Heinz, MD

The kidneys are the second most commonly injured organ, after the brain, in the pediatric trauma patient. Anatomically, the pediatric patient is at greater risk of renal trauma because the perirenal fat and renal fascia are underdeveloped and therefore less protective. Furthermore, the secondary ossification centers of the eleventh and twelfth ribs do not completely close until the 25th year of life.[1]

TYPES OF INJURIES

Blunt trauma accounts for the vast majority of renal injuries. These injuries can be subdivided into minor and major categories. The former include contusions, shallow lacerations of the renal cortex, and disruption of the fornices. Major injuries include deep parenchymal lacerations, shattered kidney, and involvement of the pedicle, ureter, or renal pelvis.[2]

The management of minor renal injuries requires only a period of observation as there are no serious sequelae. Immediate consultation with a urologist is required for all major injuries.

Forty percent of patients with renal injuries have associated injuries.

THE DILEMMA

Hematuria with more than 5 red blood cells (RBCs) per high-power field (HPF) in the urine is considered to be the leading indicator of renal trauma. There is, however, no direct correlation between the amount of hematuria and the severity of the injury. Although gross hematuria in patients with renal contusions and other minor injuries is commonplace, several instances of major renal trauma without hematuria have been reported.

Does the presence of hematuria in patients with blunt trauma mandate renal evaluation by an intravenous pyelogram (IVP)? Historically, hematuria, flank tenderness, mass, ecchymosis, abrasion, or pain have routinely been evaluated using IVP. Furthermore, IVPs are noninvasive, and pre-existing genitourinary disease is identified in 10% to 20% of patients.

However, the yield of IVPs performed in all patients with hematuria of any degree is very low. The test involves radiation exposure, risk of allergic reactions, is expensive, and may cause a delay in the management of associated injuries.

THE ALTERNATIVES

Several recent studies focused on developing discriminating guidelines for evaluation with IVP. These studies explored the relationship between hematuria and other clinical criteria, such as shock and associated injuries, with the severity of the renal injury.

Guice et al[3] retrospectively studied 156 patients with microscopic or gross hematuria who had an IVP performed because of a high risk for genitourinary injuries. The majority had a cystogram before the IVP. Only 13 (8.3%) showed abnormal findings on IVP or cystogram. Five of these 13 patients required further diagnostic or therapeutic intervention; each had gross or 4+ (packed RBC per HPF) hematuria. If IVPs had been performed only on such patients, 75% of the patients in this study would have been spared an IVP, and no significant injury would have been missed.

Nicolaisen et al[4] prospectively followed 359 patients with renal trauma, 306 of whom sustained blunt trauma. Of those patients with blunt trauma and hematuria, 92% had renal contusions. Some patients with microscopic hematuria did sustain major renal injuries; however, all had a systolic blood pressure less than 90 mm Hg. No patient with microscopic hematuria after blunt trauma and a blood pressure greater than 90 mm Hg sustained a substantial renal injury.

Levitt et al[5] retrospectively looked at 105 patients with blunt renal trauma. Eighty-eight patients (84%) had normal IVP findings, and only three patients required urologic surgical intervention. These three patients had gross hematuria and at least one associated injury (retroperitoneal hematoma, fracture of ribs 10 to 12, pelvic fracture, or long bone fractures). Two of the three patients had flank tenderness or a flank mass; the third patient was obtunded. If IVPs had been performed only in patients with gross hematuria, an important

Table 41-1 Suggested Guidelines for the Use of an Intravenous Pyelogram after Blunt Trauma

Clinical Finding	Intravenous Pyelogram	Observe with Serial Urinalysis
Gross hematuria	Yes	No
4+ Hematuria ($\geq$ 50 RBC/HPF)	Yes	No
Microscopic hematuria (< 50 RBC/HPF) and important physical findings* or associated injury	Yes	No
Microscopic hematuria in absence of important physical findings or associated injury	No	Yes

*Significant physical findings include hypotension (BP < 90 mm Hg), flank pain or tenderness, flank mass, or ecchymosis. *Note:* Some clinicians feel that hematuria of any degree following blunt trauma requires an intravenous pyelogram.

physical finding, or associated injuries, no major injury would have been missed.

These three studies imply that major renal injury after blunt trauma is unusual, especially in patients who are normotensive and have no physical findings or associated injuries indicative of renal injury. The yield of IVPs performed in patients with suspected renal injury can be markedly improved using selective criteria in addition to the presence of hematuria (Table 41-1).

CONCLUSION

Data suggest that not all patients with hematuria after blunt trauma require an IVP. It is imperative to note, however, that the collective number of patients from the three studies summarized is quite small. Additional studies are needed to substantiate these findings, thus allowing the practitioner to adopt a conservative, selective approach to the performance of IVPs.

REFERENCES

1. Morse TS: Renal injuries. *Pediatr Clin North Am* 1975;22:379–391.

2. Guerriero WG: Trauma to the kidneys, ureters, bladder and urethra. *Surg Clin North Am* 1982;62:1047–1075.

3. Guice K, Oldham K, Eide B, et al: Hematuria after blunt trauma: When is pyelography useful? *J Trauma* 1983;23:305–311.

4. Nicolaisen GS, McAnich JW, Marshall GA, et al: Renal trauma: Re-evaluation of the indications for radiographic assessment. *J Urol* 1985;133:183–187.

5. Levitt MA, Criss E, Kobernick M: Should the emergency IVP be used more selectively in blunt renal trauma. *Ann Emerg Med* 1985;14:959–965.

Section 23

Dog or Cat Bites

Irrigation and debridement are the fundamental components of adequate treatment of dog or cat bites. Suturing is appropriate for injuries requiring cosmetic considerations, but may increase the risk of infection. This incidence can be reduced by meticulous wound care.

Conclusive clinical data do not exist regarding the efficacy of prophylactic antibiotics. They may have particular value in areas where infection would be particularly dangerous, including wounds on the face, hands, and feet and those involving extensive tissue damage or suturing.

42. Dog or Cat Bites

Donald Demetrios Zukin, MD

The treatment of dog and cat bites varies from emergency department to emergency department, and usually from physician to physician in the same department. Opinions differ as to which bacteria are most commonly associated with dog and cat bites. Some practitioners prescribe prophylactic antibiotics; others do not. Some advocate topical antiseptics, while others maintain that nothing but normal saline should ever be used in an open wound. Some close lacerations resulting from animal bites, while others maintain that no animal bite should ever be sutured.

ETIOLOGY

Authorities frequently report different organisms as the most common offenders in infections, especially in the case of dog bites. Some focus on the organisms that can be cultured from dogs' mouths, whereas others rely on data about which organisms can be cultured from infected wounds. Table 42-1 lists the results of three studies looking at the spectrum of bacteria cultured from infected dog bite wounds. Infections are most commonly caused by staphylococci, streptococci, and gram-negative enteric organisms. Note the low incidence of *Pasteurella multocida*. Although dogs frequently carry *P multocida* in their mouths, this organism is not the predominant cause of wound infections after dog bites.[1,2]

There is less confusion in the literature concerning the cause of cat bite wound infections. *P multocida* is frequently found in cats' mouths and is also the predominant organism causing infections after cat bites (and cat scratches).[3,4] *Staphylococcus aureus* and beta-hemolytic streptococci also account for some cat bite infections.

Table 42-1 Spectrum of Bacteria Cultured from *Infected* Dog Bite Wounds: Comparison of Three Studies*

	Study 1[10]	Study 2[2]	Study 3[1]
S aureus	10%	50%	16%
S epidermidis	10%	50%	7%
Gram-positive strep (total)	15%	38%	6%
Diphtheroids	5%	0%	0%
Enteric gram-negative rods	10%	38%	30%
Pseudomonas	10%	13%	22%
B subtillus	0%	0%	14%
P multocida	0%	25%	0%

*Rarely encountered bacteria are not listed. Several wounds grew multiple pathogens.

PUNCTURE WOUNDS VERSUS OPEN LACERATIONS

Cat bites typically result in puncture wounds while dog bites can cause both puncture wounds and lacerations. Puncture wounds, although smaller than lacerations, have a higher potential for infection.[5] For example, dog bites to the hand that cause puncture wounds have a 7% infection rate; those that cause open lacerations have only a 4% to 5% infection rate.[6] Puncture wounds to areas other than the hand have a 4% to 5% infection rate; lacerations to areas other than the hand have only a 1% to 2% infection rate.[6]

The heightened infection potential of puncture wounds most likely results from the introduction of pathogens and particles of debris into the deep tissue, as well as the increased difficulty with cleaning the wound. An eschar forms at the top of the puncture site, trapping the bacteria and debris below.

Since cat bites more commonly result in puncture wounds than dog bites, it is not surprising that cat bites have a much higher potential for infection than dog bites. Some investigators[4,6,7] noted infection rates of 50% or more after cat bites, but only 5% to 10% after a typical dog bite.

WOUND IRRIGATION AND DEBRIDEMENT

Irrigation with normal saline leads to a dramatic reduction in the incidence of infection after animal bites.[5] To be effective, irrigation must be performed under pressure. Pressures on the order of 7 pounds per square inch (PSI) are needed to remove bacteria and particulate matter from a contaminated wound.[8] In laboratory animals, contaminated wounds irrigated under 7 PSI pressure had an infection rate of 10%, compared with an infection rate above 80% in wounds irrigated with 0.05 PSI of pressure.[9]

Using a standard bulb syringe, one can generate pressures of only 0.05 PSI.[8] However, using a 35-mL syringe fitted with a 19-gauge needle and pushing on the plunger with full force will generate the necessary pressure of 7 PSI or greater. Since all animal bites are contaminated, all should be treated with high-pressure irrigation.

Debridement or sharp excision of the edges of dog bite wounds seems to lead to a lower incidence of infection than wounds treated without excision. In an uncontrolled study, Callaham[10] reported an infection rate of 1% in debrided wounds, compared with 60% in nondebrided wounds.

Only a small rim of tissue needs to be excised. Debridement of the wound edges has the added benefit of improving the final, plastic appearance of the repair, especially in the case of macerated edges.

Excision is also important in the treatment of cat bite puncture wounds. Excising a rim of tissue 1 to 2 mm from around the periphery of the puncture wound allows for both improved irrigation of the deep portion of the puncture wound and improved drainage of serous fluid from deep within the wound during the healing process.[11]

TOPICAL ANTISEPTICS

Multiple clinical studies showed a decreased incidence of infection in surgical wounds treated with povidone iodine solution before wound closure. Sindelar and Mason[12] treated surgical wounds with topical povidone iodine (applied directly into the subcutaneous tissue) or an inert control substance. There was a 26% infection rate in the control group, v 7% in the povidone iodine group (P < 0.05). Table 42-2 lists the results of controlled trials (human) of povidone iodine applied to the subcutaneous tissues before wound closure. In more than 80% of these studies, there was a lower infection rate in the groups treated with povidone iodine.

Despite the proven efficacy of povidone iodine solution in reducing the infection rate of contaminated wounds, many still resist using anything but saline on an open wound. This reluctance to use topical povidone iodine probably stems from the fact that many antiseptics are indeed highly cytotoxic. Peroxide, for example, causes almost complete obstruction of the microvasculature when used in open wounds. Isopropyl alcohol essentially fixes the tissues.

Plain povidone iodine (the aqueous solution) does not impair healing, whereas povidone iodine surgical scrub (a detergent-based product) is highly cytotoxic to the deep tissues. In one study, the aqueous solution (Betadine

Table 42-2 Efficacy of Povidone Iodine Applied Directly to Subcutaneous Tissue in Reducing Incidence of Wound Infections

Author	Type of Povidone Iodine	Infection Rate Povidone Iodine	Control	Significant
De Jong (*Surg Gynecol Obstet* 1982;155:221.)	1% solution 10% solution	11% 15%	15% 11%	No No
Gilmore (*Br J Surg* 1975;62:792.)	Powder*	8.6%	24%	Yes
Gilmore (*Postgrad Med J* 1977;53:122.)	Powder*	0%	4%	No
Gilmore (*Lancet* 1973;I:220.)	Powder*	8%	18%	Yes
Gray (*Br J Surg* 1981;68:310.)	Powder*	9.9%	24.4%	Yes
Morgan (*Lancet* 1978;I:769.)	NR	6%	14%	Yes
Rodgers (*Surg Gynecol Obstet* 1983;157:426.)	10% solution	4.6%	10.9%	No
Sindelar (*Surg Gynecol Obstet* 1979;148:227.)	10% solution	2.9%	15.1%	Yes
Sindelar** (*Surg Gynecol Obstet* 1979;148:409.)	1% solution	1.3%	10.2%	Yes
Viljanto (*Arch Surg* 1980;115:253.)	5% solution 1% solution 1% solution	19% 2.6% 50%	8% 8.5% 41%	Yes Yes NR
Walsh (*Br J Surg* 1981;68:185.)	5% solution 5% solution 5% solution	3% 9% 29%	10% 11% 39%	No No No

*The povidone iodine powder, Disadine, has 5% available iodine. Stock 10% povidone iodine solution has 1% available iodine.

**In this study, povidone iodine was applied to the peritoneal cavity. In all other studies listed, povidone iodine was applied *only* to the subcutaneous tissues just before wound closure.

NR = Not reported.

Solution) caused little or no damage to cartilage and soft tissue when injected directly into the knee joints of rabbits, but the detergent product (Betadine Surgical Scrub) caused widespread tissue necrosis, and eventually ankylosis of the joints.[13] Therefore, no detergent products should ever be used in an open wound. However, povidone iodine aqueous solution, which lowers the wound infection rate without impairing healing, is indicated for contaminated wounds, and in particular contaminated animal bites.

A 1:10 dilution of the stock 10% solution should be applied with a sterile sponge to the subcutaneous tissue for a 30 to 60 second period just before closure. The solution probably should not be applied to open joints or exposed tendons pending further study. Iodine solutions are also contraindicated in infants and neonates, in whom systemic absorption of iodine could suppress thyroid function.

DOG BITES: TO SUTURE OR NOT TO SUTURE

One of the areas of greatest controversy concerning dog bites is whether or not an open wound resulting from the bite can be sutured closed. Many children have probably had needless delays in healing because their physicians followed the time-honored adage, *"Never close an animal bite."* Although dog bite wounds that are sutured closed do indeed tend to have a higher infection rate than wounds that are left open, the difference in infection rates is quite small. Brown and Ashton[6] estimate that the overall infection rate of dog bite lacerations to the hand is 4.5% for nonsutured wounds and 5.5% for sutured wounds. For wounds to regions other than to the face, the infection rates are estimated to be 2% for sutured wounds and 1% for nonsutured wounds. It does not seem judicious to leave 99 of 100 children with open wounds in order to save 1 child in 100 from having a wound infection. This is especially true in pediatric animal bites, which have a predilection for occurring on the face.

With proper wound care, the infection rate in sutured dog bites can most likely be kept even below the 2% to 5% rate mentioned above. Using an aggressive protocol that included high-pressure irrigation, meticulous wound edge debridement, and prophylactic antibiotics, Zook et al[14] were able to keep the overall infection rate below 0.5% for dog bite puncture wounds and lacerations that were sutured closed primarily. Therefore, in most cases, the concern over infection should not lead the practitioner to leave open a gaping laceration.

In wounds that have been left open too long to close primarily, and in especially macerated wounds, the wound can be treated with irrigation and debridement, packed with xeroform gauze, and then bandaged without suturing. The patient should return in four days, and if no infection occurs, the wound can be sutured closed at that time. This technique is termed delayed primary closure, or closure by tertiary intent.

PROPHYLACTIC ANTIBIOTICS

In the case of cat bites, a single study[4] showed a significant decrease in the wound infection rate in patients treated with oral dicloxacillin sodium compared with placebo. Three of five patients in the control group developed *P multocida* wound infections, but there were no infections in the six patients treated with dicloxacillin (P < 0.05). Although dicloxacillin was used in the cited study, penicillin sodium (the drug of choice for *P multocida*) is a reasonable alternative, as is cephalexin (Keflex). Erythromycin is not a good choice, because it has only limited activity against *P multocida*.

In the case of dog bites, clinical studies have failed to show a significant benefit from the use of prophylactic antibiotics (Table 42-3). In one half the studies, the placebo group had fewer infections; in the other half, the antibiotic group had fewer infections. In none of the studies were results statistically significant.

Since infections after dog bites are relatively uncommon, huge sample sizes would be needed to show significant differences in the infection rates between treatment and control groups. None of the studies to date have been so large.

Table 42-3 Placebo-Controlled Studies on the Effects of Prophylactic Antibiotics on the Incidence of Dog Bite Wound Infections

Author	Type of Antibiotic	Infection Rate		Significant
		Antibiotic	Control	
Boenning (*Am J Emerg Med* 1983;1:17.)	Penicillin	4%	3.3%	No
Callaham (*Ann Emerg Med* 1980;9:410.)	Penicillin	7.4%	17%	No
Elenbaas (*Ann Emerg Med* 1982;11:248.)	Oxacillin	9.1%	0%	No
Rosen (*Am J Emerg Med* 1985;3:20.)	Dicloxacillin, Cloxacillin, or Erythromycin	5.7%	9.7%	No

For the time being, therefore, physicians must decide whether or not to use antibiotics without the benefit of a conclusive clinical study.

Many use antibiotics only for selected dog bite wounds, such as those involving the hands or face; those involving tendon, joint, or bone; those that are particularly macerated or large; and those that are sutured.

Once the decision is made to use prophylactic antibiotics for either a dog or a cat bite, the first dose must be given as soon as possible. In animal studies,[15] prophylactic antibiotics must be given within 3 hours of the time of injury to be effective. The first dose of antibiotic should therefore be given in the emergency department (and preferably parenterally for more serious wounds). The first dose should not be delayed until the prescription is filled.

CONCLUSION

Optimal care of children with dog and cat bite wounds consists of high-pressure saline irrigation, followed by edge debridement and topical antisepsis with dilute povidone iodine solution (not the cytotoxic povidone iodine detergent scrub). For dog bites, suturing should be performed as needed, especially for facial lacerations in which the infection rate is low; the adverse cosmetic effects of allowing the wound to heal in by granulation can be disastrous. Prophylactic antibiotics are indicated for cat bites, but the exact role of prophylactic antibiotics for dog bites has yet to be determined. If the decision is made to give prophylactic antibiotics, the first dose should be given without delay.

REFERENCES

1. Ordoq GJ: The bacteriology of dog bite wounds on initial presentation. *Ann Emerg Med* 1986;15:1324.

2. Goldstein EJC, Citron DM, Finegold SM: Dog bite wounds and infection: A prospective clinical study. *Ann Emerg Med* 1980;9:508.

3. Veitch JM, Omer GE: Case report: Treatment of cat bite injuries of the hand. *J Trauma* 1979;19:201.

4. Elenbaas RM, McNabney WK, Robinson WA: Evaluation of prophylactic oxacillin in cat bite wounds. *Ann Emerg Med* 1984;13:155.

5. Callaham ML: Treatment of common dog bites: Infection risk factors. *Ann Emerg Med* 1978;7:83.

6. Brown CG, Ashton JJ: Dog bites: The controversy continues. *Am J Emerg Med* 1985;3:83.

7. Aghababian RV, Conte JE: Mammalian bite wounds. *Ann Emerg Med* 1980;9:79.

8. Rodeheaver GT, Pettry D, Thacker JG, et al: Wound cleansing by high pressure irrigation. *Surg Gynecol Obstet* 1975;141:357.

9. Stevenson TR, Thacker JG, Rodeheaver GT, et al: Cleansing the traumatic wound by high pressure syringe irrigation. *Ann Emerg Med* 1976;5:17.

10. Callaham M: Prophylactic antibiotics in common dog bite wounds: A controlled study. *Ann Emerg Med* 1980;9:410.

11. Edlich RF, Rodeheaver GT, Thacker JG, et al: Fundamentals of wound management in surgery: Technical factors in wound management. South Plainsfield, NJ, Chirugecom, 1977.

12. Sindelar WF, Mason GR: Irrigation of subcutaneous tissue with povidone-iodine solution for prevention of surgical wound infections. *Surg Gynecol Obstet* 1979;148:227.

13. Faddis D, Daniel D, Boyer J: Tissue toxicity of antiseptic solutions: A study of rabbit articular and periarticular tissues. *J Trauma* 1977;17:895.

14. Zook EG, Miller M, Ban Beek AL, et al: Successful treatment protocol for canine fang injuries. *J Trauma* 1980;20:

15. Elenbass RM, McNabney WK, Robinson NA: Prophylactic oxacillin in dog bite wounds. *Ann Emerg Med* 1982;11:248.

PART VII

Cardiopulmonary Resuscitation

Section 24

Advanced Life Support

Numerous changes have occurred in the method of resuscitating the child. The use of calcium should be restricted to patients with hyperkalemia, hypocalcemia, hypermagnesemia, and calcium channel blocker overdose. Sodium bicarbonate should be used with greater caution in the ventilated patient, optimally while monitoring arterial blood gases. The role and dosage of atropine require further study.

Defibrillation may require re-evaluation to determine its role early in asystole and appropriate watt-seconds/kg. The optimal dose, if initial attempts are unsuccessful, requires further study.

Alternative routes of drug administration are extensively used when intravenous access is not obtained. Endotracheal administration of epinephrine, atropine, lidocaine, and naloxone seems to be safe. Intraosseous infusion of fluids and drugs was recently reintroduced.

43. Pediatric Cardiopulmonary Resuscitation: A Study of Consonant Dissonance

Jeffrey L. Blumer, PhD, MD

Our society has become quite sophisticated in recognizing the signs and symptoms of myocardial infarction. Many laymen are now quite skilled in providing cardiopulmonary resuscitation (CPR) to adults who suffer cardiac arrest outside the health care facility. Depending on the bias of the individual author, the outcome of resuscitation outside the hospital is either encouraging or discouraging.[1] Nevertheless, we continue to encourage the public to familiarize themselves with CPR techniques.

In all courses designed to train both laymen and health care professionals in the art of CPR, there is at least passing reference to the pediatric patient. Differences between children and adults in terms of heart rate, respiratory rate, and chest compression techniques are well described.[2] Unfortunately, few of these courses emphasize the true differences between pediatric and adult patients requiring CPR. As a result, there is often surprise at the dismal outcome of pediatric resuscitations even when patients are found before full arrest.[3,4]

The paucity of successful out-of-hospital resuscitations highlights what may be the most important difference between pediatric and adult patients requiring CPR. In the adult, it is seldom necessary to initiate CPR before full arrest. In contrast, in the pediatric patient, particularly the very young, full CPR must be initiated when a patient is thought, on clinical grounds, to manifest cardiac output that is insufficient to support vital organ function, or pulmonary function insufficient to maintain adequate tissue oxygen delivery or both.

CLINICAL INDICATIONS FOR CARDIOPULMONARY RESUSCITATION

Although adult and pediatric patients share a number of clinical settings in which CPR is indicated, the antecedent events in the adult are generally

335

different from those in children. In adult patients sustaining cardiopulmonary arrests, the onset is generally sudden, and the disease of origin is generally cardiac. Adult patients are also plagued by a number of self-inflicted predisposing environmental factors that lead to impairment of overall health. These include diet, stress, and alcohol and tobacco abuse. The penultimate event in their cardiac arrest is generally a ventricular dysrhythmia or coronary artery insufficiency. Cardiac standstill generally precedes the respiratory arrest, and a generic therapeutic approach may apply. Thus, many adults may be successfully resuscitated outside the hospital, and in-hospital care is directed toward their underlying cardiac disease.[5]

In contrast, infants and children requiring resuscitation often show an array of predisposing abnormalities and illnesses that may require specific therapy. Unlike their adult counterparts, the catastrophic events in children usually occur during acute illness, and generally result from the failure of an extra-cardiac system (Table 43-1). In addition, contributions from abnormal anatomy may be substantial.

These factors suggest that either a uniform therapeutic strategy will be futile, or that there is a need to identify a common pathway for these potential insults. In infants and children, the final common pathway tends to be hypoxemia.[6] Independent of underlying illness, hypoxia serves as the final common denominator leading to organ dysfunction, ischemic damage, and cardiopulmonary arrest. Hypoxia may be acute or chronic and may result from either an acquired or a congenital illness. Moreover, contributions because of abnormal pulmonary vasculature or congenital heart disease leading to right-to-left shunting maintain some patients in a tenuous status for a long period of time.

Table 43-1 Etiology of Cardiopulmonary Arrest in Children

Newborn

Prematurity	Sepsis
Uteroplacental insufficiency	Nuchal cord
Congenital malformations: brain, heart, lung	

Infancy

SIDS	Ingestions
Child abuse	Congenital malformations
Pulmonary disease	Sepsis
Congenital heart disease	

Adolescence

Trauma
Drug overdose
Dysrhythmias
Congenital heart disease

Physicians must be acutely aware of the potential damage that hypoxia and the resulting ischemia may cause to susceptible tissues such as the central nervous system (CNS), liver, and kidneys. Thus, the approach to an infant or a child experiencing cardiopulmonary arrest must extend beyond CPR to include vital organ preservation.

RATIONAL THERAPY OF CARDIOPULMONARY ARREST IN PEDIATRIC PATIENTS

To develop a rational therapeutic approach to the child who has sustained cardiac arrest, it is necessary to develop predetermined goals for the resuscitation. On a very simple level, it might be construed that a reasonable goal would be to re-establish a spontaneous cardiac rhythm and blood pressure. However, an in-depth examination of the consequences of this approach reveals that it is inadequate.[7] In fact, the goals of pediatric resuscitation should be to restore optimal cardiac output and tissue oxygen delivery. These may be accomplished through the effective use of chest compression and artificial ventilation coupled with the judicious use of pharmacologic agents.

Very little need be said regarding the mechanical aspects of CPR. Reams have been written concerning the number of chest compressions relative to the number of breaths and the technique for the application of each.[2,8] Although these mechanical efforts may generate an arterial pressure wave and move oxygen in and out of the lungs, the outcome has been less than optimal. In the child who comes to the emergency department in full arrest, the likelihood of successful resuscitation is small. Moreover, recent information[7] suggests that no modification or intervention in terms of closed-chest massage will in any way improve this effectiveness. This leads one to wonder whether a more aggressive approach involving emergency thoracotomy and open-chest massage will be more effective. Clearly, further investigative efforts along these lines are both desirable and indicated.

Intubation

Perhaps the most important procedure in a pediatric resuscitation is endotracheal intubation. Since hypoxemia is the final common pathway for most pediatric arrests, placement of an endotracheal tube through which oxygen is delivered and adequate ventilation assured may be the only lifesaving maneuver necessary. The provision for an adequate airway and the use of oxygen cannot be overemphasized. In fact, it is likely that without these, all other efforts at resuscitation will be in vain.

Drug Therapy

Drug therapy during CPR must be directed toward achieving the goals of optimizing cardiac output and maintaining tissue oxygen delivery. These can be accomplished only when a therapeutic strategy is adopted that allows individualization in dosing parameters. Such an approach is termed the "target-effect" strategy[9] and assures that the dosage adjustment of any agent will be directed toward achieving a predetermined therapeutic goal without any limit, other than supervening toxicity, imposed on the amount of drug administered. Alterations in therapy are therefore mandated either when toxicity occurs or when serial increases in dose result in no additional therapeutic effect and the predetermined goal has not been reached. The application of such a therapeutic strategy to pediatric CPR also requires that the impact of the arrest on drug biodisposition (pharmacokinetics) and the ontogeny of drug responsiveness (pharmacodynamics) be recognized.[6]

Although oxygen is the most common and perhaps the most important drug used during pediatric CPR, a number of other classes of drugs need to be discussed. These include:

- oxygen
- buffers
- intravenous fluids (IV) (crystalloid v colloid)
- catecholamines
- anticholinergic agents
- antidysrhythmic agents
- vasodilators
- endogenous compounds.

Sodium Bicarbonate

The use of buffers has been the subject of considerable controversy during the past several years. Sodium bicarbonate is the most commonly used buffer, but realization is growing that its risk may outweigh its potential benefits.[10,11]

During most arrests, the first drug requested by physicians is generally sodium bicarbonate. One of the hallmarks of poor cardiac output is acidemia. In pediatric patients, however, this acidemia is primarily respiratory rather than metabolic. There is no argument that the judicious use of sodium bicarbonate to correct the metabolic component of the acidosis is beneficial. Nevertheless, its use to correct what is primarily a respiratory problem can lead to further difficulties.

Once the bicarbonate enters the blood stream, it is rapidly converted to carbonic acid, which dissociates into carbon dioxide and water. In young infants and children for whom carbon dioxide elimination is a primary problem and pulmonary disease is a major predisposing factor to cardiac arrest, it is likely that the aggressive use of sodium bicarbonate could in fact cause the pCO_2 to rise.[12]

More recently, it was shown[11] that during CPR a marked difference in the acid-base status between the arterial and venous portions of the circulation exists. On the venous side of the circulation, CO_2 retention is more profound than one would expect based on arterial blood gas determination. This is thought to be caused by the need to buffer the lactic acid generated during the period of inadequate circulation coupled with the ineffective delivery of blood to the lung for CO_2 elimination. The administration of bicarbonate under these circumstances may only serve to worsen the acidosis. Moreover, since CO_2 can freely diffuse in and out of the CNS whereas bicarbonate may not, the aggressive use of sodium bicarbonate may result in a marked CNS acidosis once the circulation is re-established and the rest of the system has re-equilibrated.

Similar concerns are being raised in adult patients. Nevertheless, since the arrests in adult patients are primarily cardiac in origin, the establishment of a patent airway along with the reinstatement of effective circulation usually ensures adequate CO_2 elimination. In contrast, in pediatric patients in whom pulmonary disease has a prominent role, one cannot be assured that an adequate airway will automatically result in effective ventilation. Thus, the admonition against the overzealous use of bicarbonate should be amplified when dealing with resuscitations in children.

Intravenous Fluids

Less controversial is the use of IV fluid during CPR. The goal is repletion of the intravascular volume to achieve hemodynamic stability. However, controversy regarding the use of colloid- or crystalloid-containing solutions in this setting rages on.[13] This controversy need not be addressed here, since it is clear that no single answer can be found. The key points in resuscitation are simply the prompt recognition of the pathophysiology of the underlying illness and that the goal is intravascular volume repletion.

Catecholamines

As in adults, the catecholamines are the mainstay of therapy for CPR in children.[14] They are administered both as IV boluses during the acute phases of resuscitation and as continuous infusions during the maintenance therapy involved in postresuscitative stabilization.

Epinephrine hydrochloride is the primary agent employed. It is a catecholamine with mixed alpha- and beta-agonist properties. During the past several years, it has become clear that it is the alpha- rather than the beta-adrenergic effects that are most important during the acute phases of CPR.[10] No difference has been observed between epinephrine, phenylephrine, and methoxamine in experimental studies of CPR.[10] In contrast, the use of isoproterenol is not recommended, since its vasodilatory effects may be counterproductive in this setting. Re-establishment of coronary blood flow is the key to success in CPR.

Catecholamine therapy should be titrated to the desired target response. The child in full arrest is unlikely to be resuscitated; the chief consideration must be given to children with failing cardiopulmonary function before arrest. It is recommended that therapy with catecholamines be initiated with the least potent agent available, since as the agents increase in potency, for example, going from dopamine to epinephrine, they also increase in relative toxicity.

In using catecholamines in young infants and toddlers, it must be recalled that the pharmacodynamic actions of these drugs may differ from those expected in adult patients.[14] The heart in young children tends to be under a high level of sympathetic tone, and its contractile elements less organized than those in adult hearts. Infants will often respond to catecholamines with an exaggerated chronotropic response to increase cardiac output, since stroke volume has been maximized physiologically. Thus, it may be efficacious in some younger patients to add a vasodilator to the catecholamine once effective heart rate and rhythm are established. None of the currently available vasodilators have been rigorously investigated in young children. Nevertheless, the use of nitroprusside, which is a balanced arteriolar and venular dilator, may be recommended to improve cardiac output in the very young, particularly those with intracardiac shunts. As with catecholamines, vasodilators must be titrated to the desired therapeutic effect and often require volume loading for their effective use.

Anticholinergic and Antidysrhythmic Agents

Anticholinergic and antidysrhythmic therapies in pediatric patients have received relatively little attention. Atropine remains the anticholinergic agent of choice during CPR. Although several investigators in internal medicine have suggested that atropine sulfate may be used in asystolic patients to initiate spontaneous myocardial electrical activity, this cannot be recommended in children. Atropine should be reserved for patients who have true supraventricular or junctional bradydysrhythmias. The idea that cardiac standstill might be related to overstimulation by the parasympathetic nervous system requires further investigation in pediatric patients before atropine can be recommended for cardiac standstill.

The currently recommended pediatric doses for atropine may not prove generally effective. A careful review[15] of their origin reveals they were derived from data generated by anesthesiologists investigating the dose required to inhibit salivation during preanesthetic medication. It is well known that salivation is among the most sensitive autonomic responses to atropine, and that its inhibition can be achieved with little or no effect on the heart. Thus, in most pediatric patients, doses between 2 and 10 times those currently recommended should be considered in patients who fail to respond. The one caveat is the child with Down's syndrome. These patients appear to have a genetic sensitivity to atropine and may show exaggerated responses to even low doses.

Antidysrhythmic therapy for pediatric patients remains largely empiric. Dysrhythmias in children are often ill defined, and their pharmacologic management is familiar only to a handful of specialists. For many supraventricular tachydysrhythmias that impair cardiac output, drugs like digoxin are still considered the drugs of choice. The use of verapamil in children under 12 months of age is often ineffective and may be fraught with considerable hazards.[16] In fact, in this setting, electrical cardioversion may be the therapeutic maneuver of choice.

For sustained ventricular dysrhythmias, lidocaine remains the antidysrhythmic medication of choice. In using lidocaine by continuous infusion, maintenance therapy (20 to 50 µg/kg/hr) should be begun immediately after the IV bolus (1 to 2 mg/kg) is administered. This will sustain the serum concentration achieved by the bolus dose. Once lidocaine therapy is initiated, serum concentration monitoring is mandatory. Lidocaine is cleared by the liver, and its accumulation predisposes to seizures as well as other CNS toxicity.

In patients who prove refractory to lidocaine, bretylium may be used as a safe alternative. Although there are very few data concerning the use of this drug in pediatric patients, its use in a manner similar to that employed in adults can be recommended with appropriate monitoring of its sympatholytic activity.

Finally, in cases in which asystole is converted to one of the several varieties of ventricular fibrillation, electrical defibrillation is indicated. Bolus administration of lidocaine is recommended before defibrillation. Appropriate equipment for pediatric defibrillation must be available. This involves the use of small paddles and an instrument that allows for the use of low voltage. Defibrillation attempts should start with a dose of 2 watts/sec/kg and with each successive attempt the voltage should be doubled. Although these dysrhythmias are rare in pediatric patients, prompt recognition and therapy may be lifesaving.

Endogenous Compounds

Although it may be dogmatic, it is essential that a bolus of glucose be administered as a part of any pediatric resuscitation. Young infants experiencing stress are at risk for using all their metabolic reserves. In such cases, profound hypoglycemia can result with blood glucose values less than 40 mg/dL. Virtually all these patients will benefit from an initial bolus infusion of glucose; its omission may stymie all other resuscitative efforts.

In the current medical literature, there is perhaps no issue that has created more controversy than that of the use of calcium during resuscitation. The 1985 National Conference on Cardiopulmonary Resuscitation and Emergency Cardiac Care recommended that calcium not be used during cardiac arrest.[17] It went on to state, however, that the application of these recommendations to pediatric arrest situations required further investigation. There are, in fact, sound theoretical reasons for avoiding calcium during CPR. These relate to disturbances in the control of calcium movement in the myocardium that would likely result in elevated cytoplasmic calcium, and decreased myocardial function that may occur with calcium overload.

However, virtually all proposed detrimental effects of calcium during CPR are theoretical rather than proven.[18] Calcium has been used to augment myocardial contractility in patients undergoing reperfusion after hypothermic cardioplegia and cardiac arrest. Moreover, all clinical studies designed to show the potential detrimental effects of calcium when administered during cardiac arrest are retrospective in nature. Although they point out that patients who receive calcium rarely leave the hospital alive, the reason for these deaths is not always clearly associated with either calcium administration or myocardial dysfunction. In contrast, experience with the use of calcium during pediatric resuscitation has been very rewarding.

Calcium chloride has been the drug of choice since calcium gluconate, the other standard pediatric formulation of calcium, requires hepatic transformation to release the calcium in its ionic form. The drug has been useful in patients in low cardiac output states associated with chronic respiratory failure and congenital heart disease. It has been particularly effective and safe when guided by the rapid determination of plasma levels of ionized calcium, which is currently available on many blood gas machines. Thus, it must be concluded that during resuscitations in which electromechanical dissociation is apparent or a widened QRS rhythm is manifest in the face of aggressive catecholamine support, calcium chloride administration may be beneficial and may be used safely with proper monitoring. Further investigation is required.

ROUTES OF DRUG ADMINISTRATION DURING CARDIOPULMONARY RESUSCITATION

The preferred route of administration during CPR is via central venous catheter. Although resuscitative efforts may be initiated through the use of peripheral venous access, many of the drugs employed are sclerosing, and the coincident circulatory embarrassment may preclude the delivery of effective drug concentrations to the myocardium. During CPR, intratracheal administration of catecholamines, atropine, and certain antidysrhythmics is both beneficial and effective. If it is remembered that larger volumes of drug must be delivered and somewhat increased doses need to be used through the endotracheal route, the differences in clinical outcome are insignificant. Another route often used in emergency situations is the intracardiac route. This route cannot be recommended for pediatric patients. Intracardiac administration through a closed chest is frought with danger and is no more effective than either the endotracheal or central venous route. Thus, the risk-benefit ratio recommends against the use of intracardiac medication. Although intraosseous administration of drugs has received a great deal of attention in the recent literature, its superiority over IV or endotracheal administration has not been documented, and its safety is in question.

CONCLUSION

Pediatric resuscitation techniques may differ significantly from those employed for adult patients. The pathophysiology leading to cardiopulmonary arrest in infants and children is age-dependent and generally involves the failure of a noncardiac system. Resuscitations outside the hospital, because of the common denominator of hypoxemia, are generally unsuccessful; the success of in-hospital resuscitation requires careful attention to the goals of optimizing cardiac output and maintaining tissue oxygen delivery. Pharmacologic agents used during CPR in children should be employed using a target-effect strategy with clear expectations of drug effect recognized before the initiation of therapy.

REFERENCES

1. Bedell SE, Delbanes TL, Cook EF: Survival after cardiopulmonary resuscitation. *N Engl J Med* 1983;309:569–576.

2. American Heart Association: Standards for cardiopulmonary resuscitation and emergency cardiac care: V. Pediatric advanced life support. *JAMA* 1986;255:2961–2973.

3. Torphy DE, Minter MG, Thompson BM: Cardiorespiratory arrest and resuscitation of children. *Am J Dis Child* 1984;138:1099–1102.

4. Orlowski JP: The effectiveness of pediatric cardiopulmonary resuscitation, editorial. *Am J Dis Child* 1984;138:1097–1098.

5. Guerci AD, Weisfeldt ML: Cardiopulmonary resuscitation, in Kravis TC, Warner CG (eds): *Emergency Medicine: A Comprehensive Review*, ed 2. Rockville, Md, Aspen Publishers, 1987, pp 1039–1050.

6. Blumer JL: Pharmacologic approach to cardiopulmonary resuscitation in children. *Pediatr Ann* 1985;14:313–322.

7. White DJ: The new CPR, in Jacobson S (ed): *Resuscitation Clinics in Emergency Medicine.* New York, Churchill Livingstone Inc, 1983, vol 2, pp 27–37.

8. Pierog JM: CPR, in Kravis TC, Warner CG (eds): *Emergency Medicine: A Comprehensive Review,* ed 2. Rockville, Md, Aspen Publishers, 1987, pp 521–532.

9. Koch-Weser J: Serum drug concentrations in clinical perspective, in Richens A, Marks V (eds): *Therapeutic Drug Monitoring.* New York, Churchill Livingstone Inc, 1981, pp 1–22.

10. Yakartis RW: The pharmacology of cardiopulmonary resuscitation, in Jacobson S (ed): *Resuscitation Clinics in Emergency Medicine.* New York, Churchill Livingstone, 1983, vol 2, pp 27–37.

11. Weil MH, Rackow EC, Trevino R, et al: Difference in acid-base state between venous and arterial blood during cardiopulmonary resuscitation. *N Engl J Med* 1986;315:153–156.

12. Berenyi KJ, Wolk M, Killip T: Cerebrospinal fluid acidosis complicating therapy of experimental cardiopulmonary arrest. *Circulation* 1975;52:319–324.

13. Shoemaker WC: The crystalloid-colloid controversy, in Chernow B, Lake CR (eds): *The Pharmacologic Approach to the Critically Ill Patient.* Baltimore, Williams & Wilkins Co, 1983, pp 204–219.

14. Zaritsky A, Chernow B: Use of catecholamines in pediatrics. *J Pediatr* 1984;105:341–350.

15. Unna KR, Glaser K, Lipton E, et al: Dosage of drugs in infants and children: I. Atropine. *Pediatrics* 1951;6:197–207.

16. Garson A Jr: Medicolegal problems in the management of cardiac arrhythmia in children. *Pediatrics* 1987;79:84–88.

17. American Heart Association: Standards for cardiopulmonary resuscitation and emergency cardiac care: III. Adult adrenal cardiac support. *JAMA* 1986;255:2933–2953.

18. Hughes WG, Ruedy JR: Should calcium be used in cardiac arrest? *Am J Med* 1986; 81:285–296.

44. Pediatric Advanced Life Support: A Critical Analysis

Ronald A. Dieckmann, MD, MPH

Scrutiny of the scientific foundations of the new American Heart Association (AHA) guidelines for advanced life support (ALS) reveals disquieting deficiencies in our understanding of both the complex pathophysiology of cardiopulmonary arrest in children and our methods for treatment.[1] Although controlled clinical studies in adult populations have helped clarify certain areas of practice, similar data for children are unavailable. Current ALS guidelines are derived from animal models, adult models, anecdotal reports, and small studies in children—some of which are poorly extrapolated to the setting of pediatric resuscitation.

PREHOSPITAL ALS MANAGEMENT OF PEDIATRIC ARRESTS

The prognosis in prehospital pediatric arrests is dismal. In about 90% of cases, the child arriving in full arrest to the emergency department dies. Typically, the child was transported, after an unwitnessed arrest, by a life squad administering basic life support (BLS). Technical problems with effective airway management and rapid intravenous access in children severely limit therapeutic options in the prehospital setting.

What "modern" modalities of ALS care of children in arrest are available to the prehospital provider that might enhance survival? Practical interventions holding greatest promise include early defibrillation; pediatric intubation training for paramedics; endotracheal drug administration; and prehospital use of intraosseous (IO) drugs and fluids in cases of extended transport time.

346 Cardiopulmonary Resuscitation

Defibrillation

For adults in cardiac arrest, *time to defibrillation is most closely related to survival*. The rhythms of adult arrests are ventricular fibrillation and ventricular tachycardia—dysrhythmias known to respond to electrical countershock. In children, the arrest rhythm is usually *bradyasystole*—a terminal spectrum of electrical deterioration that probably begins with bradycardia and ends with asystole.

Complex ventricular dysrhythmias are rare in children, except for patients with congenital heart disease, myocarditis, or traumatic myocardial contusion. Ventricular fibrillation may, in part, depend on myocardial mass and age-related maturity of beta-adrenergic receptors. The parasympathetic and alpha-adrenergic pathways predominate in autonomic cardiac regulation in children experiencing a medical arrest, which occurs at a mean age of 5.9 months; this milieu predisposes to bradysystole, rather than ventricular fibrillation.[2] Nonetheless, literature reviews[3,4] correlating pediatric arrest outcome with presenting rhythm suggest that meaningful *survival from arrest is still most likely to occur in those few patients with ventricular dysrhythmias*. Return of spontaneous circulation is occasionally achieved through resuscitation of severe bradycardia, but only rarely with true asystole.[4,5]

Since optimal outcomes seem most often effected through defibrillation, should electrical therapy be routinely administered in all pulseless children? AHA guidelines recommend that "only if ventricular fibrillation is shown on the electrocardiographic monitor should defibrillation be attempted." Our algorithm (Figure 44-1) for prehospital and initial emergency department care, in contrast, *emphasizes early use of countershock* presuming that oxygenation and ventilation are ongoing:

(1) Once full arrest is recognized, the airway is managed and quick-look paddles or a cardiac monitor is applied for rapid rhythm readout. *If asystole or ventricular fibrillation is present, defibrillate twice with 2 watt-sec/kg*. If no pulse returns, a second series of shocks is delivered at 4 watt-sec/kg.

(2) If fibrillatory electrical activity is present without return of spontaneous circulation after the second defibrillation at 4 watt-sec/kg, bretylium tosylate (5 mg/kg IV) is given. The drug is also administered if sinus rhythm is immediately restored by defibrillation. The dose may be repeated at 10 mg/kg twice, every 10 minutes, for refractory or recurrent ventricular fibrillation. Usually, electrical countershock must follow IV therapy to convert ventricular tachydysrhythmias. In adults, effective myocardial levels of bretylium are probably achieved in 2 to 5 minutes. Although pharmacologic data have not shown superiority of bretylium over lidocaine in adults (except for isolated reports of "chemical" conversion by bretylium of ventricular fibrillation), we

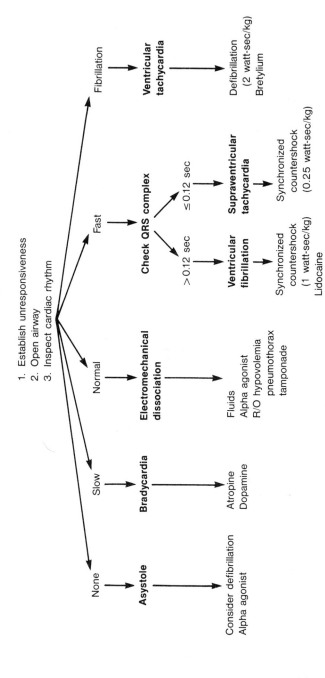

1. Establish unresponsiveness
2. Open airway
3. Inspect cardiac rhythm

None → **Asystole** → Consider defibrillation / Alpha agonist

Slow → **Bradycardia** → Atropine / Dopamine

Normal → **Electromechanical dissociation** → Fluids / Alpha agonist / R/O hypovolemia / pneumothorax / tamponade

Fast → **Check QRS complex**
- >0.12 sec → **Ventricular fibrillation** → Synchronized countershock (1 watt-sec/kg) / Lidocaine
- ≤0.12 sec → **Supraventricular tachycardia** → Synchronized countershock (0.25 watt-sec/kg)

Fibrillation → **Ventricular tachycardia** → Defibrillation (2 watt-sec/kg) / Bretylium

Figure 44-1 Pediatric resuscitation management algorithm.

have good success with this drug and use it as a first-line agent. There are no data to evaluate bretylium *v* lidocaine in children.

(3) If the cardiac monitor on the pulseless child displays tachycardia, the QRS complex is inspected. When the complex is greater than 0.12 second, presumptive ventricular tachycardia is diagnosed, and a synchronized counter-shock is delivered, at 1 watt-sec/kg. Repeat cardioversion is applied at 1 watt-sec/kg, and then doubled to 2 watt-sec/kg for no response. After the first series of synchronized shocks, we administer lidocaine at 1 mg/kg, with a continuous infusion at 20 to 50 µg/kg/min.

(4) If the QRS complex in pulseless tachycardia is less than 0.12 second, and the rate is greater than 150 per minute (greater than 200 per minute in infants), supraventricular tachycardia (SVT) is likely. In this situation, synchronized countershock is begun with 0.25 watt-sec/kg, and the electrical dose doubled, thereafter, to achieve electrical conversion.

(5) If a narrow complex rate is less than 150 per min (or 200 per min in infants), without pulses, electromechanical dissociation (EMD) is the most likely diagnosis. *Neither EMD nor sinus bradycardia should be shocked*, since these rhythms may degenerate into terminal patterns if electrical energy is delivered inappropriately.

When countershock is administered, 4.5-cm paddles are suggested *for infants only*, and 8-cm paddles for patients who weigh more than 10 kg. The paddles are placed in the standard sternoapical location. If no pediatric paddles are available, adult paddles placed anteroposterior are acceptable. A good conductive agent is also necessary, along with firm application of the paddles to the chest wall. Such details as paddle size and location, and exact dosages of energy are probably less important than the optimal technique of delivery of electrical energy: assurance of tight contact and timely repeat administrations.

Electrical countershock is less effective over time, with increasing hypoxia and acidosis. Control of ventilation and oxygenation will increase success. When properly used, early use may save the child with ventricular fibrillation, ventricular tachycardia, or SVT as well as an occasional child with fine ventricular fibrillation masquerading as asystole.

The role of countershock in apparent asystole requires further delineation. Although no deleterious effects are reported from electrical therapy in patients with asystole, the benefit is unknown. In true asystole, defibrillation is useless. Yet, at least one study[6] revealed significant errors in analysis of electrocardiographic asystole when only one electrical plane was monitored. Apparent "asystole" may be fine ventricular fibrillation. Before withholding potential definitive electrical therapy, a prudent approach may, at minimum, include review of a second electrocardiographic plane.

Controlled, prospective clinical studies of the appropriateness of defibrillation in asystole are needed. Potential exists for undue delay of pharmacologic intervention for asystole if early defibrillation attempts are prolonged. Our approach allows rapid, immediate defibrillations at 2 watt-sec/kg and 4 watt-sec/kg, in apparent asystole, while oxygenation and ventilation are achieved and intravascular cannulation assembled.

Endotracheal Intubation

Seventy-five percent of the emergency medical systems have personnel trained in pediatric intubation.[7] Yet, many paramedics do not intubate children successfully because of skills decay or restrictive prehospital policies. Complications of field intubations of children are well known, including transport delays, esophageal intubation, airway trauma, and mainstem bronchus intubation. Proper equipment is difficult to maintain. Nevertheless, several factors argue in favor of prehospital pediatric intubation training.

First, airway and ventilation control by mechanical airway device and bag-mask or mouth-to-mouth ventilation is usually ineffective. Improper mask size and faulty seals cause gastric insufflation, aspiration, and inadequate ventilation—which jeopardize the resuscitation. Control of airway and breathing by endotracheal intubation is simpler and more efficacious.

Second, respiratory arrest is the commonest cause of out-of-hospital medical arrests in children.[8] When respiratory arrest alone is present, early definitive airway control combined with proper ventilation/oxygenation revives more than 75% of patients. When respiratory arrest has advanced to full cardiopulmonary arrest, optimal ventilation/oxygenation, via the endotracheal tube, facilitates subsequent electrical and pharmacologic interventions. Furthermore, endotracheal intubation permits slower, more controlled chest inflation—a technique now recognized as optimal for adequate ventilation.

Third, in life-threatening pediatric trauma, especially closed head and chest trauma, control of airway and breathing is probably the most useful prehospital intervention to minimize neurologic disability and overall mortality.

Fourth, an endotracheal tube provides a safe and reliable conduit for delivery of several important ALS drugs including epinephrine, atropine, lidocaine, and naloxone. Rapid intubation permits delivery of essential drugs when IV access is impossible or delayed.

To implement prehospital pediatric intubation successfully, a comprehensive system for training, certification, and ongoing medical quality assurance is imperative. Manikin and animal (usually cats) models for pediatric intubation provide practical bases for initial provider training, and then for mandatory ongoing retraining of personnel. A framework for on-line, immediate physician control must assure expeditious transport of pediatric patients in arrest. *Prehospital protocol might allow two attempts in 2 minutes at endotracheal intubation in the field before hospital transport.* Last, mandatory retrospective review of all prehospital and emergency department pediatric resuscitations further safeguards high treatment standards.

Intraosseous Drugs and Fluids

For pediatric patients in arrest or near-arrest, definitive airway management and rapid transport are hallmarks of optimal care. But, for both medical and trauma victims in the field *facing transport times greater than 30 minutes*, salvage may require both definitive control of airway/breathing and speedy drug and fluid resuscitation. While en route to the emergency department, IV access is usually attempted; in children under 2 years of age, it is often unsuccessful. In these circumstances, IO cannulation in the field may be considered.

Needles may be inserted in either the distal femur or the proximal tibia (Chapters 46 and 47). The method is safe, reliable, and effective. Yet, complications are possible. Again, well-designed quality assurance mechanisms for on-line, prospective, and retrospective medical control must assure appropriate field use of this technique.

Extensive experience with the IO approach supports its usefulness for delivery of most ALS drugs.[9] Indeed, IO drugs and fluids are quickly becoming a crucial ingredient of most pediatric emergency care systems. However, as with endotracheal drugs, pharmacokinetic data and flow-volume data for children are lacking. Important missing data include efficacy of volume resuscitation via the IO route in traumatic shock; IO pharmacokinetics for ALS drugs in nonperfusing patients; and safety on a short- and long-term basis.

EMERGENCY DEPARTMENT APPROACH TO PEDIATRIC RESUSCITATION

Once the child in full arrest arrives in the emergency department, a calm, prepared team with a designated leader must assume care. A pocket-size or wall-mounted guide to age-adjusted weights, endotracheal tube sizes, blood pressures, heart rates, and respiratory rates, as well as exact drug doses per kilogram, will help avoid common errors of management (Table 44-1). Drugs and fluids must be delivered precisely, in proper sequence.

Airway and ventilation/oxygenation are assured by endotracheal intubation, or careful evaluation of field-placed endotracheal tubes. A nasogastric tube is inserted in the child's stomach and the contents evacuated. Efficacy of closed chest massage is assessed, and a cardiac monitor inspected for rhythm. Coun-

Table 44-1 Pediatric Resuscitation: Age-Adjusted Normal Values

Age	Mean Wt in Kg	Minimum Systolic Blood Pressure	Normal Heart Rate	Normal Respiratory Rate	Endotracheal Tube Size
Premature	2.5	40	120–170	40–60	2.5–3.0
Term	3.5	50	100–170	40–60	3.0–3.5
3 mo	6	50	100–170	30–50	3.5
6 mo	8	60	100–170	30–50	4.0
1 yr	10	65	100–170	30–40	4.0
2 yr	13	65	100–160	20–30	4.5
4 yr	15	70	80–130	20	5.0
6 yr	20	75	70–115	16	5.5
8 yr	25	80	70–110	16	6.0
10 yr	30	85	60–105	16	6.5
12 yr	40	90	60–100	16	7.0

tershock is then administered immediately for asystole, ventricular fibrillation, ventricular tachycardia, or SVT, as previously outlined. Access is established by IV or IO technique. The sequence of drug delivery then follows a set algorithm (Table 44-2).

Epinephrine (1:10,000) is administered at 0.01 mg/kg endotracheally, IV, or IO. If there is no response after the first dose, we double the dose, then repeat the bolus every 5 minutes. (Higher doses may be required endotracheally.) Epinephrine is the most useful drug in cardiac arrest because of its established alpha-adrenergic property of increasing aortic diastolic pressure and critical coronary artery perfusion.

Isoproterenol hydrochloride, on the other hand, once part of the resuscitation pharmacopoeia, is no longer used in cardiac arrest. Its beta-adrenergic reduction of aortic diastolic pressure reduces coronary perfusion and diminishes likelihood of survival.

Sodium bicarbonate has historically enjoyed wide usage in cardiac arrests to treat metabolic acidosis—a condition purported to decrease cardiac function, lower fibrillation threshold, and attenuate pressor response to exogenous catecholamines. However, recent investigations have seriously questioned its routine use, especially at high doses (Chapters 43 and 45).

Detrimental effects from bicarbonate therapy in humans are well recognized: hyperosmolality, hypernatremia, hypokalemia, and hypocalcemia occur, as well as leftward shift of the oxyhemoglobin dissociation curve and

Table 44-2 Pediatric Resuscitation Drug Sequence

Drug	Dose	Route	Special Considerations
Defibrillation	2 watt-sec/kg 1 watt-sec/kg 0.25 watt-sec/kg	for for for	ventricular fibrillation ventricular tachycardia SVT
Epinephrine, U.S.P. (1:10,000) 10 mL syringe = 1 mg	0.01 mg/kg	Endotracheal Intravenous Intraosseous*	Double if no response Consider constant infusion
NaHCO$_3$ (1 mEq/mL) 10 mL = 1 ampule	1 mEq/kg; then, 0.5 mEq/kg	Intravenous Intraosseous*	Only after intubation Use caution when pH > 7.15. Do not overdose
Atropine sulfate (0.1 mg/mL) 10 mL syringe = 1 mg	0.02 mg/kg	Endotracheal* Intravenous Intraosseous*	Minimum dose = 0.1 mg
Dopamine hydrochloride (5 mL ampule = 200 mg)	5–20 μg/kg/min	Intravenous Intraosseous*	Use > 20 μg/kg/min for alpha effect.
D25W	2 mL/kg	Intravenous Intraosseous*	Check Chemstrip or Dextrostik first.
Naloxone 1 mL ampule = 0.4 mg	0.01 mg/kg	Endotracheal Intravenous Intraosseous*	Opiate antagonist. Many recommend higher dose (0.1 mg/kg/dose).
Bretylium 10 mL ampule = 500 mg	5 mg/kg; then, 10 mg/kg	Intravenous Intraosseous*	Best with ventricular fibrillation
Lidocaine hydrochloride, 2% 5 mL syringe = 100 mg	1 mg/kg; then, 20–50 μg/kg/ min	Endotracheal Intravenous Intraosseous*	Best with ventricular tachycardia; seizures common after 3 mg/kg

*Limited experience.

reduction of tissue oxygen delivery. In addition, metabolic alkalosis from overuse of bicarbonate—a frequent complication of resuscitation into children—may be more harmful than metabolic acidosis. One human resuscitation study[10] showed a 45% survival with pH 7.15 to 7.35; 65% survival with pH 7.35 to 7.45; and 25% with pH 7.55 or greater.

The prudent clinician must exercise great caution in routine bicarbonate usage during resuscitation. Certainly, *before any bicarbonate is administered, adequate ventilation by endotracheal tube is imperative*. Possible candidates for bicarbonate include unwitnessed in-hospital cardiac arrests; out-of-hospital arrests with prolonged time (greater than 10 minutes) to ALS; and nonperfusing patients with arterial pH less than 7.15, and pCO_2 less than 40. When any of the criteria are present, we administer 1 mEq/kg of bicarbonate, and further doses at 0.5 mEq/kg every 10 minutes as needed. Obviously, objective clinical data in this critical area are sorely needed, both to define an optimal pH range for cardiac and cerebral resuscitation and to establish accurate methodologies for measuring tissue level acid-base status.

Atropine sulfate is indicated in the child with asystole or sinus bradycardia. A dose of 0.02 mg/kg is suggested, with a minimal dose of 0.1 mg to avoid paradoxical central medullary vagal stimulation and exacerbation of bradyasystolic rhythm. Although atropine may undergo revised use in adults in asystole—since recent clinical studies failed to show effectiveness in this setting—the drug is still indicated in children. As noted earlier, infants may have a predominance of parasympathetic regulation of myocardial function, which possibly predisposes to bradycardia.

Calcium administration is no longer advised by current ALS guidelines. Use of calcium in pediatric resuscitation developed largely from anecdotal experience in intraoperative open-heart patients, in varying degrees of cardiac collapse, who also received epinephrine. These special circumstances are quite disparate from the cardiac arrest in the emergency department. Blinded, prospective, randomized clinical trials in adults have not shown value for calcium in arrest management.[11] Possible exceptions are patients with specific metabolic disturbances: hypocalcemia, hyperkalemia, hypermagnesemia.

A principal concern with routine calcium administration during resuscitation is neuronal and, possibly, cardiac injury. Our model for brain cell death after cardiac arrest has two phases: the anoxic-ischemic phase, followed by the reperfusion phase, when return of spontaneous circulation is achieved. An important revelation of recent investigations of neuropathophysiology is that most brain cell injury develops during the reperfusion phase.

Calcium is among a host of vascular and chemical factors that mediate this reperfusion injury. (Other toxic mediators include free iron and oxidative free radicals.) Rapid entry of calcium ions intracellularly, through membranes damaged during the anoxic-ischemic phase, eventuates in calcium overload and cellular dysfunction.[12] Indeed, a clear causal relationship is now established between intracellular calcium intoxication and cell death. Vulnerability to postischemic calcium influx is greater in selected tissues; and myocardial cells may also be especially susceptible. Known additional practical problems with calcium are its interactions with digitalis glycoside and bicarbonate, as well as increased frequency of ventricular fibrillation.

Therefore, unless future experimental models establish benefit to long-term outcome from calcium administration, this agent should be withheld from the pharmacologic sequence in pediatric resuscitation. The exception is the child with a suspected metabolic disturbance amenable to calcium therapy, particularly hyperkalemia.

CONCLUSION

As our techniques and preparedness for pediatric CPR become increasingly refined, we must apply similar vigor to development of methods for brain resuscitation of children. Trials in adults with calcium channel blockers, iron chelators, and free radical scavengers are underway, or in planning. Results from these studies and from appropriate animal investigations must be applied to organized, prospective, collaborative trials in children. The specter of the neurologically disabled child postresuscitation should motivate ongoing modifications of ALS to enhance brain salvage. Last, future ALS guidelines might also address the difficult *ethical* dilemma posed by the resuscitated child who regains cardiovascular function, but is brain dead.

REFERENCES

1. American Heart Association Pediatric advanced life support standards and guidelines for cardiopulmonary resuscitation (CPR) and emergency cardiac care (ECC). *JAMA* 1986; 255:2905–2989.

2. Walsh CK, Krongrad E: Terminal cardiac electrical activity in pediatric patients. *Am J Cardiol* 1983;51:557–561.

3. Friesen RM, Duncan P, Tweed WA, et al: Appraisal of pediatric cardiopulmonary resuscitation. *Can Med Assoc J* 1982;126:1055–1058.

4. Eisenberg M, Bergner L, Hallstrom A: Epidemiology of cardiac arrest and resuscitation in children. *Ann Emerg Med* 1983;12:672–674.

5. Nichols DG, Kettrick RG, Swedlow DB, et al: Factors influencing outcome of cardiopulmonary resuscitation in children. *Pediatr Emerg Care* 1986;2:1–5.

6. Ewy CA: Ventricular fibrillation masquerading as asystole. *Ann Emerg Med* 1984; 13:811–812.

7. Seidel J: Emergency medical services and the pediatric patient. Are the needs being met? II. Training and equipping emergency medical services providers for pediatric emergencies. *Pediatrics* 1986;78:808–812.

8. Ludwig S, Kettrick RG, Parker M: Pediatric cardiopulmonary resuscitation. *Clin Pediatr* 1984;23:71–75.

9. Rossetti VA, Thompson BM, Miller J, et al: Intraosseous infusion: An alternative route of pediatric intravascular access. *Ann Emerg Med* 1985;14:885–888.

10. Weil MH, Ruiz CE, Michaels S, et al: Acid-base determinants of survival after cardiopulmonary resuscitation. *Crit Care Med* 1985;13:888.

11. Stueven H, Thompson BM, Aprahamian C, et al: Use of calcium in prehospital cardiac arrests. *Ann Emerg Med* 1983;12:136–139.

12. Reempts JA, Borgers M: Ischemic brain injury and cell calcium: Morphologic and therapeutic aspects. *Ann Emerg Med* 1985;14:736–742.

45. Calcium Chloride and Sodium Bicarbonate in Treating Cardiac Arrest: Should There Really Be a Controversy?

Richard W. Talley, MD

Currently recommended procedures for advanced life support (ALS) in the pediatric age group are largely based on a small number of legitimate laboratory and clinical studies to guide the resuscitator.[1] This is no doubt because of the relative infrequency of pediatric arrests (about 1 in 5,000 to 7,000 emergency department admissions).

The underlying mechanism of cardiac arrest is markedly different in children than that noted in adults. Children arrest from hypoxic/hypercarbic events (sudden infant death syndrome, near-drowning, suffocation, child abuse, etc.); adults suffer cardiac arrest because of ventricular dysrhythmias secondary to an ischemic cardiac event if thoraco-abdominal trauma arrest victims are excluded. Despite the seeming resiliency of children to various calamities, when the process ultimately leads to cardiac (as opposed to isolated respiratory) arrest, the rhythm is almost always bradyasystolic and the outcome fatal (Table 45-1). In contrast, comparing these data to the 20%-60% survival for the nontrauma adult arrest victim makes it obvious that a great deal of study is required to improve the survival of the pediatric cardiac arrest victim.

CALCIUM CHLORIDE

Pathophysiology

Calcium is critical to the maintenance of homeostasis in the human organism. It is a mediator of excitation-contraction coupling, enzyme regulation via the second messenger concept, and endocytosis and exocytosis.[7] Calcium has a central role in myocardial ischemia and myocardial damage during cardiac arrest.[8,9]

356

Table 45-1 Cardiac Arrest Rhythms in Children

Author	Number of Patients	Asystole	Survival from Asystole
Rosenberg (1984)[2]	26	90%	12.5%
Gillis et al (1982)[3]	42	90%	10%
Eisenberg et al (1983)[4]	119	77%	4%
Torphy et al (1984)[5]	91	91%	0%
Friesen et al (1982)[6]	66	80%	3%

Calcium balance primarily affects bone, muscle, and nerve function. Proper functioning of muscle fibers depends on a precise balance of ionized calcium in the cytosol. The coupling and uncoupling of actin and myosin fibers to cause contraction and relaxation occur at this level. The entry of calcium is through voltage-dependent calcium ion channels, and its extrusion is via the Na^+/Ca^{++} exchanger; interference in either mechanism affects contraction.[9] This latter mechanism is energy dependent via adenosine triphosphate (ATP) production, which is markedly reduced under conditions of cardiac arrest.

During a period of global anoxia as in a cardiac arrest, substrate (oxygen and glucose) is absent because circulation stops. Cell membrane disruption occurs, and calcium (and other ions) can freely enter the cell. During reperfusion (resuscitation), a low flow state (approximately 10% of normal coronary and carotid artery flow) occurs, and further intracellular damage may occur because of the production of oxygen-free radicals, hydroxyl ions, and ferrous ions. The interaction between calcium ions and oxygen-free radicals leads to damage of the mitochondrial electron transport chain and irreversible cellular death.[10]

Clinical Experience

Before 1985, AHA had recommended calcium administration in electro-mechanical dissociation (EMD) and asystole.[11] Its use in asystole was based largely on observations in the operating theatre of the stimulant effect of calcium on the flaccid heart. This was reported by Kay and Blalock[12] in 1951 in a group of four pediatric cardiac patients. However, its validity is questionable; there were too many unreported variables—potassium levels, volume of citrated (and hence hypocalcemic) blood used, monitored rhythms, etc.

Four clinical studies investigated the use of calcium in asystole—unfortunately, none of them included pediatric cases (Table 45-2). None of the 289 patients given calcium survived although the rhythm was at least successfully converted transiently in some; only one not given calcium and in documented

Table 45-2 Clinical Outcome of Asystolic Patients Related to Use of Calcium

Author (Year)	Number of Patients	Outcome in Patients Given Calcium	No Calcium
Stueven et al,[13] 1983	129	success 8/105 survival 0/105	8/24
Harrison and Amey,[14] 1983	52	success 0/52 survival 0/52	———
Stempien et al,[9] 1986	93 (includes EMD)*	success ? survival 0/93 (includes EMD)	4/17 (includes EMD)
Stueven et al,[15] 1985**	73	success 3/39 survival 0/39	1/34 0/34

*Electromechanical dissociation
**Prospective study

asystole survived. The conclusion of these studies is that asystole is a fatal terminal rhythm whose outcome is unaltered by calcium.

The outcome of EMD is similar. However, EMD is a common presentation in several processes; some are reversible, others are not:

Reversible Causes of EMD	(Usually) Irreversible Causes of EMD
Hypovolemia	Massive myocardial infarction
Tension pneumothorax	Myocardial rupture
Pericardial tamponade	Massive pulmonary embolus
Severe acidosis	

Few studies in the literature report autopsy findings, and most exclude trauma; in interpreting the role of calcium it must be assessed that reversible causes were dealt with appropriately. The results comparing groups who received calcium and those who did not are summarized in Table 45-3. Of 386 patients reported, there were 10 survivors (2.6%), and only 1 of 230 given calcium survived. Although there was methodologic variability among the studies, the results were uniformly dismal.

Stueven et al[16] reported a subset of patients with widened QRS (greater than 0.12 msec), peaked T waves, or elevated ST segments who seemed to respond better to calcium (20%) than did the group in general (17%). In fact, the only responders to calcium were in this group despite the fact that none was hyperkalemic, and only one was hypocalcemic.

Table 45-3 Clinical Outcome of Patients with EMD Related to Use of Calcium

Author	Number of Patients	Outcome in Patients Given	
		Calcium	No Calcium
Stueven et al,[13] 1983	81	success 10/63 (16%) survival 0/63 (0%)	8/18 (44%) 4/18 (22%)
Harrison and Amey,[14] 1983	119 (no statement that trauma was excluded)	success 13/119 (11%) survival 1/119 (<1%)	
Stempien et al,[9] 1986	93 (includes asystole)	success 0 (0%) survival 0 (0%)	4/17 (22%) 0/17 (0%)
Stueven et al,[16] 1985*	93	success 8/48 (17%) survival category not stated	2/42 (5%)

*Prospective study

Calcium has not been shown to be beneficial in cardiac resuscitation, but the rhythms it is used for are associated with a distressingly poor survival rate. In the nontrauma victim without a reversible etiology, these rhythms may be terminal, and the focus must be on preventing asystole or EMD. It must however be remembered that calcium does have specific indications in the resuscitation of children:

- hyperkalemia (as in dialysis patients)
- hypocalcemia (as in long-term ICU patients)
- calcium channel blocker overdose
- fluoride poisoning (fluoride removes calcium)
- hypermagnesemia.

Another factor in evaluating the role of calcium in the outcome of arrest victims is the impact on cerebral function and protection. Calcium appears to be the catalyst in the formation of superoxide radicals, which in combination with the ubiquitous ferric ion and products of anaerobic metabolism produce perferoxyl compounds that cause cell membrane destruction by lipid peroxidation.[17,18] The needless addition of extraneous calcium in this setting can only accelerate cellular destruction.

Specific studies on the use of calcium in the pediatric age group are limited; published adult studies with few exceptions fail to show any benefit. The potential for enhancing further cell damage by using calcium is present and must also be considered.

SODIUM BICARBONATE

Experimental and clinical evidence mandate a reassessment of the routine use of sodium bicarbonate as therapy for the metabolic acidosis of cardiac arrest.

Current AHA guidelines recommend its limited use: ". . . may be used in the patient with prolonged cardiac arrest, or in an unstable hemodynamic state with documented metabolic acidosis."[1] Sodium bicarbonate should be used "if at all" only after proven modalities such as defibrillation, compressions, ventilation, epinephrine, and antidysrhythmics have been used (a sequence that should take about 10 minutes). "Thereafter, bicarbonate, although not recommended, may be used at the discretion of the team leader."[1] This is quite a change from 10 years ago when sodium bicarbonate was given to the arrest victim without hesitation and certainly every 5 minutes.

Acidosis has historically been considered to have an undesirable physiologic impact because it depresses myocardial contractility, decreases the threshold for ventricular fibrillation, impairs normal cardiac automaticity, and blocks the cardioaccelerator and vasopressor action of catecholamine. These alterations are, however, more dramatic in vitro than in vivo and may be inconsequential in the early moments of a cardiac arrest, when oxygenation, ventilation, and administration of epinephrine are initiated.

In the pediatric age group, acidosis is almost exclusively respiratory. In the adult populations studied,[19] if the decreased pH is corrected for the elevated $PaCO_2$, then it falls well within the physiologic range.

In experimental hypoxic lactic acidosis in which the arterial pCO_2 is maintained at normal values, the administration of sodium bicarbonate *lowered* arterial pH.[20] The combination of hypoxia and hypercapnia (classic findings in respiratory arrest) is responsible for the acidosis in cardiac arrest; the treatment is oxygenation and ventilation, not sodium bicarbonate. Without adequate removal of CO_2 (ventilation), intracellular pH falls rapidly.

Our inability to measure changes readily at the cellular level may confuse the impact of our therapeutic interventions. Weil et al[21] showed that the arterial pH, pCO_2, and bicarbonate deficit obtained from an arterial blood gas specimen do not correlate with mixed venous values, which more accurately reflect intracellular physiology. In fact, therapy with sodium bicarbonate raises mixed venous pCO_2 while lowering its pH, and this sequence has been postulated clinically in the cerebrospinal fluid. The latter finding has been termed paradoxical, and yet it is quite easily explained by the permeability of cell membranes to carbon dioxide as opposed to bicarbonate.

If the benefits of sodium bicarbonate are unclear, its detriments are better defined: Sodium bicarbonate does not improve the ability to defibrillate experimental animals; shifts the redox state of oxyhemoglobin causing it to bind oxygen more tightly, thus inhibiting oxygen release to hypoxic cells; causes hyperosmolality, which may contribute to mortality; creates hypernatremia, which may induce volume overload; creates an intracellular acidosis; induces adverse effects of extracellular acidosis; worsens mixed venous acidosis; and may inactivate simultaneously administered catecholamines.[22] These examples seem more than adequate to cause a reappraisal of our use of sodium bicarbonate.

In addition, a clinical study[23] of pH determinants of survival after cardiopulmonary resuscitation shows no difference in survival between patients with an initial arterial pH of 7.15 *v* a pH of 7.55. An initial or subsequent pH of 7.60 or greater, however, is associated with 100% mortality, thus underscoring the danger of alkalemia.

Sodium bicarbonate may be beneficial in ameliorating the effects of hyperkalemia or transiently correcting a hypo-osmolar state. Furthermore, metabolic acidosis may require specific treatment. If adequate oxygenation, ventilation, and circulation fail, then other drugs may be of benefit. Currently, researchers are exploring dichloracetate and tromethamine, two non-CO_2 generating buffers, as alternatives to sodium bicarbonate.

Acidosis in cardiac arrest is predominantly, if not exclusively, a problem with ventilation and oxygenation and should be so treated. *If* after 10 minutes of appropriately administered ALS, reversal of acidosis by pharmacotherapy is deemed necessary, then any detriments of acidosis must be balanced against the risks of sodium bicarbonate. Hopefully, more satisfactory agents will be developed; in the meantime it seems prudent to exercise great caution and restraint in reaching for sodium bicarbonate.

CONCLUSION

Two recent changes in the recommendations regarding resuscitation are:

1. Calcium use should be avoided except in extremely unusual circumstances as it contributes to excessive mortality.
2. Sodium bicarbonate should be withheld for the first 10 minutes after ALS measures are instituted and used only sparingly to treat severe metabolic acidosis, and even then with no assurance of improving outcome.

Much more research remains to be done before we can clearly make recommendations, but other modalities such as new CPR techniques, allopurinol, calcium channel blockers, and desferroxamine may eventually become part of our approach.

REFERENCES

1. American Heart Association: Standards and guidelines for cardiopulmonary resuscitation and emergency cardiac care. *JAMA* 1986;255:2843–2989.

2. Rosenberg N: Pediatric cardiopulmonary arrest in the emergency department. *Am J Emerg Med* 1984;2:497–499.

3. Gillis J, Dickson D, Rieder M, et al: Results of inpatient pediatric resuscitation. *Crit Care Med* 1986;14:469–471.

4. Eisenberg M, Bergner L, Hallstrom A: Epidemiology of cardiac arrest and resuscitation in children. *Ann Emerg Med* 1983;12:672–674.

5. Torphy DE, Minder MG, Thompson BM: Cardiorespiratory arrest and resuscitation of children. *Am J Dis Child* 1984;138:1099–1102.

6. Friesen RM, Duncan P, Tweed WA, et al: Appraisal of pediatric cardiopulmonary resuscitation. *Can Med Assoc J* 1982;126:1055–1058.

7. Rasmussen H: The calcium messenger system. *N Engl J Med* 1986;314:1094–1101, 1160–1170.

8. Cheung JY, Bonventre JV, Malis CD, et al: Calcium and ischemic injury. *N Engl J Med* 1986;314:1670–1676.

9. Stempien A, Katz AM, Messineo FC: Calcium and cardiac arrest. *Ann Int Med* 1986;105:603–606.

10. McCord JM: Oxygen-derived free radicals in post ischemic tissue injury. *N Engl J Med* 1985;312:159–163.

11. *Textbook of Advanced Cardiac Life Support*. Dallas, American Heart Association, 1981.

12. Kay JH, Blalock A: The use of calcium chloride in the treatment of cardiac arrest in patients. *Surg Gynecol Obstet* 1951;93:97–102.

13. Stueven H, Thompson BH, Aprahamian C, et al: Use of calcium in pre-hospital cardiac arrest. *Ann Emerg Med* 1983;12:136–139.

14. Harrison EE, Amey BD: The use of calcium in cardiac resuscitation. *Am J Emerg Med* 1983;3:267–273.

15. Stueven H, Thompson BH, Aprahamian C, et al: Lack of effectiveness of calcium chloride in refractory asystole. *Ann Emerg Med* 1984;13:387.

16. Stueven H, Thompson BH, Aprahamian C, et al: The effectiveness of calcium chloride in refractory electromechanical dissociation. *Ann Emerg Med* 1985;14:626–629.

17. White BC, Wiegenstein JG, Winegge CD: Brain ischemic anoxia. *JAMA* 1984;251:1586–1590.

18. Krause GS, Joyce KM, Nayini NR, et al: Cardiac arrest and resuscitation: Brain iron delocalization during reperfusion. *Ann Emerg Med* 1985;14:1037–1043.

19. Ornato JP, Gonzalez ER, Coyne MR, et al: Arterial pH in out-of-hospital cardiac arrest. *Am J Emerg Med* 1985;3:498–502.

20. Graf H: Evidence of a detrimental effect of bicarbonate therapy in hypoxic lactic acidosis. *Science* 1985;227:754–756.

21. Weil MH, Grundler W, Yamaguchi M, et al: Arterial blood gases fail to reflect acid-base status during cardiopulmonary resuscitation. *Crit Care Med* 1985;13:884–885.

22. Stactpoole PW: Lactic acidosis: The case against bicarbonate therapy. *Ann Int Med* 1986;105:276–279.

23. Weil MH, Ruiz CE, Michaels S, et al: Acid-base determinants of survival after cardiopulmonary resuscitation. *Crit Care Med* 1985;13:888–891.

Section 25

Vascular Access

The need for secure venous access in the critically ill child has led to the resurgence of the intraosseous (IO) infusion technique. Although there has been tremendous enthusiasm for what promises to be a major technique during resuscitation, several cautions are needed. The IO route should be used only when other access is not quickly achieved and fluids or drugs may be lifesaving. It should be considered a temporizing measure while a venous cutdown or other route is established.

Pharmacodynamic and histologic studies must further explore not only the clinical efficacy of drugs and fluids but the drug levels achieved. There is little or no long-term follow-up to show the true safety of this technique with respect to its effects on bone marrow, hematopoiesis, and bone growth. Alpha-adrenergic agents may theoretically lead to ischemic areas and subsequent embolization.

Intraosseous infusion is appropriate in life-threatened children; the risks and benefits require further delineation.

46. Vascular Access in Children: Alternative Routes

John D.G. Neufeld, MD

In children under 3 years of age, venous access may pose an important obstacle to initiating care. One study[1] showed that 6% of children in shock or cardiopulmonary arrest could not have venous access established; 24% required 10 minutes or more to achieve access.

Although no single technique is uniformly reliable and rapid, it is essential to be familiar with alternatives to venous cannulation. The optimal choice and rationale for selection becomes a matter of tremendous controversy.

NONVENOUS ACCESS

The subcutaneous or intramuscular routes are rapid modes of access. However, poor circulation, drug characteristics, tissue injury, and pain limit their use. Intubation provides immediate access for five drugs: (1) epinephrine hydrochloride, (2) atropine sulfate, (3) lidocaine hydrochloride, (4) naloxone hydrochloride, and (5) diazepam (Valium).[2] The weight-specific dose should be diluted to a total volume of 3 to 5 mL of sterile water and administered by the endo- (or naso-) tracheal tube. Manual ventilation disperses the drug over the 65 m^2 of alveoli surface area where absorption occurs.

PERIPHERAL VEINS

Cannulating a peripheral vein should be attempted first, but may be difficult to achieve because of vascular collapse, increased body fat, burns, edematous or traumatized extremities, or the small size of the vessels. Even if there is not a visible vein, cannulation may be attempted at defined sites because of the constancy of the anatomic position. These include the external jugular vein,

365

the median cephalic and basilic veins in the antecubital fossa, the greater saphenous vein anterior to the medial malleolus, and the fifth interdigital vein between the fourth and fifth metacarpal heads on the dorsum of the hand.

Venous access can be achieved in as many as 95% of patients using the peripheral route, but in one study[3] only 24% were cannulated within 1.5 minutes.

A modification of the peripheral vein access technique was developed by Seldinger.[4] This approach allows percutaneous catheterization with a small needle through which a guidewire is placed.[4] Advancing the needle with the bevel upward reduces the risk of perforation of the posterior venous wall. The vein may be dilated, once punctured, by gently flushing 1 to 2 mL of saline through the catheter before advancing it.[4]

The external jugular vein is particularly useful and is frequently overlooked in the younger child, whether the traditional or guidewire technique is used. The Trendelenburg's position helps distend the external jugular vein to facilitate cannulation.

CENTRAL VEINS

Central venous access via the femoral, internal jugular, or subclavian approaches should be employed last or concurrently with attempts at venous cutdowns because of the potentially serious complications of these techniques. The traditional anatomic approaches are used, but the landmarks are more difficult to identify. Using the guidewire method for cannulation of the internal jugular or femoral vein reduces the risks. For subclavian veins, usually performed using a catheter-through-needle device, the needle must be inserted and withdrawn as a straight line; searching for the vein beneath the clavicle is dangerous. The catheter should never be withdrawn through the needle because of the danger of shearing.

Confirmation of placement is essential. An x-ray film is mandatory to document placement and exclude complications. Lowering the administration set below the level of the head should produce a backflow of blood through the catheter.

Although a high success rate for central venous cannulation in children was noted in controlled settings, the emergency environment may be different.[5-7] Percutaneous femoral lines were successfully cannulated only 37% of the time in one report.[3] Emergency cannulation of the superior vena cava was successful in one study[8] in two-thirds of patients.

Complications do exist. Femoral puncture can lead to local bleeding, arterial puncture, septic hip, limb gangrene, femoral artery or vein thrombosis, and peritoneal perforation.[3,9,10] Problems with the superior vena cava and internal jugular venous approaches may include pneumothorax, hemothorax, tension pneumothorax, arterial puncture, hydrothorax, brachial plexus injury, Horner's syndrome, air embolism, catheter embolization, and myocardial perforation. The reported incidence is variable, ranging from less than 1% to more than 10%.[11]

Intravenous (IV) access by a central vein does not guarantee quicker fluid infusion unless a larger diameter catheter is inserted. Fluid flow rates are related to the diameter and length of the catheter.

VENOUS CUTDOWN

A traditional approach to the child requiring rapid venous access in whom the percutaneous route is unsuccessful is the cutdown of the saphenous vein at either the ankle or the saphenofemoral junction. Both sites are away from the airway and resuscitation and carry a low risk of complications. Familiarity with venous landmarks and specific surgical skills is essential. Kanter et al[3] noted an 81% success rate, but long delays occurred. The median time for a successful cutdown was 8 minutes with a range of 2 to 40 minutes; others[1] reported an average time of 24 minutes.

INTRAOSSEOUS ACCESS

Bone marrow transfusions were first shown in 1915,[12] the technique being popularized in the 1940s by Tocantins and O'Neill.[13] Interest faded with the development of IV lines in the 1950s. Renewed interest in the intraosseous (IO) line has surfaced with the necessity for rapid and reliable access during resuscitation.

Unlike venous access, intramedullary vessels are supported by bone architecture and are therefore accessible without risk of damaging critical structures. Intraosseous infusions can be used in children up to 3 to 5 years of age because their tibial marrow is still actively producing red blood cells. This allows access into the sinusoids and ultimately the large medullary venous channels, the nutrient and emissary veins, and finally the systemic venous circulation. The marrow is infiltrated with fat cells by 5 years of age; it is presumably less effective in handling fluid administration thereafter (Figure 46-1).

Though specialized bone marrow needles are available, a plain, 18-gauge (optimally 1.5-inch) spinal needle with stylet works well. After thorough cleansing of the infusion site, the skin and periosteum may be anesthetized; in obtunded or moribund patients this latter step is unnecessary. The spinal needle is inserted perpendicular to the skin or at a 45° angle away from the epiphyseal plate, the latter preventing administration of fluids into the growth

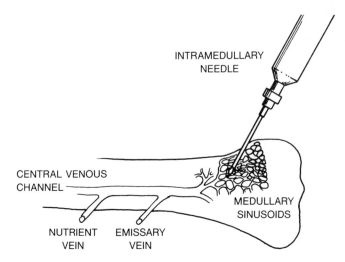

INTRAMEDULLARY
NEEDLE

CENTRAL VENOUS
CHANNEL

MEDULLARY
SINUSOIDS

NUTRIENT   EMISSARY
VEIN   VEIN

Figure 46-1 Venous drainage from marrow of a long bone with intramedullary needle in place.

plate. The proximal tibia or distal femur is preferred. Most experience exists with the tibial tuberosity, using a site one to two finger breadths below the tibial tuberosity. The femoral site located 2 to 3 cm above the epicondyle necessitates inserting the needle through the suprapatellar bursa and the quadriceps femoris muscle (Figure 46-2).

A screwing motion is used to push the needle through the cortex into the marrow. A sudden and definite give is sensed once the marrow space is entered. The position can be confirmed by aspirating marrow into a syringe, as well as by the firm position of the needle. Crystalloid and drugs can then be infused without resistance.

Volume resuscitation has been done with blood, normal saline, and plasma.[13–16] Under 300 mmHg of pressure, 41 mL/min of crystalloid has been infused.[14] Manually forced infusion with a syringe can generate flows approaching 200 mL/min. Infusion can be achieved relatively painlessly with a gravity drip infusion, but is painful when forcefully injected.

With fixed infusion rates, the IO route will correct shock as quickly as peripheral and central lines. Though more volume can be given through a central or peripheral vein, a substantial percentage of the patient's circulating volume can be restored in the time period required to secure direct venous access. Large total fluid volumes can be given. As much as 42 L have been administered through an IO line.[17]

A multitude of medications have been administered through IO lines. These include glucose, epinephrine, antibiotics, digitalis glycoside, heparin, insulin

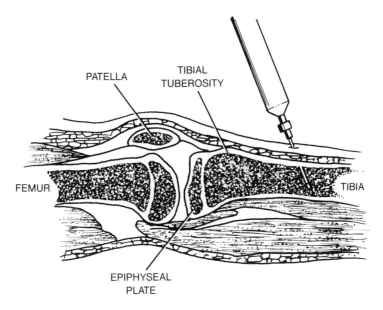

PATELLA

TIBIAL
TUBEROSITY

FEMUR

TIBIA

EPIPHYSEAL
PLATE

Figure 46-2 Intraosseous insertion of needle.

antitoxin, antiserum, morphine sulfate, sodium bicarbonate, diazepam, physostigmine salicylate, and vitamins.[16,18] Circulation times for drugs given by the IO route are comparable with those from direct venous lines.[19]

Heinild et al[16] recorded 982 IO infusions with only 18 failures and 5 complications. Kanter et al[3] had an 83% success rate with IO attempts.

The most serious complication, although rare, is osteomyelitis. A review of 3,214 infusions noted a rate of less than 1%.[20] Such bone infection is associated with infusion of caustic substances, use in septic patients, and prolonged infusions.[16] Fat embolism has not been reported in children, possibly because of the erythropoietic nature of the young marrow.

Technical complications include subperiosteal infusion, penetration of the needle through the posterior cortex, leakage of fluid from a second puncture site in the bone, compartment syndromes caused by fluid extravasation, and fracture. A case of a needle broken off in the bone caused no ill effects when left embedded for 5 months.[20]

Bone and marrow damage is a major concern of IO infusions. Roentgenographic examinations 1 week after infusion show a small hole in the bone, which disappears over 6 months.[16] Histologic studies have shown no ill effect from dextran or normal saline, but edema and fibrin deposition are associated with 20% calcium chloride, and cell necrosis has been seen with administration of undiluted uroselectan dye. Hypertonic solutions cause shrinkage because of the osmotic effect; isotonic solutions do not appear to cause injury.[21] Long-term complications to the bone marrow and growth plate have not been defined.

Contraindications are infection at the site of the intended puncture; generalized sepsis and proximal limb damage are relative contraindications. These risks may be reduced by removing the IO needle as soon as IV access is secured. Generally, definitive access should be achieved before leaving the emergency department.

The use of IO infusions in the field is not well defined. Emergency medical systems need to weigh the risks of using IO infusions against the benefits. Transport times, degree of difficulty achieving IV access in a given case, patient combativeness, and paramedic skill are just a few of the considerations.

INTRACARDIAC INJECTION

As a last option, intracardiac injection provides vascular access. Complications include cardiac tamponade, coronary artery laceration, myocardial necrosis, and pneumothorax.[22] It may be advisable to perform an open-chest thoracotomy instead.

CONCLUSION

Intravenous access is imperative in the resuscitation of the profoundly ill child. A systematic approach can reduce the delay significantly, optimally within 5 minutes in difficult situations.[2] Initial attempts should focus on percutaneous peripheral venous access. If this is unsuccessful in life-threatening conditions, an IO line should be placed as a temporizing measure for the administration of crystalloid and restricted drugs. Further study is required to explore the impact of such infusions on the bone marrow. Once such a line is established, a definitive route must be secured, either using a cutdown or central line technique. At that time the IO needle should be removed and normal resuscitation efforts continued.

REFERENCES

1. Rossetti V, Thompson BM, Aprahamian C, et al: Difficulty and delay in intravascular access in pediatric arrests. *Ann Emerg Med* 1984;13:406.

2. Ward JT Jr: Endotracheal drug therapy. *Am J Emerg Med* 1983;1:71–82.

3. Kanter RK, Zimmerman JJ, Strauss RH, et al: Pediatric emergency intravenous access. *Am J Dis Child* 1986;140:132–134.

4. Seldinger SI: Catheter replacement of the needle in percutaneous arteriography. *Acta Radiol* 1953;39:368–376.

5. Filston HC, Grant JP: A safer system for percutaneous subclavian venous catheterization in newborn infants. *J Pediatr Surg* 1979;14:564–570.

6. Groff DB, Ahmed N: Subclavian vein catheterization in the infant. *J Pediatr Surg* 1974;9:171–174.

7. Hall DMB, Geefhuysen J: Percutaneous catheterization of the internal jugular vein in infants and children. *J Pediatr Surg* 1977;12:719–722.

8. Irwin G Jr, Fifield G, Clinton J: Emergency catheterization of the superior vena cava in pediatric patients. *Am J Emerg Med* 1984;2:494–496.

9. Asnes RS, Arendar GM: Septic arthritis of the hip: A complication of femoral venipuncture. *Pediatrics* 1966;38:837–841.

10. Nasbeth DC, Jones JE: Gangrene of the lower extremities of infants after femoral venipuncture. *N Engl J Med* 1963;268:1003–1005.

11. Borja AR: Current status of infraclavicular subclavian vein catheterization. *Ann Thorac Surg* 1972;13:615–624.

12. Drinker CK, Drinker KR: A method for maintaining an artificial circulation through the tibia of the dog, with a demonstration of the vasomotor control of the marrow vessels. *Am J Physiol* 1916;40:514–521.

13. Tocantins LM, O'Neill JF: Infusion of blood and other fluids into the circulation via the bone marrow. *Proc Soc Exp Biol Med* 1940;45:782–783.

14. Shoor PM, Berryhill RE, Benumof JL: Intraosseous infusion: Pressure-flow relationships and pharmacokinetics. *J Trauma* 1979;19:772–774.

15. Arbeiter H, Greengard J: Tibial bone marrow infusions in infancy. *J Pediatr* 1944; 25:1–12.

16. Heinild S, Sondergaard T, Tudvad F, et al: Bone marrow infusions in children: Experiences from a thousand infusions. *J Pediatr* 1947;30:400–412.

17. Valdes MM: Intraosseous fluid administration in emergencies. *Lancet* 1977;2:1235–1236.

18. Berg RA: Emergency infusions of catecholamines into bone marrow. *Am J Dis Child* 1984;138:810–811.

19. Spivey WH, Lathers CM, Malone DR, et al: Comparison of intraosseous, central and peripheral routes of sodium bicarbonate administration during CPR in pigs. *Ann Emerg Med* 1985;14:1135–1140.

20. Massey LWC: Bone-marrow infusions: Intratibial and intravenous routes compared. *Br Med J* 1950;2:197–198.

21. Wallden L: On injuries of bone and bone-marrow after intraosseous injections. *Acta Chir Scand* 1947;96:152–162.

22. Schecter DC: Transthoracic epinephrine injection in heart resuscitation is dangerous. *JAMA* 1975;234:1184.

47. Vascular Access in the Child

James B. Besunder, DO
Elizabeth M. Allen, MD

Sites of venous cannulation are divided into peripheral and central locations. Peripheral sites include the superficial veins of the upper and lower extremities, the external jugular vein, and scalp veins. Central sites suitable for cannulation include the femoral, subclavian, and internal jugular veins. Recently, there has been a renewed interest in a third vascular access site for fluid and drug administration, the intraosseous (IO) site.

PERIPHERAL SITES

Peripheral venous catheterization is the access route of choice in most cases. Cannulation of peripheral veins is easily and rapidly accomplished in patients with adequate peripheral circulation. However, in low flow states such as shock or cardiopulmonary arrest, peripheral veins may be collapsed and difficult to cannulate.

The number of drugs and types of fluids that can safely be infused peripherally are also limited. Hypertonic or irritating fluids may cause pain or phlebitis, and certain drugs, such as catecholamines, may cause tissue necrosis if infiltrated into the subcutaneous (SC) tissues. A final drawback to peripheral lines is that they can easily be dislodged, causing SC infiltration.

Peripheral vein catheterization is indicated for the delivery of suitable drugs or fluids to a patient whose circulation is not markedly compromised. It can be used, for example, to treat a seizing patient with anticonvulsants, or a patient with a dysrhythmia with antidysrhythmic agents. Also, patients who are mildly-to-moderately dehydrated can be successfully fluid resuscitated via a peripheral vein.

CENTRAL SITES

In conditions associated with poor peripheral perfusion, such as shock or cardiac arrest, vascular access, particularly in young infants, may be a problem. Under these circumstances central venous catheterization is more easily accomplished than cannulation of a peripheral vein. In a 3-year retrospective review of 66 pediatric emergency department arrests at a children's hospital, Rossetti et al[1] reported that intravenous (IV) access was never achieved in 6% of patients, and that it took more than 10 minutes to secure vascular access in 24%. In addition, 33% of patients eventually required a venous cutdown for access.

Not only can vascular access be achieved in an expedient fashion via the central route allowing rapid fluid administration, but central access also allows rapid delivery of cardiac stimulants to the myocardium in a patient with a failing heart or in full arrest.

Hedges et al[2] confirmed the advantages of central placement in a canine model of cardiopulmonary arrest. They induced cardiac arrest in 13 mongrel dogs and compared drug delivery time via infusion into the superior vena cava *v* infusion into a distal forelimb vein. Drug delivery time was determined by measuring peak and half peak counts over the left ventricle after the injection of technetium[99]-labeled human serum albumin. Time to half peak counts averaged 11 and 84 seconds for central and peripheral injections, respectively. Time to peak counts was also significantly shorter after central administration (118 *v* 258 seconds).

There are several disadvantages to the use of central sites. Since central venous catheterization is not needed frequently in small children, it is difficult for the physician to maintain the level of technical skill required to perform this procedure. Complications are more serious and may occur at a higher rate than with peripheral vein catheterization. Besides complications associated with all venous catheters such as phlebitis, thrombosis, and infection, central venous catheterization is also associated with pneumothorax, hemothorax, air embolism, and injury to adjacent arteries and nerves. These complications may add substantially to the morbidity and even mortality of a patient. Fortunately, not all central venous access sites appear to have the same risk of complications.

Efficacy

Either the superior vena cava via a subclavian or internal jugular approach, or the inferior vena cava, via a femoral approach, can be cannulated. Although data concerning the relative efficacy of these venous routes in children remain scarce, studies[3] in dogs reveal supradiaphragmatic injections achieve faster and higher peak concentrations of drugs than the subdiaphragmatic route during resuscitation. Whether the site of injection in the smaller and differently proportioned pediatric patient is clinically important is not clear and may lend itself to future investigation.

Disadvantages, Complications, and Contraindications

A major disadvantage of the supradiaphragmatic approaches is the lack of operating space around the head and neck of a small child, especially if an artificial airway needs to be established. During cardiopulmonary resuscitation (CPR) it is even more difficult to establish venous access by these routes, and CPR may need to be interrupted until access is established. Placement of central venous lines through the femoral vein obviates these problems.

Although pneumothorax is a potentially serious complication associated with both supradiaphragmatic techniques, Kanter et al[4] recently reported no pneumothoraces in a series of 27 pediatric patients in whom femoral venous catheters were placed.

Arterial puncture or perforation of the vein are complications shared by both the supra- and infradiaphragmatic approaches. Uncontrolled bleeding may result from these complications. However, in contrast to the internal jugular and, particularly, the subclavian sites, direct pressure can be applied to the femoral site to obtain adequate hemostasis. In fact, the supradiaphragmatic sites should be approached with extreme caution in patients with an underlying coagulopathy. Bullous lung disease is another relative contraindication to supradiaphragmatic catheterization because of a greater risk of pneumothorax.

Another complication associated with internal jugular catheterization is Horner's syndrome.[5]

If the first attempt at internal jugular catheterization is unsuccessful and results in hematoma formation, cannulation of the opposite internal jugular should not be attempted since development of a bilateral hematoma could result in airway compromise.

Femoral Venous Catheterization

Femoral venous catheterization is our initial choice for central venous access using a modification of the Seldinger[6] technique. In 1986 alone, we placed more than 150 femoral venous catheters in patients in our pediatric intensive care unit (ICU).

Using the Seldinger technique, Kanter et al[4] reported an overall success rate of 86% in femoral venous catheter placement in 29 pediatric patients with a median time requirement of 5 minutes. Seven of the patients studied were 1 year of age or younger, 10 weighed 10 kg or less, and 14 were in shock at the time of the insertion. In a separate evaluation, the same investigators[7] reported 10 of 27 femoral line attempts were successful in the first 5 minutes of pediatric resuscitations in their emergency department. The results of these studies agree with our experience that the femoral approach allows rapid and easy access to the central venous compartment.

In our experience arterial puncture is the most common complication of this procedure but is easy to recognize and is not associated with notable complications. In the study of Kanter et al,[4] this complication occurred in 14% of patients but was quickly recognized and resulted in no complications. If arterial puncture were to go unrecognized and the artery were to be catheterized, then subsequent infusion of pressor agents could result in ischemic damage to that limb. Other acute complications of this procedure include hematoma of the femoral triangle, retroperitoneal bleeding from inferior vena caval puncture, or bladder or bowel puncture. These complications may be minimized when care is used in catheter placement. Theoretically, puncture of the bowel or bladder would seal spontaneously with negligible soiling of the peritoneum since small-gauge needles are used.

Infection remains the most feared complication of femoral venous catheters. Septic arthritis involving the hip or osteomyelitis of the proximal femur are potential complications that are rarely seen and can be minimized by proper technique. Contamination of the catheter leading to bacteremia or sepsis is the most feared infectious complication. Bozzetti et al[8] prospectively studied 112 adult cancer patients receiving hyperalimentation through central venous catheters. The catheters were used for an average of 21 days; 27% of femoral catheter tips became colonized compared with 25% of subclavian catheters. The incidence of bacteremia or sepsis was not reported according to catheter insertion site. These results were similar to the results reported by Thomas et al,[9] who found a 25% incidence of positive catheter tip cultures in patients with indwelling radial artery catheters compared with 23% in patients with femoral artery catheters. Approximately 7% of patients with central venous catheters at our institution developed bacteremia in 1986 (data unpublished), but no correlation with site of catheter placement was found.

Finally, the most common complication of chronic indwelling femoral catheters in our experience is thrombosis of the inferior vena cava or transient venous obstruction of the extremity related to the catheter. During a prospective study in 74 pediatric patients with indwelling femoral venous catheters, these complications occurred in 8 patients.[4] However, no long-term sequelae resulted from either complication.

In summary, when placed with careful, aseptic technique and cared for meticulously, femoral catheters are safe and effective in delivering drugs and fluids to critically ill children both acutely and long-term.

INTRAOSSEOUS SITE

History

The bone marrow has been recognized as a potential site of vascular access since the 1940s. In 1940 Tocantins[10] performed several experiments on rabbits to evaluate the efficacy of the IO route for the administration of fluids and drugs. In the first study, he removed 20% of the blood volume from each of seven rabbits and then transfused them 24 hours later with a similar volume of whole blood at a rate of 5 to 7 mL/min. Four rabbits recovered their original hemoglobin content by 24 hours, two by 48 hours, and one died during removal of the blood volume. He next induced hypoglycemic seizures in four rabbits by infusing insulin, and then treated them with an IO infusion of 2 to 3 g/kg of 25% or 30% glucose. He documented a rise in blood sugar and resolution of seizures in all four rabbits. Finally, he assessed the rapidity with which fluids reach the central compartment after an IO infusion. He injected a 1% congo red solution into the tibial marrow of a rabbit. Plasma removed from the heart as early as 10 seconds after the injection contained congo red.

Tocantins then reported his experience with the IO route in humans.[11–13] Tocantins and O'Neill[11] reported substantial increases in hemoglobin content and red blood cell counts in seven patients given citrated blood through their bone marrow; two of these patients were children. Then in 1941, Tocantins et al[12] described four patients in circulatory shock who were successfully resuscitated via IO infusions of blood, plasma, crystalloids, and drugs. One patient was a 9-year-old girl who developed hemorrhagic shock after a tonsillectomy. She received 300 mL of whole blood and 200 mL of normal saline in less than 3 hours. Another patient was a 25-year-old woman in coma secondary to diabetic ketoacidosis who was successfully treated with IO infusions of insulin and a 5% glucose solution at 11 mL/min (total of 1,500 mL in 3 hours). Finally a 45-year-old woman without a recordable blood pressure after abdominal surgery was successfully resuscitated with 1,150 mL of blood, plasma, and crystalloids given over 20 minutes. These initial studies established the IO route as an effective means of restoring blood volume and peripheral circulation in adults and suggested that at least some pharmacologic agents can be administered via this route.

One of the first studies evaluating the IO route for infusion of fluids in children was published in 1941. Tocantins et al[13] successfully administered citrated blood to nine infants, 2 days to 19 months of age, via the bone marrow. All infants showed substantial increments in their hematocrit without any untoward effects. Infusion rates ranged from 0.5 to 8 mL/min. In the same paper, they reported the results of a comparison of the action on blood pressure of 0.1 mg epinephrine hydrochloride administered IV and IO to an anesthetized, intubated dog. The response to epinephrine by either route was similar in onset, duration, and intensity.

After these studies, several other reports[14–17] described the safety of IO infusions of fluids in children. The largest of these was the study by Heinild et al[14] who reported their experience with 982 IO infusions in 495 children between the ages of 2 days and 4 years. Fluids and drugs administered included blood, serum, sodium bicarbonate, 50% glucose, antitetanus serum, 30% sodium sulfate, and calcium gluconate. Clinically important complications such as osteomyelitis were rare and may have been related to infusion of hypertonic solutions.

Other reported complications of IO infusions include SC infection or infiltration, and leakage from the puncture site after multiple punctures of the same bone.[16]

With the advent of improved techniques for venous catheterization, IO infusion of agents became less common. This technique has been reintroduced into clinical practice.[18,19] In recent case reports, infants under 1 year of age received various fluids and drugs via the IO route. Since both children died it is difficult to assess the safety or efficacy of the agents administered, but one child[18] appeared to have a transient increase in blood pressure after the infusion of fluids and dobutamine hydrochloride. Other case reports have since purported to show great benefit from the IO administration of fluids and drugs.

Disadvantages

There are several reasons why the IO site is not our first choice for line placement. First, data regarding the safety and efficacy of drugs given by this route are available only for a few drugs and have been used only in a limited number of patients. Secondly, hypodermic or IV needles, which are the most readily available needles for use in an emergency department, should not be used for this technique. Hollow cutting needles without stylets can be obstructed by bone or tissue and rendered ineffective or might cause an embolus consisting of bone fragments or fat. Third, the tibial surface accessible for puncture in a young infant is quite small, and the technique requires considerable skill and experience. Finally, no modern controlled study looking for long-term complications such as osteomyelitis, growth plate deformation, or bone marrow infection has been performed.

In conclusion, the IO route may be a viable alternative when vascular access cannot be readily achieved, particularly when emergent crystalloid or colloid therapy is necessary. However, controlled human studies evaluating the safety and efficacy of commonly used drugs via this route are necessary before routine use of this technique can be advocated.

CONCLUSION

The femoral route is the access port of choice in a critically ill child with cardiovascular compromise. At our institution, residents are quite proficient at this technique after completing a 6-week rotation in the pediatric ICU where this procedure is commonly employed. This technique has proven to be safe, rapid, and easy to perform. In addition, airway stabilization or CPR can continue uninterrupted while the femoral vein is cannulated. When a critically ill pediatric patient arrives, we recommend attempting a peripheral line while a femoral line is being placed. If a peripheral or a femoral line cannot be established within a reasonable amount of time, then we recommend the insertion of an IO line for fluid administration only. During CPR, if necessary, the endotracheal route can be used for the administration of certain drugs such as epinephrine, atropine sulfate, and lidocaine[20] until vascular access is secured. During efficient CPR, cerebral blood flow can usually be adequately maintained for at least 10 minutes. We, therefore, would recommend inserting an IO line if vascular access has not been obtained by 5 minutes. This allows a safety margin of 5 minutes. An IO line even during CPR should be used primarily for fluid administration until a central venous line is established. We feel a standard approach to line placement is paramount. Kanter et al[7] prospectively evaluated the effectiveness of a protocol during pediatric resuscitation similar to ours for IV access. Vascular access was achieved in a median time of 4.5 minutes (range 2 to 10 minutes) in 16 patients for whom the protocol was followed. The median time necessary to establish vascular access in 13 patients who deviated from the protocol was significantly longer (median time 10 minutes; range 2 to 40 minutes).

Prospective studies of efficacy and short- and long-term complications of IO infusions of drugs and fluids in the pediatric population are sorely needed.

REFERENCES

1. Rossetti V, Thompson BM, Aprahamian C, et al: Difficulty and delay in intravascular access in pediatric arrests. *Ann Emerg Med* 1984;13:406.

2. Hedges JR, Barsan WB, Doan LA, et al: Central versus peripheral intravenous routes in cardiopulmonary resuscitation. *Am J Emerg Med* 1984;2:385–390.

3. Dalsey WC, Barsan WG, Joyce SM, et al: Comparison of superior vena caval and inferior vena caval access using a radioisotope technique during normal perfusion and cardiopulmonary resuscitation. *Ann Emerg Med* 1984;13:881–884.

4. Kanter RK, Zimmerman JJ, Strauss RH, et al: Central venous catheter insertion by femoral vein: Safety and effectiveness for the pediatric patient. *Pediatrics* 1986;77:842–847.

5. Cote CJ, Jobes DR, Schwartz AJ, et al: Two approaches to cannulation of a child's internal jugular vein. *Anesthesiology* 1979;50:371–373.

6. Seldinger SI: Catheter replacement of the needle in percutaneous arteriography. *Acta Radiol* 1953;39:368–376.

7. Kanter RK, Zimmerman JJ, Strauss RH, et al: Pediatric emergency intravenous access. *Am J Dis Child* 1986;140:132–134.

8. Bozzetti F, Terno G, Camerini E, et al: Pathogenesis and predictability of central venous catheter sepsis. *Surgery* 1982;91:383–389.

9. Thomas F, Burke JP, Parker J, et al: The risk of infection related to radial vs femoral sites for arterial catheterization. *Crit Care Med* 1983;11:807–812.

10. Tocantins LM: Rapid absorption of substances injected into the bone marrow. *Proc Soc Exp Biol Med* 1940;45:292–296.

11. Tocantins LM, O'Neill JF: Infusion of blood and other fluids into the circulation via the bone marrow. *Proc Soc Exp Biol Med* 1940;45:782–783.

12. Tocantins LM, O'Neill JF, Price AH: Infusions of blood and other fluids via the bone marrow in traumatic shock and other forms of peripheral circulatory failure. *Ann Surg* 1941;114:1085–1092.

13. Tocantins LM, O'Neill JF, Jones HW: Infusions of blood and other fluids via the bone marrow. *JAMA* 1941;117:1229–1234.

14. Heinild S, Sondergaard T, Tudvad F: Bone marrow infusion in childhood. *J Pediatr* 1947;30:400–412.

15. Arbeiter HI, Greengard J: Tibial bone marrow infusions in infancy. *J Pediatr* 1944; 25:1–12.

16. Quilligan JJ, Turkel H: Bone marrow infusion and its complications. *Am J Dis Child* 1946; 71:457–465.

17. Meola F: Bone marrow infusions as a routine procedure in children. *J Pediatr* 1944; 25:13–16.

18. Berg RA: Emergency infusion of catecholamines into bone marrow. *Am J Dis Child* 1984;138:810–811.

19. Glaeser PW, Losek JD: Emergency intraosseous infusions in children. *Am J Emerg Med* 1986;4:34–36.

20. Ward JT Jr: Endotracheal drug therapy. *Am J Emerg Med* 1983;1:71–82.

Section 26

Paralysis before Intubation

Intubation is a crucial aspect of resuscitation; paralysis may facilitate this process. Those who are difficult to intubate as well as children with increased intracranial pressure may benefit from paralysis. The technique obviously requires experience in airway management and careful attention to the personnel and equipment required.

48. Paralysis before Intubation

Dee Hodge III, MD

Controlling the airway and managing respiration are the two basic life support treatments that must be mastered by the emergency physician. Endotracheal intubation is the surest way to protect the airway and assure adequate ventilation in the critically ill pediatric patient. Even in the emergency department, drugs are not administered routinely to facilitate endotracheal intubation. The moribund child needs no pharmacologic aids before intubation.

When to paralyze a patient for intubation is not an easy question to answer; but some situations are often agreed upon. Paralysis is indicated in patients with intractable seizures or increased muscle tone in whom an adequate airway cannot be maintained, coma of central origin requiring treatment of increased intracranial pressure, and head trauma with decreasing level of consciousness and loss of protective airway reflexes.[1]

Patients with a presumed full stomach who require immediate intubation have a decreased risk of aspiration using a "rapid sequence" induction technique. The pediatric patient is more vulnerable to regurgitation and aspiration because of the short length of the esophagus and the higher resting intragastric pressures.[2]

EQUIPMENT AND PERSONNEL

The equipment required include drugs and instruments for performing the procedure as well as devices for monitoring the vital functions of the patient.

The patient should be placed on an adjustable bed or stretcher that can be positioned quickly into Trendelenburg's position if necessary. Continuous ECG monitoring is mandatory, and blood pressure should be measured every 3 to 5 minutes. An intravenous (IV) line should be in place.

381

For the actual intubation, an oxygen source and a bag and mask permitting delivery of 100% oxygen are required. Suction must be available. A complete range of laryngoscopic blades and endotracheal tubes are needed.

Adequate personnel must be present. A clinician skilled in airway management must serve as the airway manager and endoscopist. There must also be someone to administer drugs and perform the Sellick maneuver (cricoid pressure).

PHARMACOLOGIC AGENTS

The rich sensory innervation of the naso-oropharynx, larynx, and trachea necessitates a combination of sedation, analgesia, and anesthesia in addition to muscle relaxation.

Atropine sulfate is used to reduce secretions and for its vagolytic effect, primarily the reversal of bradycardia. The bradycardia is associated with vagal stimulation during intubation as well as being secondary to the use of succinylcholine chloride.

Thiopental sodium, a short-acting barbiturate, is used to decrease level of consciousness and as an amnestic. It has a rapid onset of action, approximately 30 to 50 seconds, and a duration of action of 5 to 10 minutes when given IV. It also has anticonvulsant properties and can decrease cerebral blood flow and cerebral metabolic rate, making it useful in treating closed head injuries. It can sharply decrease blood pressure, limiting its use in the hypotensive patient.

Paralysis is achieved with either succinylcholine or pancuronium bromide injection. Succinylcholine is a depolarizing noncompetitive neuromuscular blocking agent. Onset is rapid (60 to 90 seconds), and the short duration of action (< 10 minutes) is advantageous if intubation is unsuccessful and the patient must be bag-and-mask ventilated. The degree and duration of blockade are determined by the concentration of the drug reaching the neuromuscular junction and the presence of plasma cholinesterase. Increased serum potassium, decreased body temperature, liver disease, malnutrition, or the presence of an aminoglycoside antibiotic all prolong blockade and are relative contraindications to its use. Muscle fasciculations after administration of succinylcholine are mostly a problem in the adolescent patient. Fasciculations increase intragastric, intra-abdominal, and intraocular pressure. Succinylcholine should not be used in patients with trauma to the globe of the eye or glaucoma. Fasciculations are preventable with a small subparalytic dose of a nondepolarizing blocker such as pancuronium.

Pancuronium is a competitive nondepolarizing muscle relaxant. It acts by occupying postsynaptic receptor sites, thus preventing access to acetylcholine. There is a gradual onset of paralysis over approximately 3 minutes. The duration of action is 30 to 60 minutes, making it a good drug for ongoing paralysis after intubation if controlled ventilation should be necessary. Factors that increase the length of blockade include acidosis, hypokalemia, decreased renal function, local anesthetics, and the presence of aminoglycoside antibiotics. Ventilation must be assisted with bag and mask until paralysis occurs and intubation can be accomplished. The drug is reversible with anticholinesterase agents such as neostigmine methylsulfate; however, at least 30 minutes should elapse after the dose is administered before reversal is attempted.[3,4]

Drug doses should be based on the patient's weight, drawn as single-dose injections, and labeled.

METHODOLOGY

Expertise in positive-pressure ventilation by mask and familiarity with techniques in overcoming airway obstruction are mandatory. The technique must be used with caution in patients with a partially obstructed airway since paralysis can cause total obstruction.

Before induction, patients should be ventilated with 100% oxygen. In the emergency department the physician must assume that the patient has a full stomach. To prevent regurgitation of stomach contents, the Sellick maneuver is performed in the following manner: Before induction, the cricoid ring is palpated. An assistant then applies pressure to the cricoid ring with the thumb and index finger while the neck is kept extended. This maneuver obliterates the esophageal lumen, thereby preventing regurgitated material from reaching the pharynx. The Sellick maneuver is effective with a nasogastric tube in place. Cricoid pressure is maintained until the endotracheal tube is in place.

The drugs are administered intravenously. Atropine sulfate is usually given first at a dose of 0.02 mg/kg with a minimum dose of 0.15 mg and a maximum dose of 1 mg. If succinylcholine is used, then a defasciculating dose of pancuronium bromide injection, 0.01 mg/kg, should be administered 3 minutes before the succinylcholine is given. In noncomatose or stuporous patients, thiopental 2 to 4 mg/kg or diazepam 0.05 to 0.1 mg/kg is then given. This is followed by a muscle relaxant (succinylcholine chloride 1 to 2 mg/kg or pancuronium bromide injection 0.1 mg/kg). Muscle relaxant should not be administered (except when treating laryngospasm) until it is proven that the patient can be ventilated manually. Lidocaine may be administered before intubation if there is any concern about increased intracranial pressure. Once paralysis is complete, the trachea is intubated, and tube placement is confirmed.

CONCLUSION

Major complications can be prevented by using paralysis only when necessary and under the direction of the individual present most experienced in airway management. Major risk in paralysis for intubation is failure to intubate. Having to bag-mask ventilate a patient with a full stomach and an unprotected airway can be harrowing under the best of circumstances. The inability to ventilate a paralyzed patient is a most difficult situation, and is best treated by avoiding it. Controlled positive-pressure ventilation may depress cardiac output and compromise the blood pressure in the hypovolemic patient. Finally, as mentioned, thiopental can also decrease blood pressure.

REFERENCES

1. Natnson C, Shelhamer JH, Parrillo JE: Intubation of the trachea in the critical care setting. *JAMA* 1985;253:1160–1165.

2. Salem MR, Wong AY, Collins DJ: The pediatric patient with a full stomach. *Anesthesiology* 1973;39:435–442.

3. Nugent SK, Larauuso R, Rogers MC: Pharmacology and use of muscle relaxants in infants and children. *J Pediatr* 1979;94:481–487.

4. Patl RB: Pharmacologic aids to endotracheal intubation. *Resident Staff Physician* 1986;32;47–54.

Section 27

Death in the Prehospital Setting

In many prehospital systems, children without vital signs are usually transported to the receiving hospital, irrespective of the initial assessment of probable outcome. This approach has evolved because of the need for extensive support services to the family and friends and the desire of health professionals to deliver aggressive care to all children. Indeed, in some circumstances, children may survive insults that would have been considered fatal in an older patient. In others, for whom the outcome is clearly death, other options may need to be considered.

49. When a Child Dies

James A. Dernocoeur

The death of a child is stressful for all involved. Individual experiences[1] and emotions make it difficult to handle such circumstances.[2] Because of this, our actions may be misguided by a set of assumptions concerning what is appropriate for the prehospital care of children and infants in cardiac arrest:

- All children found in cardiac arrest in the field should always have full resuscitative measures performed regardless of clinical presentation.
- Parents are always better off if the child receives resuscitative measures in the field.
- Parents will always receive better counseling in the emergency department.
- It is always medicolegally safer to resuscitate a child regardless of clinical condition.

Exploring the validity of these statements permits both the paramedic and physician involved in the prehospital system to broaden their views of what actions are appropriate.

Few guidelines exist in the medical literature. One's approach to such circumstances must therefore be based on personal and collegial experiences, discussions with parents of children who have died, and interviews with individuals intimately involved in the support of families who have experienced sudden infant deaths.

ALWAYS RESUSCITATE?

Many prehospital care systems take the approach that cardiac arrested children should *always* be resuscitated. The belief is that this approach is better for everyone involved. But there are times when it may not be ideal.

386

Judgment, not rigid rules, must form the basis for the management of emergency situations. Prehospital care providers, like other medical professionals, develop judgment as they gain clinical experience in the field. Judgment is the skill that guides them through tough calls, the ones that are not defined by textbooks or classroom experience.

The prehospital care worker enters the patient's environment; with physicians and nurses, the patient enters their environment. Because of this, the paramedic and emergency medical technician (EMT) must develop "streetsense."[3] It is this skill that, above all others, allows paramedics to make order out of chaos, to "read" the scene, the people, and the emotions that exist. This is essential at scenes where a child has died.

The first caveat of patient care is that if there is any chance for resuscitation, full resuscitative efforts should be made. This applies to adults as well as children. But, just as there are adults who are clearly "unresuscitable" at the scene, there are infants and children in this category as well.

In infants, sudden infant death syndrome (SIDS) is an unusual trap. Since it is well known that infants who suffer SIDS do not respond to resuscitative efforts, an emergency care provider may decide not to begin resuscitation. The diagnosis of SIDS occurs in the pathology department, not the emergency department or the field. The infant may have arrested for a different and correctable reason. Resuscitative efforts should never be withheld because of an assumption that an infant is a victim of SIDS.

When making the decision whether or not to begin resuscitation, the paramedic must use the same general clinical guidelines for children as for adults. When a child is obviously dead, the decision to try to resuscitate can be complex. In the days when prehospital care meant "grab 'em and rush to the hospital," the decision to resuscitate was simpler: resuscitation was always attempted. With the increased sophistication of prehospital care, this approach was soon regarded as harmful in many situations. Many patients benefit from on-scene care before being transported. Indeed, most situations of prehospital pediatric death do warrant resuscitation efforts and transport.

READING PARENTS

However, some parents are very aware that their child has clearly died. They are not hysterical when the paramedics arrive. If the "always resuscitate" approach is taken, these parents could well be harmed in several ways.

Medicine is often the application of inhumane-looking acts in the most humane manner possible. Resuscitation is filled with inhumane-looking acts: pounding on chests, pushing tubes down throats, sending electrical current through bodies, etc. From the lay person's perspective, the act of resuscitation is frightening. Even if parents understand that it may revive their child, they are forced to watch something awful. For those who understand that their child is already dead, these gestures become grotesque, inhumane acts that disgrace their child's body.

Another harmful effect of inappropriate resuscitation is that it can give parents a feeling of false hope. Some people believe that a call to the paramedic system is a call for help and, therefore, a call to resuscitate. Yes; the call to 911 is a call for help. However, "help" does not always mean providing medical procedures. Sometimes, it is a call to guide survivors through an overwhelming situation. Some parents *know* their child is dead, but they do not know what to do. What should they do with the body? Whom are they supposed to contact? The police? Who is going to help them through this awful tragedy? They are emotionally exhausted and need guidance. Therefore, they call the paramedics. It is a reflex action. Prehospital care systems have worked to develop in the general public the idea that when they have a medical problem that is too large for them to handle, they should call 911.

When a child is clearly dead, the parents become the patients. On-scene activity shifts to caring for their emotions and providing a smooth transition into the grieving process.[4]

The key to whether or not to resuscitate is to read the parents. Parental reaction usually comes in one of two ways: either they are panicked, dazed, and indecisive; or they are all too aware of what has happened and are thinking clearly.[5,6] If the parents are still trying to understand the situation and are panicked, resuscitation should be started regardless of clinical hope for the child.

But not all parents respond in this manner.[7] With parents who are thinking clearly, many understand that their child is dead and beyond resuscitative efforts. They may answer the door with statements like "He's dead; It's too late; There's nothing we can do. . . ." This is the group of parents at risk for emotional injury due to a knee jerk response of the emergency medical services (EMS) system. To pick up their dead child and begin resuscitation—to rekindle hope—is wrong. It is unfair for these parents to relive the death of their child. Parents will later wonder why their baby was put through the resuscitation and why the death certificate lists a time of death that indicates the baby was already dead at the scene.

SUPPORTING PARENTS

What is the best approach for parents who understand the situation? Again, one of the presumptions of "always resuscitate" is that parents receive better emotional care at the hospital. People in many EMS systems are under the illusion that the hospital can provide a better environment for facing the death of a child. Psychologic support for the parents of a child who has died may, by necessity, be low on the triage scale. A very busy emergency department can be a very frightening place for lay people. In such situations, appropriately trained paramedics can provide initial psychologic support and become the parent's advocate in assuring appropriate support.

The parents of an obvious SIDS victim may not want to leave their home. The home may be the best environment in which to begin the grieving process—yet the child may have been transported, which causes conflict. If an EMS system takes the stand that the emergency department is a better place to counsel the parents, then it is essential that the parents are in fact transported to the hospital to begin the separation process in a controlled fashion.

Resources must be mobilized as the highest priority.[8] Many communities have very good support systems for parents who have lost children; it is essential that these systems be identified and mobilized, and that the EMS system not feel that it must be all things to all people.

MEDICOLEGAL ISSUES

Another presumption in favor of "always resuscitate" dead children is that it is *always* medicolegally safer, regardless of a child's clinical condition. There are two parts to litigation: due process and the "human trigger." The human trigger is what starts due process in motion. When people feel they have been injured or violated, they often respond with litigation. Prehospital personnel can have a major impact on this feeling. If the parent's emotional state and the child's clinical presentation are ignored, and resuscitation is always begun, the parents can easily feel violated. As with any medical situation, doing what is right for the patient is the best guide. In a situation where the child is dead, the *parents* are the real patients. Competent care of their emotional state can help reduce feelings of violation and helplessness, and can therefore help reduce the human trigger of the medicolegal spectra.

HEALTH PROFESSIONAL STRESS

If there is one factor that frequently influences our response to scenes where a child has died, it is stress. It is important to understand how very stressful these scenes are on everyone. The death of a child is the most stressful situation for all prehospital care providers. To reduce stress levels, some paramedics pick up the child and always begin resuscitation. That way, they do not have to make any decisions, and it makes them feel that they tried.

The lack of success exacerbates the stress. Only seven to twenty-nine percent of pediatric patients with prehospital or emergency department cardiac arrest are discharged alive.[9] Because of this, there can be a lack of confidence in handling pediatric death, when in fact, the outcome may not reflect the care the patient received. If the resuscitative efforts were flawless and the patient dies, excellent care is still excellent.

Reduction of stress must not guide actions. The rescuer's emotional support should be addressed *after* the call, not during it. By choosing the career of paramedic, a person makes a conscious decision to confront life and death situations. A paramedic is presumably more willing, therefore, to face stressful situations—including the death of a child.

CONCLUSION

The death of a child is a difficult situation no matter where it occurs. However, automatic resuscitation orders are not uniformly appropriate. Prehospital care systems must be allowed to activate options and, when appropriate, integrate care of survivors into the treatment plans. There are times when the child is clearly dead at the scene, and the parents must be regarded as the patients. Care should be directed toward them because they are the ones who can benefit from good prehospital guidance and care.

REFERENCES

1. Sanders C: A comparison of adult bereavement in the death of a spouse, child, and parent. *Omega: Journal of Death and Dying* 10:303–320.

2. Crawshaw L: The sudden infant death syndrome: A psychophysiological consideration. *Smith College Studies in Social Work* 1978;48:132–170.

3. Dernocoeur K: *Streetsense*. Bowie, Md, Brady Communications Co, 1985.

4. Williams A, Nikolaisen SM: Sudden infant death syndrome: Parent's perceptions and responses to the loss of their infant. *Res Nurs Health* 1982,5:55–61.

5. Panides W: Helping parents deal with loss: A psychoanalytic perspective. *Pediatric Social Work* 1984;3:53–57.

6. Morgan J, Goering R: Caring for parents who have lost an infant. *Journal of Religion and Health* 1978;17:290–298.

7. Mandell F, McAnuity E, Reece R: Observation of paternal response to sudden unanticipated infant death. *Pediatrics* 1980;65:221–225.

8. Price M, Carter BD, Shelton TL, et al: Maternal perceptions of sudden infant death syndrome. *Children's Health Care* 1985;14:22–31.

9. Barkin R, Rosen P (eds): *Emergency Pediatrics*, ed 2. St. Louis, CV Mosby Co, 1986.

50. Responding to the Death of a Child

Peter Rosen, MD

There are few events in medicine that are as emotionally laden as sudden death. No matter how old the patient, no matter how alone, there is inevitably a relative who will grieve, and whose grief will be distorted by being unprepared. I have seen four generations of relatives mourn the cardiac arrest of a 97-year-old "patriarch" of the family, and express as much grief and sense of loss as for many younger patients.

When the sudden death of a child is encountered, the emotions rise geometrically in intensity. Children are not supposed to die and in fact they do not often succumb. Fewer than 2% of pediatric emergency visits are even admitted to the hospital. Moreover, there is a cultural concern for children, even if unrelated (perhaps a biologic imperative for species survival), that affects all involved adults far more than with a stranger of adult age.

When faced with the sudden death of a child, all concerned have an emotional load of grief with which to cope. This is difficult enough in the emergency department where there is usually an established team of responders. In the field, it becomes a task of forbidding magnitude.

Compounding the field difficulties is the reality that most pediatric sudden death is due to hypoxia. Cardiac arrest is a rare primary event confined to a very small number of congenital valvular and conduction disturbances, and an even smaller number of acute dysrhythmias precipitated by infection or blunt trauma. Paramedics are not as skilled in pediatric airway management as they are in adults'. Because the patient has a smaller, and therefore a more difficult, anatomy and fewer cases are encountered within individual emergency management services (EMS) systems, few paramedics can successfully acquire and maintain the requisite skills. These factors result in an understandable psychologic reluctance to initiate demanding resuscitation, which quickly becomes a self-fulfilling prophecy.

When combined with the field difficulties of obtaining reliable vital signs, a task fraught with error even under ideal circumstances in normal children, we have felt it wisest to define death in the field as: "a failure to respond to resuscitation" except under the most extreme conditions. Special circumstances include: decapitation or other clear and obviously destructive injuries, decomposition, or clear homicide scenes. In other instances in which the child appears dead but the down time is undefined, or the mechanism of disease or injury and events are unknown, we ask the paramedics to commence resuscitation, and make a decision about field pronouncement in conjunction with the base station physician. Since there is a well proven ability to salvage a percentage of hypothermic arrests, especially in the context of cold water near-drowning, we prefer to continue resuscitative efforts in the emergency department.

This is not to demean the paramedics, exclude their independent judgments that they make so capably and upon which we so frequently rely, nor to treat them as inferior team members. In fact, it represents the exact opposite. We expect them to commence the management of the grief process as well as to deliver the demanded expertise of the technical tasks of resuscitation. It has been our experience[1] that the psychic pain spike of an acute grief reaction can be attenuated by not having to deal immediately with the reality of sudden death.

However, it is important for the relatives to believe that the child has not been kept from any possible life-sustaining or restoring care. A further issue the paramedics must recognize and accept is the feeling expressed by many relatives that if no physician is involved in the care of their child, the child never received any care.[2,3] This again is in no way meant to denigrate the paramedics' contributions, but to reinforce their place on the team of care givers. Moreover, this begins a healthy as opposed to a pathologic grieving process.

It takes much time to deliver appropriate and concerned grief care. In emergency departments, it averages about one hour. While it is clear that few emergency physicians will be able to spend this amount of time with the relatives, it is also true that few EMS systems will be able to have an ambulance crew out of service for the required time. Moreover, at the emergency department, the full gamut of the grief team members—physicians, nurses, social workers, clergy, and responsible and interested friends—can interact with the relatives.

Another serious issue to be considered is nonaccidental trauma (NAT). Even pediatricians, emergency physicians, family physicians, nurses, and social workers experienced in NAT require significant time to identify and manage it. Nonaccidental trauma is often confirmed only after extensive diagnostic testing and multiple interviews with family and neighbors. Not only will these resources be unavailable in the average field situation but also it represents a dysfunctional interaction between the primary field mission—stabilization, resuscitation and transport. Moreover, there may be other children who need protection and removal from the home who are at school or out playing. Once again, it reaffirms the need for team function as opposed to solo virtuosity on the part of the paramedics.

Sudden infant death syndrome (SIDS) is another very difficult field issue. Its diagnosis rests on exclusion of other causes, and certainly is often hard to distinguish from NAT. The emotional impact of SIDS is extreme, with a very high incidence of divorce in the surviving parents. The field is definitely not the locus for management of this emotional crisis.

We therefore feel that in the absence of the special circumstances described above, the standard procedure for the field will be to commence all-out resuscitative efforts. These can be modified in conjunction with the base station. In general we prefer to continue all resuscitative efforts in the emergency department, and to reserve pronouncement of death, and continue grief management in the hospital setting.

Each EMS system will have to define its own protocols. Dealing with the death of a child is one of the most difficult dilemmas we face.

REFERENCES

1. Rosen P, Honigman B: Life and death, in Rosen P (ed): *Emergency Medicine: Concepts and Clinical Practice*, ed 2. CV Mosby Co, St. Louis, MO, 1987.

2. Wiener J: Reaction of the family to the fatal illness of a child, in Schoenberg B, et al (eds): *Loss and Grief*. Columbia University Press, NY, 1976.

3. Jones WH: Emergency room death: What can be done for the survivors? *Death Education* 1978;2:231.

Index

febrile seizure and, 206
gastrointestinal foreign bodies and, 225,
226, 227–28, 230, 231, 233–35, 239,
241
head trauma
and CT, 282, 285
and skull studies, 282, 285–86
hyperinflation
and bronchiolitis and, 169
of children with wheeze, 120
intraosseous infusion and, 369
limp and, 259
diagnostic value of, 266
periorbital cellulitis and, 65–66
renal trauma, 315–16, 318
and CT, 314–15, 318
and IVP, 313, 315, 317, 321–22
urinary tract infection evaluation
anatomic abnormalities and, 80, 82, 83,
84–85
excretory urography (IVP) and, 83–84,
85
radionuclide scintigraphy and, 84, 85
renal scarring and, 71, 85
ultrasonography and, 83, 84, 85, 86
voiding cystourethrography (VCUG)
and, 82–83, 84, 85
Radionuclide scintigraphy, 84, 85
Rape, pregnancy testing and, 275
Red blood cell (RBC) count, meningitis and,
93, 94
Referral, periorbital cellulitis and
ophthalmologic, 56
Rehydration (oral). *See also* Dehydration as
alternative to IV rehydration, 244
study of parenteral rehydration and, 256
dehydration assessment and, 248–52
in developed countries, 247–48
in developing countries, 247
emergency department management and,
255
fluids for, 244, 245, 248
hypernatremic dehydration and, 251
mild or moderate dehydration and,
249–50
parenteral rehydration and, 256
severe dehydration and, 250–51
WHO solution for, 246–47
gauging severity of dehydration and, 253
hospitalization and, 256–57

pathophysiology of dehydrating diarrheal
agents and, 245–46
refeeding and, 251–52
Renal function
urinary tract infection and, 72, 77
radiologic examination and, 71, 74
Renal trauma. *See also* Hematuria (after blunt
trauma)
categorization of, 316–17
hematuria and, 313, 314, 315, 316, 317,
318, 319
hemorrhaging and, 315, 317, 318
intravenous pyelogram (IVP) and, 313,
315, 317
isotopic renal scanning and, 315
laparotomy and, 317, 318
life-threatening conditions and evaluation
of, 315–16
nonoperative management of, 318
pedicle injury and, 317
renal arteriography and, 315
radiographic analysis and, 315–16, 318
CT and, 314–15, 318
surgery and, 314, 318–19
vascular damage and, 317
Respiratory arrest, CPR and intubation and,
349
Respiratory difficulty, lumbar puncture and,
91
Respiratory diseases. *See* Apnea (infantile);
Asthma; Bronchiolitis; Croup; Epiglottitis;
Wheezing in children
Respiratory infection, fever and, 16, 18
Respiratory syncytial viral (RSV) infections,
192
Rheumatic fever, 51
Rhinorrhea, 169
Ribavirin, 168, 170–71, 172

S

Salmonella, fever and, 5, 6, 17, 24, 25, 30
Scarlet fever, 38, 51
Seizure. *See also* Status epilepticus
febrile
diagnosis and, 201
laboratory evaluation and, 203–204,
206
prognostic considerations, 202
management of